INDEPENDENT
PSYCHOANALYSIS TODAY

INDEPENDENT PSYCHOANALYSIS TODAY

Edited by

Paul Williams, John Keene,
and Sira Dermen

KARNAC

First published in 2012 by
Karnac Books Ltd
118 Finchley Road, London NW3 5HT

British Library Cataloguing in Publication Data

A C.I.P. for this book is available from the British Library

ISBN 978 1 85575 737 0

Edited, designed and produced by The Studio Publishing Services Ltd
www.publishingservicesuk.co.uk
e-mail: studio@publishingservicesuk.co.uk

www.karnacbooks.com

CONTENTS

ACKNOWLEDGEMENTS

A different version of Rosine Perelberg's paper appeared in *The Dead Mother* (1999) edited by Gregorio Kohon, London: The New Library of Psychoanalysis/Routledge. We are grateful to the *International Journal of Psychoanalysis* for permission to reproduce the papers by Paul Williams and Roger Kennedy, to *Psychoanalytic Dialogues* for permission to reproduce the paper by Michael Parsons, and to Routledge/ The New Library of Psychoanalysis for permission to reproduce Gregorio Kohon's paper "The Oedipus complex", published in *Introducing Psychoanalysis: Essential Themes and Topics*, edited by Susan Budd and Richard Rusbridger (2005). A similar version of Chapter Eight, by Kenneth Wright, was published in 2009 by Routledge in *Mirroring and Attunement: Self-realisation in Psychoanalysis and Art*. Chapter Seven, by Sira Derwen, "Endings and beginnings", was first published in © The Psychoanalytic Quarterly, 2010, *The Psychoanalytic Quarterly*, Volume LXXIX, No. 3, pp. 665–685.

ABOUT THE EDITORS AND CONTRIBUTORS

Bernard Barnett is now in semi-retirement after a long career in adult and child psychoanalytic practice which has included major responsibilities for training and administration. Apart from teaching and education, his major interests have been, and continue to be, in Holocaust related issues and in the relationship between insights to be found in psychoanalysis and in the work of poets and novelists.

Susan Budd was a Fellow of the British Psychoanalytical Society and a member of the Independent Group. She was for many years involved with teaching and supervising psychoanalytical psychotherapists in London, Oxford, and Birmingham. She was Editor of Books for the British Society, and has published papers on the history of psychoanalysis and its relationship with other disciplines. She is now retired, and lives in London and Devon.

Sira Dermen is a training and supervising analyst of the British Psychoanalytical Society. She originally trained as a child psychotherapist at the Tavistock Clinic. She is Honorary Senior Consultant at the Portman Clinic, where she worked for seventeen years and held a number of posts, including Vice Chair. She is now in full-time private practice. She has written on violence and perversion.

Ann Horne trained as a child and adolescent psychotherapist in the independent tradition at the British Association of Psychotherapists, where she has been Head of Training and Head of Post Graduate Education. Retired from the Portman Clinic, London, and clinical work, she retains an interest in children who act, unable to access thought, and continues to write, talk, and teach. *Winnicott's Children*, the third book in her independent series on child psychoanalytic work, edited with Monica Lanyado, appears later this year (2012).

John Keene is a training and supervising analyst of the British Psychoanalytical Society, having trained at the Institute of Psychoanalysis and at the Tavistock Clinic. He is now in private practice. He has taught widely on clinical issues, and on the independent tradition and the Controversial Discussions. His early interest in group relations has led to consultancy and training work with organisations, mainly in the National Health Service (NHS). His paper, "Unconscious obstacles to caring for the planet: facing up to human nature", given at a "Psychoanalysis at the Science Museum" Conference in 2010, is to be published later this year (2012).

Roger Kennedy is a training and supervising analyst and Past President of the BPAS, Consultant Child and Adolescent Psychiatrist at The Child and Family Practice, London, and author of several books, including *Couch Tales* and *The Many Voices of Psychoanalysis*.

Leon Kleimberg is a training analyst of the British Psychoanalytical Society and visiting lecturer at the Adult Department, Tavistock Clinic. He has published papers in the UK and abroad in areas of psychoanalysis and creativity, psychoanalysis and psychopathology, and psychoanalysis and immigration. He is in full-time private practice in London.

Gregorio Kohon is a training analyst of the British Psychoanalytical Society. He was Visiting Professorial Fellow for the year 2010–2011 to the School of Social Sciences, Birkbeck College, University of London. His forthcoming book is entitled *Kafka at the Borders: The Aesthetics of Estrangement*.

Michael Parsons has been in psychoanalytic practice in London for thirty years. He is a member of the British Psychoanalytical Society and the French Psychoanalytic Association. He is the author of *The Dove that Returns, The Dove that Vanishes: Paradox and Creativity in Psychoanalysis* (Routledge, 2000). A new book, *Living Psychoanalysis: From Theory to Experience*, is forthcoming.

Rosine Jozef Perelberg, PhD, is a training analyst and supervisor, and a Fellow of the British Psychoanalytical Society. She is Visiting Professor in the Psychoanalysis Unit at University College London, and Corresponding Member of the Société Psychanalytique de Paris. She has published widely in the main psychoanalytic journals. Her latest book, *Space, Time and Phantasy*, has been published by Routledge and the New Library of Psychoanalysis.

Caroline Polmear is a training and supervising analyst, British Psychoanalytical Society. She is joint author of *A Short Introduction to Psychoanalysis*, with Jane Milton and Julia Fabricius (Sage, first edition 2004, second edition 2011) and has written about the psychoanalytic understanding of adults with autistic features.

Joan Raphael-Leff, psychoanalyst (Fellow, British Psychoanalytical Society) and social psychologist, is Leader of UCL/Anna Freud Centre Academic Faculty for Psychoanalytic Research. Previously, she was Head of University College London's MSc in Psychoanalytic Developmental Psychology, and Professor of Psychoanalysis at the Centre for Psychoanalytic Studies, University of Essex. In 1998, she founded COWAP, the IPA's committee on Women and Psychoanalysis. She specialised in reproductive and early parenting issues, and is the author of 100+ publications, and eleven books. She trains primary health workers and perinatal practitioners working with teenage parents in many low- and high-income countries.

Paul Williams is a training analyst of the British Psychoanalytical Society and a Member of the Royal Anthropological Institute. From 2001–2007 he was Joint Editor-in-Chief, with Glen O. Gabbard, of *The International Journal of Psychoanalysis*. Until he retired from the NHS in 2010, he was a Consultant Psychotherapist and a Professor at Queen's University, Belfast. He is a Visiting Professor at Anglia Ruskin University, works in private practice, and writes on the subject of severe disturbance.

Kenneth Wright is a psychoanalyst and Tavistock trained psycho-therapist living and working in Suffolk. He lectures widely and has published two books: *Vision and Separation: Between Mother and Baby* (Free Association Books, 1991, Mahler Literature prize, 1992) and *Mirroring and Attunement: Self-Realisation in Psychoanalysis and Art* (Routledge, 2009). He is a Patron of the Squiggle Foundation.

PREFACE

It is not often that collections of papers by Independent analysts appear in book form. This is perhaps because Independents do not see themselves as constituting a group in the accepted sense: like-minded individuals whose efforts yield a body of work that is representative of the group's members. Independents, as has often been noted, constitute a relatively loose alliance of psychoanalysts in Britain and elsewhere that reflects their wish to remain free of a single analytic approach in order to make use of a range of conceptual orientations and forms of technique in the best interests of individual patients. At the same time, there is a history and body of literature that expresses the common elements of this open stance, which has been well named "the Independent tradition". It is hoped that this collection will become a significant part of that tradition. One established area of interest for the majority of Independents has been, and remains, the interplay between internal psychic reality and the environment. The complexity of infantile mental life within a prevailing environmental set-up, and the consequences of this relationship for psychic development and psychopathology, is a subject about which much remains unknown, and one that is extensively discussed in these pages. A second area of interest has been the resurgence of work with patients seeking analytic help who suffer from serious personality difficulties, including the consequences of trauma and even frank psychosis. These patients present clinical and technical challenges to which Independents have responded, evidence of which is presented here in the work of a number of contributors.

This book does not claim to represent all Independents; neither does it aim to cover all the interests and concerns of independent psychoanalysts. It is a staging post in the development of Independent thinking and technique, a grouping of contemporary papers that articulates Independent psychoanalytic ideas and ways of working. The book is organised under two broad headings—"Orientations" and "Interventions". While it is possible for the reader to pick out any paper that is of interest, we have contextualised their place in the book according to the extent to which they address conceptual advances or clinical approaches to the kinds of problems that face most psychoanalysts today.

Paul Williams, John Keene, and Sira Dermen

PART I
ORIENTATIONS

CHAPTER ONE

Reflections on the evolution of Independent psychoanalytic thought

John Keene

Many psychoanalysts outside and inside the UK have been puzzled, if not frustrated, at the failure of the Middle Group, later the Independents, to function as a group or school in the way that the Kleinians have been seen to have done. In contrast, in spite of the effort of Gregorio Kohon (1986) and Eric Rayner (1991)[1] to put the Independent approach together in their books, the Independent Group can appear diffuse and unco-ordinated. This quality of the "group" can really only be understood in relation to the political processes which led to its formation and which have frequently drawn attention away from the Independents' key role in the development of the object relations approach in psychoanalysis which was pioneered by Balint, Winnicott, and Fairbairn in a prolonged dialogue with Klein's and her followers' technical and theoretical innovations. I suggest that the domain of Independent thinking is better defined as the elaboration of an underdeveloped assumption in Freud's theorising which seriously overestimated the capacity of average maternal care to satisfy an infant's needs. This line of exploration was largely pioneered in Europe by the Hungarians, led by Ferenczi, and by their counterparts in the British Psychoanalytical Society, who were eventually largely concentrated in the Independent Group. I believe it is helpful to set out the organisational political context in which the group's theoretical thinking developed, because philosophical and organisational issues at times were as important as the theoretical stances which were taken up by most members of the group.

Politics, history, and ideas

I see the particular ambience of the Independents as following from the role that those who became Independents played in the history of psychoanalysis in the UK. This has left them operating more as an association of fellow travellers rather than a tightly knit "school". The Middle Group, which changed its name to "The Group of Independent Psychoanalysts" in the 1960s, was the container for two groups of people whose interests and grounds for becoming Independents derived from distinct preoccupations, often, but not necessarily, overlapping. The first motivation can be designated broadly as political. Psychoanalysis in the UK developed with the benefit of Ernest Jones' powerful personal connection to Freud. However, London, in its island kingdom off the European mainland, was sufficiently far away from the heartland of psychoanalysis to pursue its own interests without undue concern for the questions of orthodoxy that preoccupied the continental societies. For this reason, Jones felt Mrs Klein would have an easier time in Britain. From her arrival in 1926, a lively debate about her ideas took place between those who regarded themselves as her followers and those who were merely interested in working out how far her ideas could be incorporated into their own work and thinking. This debate about the validity of her theoretical and technical innovations was gradually complicated by anxieties about influence, patronage, and dominance in the British Psychoanalytical Society that focused on Klein and her followers, anxieties that were exacerbated by the lack of democratic structures in the society. An atmosphere of suspicion and rancour grew, powerfully fuelled by the animosity towards Klein of her daughter, Melitta Schmideberg, and Melitta's analyst, Edward Glover. Outside the society, the doubts of Viennese colleagues increased about the compatibility of Klein's and Freud's ideas. These two concerns became acute with the arrival in London of Anna Freud and her father and a number of European colleagues in 1939. Anna Freud objected to her students of psychoanalysis being taught theory and technique that differed significantly from her father's views. The emotionally heated "Controversial Discussions" which resulted, and took place in London between 1941 and 1945, started as a three-cornered debate between staunchly pro-Klein and anti-Klein members with a third "non-aligned" group who approached Klein's work with a questioning and analytical stance (in the ordinary sense of the word). The three-sided nature of the discussions did not last until the end of the series of meetings, as Anna Freud and her supporters mostly withdrew to Hampstead, while Edward Glover, who had wished to follow Ernest Jones as president, resigned from the society.

This left the later discussions more or less to the Kleinians and the interested remainder of the society, who were then referred to as the "Middle Group", as had been the case before relationships within the society turned rancorous. This remainder included Sylvia Payne, who was elected President rather than Glover, and formulated the "Gentleman's Agreement". This would have been better called the Ladies' Agreement, as it was concluded between Payne, Klein, and Anna Freud, and it kept the British Psychoanalytical Society in one piece by devising a two-stream structure for training within the Society. This allowed Anna Freud to control what was taught to her students on her alternative training, which was known as the "B" Course. Its graduates were, for a long time, referred to as the "B groupers" before most identified themselves as "Contemporary Freudians". The original course became the "A" Course and continued as before, being taught by a mixture of Kleinians and the remainder, generally called the "Middle Group". This middle group, under Payne, led the democratisation of the society with the introduction of regular elections for key posts within the society. These revolutionised the previously autocratic, if not tyrannical, actions of the presidents of the society.

Alongside Payne throughout the discussions were Marjorie Brierley and Ella Sharpe. Lesser contributions to the discussions were made by analysts who would come to prominence in the post-war period, John Bowlby, Ronald Fairbairn, and Donald Winnicott. These were not regarded by Klein as members of her group, and a process began in which the Kleinians became more and more clearly separated out from the remainder.

A separate political reality lay behind a further wave of recruits to the Independents. The wish to remain free of the partisan and controlling nature of the Klein and Freud groups as organisations and distaste for their groups' often dismissive attitude towards others was a powerful reason for some influential Kleinians to opt for the intellectual freedom of the Middle/Independent group. Here, there was no "party line" as to what theoretical or technical approaches were acceptable. By the middle 1950s the "A" course was more sharply delineated into a "Klein Group" and the "Middle Group" remainder. This was made emphatic by Paula Heimann's leaving the Klein Group for the Middle Group, as John Rickman and Thomas Hayley had done. Heimann's departure was most significant as she had been such a key player in the exposition of Klein's views in the Controversial Discussions. She proposed the name change to the Independent Group, although the ambiguous character of the group remained unresolved. By that, I mean that the people who became Independents for reasons of aversion to the unpleasant behaviour of the polarised groups had varying degrees of overlap with those who remained outside the Klein and Anna Freud camps, mainly on the basis of their theoretical preoccupations.

Key lines of development in Independent thinking

Some commentators, such as Rayner (1991), have put great emphasis on the above antiauthoritarian, antihierarchical stance and the freedom to use ideas that are found to have value from whatever source (the essence of the scientific method, of course) as a defining characteristic of the Independent Group, along with its commitment to democratic procedures. Rayner sees the Independents as combining the best features of romanticism and empiricism in European thought. It is, therefore, not possible to pick a single individual as the defining figure or leader of the group. Even Winnicott, who is an emblematic figure of the group, and was quintessentially an Independent from a theoretical point of view, was never actually a member of it, since he eschewed groups in every guise and would not accept membership of even a group of "Independent" psychoanalysts.

I think that such philosophical and attitudinal characteristics, important as they are, are not the most crucial definers of the Independent tradition, and frequently divert attention away from the group's contribution to the development of object relations theory and its technical consequences. In this, it is more productive to concentrate on the interrelated clinical and theoretical issues that have been extensively pursued by workers in the Independent tradition. These are highly interwoven and need to be approached from a variety of angles. They emerge from a particular set of tensions within Freud's own contributions and with the way that theory and practice were evolving between 1910 and 1939. Freud himself embraced two contrasting stances in his work. On the one hand, he never lost the reductionist approach of the *Project for a Scientific Psychology* (Freud, 1895), with its wish to furnish a psychology that is a natural science with psychical states represented as quantifiably determinate states of specifiable material particles. On the other hand, his clinical and theoretical writing is so acute and preoccupied with explicating nuances of meaning and emotion.[2] Freud's ambition would have been realised much more easily had he been working later, when the contributions of general systems theory and communications theory would have been available to him. The tension is expressed in a number of competing dualities within psychoanalytic thinking: *cause and instinct* as contrasted with *meaning and affect*; internal *vs.* external sources of anxiety and trauma; the derivation of psychic structure from the instincts or from object relationships. Freud's thinking was constrained by his lifelong belief that he needed to provide an account of development, conflict, and psychopathology derived from a fundamentally dualistic opposition of two biologically based groups of instincts.[3] In this period, there is a move to much greater emphasis on the *processes* involved in both the psychological development of the individual and in psychoanalytic treatment, as against the early stage of describing and delineating novel unconscious content. Similarly, while quantitive considerations remain of great theoretical interest, it is the centrality of affect in organising mental life and the need for defences against unbearable feelings that become predominant. In the same period, while Freud's theorising contains essentially internal—"one body"—accounts of behaviour within the individual, the increasing attention to interaction, process, and communication moves the theoretical and technical focus on to aspects of the relationships within which the defences are formed and development takes place. The move to thinking more explicitly in terms of interaction and conscious and unconscious communication in the impact of one psyche on another also helped to develop a better account of instincts and drives. The shift from Freud's "one-person psychology" to a two and multi-person psychology of interaction can be attributed particularly to the Hungarians. With their interest in ethology and observational studies of the earliest relationships and behaviours of infant humans and other primates, they drove the change towards the study of process in relationships and in psychoanalysis and a more interactive model of earliest developments than the standard model of the time.

From the viewpoint of the development of British psychoanalytic thinking, it is notable that Klein had her first analysis with Ferenczi, who encouraged her to work with children. Later, Jones felt that her work would flourish better in the growing psychoanalytic culture in London, so that both Klein's devotees and her generally enthusiastic questioners had similar interests. The English analytic scene was enlivened from the start by its association with the Bloomsbury Group and the assumption that a medical training was not an inevitable prerequisite to becoming an analyst. Thus, the intellectual milieu included those with interests and training in the arts, education, psychology, literature, and philosophy, and these disciplines contributed, as Rayner pointed out (1991), to the approaches taken to the analytic endeavour, both theoretically and technically.

I suggest that the most illuminating and unifying of the threads in the Independent tradition, which can seem diffuse, is afforded by Ferenczi's and Winnicott's responses to Freud's (1911b) "Formulations on the two principles of mental functioning". This sketch of the infant's need to shift from the "pleasure principle" to the "reality principle" rapidly prompted Ferenczi to describe in detail how this shift might be achieved. Ferenczi's 1913 paper, "Stages in the development of a sense of reality", provides a properly interactional account of the stages the infant passes through as it develops its ways of getting its needs met from its first encounter with people in its post-natal world to adulthood. Unsurprisingly, but slightly paradoxically, it is Winnicott, the rejecter of groups, who points to what I regard as the heart of the Independent tradition in his 1960a paper, "The theory of the parent–infant relationship". In the main text of Freud's 1911b paper, Freud suggests that the baby starts out by hallucinating the satisfaction of his desires without having to concern himself with the demands of reality. Only in a footnote does Freud acknowledge that no infant could survive on this basis. Freud argues that the employment of a fiction like this, which he calls "the pleasure principle", is justified "when one considers that the infant – provided one includes with it the care it receives from its mother – does almost realise a psychical system of this kind" (pp. 219–220). Winnicott knew from his extensive knowledge of mothers and babies, gained through his work as a paediatrician, how many things could go wrong in the mother and baby relationship, with profound consequences for the psychic health and development of the child. Freud's confidence in this enormous proviso, with its heart-warming optimism about the satisfactoriness of the care that infants would automatically receive, could not be justified. The maternal environment cannot guarantee that infants will inevitably have a real experience of hallucinatory wish fulfilments. This led to Winnicott's well-known epigram, "there is no such thing as a baby"—only a baby considered in the context of its relationship to its mother.

I see much Independent work as exploring the implications for both psychological development and for the understanding of the transference in analysis that arise in this fully interactional model when the parental care (in conjunction with the state of the infant) is not sufficient to give the infant a sequence of experiences that lead to a secure sense of self, a sense of power and agency, with a reliable sense of the relationship between inner and external reality. Instead, it might be exposed to various forms of primitive anxiety, excessive frustration, lack of response to its attempts to communicate, over- or under-stimulation, experiences of pain, intrusion, and being projected into. In this context, responses to trauma remain an issue of major concern for the analyst, as they do generally for the patient, and I will review this complex matter for psychoanalytic theory and practice later in the chapter.

Independent analysts have resisted the pressure within the Kleinian development to take explanations of all behaviour back to oscillations between paranoid–schizoid and depressive positions, and the tendency to attribute all pathology to the vicissitudes of destructiveness. This has provided for an interest in development throughout the life span and to significant contributions to the understanding of play, creativity, and sexuality. Every aspect of psychoanalysis, from the drives to the defences, to transference, technique, and interpretation, is affected by these considerations. The defences, for example, are seen by Independents as always developing in an interpersonal context, whereas, for Freud, they are the means of regulating inner tension, and for Klein, there was a tendency to see them as wholly emanating from problems in managing innate instinctual conflicts. In this, there are clear divergences as well as continuities in the developments from Ferenczi to Michael and Alice Balint, and to Abraham and Klein. In the UK, from the 1920s, key themes develop in the work of Jones, Ella Sharpe, Marjorie Brierley, Sylvia Payne, Rickman, and Strachey, leading into the work of Fairbairn, Milner, Bowlby, Winnicott, and Gillespie. These, in turn, stimulate a body of work developed from the 1940s by King, Khan, Main, Malan, Klauber, Heimann, Limentani, Rycroft, Stewart, and Coltart, which inspires the contemporary Independent scene with its sustained contributions from Bollas, Casement, Kennedy, Kohon, Parsons, Perelberg, Symington, Williams, and Wright, to name some of the group's most prolific writers.

In suggesting a central unifying thread in the Independent tradition it is important to recognise that it is intertwined with a number of interrelated themes in the evolution of psychoanalysis over the past hundred years. I have mentioned the increasing interest in the detailed processes uncovered in the psychic development of the individual and in the subtleties of the analytic relationship. This research moved the analytic process from a devotion to the uncovering of unconscious pressures and contents to new ways of conceptualising how change and recovery take place. These threads intertwine to form a matrix of connected issues. The first is a change of focus from instinctual discharge to affects. An overall paradigm shift saw a change of emphasis in deriving structures in the personality from internalised object relationships, rather than from Freud's early theory based on drives and their transformations through developmental phases and experience. In this shift, the focus changed away from the explanatory emphasis on the merely quantitative aspects of the reduction of drive tension. In its place was a reassertion of the key role of the affects in the development of object relations and to affects as primary sources of the meaning of objects and actions. Brierley saw affects as part of highly functional ego activities in everyday adaptation. This view is complemented by that of Bowlby, who saw that affects are continuous appraisals of the individual's internal states and the external situation. Both were influenced powerfully by the philosopher Susanne Langer. Primary affective responses to the self, objects, and actions can be regarded as primary sources of meaning for the infant, and this contributes to the elaboration of Freud's ideas about psychic causation into a richer explanatory world of meanings.

The second main area concerns assumptions about the earliest phase of life. The views of development adopted by different psycho-analytic pioneers reflected their assumptions about the infant's fundamental attitude to the world and its basic repertoire of primary drive dispositions. In many ways, Freud's first distinction between the ego instincts promoting the survival of the individual and the sexual instincts promoting the reproduction of the species has an evolutionary logic to it which his later dualism of the life and death instincts did not achieve. As I shall suggest later, both of Freud's models had problems. The early duality had an empirically incorrect view as to how objects became significant: only by being connected with experiences of pain and pleasure (the anaclitic model) as opposed to there being a primary drive to maintain connections to attachment objects. This is captured in the question as to whether Freud's libido is better characterised as "object seeking" rather than "pleasure seeking".

The theory of the life and death instincts conflated a greater interest in the role of aggression in character development with the idea that it had to derive from a simple and unitary biological source. This fails to do justice to the subtleties of aggressive behaviour, which range from self protection and the protection of territory and kin, responses to frustration and their sexualisation, which give rise to sado-masochistic trends, and, ultimately, attempts to destroy the self or the object of hatred.

The positions and researches taken up by the Independent psychoanalysts on these issues contribute powerfully to the account given of the complex processes involved in the development of the sense of self and its relationship to external and internal reality. These affect the sense agency and the capacity to utilise one's inner resources, in contrast with states of inhibition, unreality, falseness, and withdrawal. In the process, the account of the diversity of environmental deficiencies, impingements, and trauma on development is significantly enhanced.

In the following sections, I will illustrate aspects of these themes and their historical development.

The Controversial Discussions and assumptions about mothers and babies

As it was the separation of Anna Freud's followers from the Kleinians during the Controversial Discussions that precipitated the formation of a "Middle Group", it is important to review the state of theorising in which the discussions took place. The contributors to the Controversial Discussions deployed a range of arguments based on varied sources, including *a priori* philosophical assumptions, extrapolations from the treatment of adults and children, combined with varying kinds of psychological and observational evidence. For the purpose of understanding Independent thinking, it is the earlier Budapest contributions which remain the most relevant. Ferenczi's suggestion that Klein should work with children went along with an observational approach to mother–infant behaviour in humans and other primates. The Hungarian group described in infants, and also saw equivalents in the analysis of patients, forms of early object-related gratifications that led to states of *tranquil wellbeing*. These included being picked up, being responded to, being allowed to hold something, indications of concern, and prompt adaptation to the infant's needs. These gratifications are not given any significant economic importance in the Freudian scheme, and I will return to this in more detail later. They are also essentially examples of *fore pleasure* rather than *end pleasure* in Freud's libidinal theory, which was focused on pleasure deriving from the discharge of accumulated energy. It was clear by this time that many things other than sucking were rewarding to infants and were required for the healthy development of the newborn. A baby can be physically adequately fed, but emotionally fail to thrive. Current infant research shows remarkable interactive propensities from birth and capacities such as being able from birth to discriminate mother's and father's voices by differentiated responses. Imre Hermann's work in the 1920s and 1930s on the clinging response as a primary motivational system (see Hermann, 1976) was part of a wave of interest in situations which adversely affected infant development and paved the way for significant theoretical developments. These researchers included Bowlby (1940, 1944), Spitz, (1945, 1946), and Dorothy Burlingham and Anna Freud (1942, 1946). Bowlby's interest led him to a clinical and research focus on the vicissitudes of attachment and the psychical consequences of separation and loss, linking the non-Kleinian Hungarians to modern attachment theory.

In her paper of 1939, Alice Balint noted the clear instinctual interdependence between mother and child. She observed that the concept of mutuality, which Ferenczi also raised in relation to coitus, applies *par excellence* to the mother and the baby: what is good for one is good for the other. This sense of reciprocal roles does not imply equality, or being the same as. Mutuality and interdependence are highly asymmetric, as with the complementary functions of mother and infant. Later, there is a similar asymmetry in the analytic relationship. Both Fairbairn and Balint agreed about the necessity for the concept of "primary object love", which Balint (1937) suggested the infant experiences wordlessly as something like "I shall be loved and satisfied without being under any obligation to give anything in return". He saw that frustration of this can give rise to two main groups of responses. The first is a limited and narcissistic one, while the other (following Ferenczi's 1913 account) is to work towards the ultimate achievement of active object love, in which the infant or adult learns how to "give in order to get".

The different starting assumptions between analytic communities were flagged up in the Four Countries Conference of 1937, where Michael Balint (1937) provided a bravura account of the prevailing views as to the essential nature of the human infant. He described how the Viennese framed everything in terms of conflict and struggled to relate their observations to the Oedipal phase as the source of all pathology. In contrast, the London Kleinians were happy to reconceptualise the earliest phase in pre-Oedipal terms, but shared with the Viennese an emphasis on the infant as fundamentally greedy, insatiable, and hostile. On the basis of the research outlined above, Balint criticised these two schools for their emphasis on the noisy phenomena of infancy arising from acute frustration, while ignoring the early object-related gratifications that lead to states of tranquil wellbeing: being responded to, being picked up, soothed, rocked, and comforted. He had already made the point that when an infant is making the noisy phenomena of distress, need, and frustration, the behaviour already has an interpersonal history and cannot just be taken as the expression of an instinctual impulse *per se*. Klein made reference to these findings in her paper for the Controversial Discussions, and there were many references to Middlemore's (1941) study, *The Nursing Couple*, as well to many of the participants' personal experiences as mothers. So, it was clear by this time, and widely acknowledged by a wide range of parties in the discussions, that many things were gratifying to the newborn in contrast to classical theory, which held that the satisfaction of oral needs was the only ground on which the infant became interested in the person who fed him or her.

It was clear that all three groups were interested in the new observational findings of infants and their mothers, but, politically, these
discussions were about theoretical legitimacy, heresy, and the Freudian succession, so evidence itself was not the only significant factor.
Thus, while Klein could insist that object relations were present from
the beginning of life, her need to represent herself as essentially a
Freudian instinctivist seemed to dictate that the object's qualities were
entirely the creation of the infant's drives, while the actual behaviour
and attitudes of the object found no proper and convincing place in
the theory until Bion (1959) introduced the container–contained
dimension into Kleinian theory (see, for example, Hughes, 1989). Similarly, Anna Freud found some trouble in asserting, against considerable disagreement, that it was only the pleasure–pain aspects of early
experience that counted and the personalised source of the care was
irrelevant to the infant. Ideally, of course, the situation between
mother and infant is dominated by *mutuality and mutually gratifying*
reciprocal roles, in which the mother is attuned and responsive to the
infant's needs. In similar vein is the understanding that, for satisfactory development, infants need to be loved and have their needs and
communications recognised by the other.

This picture of an infant powerfully primed to seek objects,
develop relationships, and to explore its world is at one end of a
continuum of psychoanalytic assumptions about the attitude of the
infant to the world, which Hamilton carefully elucidated in her 1982
book. She noted that the most extreme position, assuming the infant's
overwhelming hostility to the world, is an essential element in the
notions of primary narcissism and primary union/fusion described by
Freud, and later taken up by Mahler and Kohut. In intermediate place
is Klein's theory of internal object-relationships, which dispenses with
the idea of primary narcissism and conceives of relationships to internal objects from the start of life, while deriving these from instinctual
representations. The remaining points on the continuum, which take
this move into fully interpersonal as well as intrapersonal schemas,
are the primary domain of the Independents, starting with Ferenczi,
Michael and Alice Balint, Fairbairn, Bowlby, and Winnicott.[4] Hamilton
characterises these in terms of their emphasis on primary object love
and primary affectional bonds, interactional synchrony and mutuality,
emphasising the infant's need to be loved and not only physically
gratified. This work is enhanced, from a research point of view, by

Bowlby, Main, Stern, Trevarthen, Brazelton, and Tronick. This shift in emphasis gave the Independents two clear fields of study. The first is the vicissitudes of relationships throughout development, and the second is the necessary revision of instinct or drive theory with some metapsychological adjustments.

Early integration and ego development: precursors of selfhood

While no key text integrates the workings of the Middle Group pioneers, together they provide a stable platform for later theoretical and technical developments. At this point, I will leave aside the question of the fundamental instinctual inheritances of each infant, with their implications for the formation of object relationships and character, and concentrate on key processes in becoming a "self", or a person. Balint, Winnicott, and Fairbairn each made significant contributions to understanding the first phases of development as the infant begins to negotiate its way from the initial period of absolute dependence on others towards individuation and interdependence.

Winnicott

All three theorists presuppose a rudimentary ego with a powerful need to relate to "a person who should be there". (This seems to me to compare with Bion's notion of "preconception" (Bion, 1959).) Winnicott, like all psychoanalysts, saw the infant as inheritor of blueprints and drives for a maturational and developmental process, envisaged by him as the True Self, which can only be healthily realised in the context of reliable and loving (good enough) maternal care. There are subtle differences in their positions on the subject of the presence of an integrated ego from the start of post-natal life, but these, I believe, can be comfortably reconciled.

   Winnicott, while generally agreeing with Klein that there is an ego, or self, capable of relationships with objects from birth, saw neither the integration of this self nor the sense of what is self and not self as securely established from the start. He argued that many other sorts of response are needed from the mother apart from suckling for proper ego-development to take place, for the infant *to feel real* and become a person. Winnicott set out these earliest developmental achievements in

"Primitive emotional development" (1945). They depend on the "good enough" behaviour of "an ordinary devoted mother", which he thought of as "holding the infant" both physically and psychically. His picture of the infant proposes that where the infant care is responsive and attuned to the states of mind and needs of the infant (as presumed in Freud's footnote), then the infant can remain in states of unintegration without anxiety. The infant who is well held and responded to in this way has the experience of being seen and responded to as a potential "person" and not just a thing: a person with a mind who wishes to communicate and engage with the people and the world around it. When satisfactory, this "holding" by the care-taking environment facilitates psychic development from a primary state of unintegration to one in which there is a reasonably persisting sense of the localisation of the self as indwelling in the body, a sense of being a person with continuity of existence and, therefore, a sense of location in time and space. These developmental achievements can usually be taken for granted in the treatment of neurotic patients, but Winnicott argued (1945) that they cannot be assumed in more disturbed patients. Where there are failures to meet these developmental needs in what the environment provides, or the infant is unable to respond to what is offered for physiological or psychological reasons, the infant is exposed to one or more of a number of primitive agonies, which are experienced with great intensity. They include the fear of a catastrophic return to an unintegrated state, loss of the sense of the self as related to the body, and a loss of a sense of the real and the capacity to relate to the world, including loss of the sense of location in space and time, and fears of falling for ever.

The original state of unintegration is not, in itself, a source of discomfort if the mother attends to the infant's needs within a manageable time, as assumed by Freud and later by Klein, but it must be distinguished from the defensive processes of psychic disintegration. (From a Kleinian point of view, this is confirmed by Bick's (1968) observations regarding the infant's passive experience of being held together by an external object, sensed through the skin and of passively falling apart if this object fails. She regarded the experience of internal space as something depending on the behaviour of the mother, which could not be taken for granted.) These experiences function prior to a clear distinction being established between what is inside the body and what is outside it. In this model, a stable distinction between self and not-self cannot be taken for granted from the beginning of extra-uterine life, and this leads to confusion in attempts to use projective and introjective processes as defences against anxiety.

In Winnicott's view, the patient who has a fear of breakdown (Winnicott, 1974) is partly aware of an infantile breakdown that occurred in this early stage of development which could not be properly remembered because, at the time that the breakdown occurred, there was not truly a person there for the breakdown to have happened to. Winnicott suggests ways in which fear of breakdown and related states (fear of death, futility, and the wish for non-existence) can be traced to an individual's anxiety about the sufficiency of early defences against the breakdown of, or the incomplete sense of being, a "unit self". The fear of breakdown refers to something that could not be encompassed by the immature ego and, thus, remains unmetabolised, in some way known, but unable to be thought about. In this state, it is unavailable to be experienced in space and time, which is necessary before it can be recognised as belonging to the past and not to the continuous present/future. Winnicott adds this further detail to Fairbairn's understanding that analysis is feared and resisted because it requires the re-experience of repressed bad experiences for healing to take place. Winnicott suggests that the symptomatic fear of breakdown refers to something that has to be experienced in the transference before it can be relegated to memory, rather than remaining an ever-present threat, a timeless threat in the unconscious.

Fear of breakdown is a particular example of Winnicott's emphasis on the individual's need for regression to an earlier failure situation in patients where the wholeness of the personality is not securely founded. The use of the term "failure situation" is in accord with Winnicott's emphasis on the interaction between the child's developmental needs and the capacity of the human environment to meet them. Winnicott assumes that it is normal and healthy for the individual to defend against such failures by freezing the failure situation until such time as circumstances arise when a more adequate response from the environment is felt to be possible.

Balint

Balint's contributions to this stage focus on the impact on the infant's psyche of the sudden and potentially traumatic transition at birth from the intrauterine existence, where Balint believed the infant felt engaged in an interpenetrating harmonious mix up with the substances, rhythms, and generally softer objects of life, to the post-natal world of much more sharply defined objects. As with Freud, Winnicott, and Bion, there is an assumption that, apart from the trauma of birth itself, there is no demand on the ego for work: that is, for thinking, and minimal anxiety, as long as maternal care is sufficiently attuned to the infant's needs. The early presence of the mother is seen as like the air we breathe—only noticed when there is a problem. Balint envisages two primary options in the splitting of values given to the primary qualities of the post-natal world of objects and spaces. He saw the infant as choosing either to positively cathect the objects/people as the primary source of security (ocnophilia), with the infant clinging fast to its objects and dreading the empty spaces between, or the opposite choice (philobatism), which locates the things to be feared in people, while the empty spaces are to be welcomed for the freedom and thrills that the amniotic fluid and, later, the air, provide, which are neither part of the self nor of the outside. These flow between them, forming a significant part of our kinaesthetic foundations. He also adds, in his description of the phenomena of the *Basic Fault* (1968), a series of emotional and interpersonal phenomena that seem to derive from particular sorts of discrepancy in the earliest phase between bio-psychological needs and the care and attention received. This can lead to a pervasive sense of a lack of fit between individuals and the people around them, resulting in a sense of fault (in both its geological meaning of a rupture and displacement in an underlying structure and its psychological meaning: a problem leading to a sense of fault in the other and the self which has to be put right, giving rise to blame and grievance).

Fairbairn

Fairbairn's (1940) contribution to the understanding of the earliest phase took for granted the early steps in ego integration outlined above, as well as an early capacity to distinguish a hallucinated breast from a real one. (It is interesting, considering the polarisation of positions that took place following the Controversial Discussions, that Joan Riviere, a prominent Kleinian, made a forthright statement that there was always a reasonably accurate perception of reality alongside the modification of attitudes to external objects coloured by phantasy

(King & Steiner, 1991, p. 282).) Fairbairn followed Ferenczi in seeing omnipotence and internalisation as desperate defences against helplessness and dependence, in the context of really bad experiences with external objects.

Of particular significance are the consequences if the mother fails to convince the infant through spontaneous and genuine expression that she cares for him or her as a person. Fairbairn suggested that this leads to part object relationships to the breast and its functions, rather than to the mother as a person. Crucially, the mother's rejection or distaste for the child's passionate "libidinal" true self desires, its infantile "love" for the mother and her body, lead to a sense of futility and shame in the infant. As I shall discuss later, this needs to be carefully distinguished clinically from guilt and its origins in hatred. A combination of possessiveness and emotional indifference is also potentially unmanageable, except by depersonalisation and de-emotionalisation of the relationship. Regular defences against this situation are an over-valuation of internal processes and ideas. Similarly, amassing possessions, physical, bodily, and mental, defends against the experience of emptiness within. Intellectualisation, with or without erotisation and perverse elements, substitutes for the desired relationships with the parents. Primitive elements of these are split off and relationships inside are full of secret control and grandiosity. The playing of roles and a preference for "showing" rather than giving helps to manage the anxieties concerning emptiness, loss, and the surrender of control.

In summary, these theorists suggest a range of consequences following problems in early relationships, with Winnicott noting failures of ego integration, premature ego development with a preoccupation with "doing" over "being", quasi mental defect, schizophrenia, and false self organisations. Balint adds a primary attachment either to objects (people) or to the spaces between them. Fairbairn notes the over-investment in thinking and its products, with other schizoid and narcissistic phenomena, such as depersonalisation and a narcissistic preference for "showing", to gain admiration over genuine giving and receiving.

Drives, internalisation, and structure

Winnicott, like Klein, was foremost a clinician, revelling in the elucidation of the therapeutic encounter. The fact that his observations, like

Klein's, and Anna Freud's own evidence from studies in her War Nurseries (Burlingham & Freud, 1942, 1946), caused increasing strain in attempts to reconcile them with some of Freud's hypotheses did not bring forth a systematic re-examination of basic assumptions and metapsychology to accommodate the new findings. Instead, it was Fairbairn, a Scottish psychiatrist and psychoanalyst with a background in philosophy, who sought to realign the Freudian models of the mind to take account of the new data on the significance of affect and relationships as the building blocks of mental structure and character to create an object relations theory of the personality.

Fairbairn's critique of Freud's libido theory, developed in a series of papers collected in 1952 under the title *Psychoanalytic Studies of the Personality*, echoed Balint's (1935) in pointing out that the maturity of object relationships is in no way guaranteed by the reproductively appropriate use of the genital organs, just as an infant who was well fed could fail to thrive for psychological reasons. Fairbairn saw the early psychoanalysts' emphasis on the erotogenic zones as resulting from a misplaced stress on instinctual discharge and a corresponding lack of a theoretical place for the need for relationships. The revised view sees the function of libidinal pleasure and the erotogenic zones as providing signposts to the object. None of this reduces the importance of the mouth and feeding, since these provide the dominant bodily phantasy of the way in which objects are incorporated, identifications built up, and the individual's favoured techniques developed for dealing with these internalised objects.

The clear evidence that was amassing that behaviourally the normal newborn infant is primed for a relationship led Fairbairn to assert that fundamentally "libido", as described by Freud, should be regarded as "object-seeking" rather than purely "pleasure-seeking". The question as to just what are the detailed preconceptions (to use Bion's term for the situations that the infant is programmed to seek) and the nature of their psychic representations has not been fully set out even today. However, the absolute quality of Fairbairn's statement rather contradicts his usually more nuanced discussion of the different motivational systems generating human behaviour, and represents the tendency for argument by slogan or soundbite that can afflict psychoanalytic discourse as much as any other. Balint correctly observed that human motivation contains elements that require a climactic satisfaction (Freud's "end pleasures") in addition to those which are essentially satisfied by proximity to, and connection with, the desired object.

Fairbairn, who was well versed in Klein's writings, found her version of Freud's life and death instincts, in which the infant is the battleground for a primal clash between loving and hating urges, psychologically unconvincing and less than useful in understanding the complexities for the infant of maintaining relationships with objects which have combinations of exciting and frustrating aspects. Fairbairn's work with abused children and the victims of war showed him how individuals will persist in relationships with objectively bad figures to whom they are attached, identify with them, and support them in preference to being alone, suggesting a primary instinct for attachment and maintaining relationships which, in many situations, would take preference over matters of pleasure and pain.

Fairbairn's study of contemporary biological and psychological accounts of motivation showed that human instinctual behaviour divides into two broad categories. The first covers the regulation of internal tensions caused by physiological need: hunger and thirst, evacuation of bodily waste products, and, eventually, sexual release. These *appetitive* instincts, in which there is a build-up of need and tension which is released by a consummatory pleasurable act, are the paradigm Freud had adopted for his account of all instincts. Freud was well aware of *situational* (i.e., external) threats to the individual, as he noted that different psychological defences were required to deal with internal dangers because fight or flight, which are the prime options for external dangers, were not available. Fairbairn criticised Freud's last schema of the life and death instincts, with its emphasis on the strength of internal tensions, because it gave a poor account of those drives which are *situational* rather than appetitive. The appetitive version of the death instinct (generally a poor term to connote the question of destructiveness) suggests a build-up of aggressive energy that will eventually require a climactic discharge, or else defences against the build-up, and alternative forms of disposal will have to be found. Undoubtedly, in certain character structures, just this propensity is found, but, as Paula Heimann (1964) concluded and Kernberg (2009) has argued in a recent discussion, this is a later character problem rather than a fundamental quality of destructiveness. For Fairbairn, it seemed much more appropriate to regard aggression as primarily a situational drive, in that it is a response to danger, frustration, or threat to self or people to whom one is attached. Predatory aggression, which has an appetitive structure, results from the addition of sadism to the ordinary protective dispositions. In Fairbairn's model, the appetitive drives and the situational ones, including aggressions, are all developments of inherited dispositions, and this completely refutes the old accusation that Fairbairn did not believe in instincts.

Fairbairn felt that Freud's conception of the ego as a structure without its own energy, which develops on the surface of the psyche for the purpose of regulating id-impulses in relation to the demands and constraints of external reality, did not adequately describe the situation. He felt that it made more sense conceptually to see the central ego, or self, as the agency which experiences needs, has desires, and has to manage both internal and external reality in trying to satisfy these, negotiating the conflicts that are aroused in the process. His reworking of Freud's structural theory removed Freud's unhelpful distinction between energy and structure and created a model based fully on object relationships and the ways in which they become internalised unconscious schemas, or models of reality in the mind. All psychoanalytic theories recognise that the immature self has to organise the world primarily into good, welcoming, loving, satisfying objects and those that are frustrating, hostile, and, therefore, bad. For Freud, the psyche organised itself initially around the seeking of pleasure and the avoidance of unpleasure, with the phantasy of making the good objects part of the self and expelling the bad. Klein's persistent emphasis theoretically (for discussions, see Greenberg & Mitchell, 1983; Grotstein & Rinsley, 1994; Hughes, 1989; Petot, 1990) was that internal reality is primary, with good and bad objects seen as constructions of the instincts which are then found in the world. The knowledge of real trauma occurring to infants gives a surreal quality to the subsequent Kleinian accounts, to which I will return later in this discussion, which, for many years, portrayed external reality as all good while the infant is the source of all the badness and problems in the relationship. Hamilton describes this Kleinian model as one of internal object relations, because the nature of the object is defined by the instinct/drive and the only role of the environment is to help the infant to moderate its destructiveness. For the infant, the struggle is to preserve the good internal object and keep it from being destroyed by the bad.

Fairbairn's model sees the external reality as a major source of the objects that become internalised in the infant's mind. The young infant, in its absolute dependence, has to find a way of adapting to its objects to get its needs met, or it would face death. Internalisation is a way of dealing with unmanageable aspects of reality by bringing them inside the self, where they can be modified by wish-fulfilling phantasy, which is, by its nature, omnipotent. In this, it is always the relationship that is internalised and the most unbearable aspects repressed. Once repressed, the central ego, or self, can unconsciously identify itself with either the self or object side of the relationship. There are structural consequences that follow, as loving parts of the self, which are in relation to loving objects, have to be kept apart from the hating parts of the self, which are connected to the depriving, frustrating, or cruel aspects of external objects. Fairbairn refers here to the accepted and the rejected objects, following Freud's observations that there is a wish to hold on to and incorporate the good object while those generating bad experiences are to be rejected and evacuated. The relationships to the bad, rejecting, and rejected objects have to be held out of consciousness by repression, consuming emotional resources and impoverishing the ego/self. The conscious and preconscious ego contains the parts of the self and its relationships to both good and bad objects that can be tolerated in consciousness. Fairbairn suggests that the hatred of these purified frustrating and rejecting aspects of the object is the emotional source of repression. It is turned against both the experience of the self in relation to the bad object and also against the loving, libidinal parts of the self, with its urges to seek out libidinally satisfying relationships with good objects. This forms the basis of fundamental splits in the personality, which, for Fairbairn, are the basal layer of the personality. The primitive superego, therefore, contains both a cruel and rejecting element and an antilibidinal element, which acts as a "fifth column" within the personality, sabotaging benign functioning. Even in relatively healthy and integrated individuals, this factor is liable to come to prominence when stress and anxiety in the individual threatens more balanced and sophisticated functioning, since it attacks healthy and loving impulses. This fifth column functions just as Rosenfeld later described his internal mafia, mocking any attempts to believe in and seek out good objects, arguing that the rewards of triumph and manipulation are safer and superior to a doomed belief in love and goodness.

This revised picture of the mental apparatus should not be seen as rigid, but comprised of many layers of self and object representations from different experiences with objects at different developmental stages. Bowlby's (1969) description of the child's need to develop multiple models of the world which are derived initially from repeated sequences of interactions with care-givers around particular patterns of need, anxiety, and gratification closely parallels Fairbairn's conception. Fairbairn's view of the internalised schemas of the relationship to reality implied that all objects in dreams represent different versions of the self and its objects. Dreams, at an important level, always represent elements of the current state of internal reality.

Fairbairn (1941) saw the classically described neuroses as various ways of structuring the psyche's attempts at managing the threat of the eruption of these schizoid phenomena from the basal layer of the personality. Schematically, he sees these as depending on the predominant preferences in the ego/self as to where the split-off good and bad objects are felt to be located. Thus, for the phobic individual, or, perhaps more accurately, "an individual in a phobic configuration", both good and bad objects are felt to be outside the self and the depleted self urgently seeks for the good object but always fears getting the bad object instead. In paranoia, the good object is clearly felt to be inside, and is, therefore, an object of envy and hostility from an external world entirely peopled with bad objects. The obsessional has good and bad retained inside, but, in wishing to keep the good and evacuate the bad, is constantly persecuted by the thought of losing the good by mistake and by doing untold damage in the evacuation of the bad. The hysteric projects the good because it is associated with unmanageable sexuality, but has to constantly seek external objects to deal with the bad that remains inside.

Symbolism, creativity, illusion, and culture

The Independent line of development on this theme can be seen as including Jones's work on symbolism, which is then interwoven with developments on dreaming and creativity. Ella Sharpe's (1937, 1950) series of papers emphasise the dramatic, poetic, and metaphorical content of dreams, which is echoed in Fairbairn's emphasis on dreams as dramatic snapshots of relationships in the inner world, in contrast to Freud's focus on their wish-fulfilling function. The later contributions of Klauber, Rycroft, Stewart, Bollas, Parsons, and Wright can be seen to build on important contributions by Winnicott and Milner. These return to the quality of the early interactions between mother and infant, where key notions in the development of the self have ramifications for authenticity, play, creativity, and culture. For the newborn infant, good environmental responsiveness provides a form of magical hallucinatory omnipotence which forms the basis of confidence in the self and the world. (This is in contrast to the defensive omnipotence discussed in relation to internalisation by Fairbairn, above.)

Winnicott, from early in his career, observed the proto-conversations between babies and mothers which later infant research confirms is something we are all programmed for. The way that these early, non-verbal dialogues develop is crucial for later development. In "Ego distortions in terms of the true and false self" (1960b, p. 146), Winnicott describes the benign case as follows:

In the first case the mother's adaptation is good enough and in consequence the infant begins to believe in external reality which appears and behaves as by magic (because of the mother's relatively successful adaptation to the infant's gestures and needs), and which acts in a way that does not clash with the infant's omnipotence. On this basis the infant can gradually abrogate omnipotence. The True Self has spontaneity, and this has been joined up with the world's events. The infant can now enjoy the illusion of omnipotent creating and controlling, and then can gradually come to recognise the illusory element, the fact of playing and imagining. Here is the basis for the symbol which at first is both the infant's spontaneity or hallucination, and also the external object created and ultimately cathected.

In between the infant and the object is some thing, or some activity or sensation. In so far as this joins the infant to the object (via maternal part object) so far is this the basis of symbol formation. On the other hand, in so far as this something separates instead of joins, so is its function of leading on to symbol formation blocked.

The consequences of overdoses of unsympathetic reality for the infant, which Winnicott names *impingements*, are twofold. First is the premature development of ego functioning, noted above, meaning the premature resort to thinking and the instigation of self-protective activities as a way of surviving, in which a kind of integration and adaptation is mobilised that is superficial and fragile. This anxious adaptation to the mother's substitution of her reality for a meaningful response to the baby leads to the baby's adopting the mother's meanings in place of its own. The infant builds up a false set of relationships on the basis of compliance, and, by means of introjections, attains a show of being real. The extent to which this falsity operates in the individual determines how much of a person's activity is essentially a *false self* activity.

As well as giving the infant a sense of agency and potency, good enough care allows the infant to remain for periods in an unintegrated state, without the need to become anxiously concerned about what is happening and without undue concern for boundaries between the self and the not-self. The infant in a secure and comfortable state is free to exercise its curiosity about its body and the world. If the infant's spontaneous gestures receive a response from the mother that recognises the infant's creative intention, the scene is set for the establishment of a model of meaningful communication within the self as well as a fluid space where the boundaries of self and other and what is found and what is created do not obtrude. For Winnicott, this fluidity is at the heart of creativity, and the transitional space is the location of cultural experience. (See, for example, Winnicott, 1953, 1971.) A key element that enables the potential of the transitional space is the way in which the mother's attunement to the infant's needs renders unimportant the question as to who did what or who created what. This is a space that sustains a belief in creativity. In this developmental sequence, Winnicott identified the crucial role of the transitional object as the first "'not me' possession", which, through the capacity for illusion, can also represent the crucial primary objects and provide a link in the achievement of greater psychic separateness.

Winnicott saw a primary splitting of the maternal object as between the mother who meets the infant's powerful physiological needs and the "environment mother", who provides the overall holding environment, meeting the non-appetitive needs. Bollas (1987) adds a further detail of the way that Winnicott's "environment mother" is internalised. The environment mother is distinct from the mother who satisfies the appetitive drive needs of the infant. The environment mother holds the baby in mind and provides the physical security which satisfies the attachment needs and allows the self development processes to unfold relatively free of impingements. Bollas believes this function is inter-nalised not as a particular object, but more as an existential "experience of being". He sees this as being revealed in later life in an individual's search for something, which he names a transformational object, whether it is a person, place, or ideology that promises to transform the self. In analysis, this search for ego repair might not be immediately focused on the analyst, and so might be mistaken for resistance.

Milner made a number of seminal contributions to the psycho-analytic understanding of creativity. In *On Not Being Able To Paint* (1950), she explores the fact of emptiness as a beneficent state for creation, which also necessitates an encounter with the temporary terror of a plunge into the chaos of non-differentiation. Her 1952 paper on the role of illusion in symbol formation elaborates this need to return to states of unintegration and oneness in order for psychic development to proceed satisfactorily. She describes the analysis of a boy whom she concluded suffered a premature loss of belief in the illusion of oneness, and who needed, through some quite apparently aggressive and dangerous activities, to gain a symbolic return to an earlier sense of self-object confusion. In her view, the act of creation goes beyond the attempt to preserve or re-create the lost good object, which she sees as a secondary aim. Anna Freud agreed with her that in creative work there is, along with reparation, the primary aim of "creating what has never been". Anna Freud also saw this in the ther-apeutic relationship, which should go beyond the mere recovery of lost feelings and abilities and provide the basis for new attitudes and relationships derived from newly created insights into the inner world. The application of these ideas in a long analysis is vividly described in Milner's *The Hands of The Living God* (1969).

At the end of his life, it is the idea of the transitional space that Winnicott makes the bedrock of his last book, *Playing and Reality* (1971). In this, he develops his ideas on the origins of creativity; dis-tinctions between dreaming, fantasying, and living; playing, creativ-ity, and the search for the self; and the location of cultural experience.

Trauma and its place in psychoanalytic theory

The psychoanalytic project has more or less continuously grappled with theoretical tensions concerning the contributions of internal

factors and external events and their interactions to psychic development and to pathology, in ways that have had political as well as
scientific purposes and consequences. As a consequence, the issue of
trauma lies across the whole matrix of issues already discussed,
which, from their point of view, Independent thinkers probably regard
as having caused more problems for other psychoanalytic schools
than was really justified. Although the issue *per se* was not headlined
in the Controversial Discussions, it can be seen to have been a fault-
line beneath the ensuing splits between the three groups, so that, in
this discussion of Independent lines of thought, I must inevitably
return to the interplay between "political" and scientific matters with
which this introduction started. With her British School or Middle
Group stance, Pearl King could describe a straightforward trajectory
for the Independent approach to the issue.

> In the first period when Freud and Breuer were working together they
> employed the hypothesis that here was a single trauma, which became
> dissociated, through some trick of accident in recall, and which was
> not therefore available to the memory. If it were possible to abreact the
> original trauma in the treatment situation, there would then be a reso-
> lution of the problem and the symptom would disappear. . . .
>
> The second period covers the classical concepts of psychoanalysis.
> During this phase the concept of trauma was enlarged and damage
> was seen to occur through instinctual agencies or energies, through
> phantasy, and through attendant object relations, which can then
> become traumatic through phantasy and psychic elaboration. The ego
> has to defend itself against this trauma. Examples of this are familiar,
> and include the castration complex and the Oedipus complex. In these
> cases, the psychic traumata continue to influence all later stages of
> development. Thus a trauma, instead of being a once-and-for-all affair
> had become extended through time. . . .
>
> The third period developed following work in two areas of research
> . . . clinical experiences with borderline patients and the observation
> and development of infants, with special emphasis on . . . the subtle
> innuendos in the mother–child relationship. It has become clear
> through this work that patterns of ego development start early and are
> dependent on how the environment permits the instinctual and
> perceptual components of the infant's experience to be released and
> structured. (King, 2005[1963], pp. 189–190)

Fifteen years later, she added,

Analysts have been familiar with the effects from broken or damaged early object relationships in their analyses of adult patients but this work with infants emphasized the importance of the mother's affective response to the child and therefore the child's vulnerability to the mother's psychopathology. . . . It became clear . . . that if the patient's mother was psychologically very disturbed during the early infancy of her child, if she was operating on a 'part-object' level, using the infant for the gratification of her own neurotic needs and as a receptacle for her unwanted impulses and affects, the infant's affective development would be seriously distorted, his basic trust precarious, and his relation to objects inhibited by fear of 'invasion' by the other person. Thus instead of contributing progressively to the maintenance of the infant's protective shield (Freud 1920) her psychopathology would have resulted in the protective shield being cumulatively damaged (Khan, 1963) and consequently her infant's sense of himself as a person with a viable ego boundary would also have been damaged. (King, 1978, p. 329)

King noted also the contributions of Brierley, Middlemore, Winnicott, and Bowlby to this development. I would add Ferenczi, the Balints, and Fairbairn to this list, and later contributions of Paula Heimann. Set against this reasonable set of assumptions, a repetitive counterpoint occurs complaining that these facts of life are ignored in favour of an over-emphasis on constitutional factors. The tension appears early in the development of psychoanalysis and Freud's ambiguous change of emphasis on giving up the seduction hypothesis led a number of people to take this as establishing that all abuse is mere fantasy. It surfaces clearly again in 1933, when Ferenczi apologises in his controversial paper for not being able to cover adequately the exogenous origin of character formations and neuroses within his congress paper. A few lines further on he comments on the

recent, more emphatic stress on the traumatic factors in the cause of neurosis which had *been unjustly neglected in recent years. Insufficiently deep exploration of the exogenous factor leads to the danger of resorting prematurely to explanations—often too facile—in terms of 'disposition' and 'constitution'.* (Ferenczi, 1955b[1933], p. 156, my italics)

This refrain is inherent in Balint's 1937 congress paper, "Early developmental stages of the ego: primary object love", and in Paula Heimann's 1965 paper, "Comments on Dr Kernberg's paper on

'Structural derivatives of object relationships'". Bowlby assumed in the mid 1980s (personal communication) that psychoanalytic trainees at the Tavistock Clinic would be as single-minded in seeing all pathology as deriving from the infant's phantasies as had Klein and Bion during his own analytical training, which he completed in 1937. He set this out clearly in a lecture in 1983, which refers specifically to parental violence, although his thesis had applied equally to sexual abuse for many years.

> Why family violence as a causal factor in psychiatry should have been so neglected by clinicians – though not of course by social workers – would be a study in itself and cannot be entered on here. But the concentration in analytic circles on fantasy and the reluctance to examine the impact of real life events has much to answer for. Ever since Freud made his famous and in my view disastrous volte-face in 1897, when he decided that the childhood seductions he had believed to be aetiologically important were nothing more than the products of his patients' imaginations, it has been extremely unfashionable to attribute psychopathology to real life experiences. It is not an analyst's job, so the conventional wisdom has gone, to consider how a patient's parents may really have treated him, let alone to entertain the possibility, even probability, that a particular patient may have been the target for the violent words and violent deeds of one or both parents. To focus attention on such possibilities, I have been told, is to be seduced by our patient's prejudiced tales, to take sides, to make scapegoats of perfectly decent parents. And in any case, it is asserted, to do so would be no help to the patient, would in fact be anti-therapeutic. It was indeed largely because the adverse behaviour of parents was such a taboo subject in analytic circles when I was starting my professional work that I decided to focus my research on the effects on children of real-life events of another sort, namely separation and loss. (Bowlby, 1998[1983], pp. 77–78)

In another fifteen years, Hyatt Williams makes essentially the same point in his *Cruelty, Violence, and Murder* (1998):

> The role of what may be broadly called traumatic experiences has not been entirely neglected in attempts to understand how violent states of mind are initiated and maintained: however, I do not think that its importance has been sufficiently stressed. (p. 83)

Stephen Mitchell (1981) had noted that psychoanalysts are just as liable to take up extreme and polarised positions as non-analysts, and this is particularly so regarding the causation of pathology. After the retreat from the seduction theory to the finding of internal causes of neurosis in the child's incestuous desires and murderousness, the role of the actual parents in the aetiology of neurosis was minimised. In his view, Klein represents the furthest swing of the pendulum in that direction, while the position developed by Fairbairn constitutes a polar over-reaction to it: for Fairbairn, neurosis derives from parental failure. I regard the post-war relationships between the groups in the British Psychoanalytical Society as subtly dominated by this false dichotomy, which was, in fact, never as clear cut as the above sound-bite might suggest. Judith Hughes illustrates this in a pair of quotes from her book:

Klein has been faulted as an extremist of the naturalist variety. (In this connection, her adherence to the death instinct has offered her critics ample ammunition.) Paradoxically, however it was she, and not Freud, who considered external objects as psychologically, and not simply biologically significant from birth onwards. For Freud it was mother's breast alone but only as a source of nourishment and physical gratification that mattered. (1989, p. 50)

What about external objects, more particularly mother, who, for all three protagonists (Klein, Fairbairn and Winnicott) in contrast to Freud, ranked as the external object par excellence. Though Freud, in replacing sexual seduction by sexual phantasy, had made early external object ties problematic (and they remained so ever after), no one was prepared to dismiss them out of hand. Not even Melanie Klein. Her views were merely asymmetrical: bad objects derived from a child's aggression, good objects from the external world: wicked mamas of whom "everything evil . . . was anticipated . . . differed fundamentally from real objects"; fairy mammas—and good breasts— more closely approximated actual mothers who had been on hand in early infancy. Fairbairn did not waver: he regarded the real mother, not a mere fantasy as central to development and psychopathology. Yet in the work of both Klein and Fairbairn, mother remained an elusive figure as a concept, she was still, by and large an empty box. It was Winnicott who did most to fill in that box and along the way tried to convince Klein that the effort was worthwhile. (1989, p. 174)

I think the key to understanding the confusion regarding these positions is to recognise that developments in psychoanalytical theory in the twentieth century led in two apparently antithetical directions. Freud, with his own internal requirement for a dualistic theory of instincts and an inherent preference for one-body theorising, led psychoanalytic conceptualisations away from the experience-near and differentiated notion of component instincts which characterised his earlier work to the rarefied abstracted qualities and philosophical speculation of the life and death instincts. Throughout his life, too, he retained a restricting assumption that complex psychical phenomena had to evolve from simpler essential forms: that is, one ultimate instinct propelling development and another instinct driving regression. Greenberg and Mitchell (1983, p. 67) observe that in the early days trauma occurred at the moment an "incompatible idea" had forced its way into consciousness. In Freud's late theory, however, trauma relates to helplessness in the face of drive demand; for example, the loved person would not cease to love us nor should we be threatened with castration if we did not entertain certain feelings and intentions within us. The intentions are always the derivatives of fully specified instinctual drives.

They make the point that in defining the traumatic situation as relating back to the demands of the drive,

> Freud stops short of attributing to reality circumstances all that he might have, and fails to develop the implication that in different circumstances the castration threat might be experienced more intensely. Freud's emphasis on phylogeny turns us away from the idea that different parents react with different levels of hostility to the child's impulse and, in fact to the child himself. (1983, pp. 66–67)

In *Inhibitions, Symptoms and Anxiety* (1926d), Freud makes the point that traumatic neurosis is inexplicable without recourse to infantile anxiety situations. This, however, does not eliminate the contributions of the environment in exacerbating these anxiety situations. Greenberg and Mitchell note that, within the drive model, it is twenty years before Hartmann, Kris, and Loewenstein (1949) suggest that the intensity of the child's castration anxiety reflects the intensity of the parent's aggression towards him, aggression that might be veiled and which would have begun long before the Oedipal period. None the less,

Ferenczi and the Budapest School, with their perspective, which took a great interest in the fine detail of interaction, meaning, and communication, steadily added specificity and number to the environmental responses to the infant's needs that might become traumatic. It was, no doubt, uncertainties about his position in the psychoanalytical movement that meant that Ferenczi's similar contribution of 1929, entitled "The unwelcome child and his death instinct" (1955a), made little impact. The metapsychology or metaphysics of Freud's personal trajectory came, therefore, to be significantly at odds with the growing observational data and the need to construct a more complete psychoanalytic theory of development represented by this second trend.

This question about the relevance and quality of the external object's behaviour rehearses the problem of the footnote in Freud's "Formulations on the two principles of mental functioning"(1911b). Freud and Klein can be seen to take it for granted that the mother's care is such that the baby's desires will automatically be fulfilled, and, therefore, any subsequent problems for the baby are the result of excesses of greed or envy. That this situation can arise is not in dispute, and the evidence of the harshness of the superego in the children of gentle and kindly parents is best explained by the nature of the child's phantasies. The problem seems to have been the difficulty in incorporating parental ineptness, unavailability or absence, insensitivity, inconsistency, hatred, cruelty, indifference, and madness into the schema to re-balance the picture.

There seem to me to be separable elements in this complex re-tooling exercise for psychoanalytic theory. I think the polarisation of the groups and the predominantly clinical focus of scientific discussions in the British Psychoanalytic Society has hindered the tidying up of various theoretical tangles, and inhibited an open re-examination of assumptions about the fundamental building blocks of mental life, the precursors of love and hate, and the way that the whole range of infantile needs and fears are represented psychically. The old debate was mired in questions of whether earliest infancy was dominated by instinct or reality, projection or introjection, whether the inner world is based on realistic perception or whether it is dominated by phantasy. The experience of danger and trauma as coming from inside or outside depends on the existence of a self–other boundary, and so views of the immediate presence or the necessary development of that discrimination will have a bearing on the matter.

Later, around fifty years ago, when Heimann was parting company with the Kleinians, they had become a tightly knit group clearly distinguished from the rest of the "A" group who became the Independents. My belief is that the impulse to continue the dialogue around these issues was countered by an unhelpful splitting and polarisation between rival versions of psychoanalysis, represented as either a tough, challenging, superegoish, "pure" psychoanalysis, deriving authority from Freud's late model of the life and death instincts, or a tender, excusing, cosy, psychoanalytic psychotherapy, based on environmental factors. For a significant period, such an approach was described as not truly analytic, as though Fairbairn had totally dispensed with a biological basis for human motivation and any attempt to deal with external factors was seen as minimising internal contributions: as convincing an example of pathological thinking in institutions as one could wish for.

Freud's final dualistic model is predicated on the basis of a pair of opposed drives, present and creating conflict from, presumably, before birth, which evolve according to a pre-ordained sequence. In this, the paradigm for the "bad object" is the object that frustrates the *oral* needs of the infant and institutes persecutory anxiety. (Rank took the source of anxiety back to birth trauma and loss of the womb, which Klein accepted.) This is contrasted with an evolving picture in which there are a number of component instincts which orientate the infant towards the mother's breast, to suck and to swallow milk, towards her body, towards her face, towards novel and interesting stimuli, along with those which express need and emotion, initiate conversation, and mastery and facilitate attachment. Conflict is not inherently present in the organism from the start. What is gratifying and what is frustrating varies from component to component.

It was unfortunate that the strain of negotiating this paradigm shift coincided with questions of orthodoxy, heresy, and allegiance to Freud. At the time of Freud's death, the question as to what constituted acceptable psychoanalytic theory was a critical issue.

It seems to me that much of the confusion of positions regarding trauma arose because Mrs Klein had used Freud's final instinct model to great effect as a stimulus to her invaluable researches on destructiveness, while, at the same time, many of her observations accorded more with the findings of the second group, who saw a number of early needs in the infant and felt that love and hate for objects and the self were a consequence of an accumulation of experiences of satisfaction and frustration in the various need systems. Mrs Klein had emphasised the importance of object relations from birth onwards, the importance of the mother as a person alongside her part-object, tension reducing functions, and the diverse needs of the baby alongside the satisfaction of sucking. My feeling is that debates on the important clinical and theoretical issues around the shifting theoretical paradigms were complicated in the Controversial Discussions by a potent brew of emotional colourings engendered by issues of orthodoxy and succession at the time of Freud's death. It is, therefore, perhaps unremarkable that asserting the primacy of the instincts would be a key claim to the Freudian authenticity of the Kleinian position in the Controversial Discussions. It seems to me that there is more overlap, at least potentially, between Klein's 1946 "Notes on some schizoid mechanisms" and Fairbairn's "Schizoid factors in the personality" (1940) and his later papers than she allows for. Her primary challenge is to repudiate his modification of instinct theory to emphasise the infant's need to sustain a relationship with its care-givers. Several readings of Klein's (1946) "Notes on some schizoid mechanisms" seem possible, depending on whether one accords destructiveness an appetitive status, as Freud's formulations in *Beyond the Pleasure Principle* (1920g) would require, meaning that destructive forces are constantly arising internally and have to be constantly projected outwards while also giving the infant a constant appetite for aggression. The other theme is to see it as reactive to the trauma of birth, which is what primes the infant to become aware of attack and prepared to respond to it, giving destructiveness the status of a reactive drive disposition, as described by Fairbairn. However, in line with clinical experience, self-protective aggression is always liable to be suffused with cruelty and to acquire the status of an autonomous drive in an individual's psychic economy.

As I have described above, Fairbairn questioned whether the former assumption was correct and argued first that the aggressive responses of the infant appeared to be reactive rather continuous. Second, adoption of the life–death instinct dualism led to a serious underemphasis on the activity and intentions of the external object in creating "bad object situations", which cause numerous developmental complications in terms of dealing with realistically bad external objects. Heimann herself, who had been a staunch proponent of the life and death instinct model in the Controversial Discussions, was happy to concede the latter point, and to contribute herself to the re-balancing of the theory. This leads conveniently into the different interpretative strategies implied by the different models. Tonnesmann (1989) discussed Paula Heimann's view that countertransference itself is closely related to the concept of the introjected object and to trauma. Heimann described two ways in which "bad" internal objects come about. They can be the result of objects that were once felt to be good, but later become bad through bad experiences (disillusionment). Alternatively, they came about when the infantile ego was helpless against the intrusion of an aggressive object, and so passively had to endure the intrusion. Tonnesmann noted that in Heimann's papers of 1964 and 1966, she starts the unbundling of the death instinct paradigm, giving early trauma a central place in her thinking.

We are now aware of a wide range of actions or experiences that, depending on the age and resilience of the individual, might overwhelm the ego, leading to an experience of helplessness and terror. As a result of these theoretical adjustments, there has been deepening understanding of the ways in which trauma will be reproduced in the transference. The situations that might traumatise have become more and more specified and range from intra-uterine difficulties (such as placental insufficiency), through birth trauma itself, to subsequent pain, medical procedures, failures to respond to various signals from the baby, ambivalence on the part of the mother, over- and under-stimulation, over-long separations from attachment figures, loss, and weaning, before we get to the classical traumata of the Oedipus situation and castration anxiety. Trauma of all kinds might continue to occur through latency, adolescence, and adulthood. Whether something becomes overwhelming or not inevitably depends on how readily primitive anxiety situations are evoked. Again, dependent on the individual's ego strength, such experiences might lead to a variety of consequences, including splitting and projection, repression, fragmentation, dissociation, identifications with bad or guilty objects, sexualisation, and, ultimately, attacks on the senses and knowing or on the body, while there might well remain a part of the self that continues to search for a situation in which the previously unmetabolisable elements can be processed.

Conceivably, it is this controversy, more than any other variable, which has led to diverse ways of integrating the contribution of the environment into the approach in the consulting room and provides a useful bridge to a consideration of some Independent contributions to technique. Tonnesmann concisely summed up the effect on technique of the different assumptions about conflict and anxiety, depending on whether anxiety is seen as deriving from the primal clash of instincts or from fear of the environmental provision.

> There is certainly a substantial difference between on the one hand an interpretation based on the assumption that there is conflict from the beginning, the anxieties aroused by it setting into motions the defence mechanisms of splitting and projection, and on the other hand an interpretation of it as a transference manifestation in a reversal of roles. (pp. 21–22)

The analysts' contribution to the analytic process: technique

It is not possible in this short essay to give a comprehensive account of Independent approaches to psychoanalytic technique, which have been well covered elsewhere and are a significant focus of the current volume. Here, I will point to some particular technical implications that follow from the developments in theory and the understanding of the early developmental needs of infants, which I have discussed above.

From the 1920s, there had been a steady realisation that merely imparting insight by the explanation of unconscious material—"making the unconscious conscious"—was not, of itself, effective. There had been a move to interpreting it in the transference context, and not only when the transference manifested itself as a resistance to free association. The institutional accompaniments to the Controversial Discussions on the scientific issues involved a lengthy debate on the constitution of the society and the principles and content of psychoanalytic training. The Independents are fortunate that, alongside Anna Freud and Melanie Klein, three members of the non-aligned analysts presented memoranda on their approach to psychoanalytic technique (King & Steiner, 1991, pp. 627–652): Marjorie Brierley, Ella Freeman Sharpe, and Sylvia Payne. These proto-Independents made a number of points about the already distinctive British approach to technique. They noted that analysts of all backgrounds tended to make more interventions than the continental analysts who had

analysed them. The imagery had shifted from the medically dominated metaphor of an emotionally detached surgeon to that of a
particular kind of emotional relationship. This change was facilitated
in Britain by the presence of prominent lay (i.e., non-medical) analysts
with connections with the intellectual and artistic traditions of the
Bloomsbury group, and others from art, literature, and education.
Sharpe (1937, 1950), for example, clearly conceived of the analytic
setting as a place for "dramatic play". They also recognised the virtue
of flexibility according to the type of pathology that they found, with
a clear statement that with borderline or psychotic patients, interpretation had to be confined to the transference relationship.

To the new ideas about unconscious contents coming from Melanie
Klein and her collaborators was added greater understanding of the
impact of the analyst's verbal and non-verbal behaviour on the
patient, and a widening of the consideration of what is curative from
Strachey's rather restricted account of what is mutative. There was an
ever deepening of interest in psychoanalysis as a process between two
people, who were consciously and unconsciously preoccupied with
the affects and intentions of the other. Freud's "Remembering, repeating and working-through" (1914g) had set the tone for this by showing how experiences from infancy, especially, but not only, pre-verbal,
were uncovered by re-enacting them with the analyst and not as
biographical memory. Klein's evocative phrase "memories in feelings"
captures some elements of this. Marjorie Brierley set this out
succinctly in her 1937 paper, "Affects in theory and practice", where
she accords affects a central place theoretically: "In practice we find
our way only by following the Ariadne thread of transference affect.
The transference relation is always affective: successful interpretations
of impulse to object are always about the affect involved" (p. 257).

In this period, the analyst's countertransference shifted from being
seen only as a problem caused by inadequately analysed aspects of the
analyst's character. There is a move from Ferenczi (1933)[1955b]
through Alice and Michael Balint (1939), Winnicott (1947), Heimann
(1950), Racker (1968), to the situation where the affective response of
the analyst to the patient's communications (as it is described by King,
1978), becomes a key tool in the psychoanalytic process and requires,
as Sharpe puts it, "the analyst to be in a profound dialogue with
his/her own feelings". This is restated by Bollas (1987) in his discussion of expressive uses of the countertransference as "the capacity to

receive messages from the self". I prefer Pearl King's phrase "affective response" to the term "countertransference", as it connotes more than just the analyst's reaction to the patient's transference by including the whole range of ordinary human responses that the patient evokes in the analyst. While emphasising that the analyst's role is not to re-mother the child, her phrase indicates how the analytic situation allows for versions of early interactions between mother and baby to be reproduced in the transference. To this insight, Klauber (1968) adds that analysts must also factor in their own needs from the patient in this experimental theatre for attempting to experience and find words for unmetabolised aspects of early interactions. This development of understanding took seriously Ferenczi's concern, expressed in 1933, that the analyst's technique could repeat early traumatic situations. There was increased sensitivity to the impact of the analyst's silence and under-activity, leading potentially to the patient's experiences of being treated cruelly, with coldness, disinterest. These can evoke feelings of abandonment, not existing, and, in certain borderline patients, the risk of disintegration, regression, and breakdown. On the other hand, over-activity might be felt as the impingements of a non-receptive mother and lead to compliance and defences against invasion, including attacks on the analyst to keep the analyst at bay. Balint's descriptions of the unobtrusive analyst contributed to the understanding of the need for the analyst to be open to very subtle shifts in atmosphere and the rhythm of the interaction to try to keep in touch with helpful re-enactments of very early interactions with the mother and to allow the patient the experience of primary creativity. As well as describing the danger of becoming an impinging mother in the transference, Winnicott alerted the analyst to the patient's sensitivity to the analyst's withdrawal and its relationships to both regression and aggression.

Rycroft's (1958) consideration of the function of words in the psychoanalytic setting focused on the paralinguistic elements of the analytic situation and contributed to the contemporary view which sees the analytic encounter as a particular type of experiential interactional encounter of affective signs in which an interpersonal meaning system evolves where every move or failure to move becomes a gesture, and every interpretation is an intervention (Tuckett, 1997). This revised model acknowledges a considerable capacity for implicit learning as well as that deriving from explicit interpretation, including, for example, the analyst's capacity for tolerating and utilising his or her countertransference (see, for example, Bollas, 1987; Carpy, 1989; Casement, 1985, 1990, 2002; Kohon, 1986, 1999a,b; Parsons, 2000).

Putting these things together, I would see the Independent approach as including the following elements. The analytic setting is a multi-dimensional theatre for repetition through re-enactment in the transference–countertransference of the patient's whole developmental history. There is a greater emphasis on the nature of what the patient *needs* to communicate through the variety of media available, even in the restricted context of the analytic setting, rather than a more restricted focus on what the patient is doing to the analyst in the present. Independents attempt to keep an eye on both aspects, according to the psychopathology, history, and stage of the analysis. It could be put that Independents try to divide their attention between the medium of communication and the message. An early technical emphasis arose on the need to interpret the patient's anxieties about the analyst's state of mind, attitudes, and intentions in relation to the patient, and to consider these anxieties in relation to versions of early experience. The interactive nature of early infancy means that Winnicott's statement that "there is no such thing as a baby" finds an echo in that, similarly, there is no such thing as a patient, except when one considers the kind of analytic care provided by a particular analyst. The consideration of what is facilitating for what type of patient at any particular moment remains a taxing one. I would suggest that the analyst keeps the question always in mind as to whether a particular intervention at a particular moment will help the patient's psychic development. Aspects of this are discussed by Casement in his explorations of the analyst's need to develop an internal supervisor (1985, pp. 29–71).

Independent contributions on technique consider the risks to the treatment of inducing compliance, of impeding the unfolding of deep unconscious dramas by becoming over-interpretative, of feigning omniscience, being a too sharply contoured object, always interpreting everything first in relation to the analyst, limiting the patient's opportunity to make creative connections, and so on. Over-interpretation risks the avoidance of states of unintegration and stimulates the patient into activity, propelling the patient into the realm of "doing" (Winnicott) rather than allowing the patient to explore the vagaries of problems in "being". These all might impede the patient's capacity to explore their true self functioning, including owning their own aggression and freeing the healthy and creative aspects of the personality from the grip of inhibitions and internal saboteurs.

The interpretation of apparently aggressive behaviour must take into account the possibility of its being part of an identification with a bad object (cf. Anna Freud's 1937 description of "identification with the aggressor"), part of a communication through reversal of the transference, or a new behaviour showing healthy resistance against an abusive object. Hence, Limentani's important papers re-evaluating acting out and the negative therapeutic reaction (Limentani, 1966, 1981). The confession of guilt by a patient needs to be carefully assessed as to whether it is true guilt about real damage done, or the moral defence, the adoption of the guilt of an aggressive object in order to sustain hope. Similarly, depression has to be carefully distinguished from the futility that results from the object's non-acceptance of the infant/patient's urgent libidinal impulses towards the object.

Without a single instinctual origin for aggression, its manifestations need to be carefully differentiated, whether it is in the service of survival, healthy assertiveness, signalling unmet needs, or summoning up firm holding. It can also function in the reversed transference, where the patient takes the place of the original object and the analyst is placed in the former role of the patient as the reversal and attempted mastery of passively endured suffering. Further options include the sexualisation of aggression, with cruelty and triumph used to reverse and defend against death-like states, providing protection from experiences of dependence, loss, disappointment, or disintegration.

The relation to trauma discussed above is relevant here and endorsed by Rosenfeld (1987). It is inevitable that the severely traumatised patient who has to relive early infantile states in the transference will have to get in touch with severe psychotic anxieties which tend occasionally to get out of control. Severely traumatised patients, who are often driven to repeat past traumatic situations in the analytic situation, have had to endure these situations on their own for considerable periods. The analyst is often the target of very forceful projections, sometimes so violent that they appear to be attacks on the analyst and his work. Understanding what is being relived in these difficult situations can help the analyst to bear experiences that the patient has had to endure.

In connection with regression to traumatic situations, Pearl King summed up succinctly the clinical headache that confronts us: it is the problem of how to discriminate between the "return of the traumatic experiences" in the transference in the analytic setting, where the main therapeutic task is the re-assimilation by the stronger adult ego of experiences that were overwhelming to the infantile ego, and the exploitation of these traumatic experiences for the maintenance of unconscious and infantile omnipotence. In this latter case, they are not re-assimilated but perpetuated (King, 2005c, p. 69). This is the long-standing and formerly controversial issue of regression, which Winnicott considered in terms of the return to the "frozen failure situation" presented in its two forms, which Balint would have described as being either benign or malignant. Although a source of controversy in psychoanalysis, its presence is inevitable. I believe most contemporary Independents regard it as something that has to be faced and neither actively encouraged or discouraged.

Notes

1. Rayner's book is an invaluable source for the study of the issues discussed in this chapter.
2. It is noteworthy that Freud called his great dream book *The Interpretation of Dreams* (1900a), rather than "The Causes of Dreams".
3. The complexity of Freud's work as "a biologist of the mind", as Sulloway (1979) characterises him, is not helped by the way that psychoanalytic authors generally use the term *instinct* to translate both *instinckt* and *trieb*, which is closer to *drive* in English (Laplanche & Pontalis, 1973, p. 214). This is confusing in that biologists tend to reserve "instinct" for species-wide and relatively invariate responses, such as responses to danger, while using the term "drive" for more complex and individualised motivational elements. For Freud, the important element in the case of *trieb* is the relatively undetermined nature of the motive force, and the variability of aim and object that are characteristic of human sexuality. The criticism levelled at Independent theorists that they do not believe in the instincts is misguided, in my opinion. The need for relationships is just as much biologically rooted as the fight/flight responses, which, for Freud, are considered as *instincts* (Laplanche & Pontalis, 1973). The criticism is only valid in as much as Independents are not inclined to treat destructiveness as a constantly arising endopsychic need, as in Freud's

version of the "death instinct" in *Beyond the Pleasure Principle* (1920g). For them, it is initially a situational response rather than an appetitive one (see p. 21). The term "drive" is generally to be preferred, but both will be used in this chapter, according to familiar usage.

4. Strictly speaking, Winnicott's description of the incommunicado aspect of the self belongs with Freud in category one, but, as this is an aspect of the self within an organism which reaches out to the world through its spontaneous gestures, Winnicott is best regarded in the interactional class of theories.

References

Balint, A. (1939). Love for the mother and mother love. Reprinted in: Balint, M., *Primary Love and Psychoanalytic Technique* (pp. 91–108). London: Tavistock, 1952.

Balint, M. (1935). Critical notes on the theory of the pregenital organizations of the libido. In: *Primary Love and Psycho-Analytic Technique* (pp. 37–58). London: Tavistock, 1952.

Balint, M. (1937). Early developmental stages of the ego: primary object-love. In: *Primary Love and Psychoanalytic Technique* (pp. 74–90). London: Tavistock, 1952.

Balint, M. (1968). *The Basic Fault*. London: Tavistock.

Balint, M., & Balint, A. (1939). On transference and counter-transference. *International Journal of Psychoanalysis, 20*: 223–230.

Bick, E. (1968). The experience of the skin in early object relations. *International Journal of Psychoanalysis, 49*: 484–486.

Bion, W. (1959). Attacks on linking. *International Journal of Psychoanalysis, 40*: 308–315. Reprinted in: *Second Thoughts* (pp. 93–109). London: Heinemann, 1967.

Bollas, C. (1987). *The Shadow of the Object: Psychoanalysis of the Unthought Known*. London: Free Association Books.

Bowlby, J. (1940). The influence of early environment in the development of neurosis and neurotic character. *International Journal of Psycho-analysis, 21*: 154–178.

Bowlby, J. (1944). Forty four juvenile thieves: their characters and home life. *International Journal of Psychoanalysis, 25*: 19–52.

Bowlby, J. (1969). *Attachment. Vol. 1 of Attachment and Loss* London: Hogarth.

Bowlby. J. (1983). Violence in the family. Reprinted in: *A Secure Base* (pp. 77–98). London: Routledge, 1998.

Brierley, M. (1937). Affects in theory and practice. *International Journal of Psychoanalysis, 23*: 107–114.

Burlingham, D., & Freud, A. (1942). *Young Children in War-time London.* London: Allen and Unwin.

Burlingham, D., & Freud, A. (1946). *Infants Without Families.* London: Allen and Unwin.

Carpy, D. (1989). Tolerating the countertransference: a mutative process. *International Journal of Psychoanalysis, 70*: 287–294.

Casement, P. (1985). *On Learning from the Patient.* London: Tavistock.

Fairbairn, W. R. D. (1940). Schizoid factors in the personality. In: *Psychoanalytic Studies of the Personality.* London: Routledge & Kegan Paul, 1952.

Fairbairn, W. R. D. (1941). A revised psychopathology of the psychoses and neuroses. *International Journal of Psychoanalysis, 22*: 250–279. Reprinted in: *Psychoanalytic Studies of the Personality.* London: Routledge & Kegan Paul, 1952.

Fairbairn, W. R. D. (1952). *Psychoanalytic Studies of the Personality.* London: Routledge & Kegan Paul.

Ferenczi, S. (1913). Stages in the development of the sense of reality. In: *First Contributions to Psycho-Analysis.* London: Hogarth, 1952 [reprinted London: Karnac, 1980].

Ferenczi, S. (1955a)[1929]. The unwelcome child and his death instinct. In: *Final Contributions to the Problems and Methods of Psychoanalysis* (pp. 102–107). London: Hogarth, 1955.

Ferenczi, S. (1955b)[1933]. Confusion of tongues between adults and the child. Reprinted in: *Final Contributions to the Problems and Methods of Psychoanalysis* (pp. 156–167). London: Hogarth [reprinted London: Karnac, 1980).

Freud, A. (1937). *The Ego and the Mechanisms of Defence.* London: Hogarth and the Institute of Psychoanalysis.

Freud, S. (1895). *Project for a Scientific Psychology. S.E., 1*: 283–397. London: Hogarth.

Freud, S. (1900a). *The Interpretation of Dreams. S.E., 4–5.* London: Hogarth.

Freud, S. (1911b). Formulations on the two principles of mental functioning. *S.E., 12*: 215–227. London: Hogarth.

Freud, S. (1914g). Remembering, repeating and working-through. *S.E., 12*: 145–155. London: Hogarth.

Freud, S. (1920g). *Beyond the Pleasure Principle. S.E., 18*: 7–64. London: Hogarth.

Freud, S. (1926d). *Inhibitions, Symptoms and Anxiety. S.E., 20*: 77–174. London: Hogarth.

Greenberg, J. R., & Mitchell, S. A. (1983). *Object Relations in Psychoanalytic Theory*. Cambridge, MA: Harvard University Press.

Grotstein, J. S., & Rinsley, D. B. (Eds.) (1994). *Fairbairn and the Origins of Object Relations*. London: Free Association Books.

Hamilton, V. (1982). *Narcissus and Oedipus: The Children of Psychoanalysis*. London: Routledge and Kegan Paul.

Hartmann, H., Kris, E., & Loewenstein, R. (1949). Notes on the theory of aggression. *Psychoanalyic Study of the Child*, 3: 9–36.

Heimann, P. (1950). On counter-transference. *International Journal of Psychoanalysis*, 31: 81–84. Reprinted in: M. Tonnesman (Ed.), *About Children and Children-No-Longer: Collected Papers of Paula Heimann*. London: Tavistock/Routledge, 1989.

Heimann, P. (1964). Evolutionary leaps and the origin of cruelty. Revised version printed in: M. Tonnesman (Ed.), *About Children and Children-No-Longer: Collected Papers of Paula Heimann* (pp. 206–217). London: Tavistock/Routledge, 1989.

Heimann, P. (1966). Comments on Dr Kernberg's paper on 'Structural derivatives of object relationships'. Reprinted in: M. Tonnesmann (Ed.), *About Children and Children-No-Longer: Collected Papers of Paula Heimann* (pp. 218–230). London: Tavistock/Routledge, 1989.

Hermann, I. (1976). Clinging—going-in-search—a contrasting pair of instincts and their relation to sadism and masochism, M. Nunberg & F. R. Hartman (Trans.). *Psychoanalytic Quarterly*, 45: 5–36.

Hughes, J. M. (1989). *Reshaping the Psychoanalytic Domain: The Work of Melanie Klein, W. R. D. Fairbairn & D. W. Winnicott*. Berkeley, CA: University of California Press.

Hyatt Williams, A. (1998). *Cruelty, Violence, and Murder*. London: Karnac.

Kernberg, O. (2009). The concept of the death drive: a clinical perspective. *International Journal of Psychoanalysis*, 90: 1009–1023.

King, P. (1978). The affective response of the analyst to the patient's communications. *International Journal of Psychoanalysis*, 59: 329–334. Reprinted in: *Time Present and Time Past: Selected Papers of Pearl King* . London: Karnac, 2005.

King, P. (2005)[1963]. Time and a sense of identity. In: *Time Present and Time Past: Selected Papers of Pearl King* (pp. 185–200). London: Karnac.

King, P. (2005). *Time Present and Time Past: Selected Papers of Pearl King*. London: Karnac.

King, P., & Steiner, R. (Eds.) (1991). *The Freud–Klein Controversies 1941–1945*. London: Tavistock/Routledge.

Klauber, J. (1968). The psychoanalyst as a person. *British Journal of Medical Psychology*, 41: 315–323. Reprinted in: *Difficulties in the Analytic Encounter*. London: Free Association Books, 1981.

Kohon, G. (Ed.) (1986). *The British School of Psychoanalysis: The Independent Tradition*. London: Free Association Books.

Kohon, G. (1999a). *No Lost Certainties To Be Recovered: Sexuality, Creativity, Knowledge*. London: Karnac.

Kohon, G. (1999b). *The Dead Mother: The Work of André Green*. London: Routledge.

Laplanche, J., & Pontalis, J.-B. (1973). *The Language of Psycho-analysis*. London: Hogarth.

Limentani, A. (1966). A re-evaluaton of acting out in relation to working through. *International Journal of Psychoanalysis*, 47: 274–282. Reprinted in: *Between Freud and Klein: The Psychoanalytic Quest for Knowledge and Truth*. London: Free Association Books, 1989.

Limentani, A. (1981). On some positive aspects of the negative therapeutic reaction. *International Journal of Psychoanalysis*, 62: 379–399. Reprinted in: *Between Freud and Klein: The Psychoanalytic Quest for Knowledge and Truth*. London: Free Association Books, 1989.

Middlemore, M. (1941). *The Nursing Couple*. London: Hamish Hamilton.

Milner, M. (1950). *On Not Being Able to Paint*. London: Heinemann.

Milner, M. (1952). The role of illusion in symbol formation. In: *The Suppressed Madness of Sane Men* (pp. 83–113). London: Routledge, 1987.

Milner, M. (1969). *The Hands of The Living God*. London: Hogarth.

Mitchell, S. A. (1981). The origin and nature of the 'object' in the theories of Klein and Fairbairn. *Contemporary Psychoanalysis*, 17(3): 374–398 [reprinted in: J. S. Grotstein & D. B. Rinsley (Eds.), *Fairbairn and the Origins of Object Relations* (pp. 66–87). London: Free Association Books, 1994].

Parsons, M. (2000). *The Dove that Returns: The Dove that Vanishes: Paradox and Creativity in Psychoanalysis*. London: Routledge.

Petot, J.-M. (1990). *Melanie Klein, Volumes I and II*. Madison, CT: International Universities Press.

Racker, H. (1968). *Transference and Counter-transference*. London: Hogarth [reprinted London: Karnac, 1982].

Rayner, E. (1991). *The Independent Mind in British Psychoanalysis*. London: Free Association Books.

Rosenfeld, H. A. (1987). *Impasse and Interpretation*. London: Routledge.

Rycroft, C. (1958). An enquiry into the function of words in the psycho-analytic setting' *International Journal of Psychoanalysis*, 39: 408–415.

Sharpe, E. F. (1937). *Dream Analysis*. London: Hogarth [reprinted London: Karnac, 1988].

Sharpe, E. F. (1950). *Collected Papers on Psychoanalysis*. London: Hogarth.

Sulloway, F. J. (1979). *Freud: Biologist of the Mind: Beyond the Psychoanalytic Legend*. New York: Basic Books, 1992.

Spitz, R. A. (1945), Hospitalism: an enquiry into the genesis of psychiatric conditions in early childhood. *Psychoanalytic Study of the Child*, 1: 53–74.

Spitz, R. A. (1946). Anaclitic depression. *Psychoanalytic Study of the Child*, 2: 313–342.

Tonnesmann, M. (Ed.) (1989). *About Children and Children-No-Longer: Collected Papers of Paula Heimann*. London: Tavistock/Routledge.

Tuckett, D. (1997). Mutual enactment in the psychoanalytic situation. In: J. Ahumada, J. Glagaray, & A. Richards (Eds.), *The Perverse Transference and Other Matters: Essays in Honor of R. Horacio Etchegoyen* (pp. 203–216). New York: Jason Aronson.

Winnicott, D. W. (1945). Primitive emotional development. In: *Collected Papers: Through Paediatrics to Psychoanalysis*. London: Tavistock, 1958.

Winnicott, D. W. (1947). Hate in the counter-transference. *Collected Papers: Through Paediatrics to Psychoanalysis*. London: Tavistock, 1958.

Winnicott, D. W. (1953). Transitional objects and transitional phenomena. In: *Collected Papers: Through Paediatrics to Psychoanalysis*. London: Tavistock, 1958.

Winnicott, D. W. (1960a). The theory of the parent–infant relationship. In: *The Maturational Process and the Facilitating Environment*. London: Hogarth Press and The Institute of Psychoanalysis, 1965.

Winnicott, D. W. (1960b). Ego distortions in terms of true and false self. In: *The Maturational Process and the Facilitating Environment*. London: Hogarth Press and The Institute of Psychoanalysis, 1965.

Winnicott, D. W. (1971). *Playing and Reality*. London: Tavistock.

Winnicott, D. W. (1974). Fear of breakdown. *International Review of Psychoanalysis*, 1: 103–108.

Appendix

Selected themes and references

In this appendix, references are given in chronological order of authorship to indicate the development of lines of thinking.

Affect as a key theoretical and clinical focus

In order to establish a scientific basis for the study of human behaviour, Freud's early models concentrate on the accumulation of psychic energy pushing for discharge as the key determinant of behaviour. In this model, unpleasure derives from the accumulation of energy, and pleasure from its discharge. A contrasting view, which was prefigured by Darwin, emphasises affects as parts of the primary signalling system between unconscious and conscious appraising functions and a major determinant of resulting behaviour, hence, affects becomes a key theoretical construct. Darwin also described in detail the importance of emotional expressions as key elements in communication between individuals. Brierley made affects central to psychoanalytic theorising and suggested that all affects "contain" object relationships, and, in the first instance, objects are indistinguishable from the affect they arouse in the subject. The interest in affects as interactional phenomena facilitated the change in view of the analyst's feelings from being a problem to being a potential asset.

References

Darwin, C. (1872). *The Expression of the Emotions in Men and Animals.* London: John Murray.

Freud, S. (1926). *Inhibitions, Symptoms and Anxiety. S.E.,* 20: 77–174. London: Hogarth.

Jones, E. (1929). Fear, guilt and hate. *International Journal of Psychoanalysis,* 10: 383–397.

Brierley, M. (1937). Affects in theory and practice. *International Journal of Psychoanalysis, 18:* 256–263.

Balint, M., & Balint, A. (1939). On transference and counter-transference. *International Journal of Psychoanalysis, 20:* 223–230.

Langer, S. (1942). *Philosophy in a New Key.* Cambridge, MA: Harvard University Press.

Winnicott, D. W. (1947). Hate in the counter-transference. *Collected Papers: Through Paediatrics to Psychoanalysis.* London: Tavistock, 1958.

Heimann, P. (1950). On counter-transference. *International Journal of Psychoanalysis,* 31: 81–84. Reprinted in: M. Tonnesman (Ed.), *About Children and Children-No-Longer: Collected Papers of Paula Heimann.* London: Tavistock/Routledge, 1989.

Little, M. (1951). Counter-transference and the patient's response to it. *International Journal of Psychoanalysis, 32*: 32–34.

Heimann, P. (1960). Countertransference. *British Journal of Medical Psychology, 33*: 9–15. Reprinted in: M. Tonnesman (Ed.), *About Children and Children-No-Longer: Collected Papers of Paula Heimann* (pp. 151–160). London: Tavistock/Routledge, 1989.

Bowlby, J. (1969). Appraising and selecting: feeling and emotion. In: *Attachment. Vol. 1: Attachment and Loss* (Chapter 7). London: Hogarth.

Brazelton, T., Kowslowski, B., & Main, M. (1974). The origins of reciprocity: the early mother–infant interaction. In: M. Lewis & L. Rosenblum (Eds.), *The Effect of the Infant on its Caregivers* (pp 49–76). New York: John Wiley.

Limentani, A. (1977). Affects and the psychoanalytic situation. *International Journal of Psychoanalysis, 58*: 171–197.

King, P. H. M. (1978). The affective responses of the analyst to the patient's communication. *International Journal of Psychoanalysis, 59*: 329–334.

The continuing theoretical significance of affects is found in work on mentalisation.

See, for example, Fonagy, P., Gergely, G., Jurist, E. L., Target, M. (2004). *Affect Regulation, Mentalization and the Development of the Self.* London: Karnac, and in neuro-psychological developments as in the work of Damasio: Damasio, A. (1994). *Descartes' Error: Emotion, Reason and the Human Brain.* London: Macmillan; Damasio, A. (2000). *The Feeling of What Happens: Body Emotion and the Making of Consciousness.* London: Heinemann

Relation to reality

Developing Freud's 1911 account of the relationship between wish-fulfilling fantasy and the recognition of reality

Freud's 1911 observations rapidly prompted Ferenczi to elaborate the developmental stages through which this takes place. Winnicott described further elements in this developmental process with his description of the transitional object, which is both an external object and largely remains under the control of omnipotent, wish-fulfilling imagination. His description of the infant's need for disillusionment from omnipotent thinking, in manageable doses, is further explored by King in the same year. Winnicott's last major contribution on the subject comes in 1969, where he argues that the final proof that an object exists in external reality, and can be regarded as independent of the subject, is that it remains unaffected by the subject's phantasied attempts to destroy it.

References

Freud, S. (1911b). Formulations on the two principles of mental functioning. *S.E., 12*: 215–227. London: Hogarth.

Ferenczi, S. (1913). Stages in the development of a sense of reality. In: *First Contributions to Psycho-analysis* (pp. 213–239). London: Hogarth, 1952 [reprinted London: Karnac, 1980].

Winnicott, D. W. (1953). Transitional objects and transitional phenomena. In: *Collected Papers: Through Paediatrics to Psychoanalysis*. London: Tavistock, 1958.

King, P. H. M. (1953). Experiences of success and failure as essential to the process of development. In: *Time Present and Time Past: Selected Papers of Pearl King* (pp. 41–52). London: Karnac, 2005.

Winnicott, D. W. (1969). The use of an object and relating through identifications. *International Journal of Psychoanalysis, 50*: 711–716. Reprinted in: *Playing and Reality*. London: Tavistock, 1971.

How we come to feel real and an agent

Ferenczi's paper gives an account of how the developing infant uses increasingly sophisticated means to get a response from the people and things in its environment. Although the sense of being a unit self, capable of initiating action, is frequently taken for granted in psychoanalytic theorising, Winnicott developed a view of the infant's needs for environmental input in order to create a sense of a mind indwelling in its body, having a boundary around itself, and having a continuity of being in time and space. The infant needs recognition of itself as a person with intentions, gestures, and a need for communication if it is to achieve an unimpaired sense of agency and make something of its "true self" potential. These themes are developed in a number of further papers, where failure of personalisation, the absence of a sense of "carrying on being", and the development of false "caretaker selves" are described. Numerous consequences follow from imperfections in this primary sense of an integrated self, which are considered anew in "Fear of breakdown".

In a parallel development, Fairbairn and the Balints emphasised the need of the infant to feel loved and valued as a person and to have its powerful needs for of the object welcomed by the object. The consequences of sustained failure in these respects are a sense of futility, withdrawal into the inner world, over-cathexis of thinking, and the adoption of narcissistic and exhibitionistic techniques as a substitute for authentic relating to others.

References

Ferenczi, S. (1913). Stages in the development of a sense of reality. In: *First Contributions to Psycho-analysis*. London: Hogarth, 1952 [reprinted London: Karnac, 1980].

Milner, M. (1934). *A Life of One's Own*. London: Virago.

Balint, M. (1937). Early developmental stages of the ego: primary object-love. In: In: *Primary Love and Psychoanalytic Technique* (pp. 74–90). London: Tavistock, 1952.

Fairbairn, W. R. D. (1940). Schizoid factors in the personality. In: *Psychoanalytic Studies of the Personality*. London: Routledge & Kegan Paul, 1952.

Winnicott, D. W. (1945). Primitive emotional development. In: *Collected Papers: Through Paediatrics to Psychoanalysis*. London: Tavistock, 1958.

Winnicott, D. W. (1949). Mind and its relation to the psyche-soma. In: *Collected Papers: Through Paediatrics to Psychoanalysis*. London: Tavistock, 1958.

Balint, M. (1952). *Primary Love and Psycho-analytic Technique* London: Tavistock [revised 1965].

Winnicott, D. W. (1957). Primary maternal preoccupation. In: *Collected Papers: Trhough Paediatrics to Psychoanalysis*. London: Tavistock, 1958.

Winnicott, D. W. (1960). Ego distortions in terms of true and false self. In: *The Maturational Process and the Facilitating Environment*. London: Hogarth Press and The Institute of Psychoanalysis, 1965.

Winnicott, D. W. (1963/1974). Fear of breakdown. *International Review of Psychoanalysis*, 1: 103–108.

Winnicott, D. W. (1965). *The Maturational Process and the Facilitating Environment*. London: Hogarth.

Grotstein, J., & Rinsley, D. (1994). *Fairbairn and the Origins of Object Relations*. London: Free Association Books.

The following papers are representative of later significant developments.

Stern, D. (1985). *The Interpersonal World of the Infant: A View from Psychoanalysis and Developmental Psychology.* New York: Basic Books.
Fonagy, P., Gergely, G., Jurist, E. L., Target, M. (2004). *Affect Regulation, Mentalization and the Development of the Self.* London: Karnac (especially Chapter 5, "The development of an understanding of self and agency").

Nature of libido and aggression: instincts, drives, and object relations

The Independent tradition embodies an approach influenced by Darwin's evolutionary theories concerning evolved strategies for surviving in an ethological niche or habitat. All Freud's models have sought to explain psychic conflict, and progression and regression in development by positing a pair of rival groups of instincts which drive a biologically programmed process of development. His first models saw the individual endowed with a number of component instincts, with a perceived general dichotomy between the life instincts, promoting the survival of the individual, and the sexual instincts, furthering reproduction of the species. This model fits better with the Independents' approach than Freud's final dichotomy of the "life and death instincts", which is more metaphysical than metapsychological in its attempt to derive human motivation from general cosmic forces promoting either agglomeration of particles or entities, or their breakdown. It also complicated Freud's earlier statement that "love" and "hate" applied to relationships to whole objects by implying a direct correlation between the instinctual forces and sophisticated adult emotions. Klein's theory followed Freud's last dichotomy in the emphasis accorded to destructiveness and in her attempt to derive good and bad objects directly from instinctual sources, rather than through the interaction of instinctual impulses with environmental responses. Independent authors proposed an alternative to these propositions, arguing for a more differentiated account of the infant's instinctual makeup, based on Freud's earlier models, and taking advantage of developments in evolutionary biology, ethology, and contemporary psychology.

These involve:

- an abandonment of Freud's need for an overarching dualism in the origins of psychic life
- recognition of a primary need for love from, and attachment to, infantile carers (rather than love and attachment being anaclitic upon instinctual gratification)
- recognition of a number of sources and reasons for aggressive behaviour: initially as part of the infant's attempt to get what it needs (Freud, 1905d), a non-sexual instinct to master that is only secondarily fused with sexuality. The original aim is not to make the person suffer: it merely fails to take the other person into account. This view, which Freud saw as preceding both pity and sadism, is taken up in Winnicott's notions of "pre-ruth" and the "stage of concern. For Winnicott, aggression is a part of the true self endowment of the individual, allied to the infant's muscular activity and its attempts at influence and mastery of its environment. Aggression is a response to frustration, anxiety, threat, mpingement, and attack. It might also be part of a wish to evoke punishment or firm holding from the environment. It can become sexualised and turned into sado-masochism, or develop into a murderous attack on the object or the self or on the capacity to perceive
- reconsideration of the infant's initial emotional and motivational endowment with recognition of an inherent need and potential for object relationships and the distinction between appetitive and situational drives
- a recasting by Fairbairn of Freud's views of psychic structure with a central ego/self endowed with energy and agency, and the structuring of the psyche as primarily the result of the internalisation of versions of relationships with real external objects, with the exciting and rejecting aspect of the object kept apart by splitting.

References

Freud, S. (1905d). *Three Essays on the Theory of Sexuality. S.E.*, 7: 125–245. London: Hogarth.

Ferenczi, S. (1913). Stages in the development of a sense of reality. In: *First Contributions to Psycho-analysis*. London: Hogarth, 1952 [reprinted London: Karnac, 1980].

Freud, S. (1915). Instincts and their vicissitudes. *S.E., 14*: 111–140. London: Hogarth

Fairbairn, W. R. D. (1930). Libido theory re-evaluated. In: E. F. Birtles & D. E. Scharff (Eds.), *From Instinct to Self: Selected Papers of W. R. D. Fairbairn. Volume II. Applications and Early Contributions* (pp. 115–156. Northvale, NJ: Jason Aronson, 1994.

Balint, M. (1935). Critical notes on the theory of the pregenital organizations of the libido. In: *Primary Love and Psycho-Analytic Technique* (pp. 37–58). London: Tavistock, 1952.

Hermann, I. (1976). Clinging—going-in-search—a contrasting pair of instincts and their relation to sadism and masochism, M. Nunberg & F. R. Hartman (Trans.). *Psychoanalytic Quarterly, 45*: 5–36.

Balint, M. (1937). Early developmental stages of the ego: primary object-love. In: *Primary Love and Psychoanalytic Technique* (pp. 74–90). London: Tavistock, 1952..

Balint, A. (1939). Love for the mother and mother love. Reprinted in: Balint, M., *Primary Love and Psychoanalytic Technique* (pp. 91–108). London: Tavistock, 1952.

Fairbairn, W. R. D. (1939). Is aggression an irreducible factor? *British Journal of Medical Psychology, 18*(2): 163–170.

Bowlby, J. (1940). The influence of early environment in the development of neurosis and neurotic character. *International Journal of Psychoanalysis, 21*: 154–178.

Fairbairn, W. R. D. (1940). Schizoid factors in the personality. In: *Psychoanalytic Studies of the Personality*. London: Routlege & Kegan Paul, 1952.

Fairbairn, W. R. D. (1943). The repression and the return of bad objects (with special reference to the 'war neuroses'). *British Journal of Medical Psychology, 19*: 327–341. Reprinted in: *Psychoanalytic Studies of the Personality*. London: Routlege & Kegan Paul, 1952.

Fairbairn, W. R. D. (1944). Endopsychic structure considered in terms of object relations. *International Journal of Psychoanalysis, 25*: 60–93. Reprinted in: *Psychoanalytic Studies of the Personality*. London: Tavistock/Routledge.

Winnicott, D. W. (1945). Primitive emotional development. In: *Collected Papers: Through Paediatrics to Psychoanalysis*. London: Tavistock, 1958.

Balint, M. (1947). On genital love. *International Journal of Psycho-Analysis, 29*: 34–40.

Winnicott, D. W. (1950). Aggression in relation to emotional development. In: *Collected Papers: Through Paediatrics to Psychoanalysis*. London: Tavistock, 1958.

Balint, M. (1951). On love and hate. In: *Primary Love and Psycho-analytic Technique*. London: Tavistock (revised 1965).

Balint, M. (1952). *Primary Love and Psycho-analytic Technique*. London: Tavistock (revised 1965).

Fairbairn, W. R. D. (1952). *Psychoanalytic Studies of the Personality*. London: Tavistock Routledge.

Suttie, I. (1952). *The Origins of Love and Hate*. London: Pelican.

Winnicott, D. W. (1953). Transitional objects and transitional phenomena. In: *Collected Papers: Through Paediatrics to Psychoanalysis*. London: Tavistock, 1958.

Winnicott, D. W. (1956). The anti-social tendency. In: *Collected Papers: Through Paediatrics to Psychoanalysis*. London: Tavistock, 1958.

Bowlby, J. (1958). The nature of the child's tie to the mother. *International Journal of Psychoanalysis, 39*: 350–373.

Winnicott, D. W. (1963). The development of the capacity for concern. In: *The Maturational Process and the Facilitating Environment*. London: Hogarth, 1965.

Heimann, P. (1964) Evolutionary leaps and the origins of cruelty. In: M. Tonnesmann (Ed.) (1989), *About Children and Children-No-Longer. Paula Heimann: Collected Papers 1942–80* (pp. 206–217). London: Routledge.

Winnicott, D. W. (1968). The use of an object and relating through identifications. *International Journal of Psychoanalysis, 50*: 711–716. Reprinted in: *Playing and Reality*. London: Tavistock, 1971.

Bowlby, J. (1969). *Attachment and Loss Volume 1: Attachment*. London: Hogarth (especially parts I, 'The task' and part II, 'Instinctive behaviour').

Gillespie, W. H. (1971). Aggression and instinct theory. *International Journal of Psychoanalysis, 52*: 155–160.

Birtles, E. F., & Scharff, D. E. (Eds.) (1994). *From Instinct to Self: Selected Papers of W. R. D. Fairbairn Volume 1: Clinical and Theoretical Papers*. Northvale, NJ: Jason Aronson.

Birtles, E. F., & Scharff, D. E. (Eds.) (1994). *From Instinct to Self: Selected Papers of W. R. D. Fairbairn Volume 2: Applications and Early Contributions*. Northvale, NJ: Jason Aronson.

In addition to Bowlby (1969) these issues are discussed by a number of authors.

Greenberg, J. R., & Mitchell, S. A. (1983). *Object Relations in Psychoanalytic Theory*. Cambridge, MA: Harvard University Press.

Eagle, M. N. (1984). *Recent Developments in Psychoanalysis: a Critical Evaluation*. Cambridge, MA: Harvard University Press.

Hughes, J. M. (1989). *Reshaping the Psychoanalytic Domain: The Work of Melanie Klein, W. R. D. Fairbairn, & D. W. Winnicott*. Berkeley, CA: University of California Press.

Grotstein, J., & Rinsley, D. (1994). *Fairbairn and the Origins of Object Relations*. London: Free Association Books.

Perelberg, R. J. (1999). Psychoanalytic understanding of violence and suicide: a review of the literature and some new formulations. In: R. J. Perelberg (Ed.), *Psychoanalytic Understanding of Violence and Suicide* (pp. 19–50). London: Routledge.

Impact of various environmental deficiencies, impingements, and trauma on development

These include active trauma, inappropriate responses, impingements, absence, separation, emotional unavailability, inconsistency, dehumanising withdrawal, the "dead mother" syndrome, parental hatred, violence, sexual abuse, projections into the infant, treatment of the infant as a thing or non-human: leading to splits in the ego, premature ego development, quasi mental defect, schizoid phenomena, depersonalisation, psychotic fragmentation culminating in schizophrenia, internalisation and identification with the aggressor, the moral defence, etc.

The interplay of environmental impingements with the subject's fantasy and internal object world denotes the most complex area of importance in infant development.

References

Breuer, J., & Freud, S. (1895d). *Studies on Hysteria. S.E., 2*. London: Hogarth.

Ferenczi, S. (1928). The adaptation of the family to the child. In: *Final Contributions to the Problems and Methods of Psychoanalysis* (pp. 61–76). London: Hogarth, 1955 [reprinted London: Karnac, 1980).

Ferenczi, S. (1929). The unwelcome child and his death instinct. In: *Final Contributions to the Problems and Methods of Psychoanalysis* (pp. 102–107). London: Hogarth, 1955 [reprinted London: Karnac, 1980).

Ferenczi, S. (1933). Confusion of tongues between adult and child: the language of tenderness and passion. In: *Final Contributions to the Problems and Methods of Psychoanalysis* (pp. 156–167). London: Hogarth, 1955 [reprinted London: Karnac, 1980).

Fairbairn, W. R. D. (1935). Child assault. In: E. F. Birtles & D. E. Scharff (Eds.), *From Instinct to Self: Selected Papers of W. R.D. Fairbairn Volume 2: Applications and Early Contributions* Northvale, NJ: Jason Aronson, 1994.

Fairbairn, W. R. D. (1943). Repression and the return of bad objects (with special reference to the 'War neuroses'. In: *Psychoanalytic Studies of the Personality.* London: Tavistock/Routledge, 1952.

Winnicott, D. W. (1953) Psychoses and child care. In: *Collected Papers Through Paediatrics to Psychoanalysis.* London: Tavistock, 1958.

Ferenczi, S. (1955). *Final Contributions to the Problems and Methods of Psychoanalysis.* London: Hogarth [reprinted London: Karnac, 1980].

Winnicott, D. W. (1960). Ego distortion in terms of true and false self. In: *The Maturational Processes and the Facilitating Environment* (pp. 140–152). London: Hogarth, 1964.

Khan, M. M. R. (1963). The concept of cumulative trauma. *Psychoanalytic Study of the Child, 18*: 286–306. Reprinted in: *The Privacy of the Self* (pp. 42–58). London: Hogarth, 1974.

King, P. H. M. (1963/1974). On a patient's unconscious need to have "bad parents". In: *Time Present and Time Past: Selected Papers of Pearl King* (pp. 67–87). London: Karnac, 2005.

Khan, M. M. R. (1964). Ego-distortion, cumulative trauma and the role of reconstruction in the analytic situation. *International Journal of Psychoanalysis, 45*: 272–278.

Balint, M. (1968). *The Basic Fault.* London: Tavistock.

Bowlby, J. (1969). *Attachment and Loss, Volume 1. Attachment.* London: Hogarth Press and Institute of Psychoanalysis.

Bowlby, J. (1973). *Attachment and loss, Volume 2. Separation: Anxiety and Anger.* London: Hogarth Press and Institute of Psychoanalysis.

King, P. H. M. (1978). The affective response of the analyst to the patient's communications. *International Journal of Psychoanalysis, 59*: 329–334.

Bowlby, J. (1979). On knowing what you are not supposed to know and feeling what you are not supposed to feel. In: *A Secure Base* (pp. 99–118). London: Routledge, 1998.

Bowlby, J. (1980). *Attachment and loss. Volume 3. Loss: Sadness and Depression.* London: Hogarth Press and Institute of Psychoanalysis.

Bowlby, J. (1983). Violence in the family. In: *A Secure Base* (pp. 77–98). London: Routledge, 1998.

Symington, J. (1985). The survival function of primitive omnipotence. *International Journal of Psychoanalysis, 66*: 481–487.

Sinason,V. (1986). Secondary Mental Handicap and its Relationship to Trauma. *Psychoanalytic Psychotherapy* 2(2) 131-154.

Jackson, M., & Williams, P. (1994). *Unimaginable Storms: A Search for Meaning in Psychosis*. Karnac: London.

Mollon, P. (1996). *Multiple Selves, Multiple Voices: Working with Trauma, Violation, and Dissociation*. Chichester: Wiley.

Williams, P. (2000). The central phobic position. a new formulation of the free association method, by André Green. International Journal of Psychoanalysis, *81*(5): 1045–1060.

Sinason, V. (Ed.) (2002). *Attachment, Trauma, and Multiplicity: Working with Dissociative Identity Disorder*. Hove: Brunner-Routledge.

Williams, P. (2004). Incorporation of an invasive object. *International Journal of Psychoanalysis, 85*: 1333–1348.

Symbolism play, creativity, and culture

Creativity and its destruction lies at the heart of the psychoanalytic project. Freud identified the symbolic importance of fantasies, daydreams, and the internal representational world. Donald Winnicott extended the study of the relationships between fantasy, dreaming, playing, symbolisation, and play as components of healthy, everyday living. Using an object relations framework, he describes the processes that enable or impede symbolisation and creativity, a universal, ordinary, not rare human quality that permits the engagement of a growing "self" with the external world. Failure to achieve this leads to submission, falsehood, and repression of true self potential and capacities. Winnicott's ideas on "potential" and "transitional" space in the formation of a capability within the subject to use the object denote the means by which creative impulses proceed according to the child's phased development.

The mind as "inner theatre", engaged with the external world through expressive symbolic forms, has received attention from Independent psychoanalysts with regard to art, music, forms of religion, illusion, delusion, psychopathology, and character formation.

References

Freud, S. (1900a). *The Interpretation of Dreams. S.E., 4–5.* London: Hogarth.

Freud, S. (1908e). Creative writers and daydreaming. *S.E., 9:* 141–153. London: Hogarth.

Milner, M. (1934). *A Life of One's Own.* London: Routledge (Reprint Edition 2011).

Sharpe, E. F. (1937). *Dream Analysis.* London: Hogarth.

Jones, E. (1950). The theory of symbolism. In: *Papers on Psychoanalysis.* London: Baillière, Tindall and Cox.

Milner, M. (1950). *On Not Being Able To Paint* [reprinted New York: International Universities Press, 1990].

Milner, M. (1952). The role of illusion in symbol formation. In: *The Suppressed Madness of Sane Men* (pp. 83–113). London: Routledge, 1987.

Winnicott, D. W. (1953). Transitional objects and transitional phenomena: a study of the first not-me possession. *International Journal of Psychoanalysis, 34:* 89–97.

Winnicott, D. W. (1967). The location of cultural experience. *International Journal of Psychoanalysis, 48:* 368–372.

Balint, M. (1968). *The Basic Fault.* London: Tavistock.

Winnicott, D. W. (1968). Playing: its theoretical status in the clinical situation. *International Journal of Psychoanalysis, 49:* 591–599.

Milner, M. (1969). *The Hands of The Living God.* London: Hogarth.

Winnicott, D. W. (1969). The use of an object and relating through identifications. *International Journal of Psychoanalysis, 50:* 711–716.

Winnicott, D. W. (1971). *Playing and Reality.* London: Tavistock.

Bollas, C. (1979). The transformational object. *International Journal of the Psychoanalytic Association, 60:* 97–107.

Rycroft, C. (1979). *The Innocence of Dreams.* London: Oxford University Press.

McDougall, J. (1985). *Theatres of the Mind.* London: Free Association Books.

Milner, M. (1987). *The Suppressed Madness of Sane Men.* London: Routledge,

Bollas, C. (1989). *Forces of Destiny: Psychoanalysis and Human Idiom.* London: Free Association Books.

Parsons, M. (2000). *The Dove That Returns, The Dove That Vanishes: Paradox and Creativity in Psychoanalysis.* London: Routledge.

Wright, K. (2009). *Mirroring and Attunement: Self Realization in Psychoanalysis and Art.* London: Routledge.

The understanding of sexuality within in an object relational model

While Freud's account of the variability of the "object" in sexual development remains crucial, his account of libidinal development in women, and particularly the theory of phallic monism, was substantially challenged by Ernest Jones based on the researches of a group of outstanding women analysts, including Klein, Payne, Sharpe, Brierley, Riviere, Isaacs, Stephen, and Alix Strachey. Writers in the Independent tradition have continued the exploration of object relations and identifications to the development of sexual identity and function through the lifespan.

References

Freud, S. (1905d). *Three Essays on Sexuality*. *S.E.*, *7*: 125–245. London: Hogarth.

Jones, E. (1918). Anal-erotic character traits. In: *Papers on Psychoanalysis* (pp. 413–437). London: Baillière, Tindall and Cox.

Freud, S. (1925a). Some psychical consequences of the anatomical distinction between the sexes. *S.E.*, *19*: 243–258. London: Hogarth.

Jones, E. (1927). The early development of female sexuality. In: *Papers on Psychoanalysis* (pp. 438–451). London: Baillière, Tindall and Cox.

Freud, S. (1931b). Female sexuality. *S.E.*, *21*: 223–243. London: Hogarth.

Freud, S. (1933a) *New Introductory Lectures on Psycho-analysis*. *S.E.*, *22*: 112–136. London: Hogarth.

Jones, E. (1933). The phallic phase. In: *Papers on Psychoanalysis* (pp. 452–484). London: Baillière, Tindall and Cox.

Payne, S. (1935). A conception of femininity. *British Journal of Medical Psychology*, *15*: 18–33.

Jones, E. (1935). Early female sexuality. In: *Papers on Psychoanalysis* (pp. 485–495). London: Baillière, Tindall and Cox.

Brierley, M. (1936). Specific determinants in feminine development. *International Journal of Psycho-analysis*, *17*: 163–171.

Balint, M. (1947). On genital love. In: *Primary Love and Psychoanalytic Technique* (pp. 109–120). London: Tavistock, 1952.

Mitchell, J. (1974). *Psychoanalysis and Feminism*. Harmondsworth: Penguin.

Gilllespie, W. H. (1975). Woman and her discontents: a reassessment of Freud's views on female sexuality. *International Review of Psycho-analysis*, *2*: 1–9.

Limentani, A. (1975). Object choice and bisexuality. In: *Between Freud and Klein: The Psychoanalytic Quest for Knowledge and Truth*. London: Free Association Books, 1989.

Khan, M. M. R. (1979). *Alienation in Perversions*. London: Karnac.

Limentani, A. (1979). Clinical types of homosexuality. In: *Between Freud and Klein: The Psychoanalytic Quest for Knowledge and Truth*. London: Free Association Books, 1989.

Limentani, A. (1979). The significance of transsexualism in relation to some basic psychoanalytic concepts. In: *Between Freud and Klein: The Psychoanalytic Quest for Knowledge and Truth*. London: Free Association Books, 1989.

McDougall, J. (1980). *Plea for a Measure of Abnormality*. New York: International Universities Press.

Limentani, A. (1984). To the limits of male heterosexuality: the vagina-man. In: *Between Freud and Klein: The Psychoanalytic Quest for Knowledge and Truth*. London: Free Association Books, 1989.

Limentani, A. (1986). Perversions: treatable and untreatable. In: *Between Freud and Klein: The Psychoanalytic Quest for Knowledge and Truth*. London: Free Association Books, 1989.

Limentani, A. (1989). *Between Freud and Klein: The Psychoanalytic Quest for Knowledge and Truth*. London: Free Association Books.

Limentani, A. (1991). Neglected fathers in the aetiology and treatment of sexual deviation. *International Journal of Psychoanalysis, 72:* 573–584.

Birksted-Breen, D. (Ed.) (1993). *The Gender Conundrum*. London: Routledge.

Campbell, D. (1999). The role of the father in a pre-suicide state. In: R. J. Perelberg (Ed.), *Psychoanalytic Understanding of Violence and Suicide* (pp. 75–86). London: Routledge.

Bollas, C. (2000). *Hysteria*. London: Routledge.

Parsons, M. (2000). Sexuality and perversion a hundred years on: discovering what Freud discovered. *International Journal of Psychoanalysis, 81:* 37–49.

Perelberg, R. J. (2002). Sadism, erotisme and melancolie. *Revue Française de Psychanalyse, LXVI:* 1225–1230.

Mitchell, J. (2003). *Sibling Identity and Relationships: Sisters and Brothers*. Cambridge: Polity Press.

Raphael-Leff, J., & Perelberg, R. J. (2008). *Female Experience: Four Generations of British Women Psychoanalysts on Work with Women Patients*. London: Anna Freud Centre.

CHAPTER TWO

An Independent theory of clinical technique

Michael Parsons

T he word "Independent", with a capital "I", entered the psychoanalytic vocabulary around 1950. That was when, after the so-
called "Controversial Discussions", the informal "Middle
Group" of analysts, who did not align themselves with either Anna
Freud or Melanie Klein, agreed to become formally a third group
within the British Society: the Group of Independent Psychoanalysts.

Melanie Klein settled in London in the late 1920s and became an
influential member of the British Society. A polarisation developed
between her views and those of Anna Freud about child analysis and
about early psychic development. So long as Anna Freud was at a safe
distance with her father in Vienna, these debates remained at the level
of theoretical and technical discussion. The flight of the Freud family
to Britain in 1939, however, brought Anna Freud to settle in London
as well, and from then on the arguments between Klein's adherents
and those of Anna Freud took on an acrimonious, personal quality.
The essential points of theoretical disagreement were about Klein's
emphasis on early infantile phantasies, which Anna Freud did not
believe in, Klein's stress on innate destructiveness as the main factor
around which development was organised, which Anna Freud
thought devalued the importance of infantile sexuality, and Klein's

early dating of the Oedipus complex. The Controversial Discussions in the early 1940s clarified these differences but did not resolve them.

The British Society was in danger of splitting, and the solution was to work out a scheme involving two parallel streams of training. One was for students who would follow the views of Anna Freud (known as the "B" Group) while the other training was run both by those analysts who specifically identified themselves with Melanie Klein's ideas and by those who remained non-aligned between the two factions. Within this "A" Group, the distinction between the Kleinian and the non-aligned analysts was marked by the fact that whichever stream of training a student was following, the second training case had to be supervised by one of the non-aligned analysts. The polarisation in the Society continued, and this requirement for a non-aligned supervision was dropped. The A group was replaced by a specifically Kleinian group, while those analysts who still wanted not to align themselves with either Anna Freud's B group or the Kleinians came to be known as the Middle Group. For some years, they resisted the idea of being considered as a group at all. It was their independence from any particular psychoanalytic doctrine that mattered most to them, and the fact that there might be quite striking differences amongst them was all part of that. But the pressure to become a third group within the Society was eventually too great, and so they became what is usually known as the Independent Group. It is worth noting, however, that the proper name of the group is not the "Independent Group", but the "Group of Independent Psychoanalysts", an important nicety which still shows the original unwillingness to sacrifice individuality.

This history means there have always been two aspects to the identity of the Independent Group. One is to have been defined by a negative. Its members were the residue of the Society, who would not align themselves with either of the other two groups. But it was not just a buffer zone whose inhabitants selected themselves by default. Its members also constituted, by and large, the original structure of the British Society, like the original part of a building with a new wing added on either side. This original structure had its own characteristics, and these are the roots of what may be called the Independent Tradition. The titles of Gregorio Kohon's (1986) book, *The British School of Psychoanalysis: The Independent Tradition* and of Eric Rayner's (1991) *The Independent Mind in British Psychoanalysis* noticeably make no reference to a group. The Independent Group was faced with a contin-uing question, over the years, about what kind of group it was to be. It had the options either of emphasising its negative identity as a home for all those who did not want to align themselves with any other viewpoint, or of seeking, positively, to represent and develop that Independent Tradition. The Group, as a group, implicitly but clearly went in the former direction.

The Independent Tradition does not coincide with the Indepen-dent Group. They overlap, in that analysts who have exemplified and developed that tradition have tended to belong to the Group. But there are members of the Independent Group who do not stand within the Independent Tradition, and, conversely, the Independent Tradition is not limited to the Group, or even to the British Society. There are analysts whose work places them clearly in that tradition, despite their having no connection with either.

Independent analysts have tended to organise their analytic iden-tities around underlying intellectual and human values, rather than particular analytic doctrines. To put it the other way round, the desire for freedom to do that is what makes Independents unwilling to organise their identities around a doctrine. This is not simply histori-cal, a reluctance to sign up to Melanie Klein's or Anna Freud's partic-ular viewpoints; there is a deeper sense that any theoretical position that claims overarching, universal validity should be treated with suspicion. Freud's theory of instincts, for example, evolved through various stages, but what did not change was his fundamental view of human beings as the products of a system of biologically deter-mined drives. For all Klein's differences from Freud, she also saw development in terms of an innate schema, one that was, in her view, determined at root by the need to deal with the death instinct. The two new wings were at opposite ends of the original building, but they shared a certain universalising approach, seeing particular human beings in terms of the way they exemplified a general underlying theory. The Independent Group has been politically preoccupied with dissociating itself from other viewpoints in the British Society, while analysts of the Independent Tradition have been more concerned to represent actively and positively a different cast of mind, a non-universalising approach whose emphasis is on what differentiates human beings and makes them unique, rather than on how they exemplify general principles.

One of the most passionately individual of psychoanalysts was Sándor Ferenczi. It is through him that the Independent tradition derives ultimately from Freud. Ferenczi saw psychoanalysis as grounded in experience rather than dogma and, above all, as a matter of the unique experience of the individual patient. His influence on the Independent Tradition came most directly through Michael Balint, but there is a widespread resonance between Ferenczi's thought and the ideas of many Independent thinkers.

In his paper, "The elasticity of psychoanalytic technique", Ferenczi (1928) introduced the idea of "tact" as an essential quality in the analyst's relation to the patient. This came under fire from Freud and Fenichel, who thought it relied on subjective intuition instead of systematic theory. Ferenczi, defending his concept, said, "there is no conflict between the tact we are called upon to exercise and the moral obligation not to do to others what in the same circumstances we should not desire to have done to ourselves" (Ferenczi, 1955[1928], p. 90). All analysts, of course, would agree that it is important to understand things from the patient's point of view. But different preconscious assumptions among analysts about what this means can produce distinctly different therapeutic climates. I want to emphasise not just that Ferenczi, like many people, believed in an obligation of care and concern from one human being to another. My point is that an ethical principle like this, and not a metapsychological or theoretical belief, is what he takes as the starting point for his theory of clinical technique.

Because of this humanist, rather than scientific, starting point, Ferenczi has been criticised as though he did not have any theory of clinical technique. But his papers on technique and his *Clinical Diary* (Ferenczi, 1988) show him thoroughly aware of the need for it, and struggling to develop the clinical theory he required. The concepts he needed were not available in his time: hence the frustration of his struggle. After being dismissed for years, Ferenczi's work is appreciated nowadays by analysts of various orientations. But it is the Independent Tradition in particular, I think, that has developed concepts which allow us to articulate the kind of clinical theory Ferenczi was searching for.

Ferenczi placed more emphasis on the quality of the patient's experience than on what the analyst was supposed to do. This focus is clear, for example, when he writes that his so-called "active technique" should only be used when conventional technique has been thoroughly deployed, the developmental basis of the patient's condition has been worked through, and only the "throb of experience" is lacking (1926, p. 220). Here, he points towards a central feature of Independent psychoanalysis: that what comes from the patient, and what the patient experiences as his or her own discovery in the analytic encounter, matters far more than anything that comes from the analyst. What comes from the analyst is crucial, of course, but only for the way it facilitates patients' own experience of themselves. Once this is spelt out, it might not sound controversial. What characterises the Independent Tradition is the way it takes this as a primary focus in its theory of clinical technique. Winnicott, for example, referring to therapeutic consultations with children, says that "The significant moment is that at which *the child surprises himself or herself.* It is not the moment of my clever interpretation that is significant" (1971b, p. 51); and for Christopher Bollas, the essence of psychoanalysis is that it "supplies a relationship that allows the analysand to hear from his or her own unconscious life" (2002, p. 10).

To return to Ferenczi's "moral obligation not to do to others what ... we should not desire to have done to ourselves", the positive implication is that what we *should* do to others is what we *do* desire for ourselves. The psychoanalytic reflection of this is that the kind of attention and understanding that the analyst gives to the patient, he needs also to bring to bear on himself. Since almost the beginning of psychoanalysis, of course, the need has been recognised for analysts to be alert to the dangers of their countertransference reactions, and through the second half of the past century views of countertransference expanded so as to give it a more positive function as well. Countertransference awareness is both necessary and helpful. But it is not just a safeguard and a useful adjunct to help the analyst understand the patient. Independent understanding goes beyond this to say that the analyst's psychoanalytic attention to his or her own state of mind is itself the vehicle of analytic activity (e.g., Parsons, 2006). Unless an analyst treats himself or herself in the same way that he or she is treating the patient, nothing psychoanalytic at all will happen between them.

Near the end of Ferenczi's paper, "The elasticity of psychoanalytic technique", he writes, "The ideal result of a completed analysis is precisely that elasticity which analytic technique demands of the mental therapist" (1955[1928], p. 99). That is to say that the aim of psychoanalysis is to foster in the patient a quality which, for that development to happen, needs also to be present in the analyst. This does not mean that analysts want their patients to identify with them in a compliant or mimetic sort of way, and to speak of the patient's introjecting the analyst would not be typically Independent language. More characteristically Independent would be the idea of patients' internalising a capacity—to use a Winnicottian word (Winnicott, 1958; Hopkins, 1997)—that they find in the analyst. But the essentially Independent idea prefigured in Ferenczi's formulation is that a patient is enabled to discover something in herself, because she is in a particular relationship with someone who is working at that same sort of discovery in his or her own self. I have expressed this elsewhere as follows:

> The patient is there to see further into the things that really matter about himself and his life. But for that to happen he has to sacrifice the arrangement which, until now, it has mattered very much to preserve. The analyst needs to see further into what really matters about the analysis. But to do that he must be prepared to let go of the way he has seen things so far. The two situations reflect each other, and the analyst's being open to his version helps the patient to experience his. (Parsons, 2000, pp. 43–44)

Such an emphasis on the relation between the patient's self-discovery and the analyst's own self-discovery runs through much Independent writing, with an underlying belief that unless analysts find personal meaning in their work, there will be no personal meaning in it for their patients either.

What distinguishes such a mutual effort at self-discovery as being psychoanalytic? The first thing to say is that Independent analysis tends not to wear its theory on its sleeve. When the British analyst Martin James (1979, unpublished) discussed what concepts might be essential to Independent analysis, his first point was that Independents tend towards a vernacular style, using everyday language in speaking and writing about analysis. Ferenczi's comment, that the ideal result of analysis is a kind of elasticity, is not a metapsychological statement. It refers to a quality of psychic life. Ferenczi does not characteristically invoke such terms as the resolution of intrapsychic conflict, adoption of less primitive defence mechanisms, giving up infantile fixations, or progression from one developmental stage to another. No doubt he would have agreed with these if they were put to him, but his natural way of thinking is in terms of psychic qualities such as elasticity and flexibility. If these were put to non-Independent analysts, they would probably agree in turn, like Ferenczi faced with a metapsychological formulation. For analysts in the Independent Tradition, though, it is a natural habit of mind to think primarily in terms of the quality of psychic life, using ideas like elasticity and flexibility, intellectual freedom, emotional availability, openness to relationships, tolerance and enjoyment of complexity, and the sense of being real. Thomas Ogden, for example, writes in an unmistakeably Independent vein about aliveness:

> I believe that every form of psychopathology represents a specific type of limitation of the individual's capacity to be fully alive as a human being. The goal of analysis from this point of view is larger than that of the resolution of unconscious intrapsychic conflict, the diminution of symptomatology, the enhancement of reflective subjectivity and self-understanding, and the increase of sense of personal agency. Although one's sense of being alive is intimately intertwined with each of the above-mentioned capacities, I believe that the experience of aliveness is a quality that is superordinate to these capacities and must be considered as an aspect of the analytic experience *in its own terms*. (1995, p. 696)

In the clinical situation, all analysts would probably favour simple, non-technical language. But this is especially important for Independents because of their particular stress on what patients find in themselves rather than what comes from the analyst. The special priority given in Independent clinical technique to fostering, and not getting in the way of, a patient's self-discovery is one reason why Independent analysts make a point of using ordinary conversational language. But this is important not only in talking to patients. In their own thinking as well, Independent analysts might wish to avoid language that carries too much pre-packed theoretical baggage with it. James emphasised what he called an existential point, that for an Independent analyst every clinical observation exists in its own right, and not as an example of something. One of the functions of theory in Independent psychoanalysis is to allow us to imbue with psychoanalytic understanding our use of everyday language.

This raises a general question about the role of interpretation in Independent analysis. Ferenczi (1955[1928], pp. 95–96) advises, "the analyst must wait patiently", and "Above all, one must be sparing with interpretations". As before, his emphasis corresponds to later Independent developments. Compare Pearl King's (1978, p. 334) comment that "We have to wait without any preconceptions for whatever our patients communicate to us", followed by her emphatic quotation from T. S. Eliot that "the faith and the hope and the love are all in the waiting". Winnicott stressed the need to interpret in terms of patients' own psychic realities, and said, "The analyst is prepared to wait a long time to be in a position to do exactly this kind of work" (Winnicott, 1965, p. 37). Enid Balint, in a paper about her analytic technique, highlights the tension between necessary waiting and the temptation to activity.

> The analyst must not be intrusive or lead the way, but he must be there, listening alertly. He . . . sometimes has to point out . . . obstacles, which prevent the patient from finding what he is looking for but which have been put there by the patient himself so as to avoid having to undertake this painful task. The analyst . . . may sometimes be tempted to follow an easier path without realising it . . . Usually, however, the analyst has to wait. (1993, p. 122)

And again, "In order to release himself and the patient from prison, the analyst must exercise the ability to wait" (1993, p. 129).

The implication that the analyst has to be freed as well as the patient is another example of the characteristically Independent parallelism between the analyst's internal process and the patient's.

This theme is notably explored in Neville Symington's (1983) paper, "The analyst's act of freedom as agent of therapeutic change". Symington's examples include a patient, originally seen in a reduced-fee clinic, whom he was continuing to charge a considerably reduced fee based on the assumption that she could not pay more. References in the patient's material to a patronising employer led Symington to realise that he had become "the prisoner of an illusion about the patient's capacities" (p. 283). When he brought up the question of her fee, she said, "If I *had* to pay more, then I know I would." He did raise her fee, at which "she cried rather pitifully but then became resolved that she would meet the challenge". Striking changes followed in the direction of self-sufficiency and independence, both in her work and her emotional life. Another patient regularly expressed a fear that the analyst would think him pathetic, inducing Symington each time to make an interpretation tacitly implying that he would not. The patient, says Symington, "would then obligingly tell me the thought in his mind". A passage from Bion that Symington happened across led him to realise how the patient was extracting from him a predetermined response and so limiting his analytic freedom of thought.

> I had been a prisoner of this patient's controlling impulses and at the moment of reading this . . . I had a new understanding in which I felt freed inwardly . . . The next time he expressed his apprehension that I would think him pathetic I said to him quietly, 'But I am quite free to think that'. He was much taken aback. It was then possible to see how much he operated by controlling my thoughts and the thoughts of others. (p. 284)

I said earlier that the importance of what comes from the analyst lies in how it facilitates patients' own experience of themselves, and quoted Winnicott and Bollas on patients' taking themselves by surprise and hearing from their own unconscious life. What helps a patient most towards this is the unconscious recognition of being in a relationship with someone, the analyst, who knows the importance of hearing from their own unconscious life and of being able to take themselves by surprise.

Ferenczi's emphasis on restraint in interpretation recurs in Michael Balint's work, notably in the chapter in *The Basic Fault* entitled "The unobtrusive analyst" (1968, pp. 173–181). This is concerned with patients in a state of regression, whom Balint thought needed not interpretation so much as for the analyst to provide a particular kind of environment. It might be imagined that when analysts like Winnicott and Balint write about regression, they must be meaning something on a large scale, unmistakeable and persistent. Extended episodes of profound regression do occur (Marion Milner's (1969) book *The Hands of the Living God* is a classic account of such a case), but the regressive episodes that occur commonly in analysis are on a smaller scale. Enid and Michael Balint shared and developed their ideas closely together, and Enid emphasised that "Regressive periods may be very brief, but they must be observed and respected" (1993, p. 122). This connects with her own view of the analytic stance.

> If I am asked ... what I think is essential to analytic work, I may
> answer, after I have stressed the need for a basic and thorough train-
> ing in psychoanalytic theory and practice, that it is important for the
> analyst not to be too intrusive. (ibid., p. 121)

Ferenczi and Michael and Enid Balint exemplify the interweaving
in Independent clinical theory of these themes: that regression subtly
pervades the whole analytic experience, that this needs to be accepted
as an unconscious communication, and that such acceptance of regression involves providing an environment for the patient which may
imply great restraint in interpretation, however true the unmade interpretations might have been. Winnicott (1954) and Harold Stewart
(1992, pp. 101–126), among other Independent analysts, have
addressed the same issues.

But the subtle pervasiveness of regression is not the only reason
why an analyst makes a point of not being intrusive. Independent
analysts do interpret, as well as wait, but their way of interpreting is
as much to do with creating a therapeutic environment as with
conveying particular bits of insight. Rycroft (1956, p. 472) wrote,

> In addition therefore to their symbolic functioning of communicating
> ideas, interpretations also have the sign-function of conveying to the
> patient the analyst's emotional attitude towards him. They combine
> with the material setting provided by the analyst to form the analyst's
> affective contribution to the formation of a trial relationship, within
> which the patient can recapture the ability to make contact and
> communication with external objects.

At the time Rycroft wrote that, it was controversial to value interpretations for conveying to patients that their analyst had a benign
emotional attitude towards them. This seemed too close, for some, to
Alexander's (1950) "corrective emotional experience", arousing fears
of seduction and collusion that needed guarding against by the auster-
ity of pure understanding. Segal's (1962) paper, "The curative factors
in psychoanalysis", is a classic example of this anxiety. Even today,
one can run across the careworn assumption that Independent
analysts "soft-pedal" their patients, neglect the negative transference,
and so on. This is just plain wrong. As far back as 1928, Ferenczi
himself, who is perhaps most of all caricatured as collusively indul-
ging his patients, wrote that "the analyst must accept for weeks on

end the role of an Aunt Sally on whom the patient tries out all his aggressiveness and resentment" (1955[1928], p. 93).

In her chapter on clinical technique, Enid Balint emphasises three times the need for a thorough training in basic psychoanalytic theory and technique. One of these statements is particularly worth noting.

> Imagination is a precondition of the creative life. It can be safely used only if the structure and training are there; but the structure and training are useless if the analyst's imagination, or the patient's, is imprisoned. (1993, p. 129)

And this is the point at which she says, "In order to release himself and the patient from prison, the analyst must exercise the ability to wait" (1993, p. 129). This view of the function of theoretical structure and technical discipline as being to mediate the analyst's creative imagination, is, to my mind, a characteristically Independent attitude.

The mistake of the "soft-pedalling" criticism comes from a failure to grasp the theory behind the Independent clinical stance. In their early papers, Rycroft, Balint, and Winnicott were developing the idea that the function of the analytic setting is to provide for a particular quality of object relating. To speak of the object relationship between patient and analyst might seem obviously to refer to the transference, with the interest being in how that object relationship is unconsciously affected by the patient's repetitions and projections. Of course, all analysts continually think in those terms. That is part of what Enid Balint meant by "a basic and thorough training in psychoanalytic theory and practice". But the analytic relationship is not simply a substrate for transference. What Rycroft, Winnicott, Balint, and others since them in the Independent tradition have progressively articulated is a quality of object relating that needs to be a fundamental bedrock of the analytic setting, whatever the vicissitudes of the transference. When some analysts talk about the importance of the setting, they mean, on the one hand, keeping practical boundaries about session times and so on, and, on the other, a firmness about not being drawn into non-analytic responses to the patient when interpretation is what is called for. Again, this is common analytic currency. But the emphasis on the framework that characterises Independent thinking is subtly different. Ferenczi knew that the exchange between analyst and patient needed to be at the level of ordinary human interaction. What he searched for with such difficulty, and what Independent analysts have worked to articulate, is a framework that can infuse ordinary human interaction with psychoanalytic awareness, a framework that will maintain that conjunction, so that the exchange does not stop being either human or analytic. Here are two strikingly similar statements about the nature of psychoanalysis. Enid Balint (1993, p. 129) says that the analyst needs to "see analysis more like the process of learning a language than a joint journey of explanation or research", while Khan (1972, p. 135) ends his paper, "On Freud's provision of the therapeutic frame", as follows:

> Hence in Freud's therapeutic frame, the emphasis is not only on the understanding of the meaning and resolution of the malady, but even more importantly and essentially on the discovery by the analyst and patient together of a symbolic language which is larger and richer than the individual tradition of each alone.

How to describe the specific quality of analytic relating that lies behind this? One aspect is its appreciation of the importance of a patient's external reality. I mentioned earlier the analyst's provision of an "environment". Riviere (1927, p. 376) said in a symposium on child analysis,

> Psycho-analysis is Freud's discovery of what goes on in the imagination of a child. Analysis has no concern with anything else: it is not concerned with the real world, nor with the child's or the adult's adaptation to the real world, nor with sickness or health, nor virtue or vice. It is concerned simply and solely with the imaginings of the childish mind, the phantasied pleasures and the dreaded retributions.

In 1927, Riviere was fighting the Kleinian corner against Anna Freud. I do not know how many analysts would still take such an extreme view, but it is against such a background that Winnicott (1964, p. 88) made his statement that there is no such thing as a baby without a mother, and chose to call his book *Maturational Processes and the Facilitating Environment* (1965). There is a real difference among analysts in how interested they are in a patient's environment and in his or her relation to external reality. I have quoted Rycroft on the analyst's contribution to a relationship "within which the patient can recapture the ability to make contact and communication with external objects". And, for Enid Balint, "the core of psychoanalysis is, in brief, the understanding of intrapsychic processes and states, and their relationship, or lack of it, with external reality" (1993, p. 121).

This emphasis on the interrelation of intrapsychic and external reality makes it important to locate the experience of the analysis in the historical context of the patient's life as a whole. One source of the difficulty between Freud and Ferenczi was the way that Ferenczi respected his patients' accounts of trauma, and his insistence that the analytic environment should not replicate them.

Such an analytic climate depends more on how analysts listen than on the things they say. Independent clinical technique can be considered, in fact, more as a way of listening than of interpreting. When Enid Balint writes about the analyst's need to wait, she says, "In my experience this seems more and more necessary, not less so, as the analyst becomes more experienced and more able to listen for variations and contradictions" (1993, p. 122). This is striking. One might think that the experienced analyst, understanding more quickly, would not have to wait so long before interpreting. But no. Again we see that the waiting itself and the listening itself are what matter.

It might be assumed that the point of the analyst's free-floating attention or, as we may call it, free-associative listening, is to detect what is being unconsciously communicated by the patient. This is true, but it is only part of the story. The emphasis in Independent analysis on the quality of the analyst's listening—and on how the analyst's interventions arise out of a particular kind of listening—helps patients discover how to listen to themselves in a new way and, as Bollas put it, to hear from their own unconscious lives. A basic function of this kind of listening is simply to facilitate for the patient the activity of free associating. Free association is valuable not only because it reveals unconscious mental content, but as an imaginative activity in its own right. To help somebody become less anxious about having to control the internal mobility of their thoughts and feelings is, itself, to facilitate their psychic growth and development.

In this connection, Bollas mentions several times the *use* that the patient makes of the analyst. This idea that the analyst, as well as understanding and interpreting, is there to be psychically made use of by the patient, is a key Independent concept. When a patient is speaking, it might seem obvious what the analyst is doing: listening to the patient's "material" and trying to understand it. In periods—perhaps long periods—of silence, there might seem nothing to listen to, and nothing for the analyst to do except, as I have emphasised, to wait. But the waiting analyst is not doing nothing. Just as much as to a patient's words, an analyst will listen to the silence, and not in the hope of finding something to say. This kind of listening, whether to a patient's silence or their speech, is a continuous invisible activity of the analyst's making himself available to be psychically utilised.

I have described elsewhere (Parsons, 2007) a silence that lasted throughout the session. A patient took up position on the couch and lay silent. The silence continued and dream-like images came to me. I let myself be interested in them, but not because I hoped they would give me a clue about what to say. My way of listening to the silence was not about looking for a helpful intervention. The silence was not absolute. Sometimes, one knows that any movement whatever could disturb the utter stillness that a patient needs, but this was not like that. I knew I must not move suddenly or noisily, in a way that could suggest irritation or frustration, but I also knew that absence of all sound was not called for. The patient shifted on the couch from time to time. I did the same in my chair. Not by conscious decision—I just let it happen when I felt like it, in a natural easy way that showed I was comfortable. After a while, it seemed as though our bodies were responding to each other in a kind of slow dialogue. I had the thought: two men whose bodies are moving together in response to each other? It seemed something homosexual was happening between us. But it did not feel erotic. I thought of the *Three Essays* and how Freud broadened the understanding of what sexuality means. Was I experiencing something with this man that was sexual in a wider sense? And the session ended, without either of us having spoken a word.

Two sessions later, he wondered if a man he had seen coming out of my house might be my son. Apparently overt homosexual references in the same session led me to interpret that he wanted to stop the heterosexual intercourse that had produced my son by thinking that I would have intercourse with him instead. He recapitulated my interpretation of his negative Oedipus complex in a deadening, literal sort of way. "So you mean that there is somebody that you have sex with, and I do not want this third person to be there. I want you just for myself. And that is why I want you to come into me from behind." His understanding was verbally correct, but lifeless.

In the following session, he described a dream of an enormous rabbit, which he wanted to come close to and cuddle. The subsequent material was almost totally pre-Oedipal, and full of anxiety about contact with an object that was confusedly indeterminate between genital and breast. My Oedipal interpretation in the previous session, however accurate, had been misjudged. I thought I was addressing his anxiety about one sort of genital intercourse (parental) and his wish to substitute a different sort (passive homosexual with me as his father). But the patient had no notion, at that moment, of any sort of genital intercourse. The significance of the silent session became clear at this point. I had sensed the alternating movement of our bodies and thought at first that I must be involved in a homosexual interaction. But it did not feel erotic. I thought of Freud's extension of the meaning of sexuality and, sure enough, this last session revealed that the patient had been in a state of pregenital and preverbal regression. The mutual responsiveness of our bodies was not that of two men, but of mother and infant.

This episode exemplifies the importance of listening as being the way in which the analyst makes himself available, rather than a functional way of arriving at interpretations. It also shows the patience and restraint that might be necessary for the analyst really to allow the time to take himself by surprise. And my misjudged Oedipal interpretation shows what happens when an analyst uses theory as something to fall back on and not as a stimulus to freeing his imagination. But, as well as illustrating these points I have already made, this episode shows something further about what it means for an analyst to make himself available to be utilised. Bollas (2000, p. 42) mentions times when the analyst might find, while making a comment, that the patient appears to have drifted off.

> The analyst discovers that his or her interpretation is not used for its apparent accuracy, but as a kind of evocative form: because the analyst is talking, curiously the patient is free not to listen! But in not listening, the patient seems intrapsychically directed towards another interpretation. To the analyst's observation 'You are thinking of something else?', the patient replies that as the analyst was speaking the patient was thinking of x, where x is an interpretation from the analysand's unconscious that will be different from the analyst's; but x will not have been possible without the analyst's interpretation constituting difference in that moment.

What Bollas says about interpretations can apply also to the analyst's silence. It took three sessions, following the silent session, for me to realise how differently the patient had been making use of my silence from how I had imagined at the time. It is characteristic of Independent analysts that they try to be available to be made use of in ways that they were not necessarily expecting.

In the same paper (Parsons, 2007), I report an occasion when a patient asked if she could bring her small dog to the sessions. It had a health problem, which she said meant it should not be left alone, and the person who normally looked after it was away. I might have taken the position that this was an attempt to disrupt the analysis, and said No, she must make other arrangements. But since my theory of clinical technique holds that sessions are there for patients to discover how they can use them, I simply said it was up to her. She brought the dog, lay on the couch, and settled it down on her tummy. It was easy to see, and to interpret, that this small creature, peacefully asleep in that position, represented our baby inside her: an idea that she would otherwise have found very difficult to allow into consciousness. One day the dog did not seem well, and half way through the session it was sick on the carpet. To have a dog being sick in the consulting-room might seem like a pretty thorough breach of the analytic setting. But the patient and I cleared up the mess together, and I said I thought that at this moment the dog might represent an aspect of herself, usually shut away out of sight, which felt angry and hostile towards me and would be glad to mess up my room. The patient did not retreat into the rational defences that were easily available to her, protesting that she had not made the dog sick, she could not have known it was going to happen, and so on. Instead, she seemed relieved that a way had appeared for us to talk about her aggressive feelings towards me.

When I say that "sessions are there for patients to discover how they can use them", this seemingly straightforward, ordinary-language statement is, in fact, highly theorised. However much a patient's acting-out, or acting-in, constitutes an attempt to disrupt the analysis, for someone to be in analysis at all indicates an underlying impulse towards psychic health, and it is important to try, actively and persistently, to keep contact with that area of the patient's being. However necessary it might be to interpret the negative transference (and, of course, it is), the Independent approach is always to come at that through the anxiety or conflict that makes patients feel the need to be the way they are. As Bion said, it is a question of talking the language of achievement, not the language of blame.

So, when my patient wants to bring her dog, I am interested to see what her unconscious is getting at, and specifically how she might be wanting to experiment with the analytic setting. A cardinal principle of Independent analysis is not to stand in the way of a patient's exploring what use she can make of the analytic situation, and of the analyst as an analytic object. Two classic texts in particular lie behind my clinical handling of this episode. One is Winnicott's (1971a) paper on "The use of an object". Here, he discusses the shift from object-relating to object-use, and he emphasises the role of aggression in making this possible. A patient's aggressive attacks on the analyst need not be a matter of anxiety-driven resistance, or hostile attempts to destroy the analysis, but might, rather, be attempts to establish the analyst as an object that can be made use of. If there is an element of aggression by my patient against the setting in bringing her dog, this is how I would understand it.

The other text is Milner's (1952) paper on "The role of illusion in symbol formation". She describes her work with an eleven-year-old boy, whose play could be alarmingly destructive. He devised a game that involved setting fire to the analytic toys, and once burnt a whole stack of matchboxes. Milner comments, "He makes me stand back from the blaze, and shows great pleasure". The important thing, according to Milner, was that, because he could do what he liked with the toys, and yet they were outside him and had qualities of their own, they offered him the possibility of a new way of relating to external reality. The boy regularly began sessions by treating the analyst aggressively but, Milner says,

> as soon as he had settled down to using the toys as a pliable medium, external to himself, but not insisting on their own separate objective existence, then apparently he could treat me with friendliness and consideration, and even accept real frustration from me. (ibid., p. 92)

He became able to use both Milner herself and the playroom equipment as what she calls an "intervening pliable substance". She likens this to paint for an artist or words for a poet, which they can make use of to create and express "an appetitive interest in external reality". What Milner did with this boy's aggression was to accept and survive it in a way that safely freed him to discover how to make imaginative and creative use of her.

Central again to Milner's method is her aim to make herself available for a patient to discover his own way of using her. Different clinical traditions, which do not work by this concept, might misunderstand or mistrust it. I have heard Milner criticised as though, because she did not interpret this boy's violence against herself and the analysis as being destructive, she could not be taking it seriously. Rosenfeld, in his last book, *Impasse and Interpretation* (1987), emphasised the need to attend fully to the subjective experience of patients, and not inflict on them an interpretative stance that might feel like an attack on their own sense of themselves. This rather Ferenczian position drew an adverse response from Kleinian colleagues who had admired his previous work (Segal & Steiner, 1987; Steiner, 1989). When Enid Balint presented a paper at the British Society in 1994, her discussant was moved to say, "Enid's example warns us against premature intervention; there is also in my view the danger of prolonged non-intervention, however thoughtful".

Analysts who feel this sort of anxiety about Independent technique may be reassured to remember that Enid Balint (1993, p. 126) also wrote,

> In my view the analyst has to be just as observant, perhaps even more so, about what he does not do as about what he does. What the analyst does not say must be remembered by him more carefully than what he does say, because the decision to leave it to the patient, or to wait for the right time, is a very important one.

I have tried to bring these seemingly opposed attitudes into relation with each other, with an idea developed in the last chapter of my book, *The Dove that Returns, The Dove that Vanishes* (Parsons, 2000). I described there a dimension along which an analyst needs to be able to shift his or her analytic stance, back and forth. At the near end, the analyst operates in a way that aims to extract insight from the analytic process and convey this to the patient, using interpretations with a more or less clearly intended purpose with regard to the understanding the analyst wants to bring about in the patient. At the farther end, the analyst looks to the unfolding of the process itself, according to its own direction, regardless, for the moment, of tangible results. The analyst's main concern is not to get in the way of this unfolding. He will make relatively few interventions, and these will not be aimed at producing insight in the patient. Instead, they will have an open-ended potential for all sorts of unforeseen and unforeseeable transformations in the patient's mind, transformations with the potential to reveal themselves in new forms of being and relating. Analysts work best when they can shift freely and flexibly back and forth along this dimension. But different analysts will feel more naturally comfortable at different points on it, and might tend to emphasise the kind of analytic work that belongs to the position where they feel most at home. Analytic traditions and orientations can be characterised by whereabouts on the dimension different sorts of analyst tend to group themselves.

Transference and its interpretation is an omnipresent theme in any analysis, and the following clinical examples illustrate how different locations on this dimension could give rise to different modes of addressing it.

A patient coming four times a week rolled over on the couch near the end of a session to lie on his side. The next day, he said he thought I had not realised that this was because he had been feeling uncomfortable. I picked up how important it was for him that I should understand what he felt in his body. He said that physical feelings were something he did not much like talking about, and there was a silence. After several minutes, he said he had been thinking about how uncomfortable he used to feel as a child. He would feel too hot or too cold, or restless and fidgety, but he would try to keep still and not complain, so as not to challenge his parents.

The word "challenge" struck me. It carried a resonance, like an element in a dream that catches the attention without one's being quite sure why. There was something in it about how he thought his parents would experience what he might say about his bodily feelings. But I did not take this up. I simply noted my reaction and continued listening.

Later in the session, he was talking about his hopes for a close relationship, and went on at great length in a painfully self-critical way. He did not think there was anything about him that could be attractive or interesting to a partner. Then he said he thought that now he had made me depressed as well. I must be, listening to him regurgitate all this stuff. I remarked what a physical word "regurgitate" was. We were back with his body again. I said he was telling me horrible feelings about himself—that he is worthless, unattractive, self-destructive—and I thought he was afraid I would be repelled by what he was vomiting up from inside himself. He said it was not just me who would find it repulsive. He himself did not want to know about these feelings either. He seemed to think, I said, that he should try and keep them to himself, and not challenge me with them. After a slight pause, he said that what he remembered most, from being a child and trying to tell something to others, was a sense of emptiness.

By my use here of the word "challenge", I am doing various things. I am letting the patient know that I registered, earlier in the session, that he was telling me something significant (although neither of us may yet know what) about him and his parents. I am also implying that there might be a connection between what he feels as he tells me, in bodily terms, about these horrible internal perceptions of himself, and what he used to feel about telling his parents what his body felt like. And I am offering him this idea, for him to make whatever he wants of it, or to ignore it, without adding any idea of my own about what kind of challenge he thinks he might be to me, or the nature of the possible connection with his parents.

Contrast that with the following. A patient in five-times-weekly analysis, who is quite well known in the entertainment world, came to a session shortly after giving a newspaper interview. Before it, she said, she went over in her mind the aspects of her life she was prepared to talk about and those she was not. Her life was in some turmoil. She had difficult personal decisions to make, and she was uncertain about the future direction of her work. She decided she would discuss her past work, and her current activity that the media were interested in, but she would definitely not talk about future plans nor mention any of the problems she was struggling with. She told the interviewer what she was willing to talk about, and added that she thought her work might be about to take new directions, but this was very unclear to her and she did not want to go into it. He, thereupon, said that that was just what he was interested in and pressed her to tell him about those things she had decided not to discuss. She found herself doing so, going into a lot more personal detail than she had intended. Afterwards, she was shocked at what she had done, and in the session she agonised about how she could have stepped so easily beyond the boundaries she had set herself.

This patient had clearly erotic feelings towards me that she brought into the interaction between us, being concerned to show me that she knew about them. It was evident, though, that she had deeper conflicts about her sexuality than she was yet conscious of and, even though her erotic transference was, to some extent, available, I thought its power to disturb her more than she realised needed interpreting. So I said she was telling me about herself and a man, and about boundaries that were supposed to set limits on how intimate they would be together. Then she oversteps those limits to become much more personal and intimate with the man than she had told herself she meant to. I said I thought the man that she was, in fact, wanting to do this with was myself. She was very taken aback. The interpretation had a strong impact on her, and she recognised that I had indeed been very much in her mind both before the interview and during it.

This is very different. It is a classic, head-on, "it's me you're really talking about" transference interpretation, of the sort Freud described in "The dynamics of transference" (1912b, p. 101) as "an assurance that [the patient] is being dominated at the moment by an association which is concerned with the doctor himself". Freud thought such interpretations were needed when a patient's resistance manifested itself in the transference. But resistance and communication go hand in hand, as Freud pointed out in the same paper, and overcoming resistance was not the primary aim of my interpretation. This interchange is, in fact, rather complex. The patient's feelings and fantasies about me are, it is true, a substitute for exploring the place of sexuality in her life. And she does displace her transference on to the interviewer and then enact it, rather than reflect on its meaning with me. But she is also unconsciously allowing important questions to take form. Why did she point out the forbidden area to the interviewer in the first place? If he stands for me, does her story imply that she thinks, or hopes, that I, too, wish for intimacy between us? How much does her strong response to my interpretation stem from a desire to be stirred up by me, as well from whatever truth it might contain? These are tender topics that are unconscious because, for the moment, they need to be, and I shall not necessarily hurry to put them into words. My interpretation is not simply because I think she is resisting such thoughts. I think the directness with which she tells me about this episode is a step, intentional although unconsciously so, towards making it possible for us to explore, in her relationship with myself, sexual conflicts that stretch back to her early childhood. The directness of my interpretation is a response to this, guided, as I was in the first, very different, example, by my sense of the analytic process in the immediate moment.

Both examples belong to my work as an Independent analyst. While colleagues of other orientations might have handled these situations differently, I would not expect them to feel too alienated by my approach in either case. What characterises the Independent tradition is a particular sort of openness to the farther end of the dimension I described, exemplified by my approach in the first example. As to how an analyst senses whereabouts on this dimension to locate himself at any moment, no technical prescriptions are possible. This requires an availability that depends on the inner silence of the analyst's listening.

Independent clinical theory, like the Independent analyst, is unobtrusive. Trying to grasp Independent theory and technique seems to me rather like trying to see an animal in a forest, whose colouring makes it melt into the background. You stare, and there does not seem to be anything there. All you can see are trees and shadows. And then, suddenly, the visual pattern clicks, and the shape of the animal is so clear that you cannot imagine why you could not see it before. It is itself part of Independent theory, that theory should be unobtrusive in this way. Whatever an analyst's orientation, it is the essential humanity of the psychoanalytic process that helps the human being on the couch think it might be possible to change. On the other side of the coin, the specifically psychoanalytic quality of the human process that the analyst offers is what provides patients with the means to change. The particular quality of the Independent Tradition, I think, is to keep both these aspects in view, not losing sight of either.

References

Alexander, F. (1950). Analysis of the therapeutic factors in psychoanalytic treatment. *Psychoanalytic Quarterly, 19*: 482–500.

Balint, E. (1993). *Before I was I: Psychoanalysis and the Imagination*. London: Free Association Books.

Balint, M. (1968). *The Basic Fault: Therapeutic Aspects of Regression*. London: Tavistock.

Bollas, C. (2002). *Free Association*. Cambridge: Icon.

Ferenczi, S. (1926). *Further Contributions to the Theory and Technique of Psycho-Analysis* (2nd edn). London: Hogarth, 1950.

Ferenczi, S. (1928). The elasticity of psycho-analytic technique. Reprinted in: *Final Contributions to the Problems & Methods of Psycho-Analysis* (pp. 87–101). London: Hogarth, 1955; Maresfield Reprints, 1980.

Ferenczi, S. (1988). *The Clinical Diary of Sandor Ferenczi*, J. Dupont (Ed.). Cambridge, MA: Harvard University Press.

Freud, S. (1912b). The dynamics of transference. *S.E.*, *12*: 97–108. London: Hogarth.

Hopkins, B. (1997). Winnicott and the capacity to believe. *International Journal of Psychoanalysis, 78*: 485–497.

Khan, M. (1972). On Freud's provision of the therapeutic frame. In: *The Privacy of the Self* (pp. 129–135). London: Hogarth, 1974.

King, P. (1978). Affective response of the analyst to the patient's communications. *International Journal of Psychoanalysis, 59*: 329–334.

Kohon, G. (Ed.) (1986). *The British School of Psychoanalysis: The Independent Tradition*. London: Free Association Books.

Milner, M. (1952). The role of illusion in symbol formation. In: *The Suppressed Madness of Sane Men: Forty-Four Years of Exploring Psychoanalysis* (pp. 83–113). London: Tavistock, 1987.

Milner, M. (1969). *The Hands of the Living God: An Account of a Psychoanalytic Treatment*. London: Hogarth.

Ogden, T. (1995). Analysing forms of aliveness and deadness of the transference–countertransference. *International Journal of Psychoanalysis, 76*: 695–709.

Parsons, M. (2000). *The Dove that Returns, The Dove that Vanishes: Paradox and Creativity in Psychoanalysis*. London: Routledge.

Parsons, M. (2006). The analyst's countertransference to the psychoanalytic process. *International Journal of Psychoanalysis, 87*: 1183–1198.

Parsons, M. (2007). Raiding the inarticulate: the internal analytic setting and listening beyond countertransference. *International Journal of Psychoanalysis, 88*: 1441–1456.

Rayner, E. (1991). *The Independent Mind in British Psychoanalysis*. London: Free Association Books.

Riviere, J. (1927). Contribution to symposium on child analysis. *International Journal of Psychoanalysis, 8*: 339–391.

Rosenfeld, H. (1987). *Impasse and Interpretation*. London: Tavistock.

Rycroft, C. (1956). The nature and function of the analyst's communication to the patient. *International Journal of Psychoanalysis, 37*: 469–472.

Reprinted in: *Imagination and Reality*. New York: International Universities Press, 1968.

Segal, H. (1962). The curative factors in psychoanalysis. *International Journal of Psychoanalysis, 43*: 212–217.

Segal, H., & Steiner, R. (1987). H. A. Rosenfeld (1910–1986). *International Journal of Psychoanalysis, 68*: 415–419.

Steiner, J. (1989). The psychoanalytic contribution of Herbert Rosenfeld. *International Journal of Psychoanalysis, 70*: 611–616.

Stewart, H. (1992). *Psychic Experience and Problems of Technique*. London: Routledge.

Symington, N. (1983). The analyst's act of freedom as agent of therapeutic change. *International Review of Psychoanalysis, 10*: 283–291.

Winnicott, D. W. (1954). Metapsychological and clinical aspects of regression within the psychoanalytical set-up. In: *Collected Papers: Through Paediatrics to Psychoanalysis* (pp. 278–294). London: Tavistock, 1975.

Winnicott, D. W. (1958). Primary maternal preoccupation. In: *Collected Papers: Through Paediatrics to Psychoanalysis* (pp. 300–305). London: Tavistock, 1975.

Winnicott, D. W. (1964). *The Child, the Family and the Outside World*. London: Penguin.

Winnicott, D. W. (1965). *The Maturational Processes and the Facilitating Environment: Studies in the Theory of Emotional Development*. London: Hogarth.

Winnicott, D. W. (1971a). The use of an object and relating through identifications. In: *Playing and Reality* (pp. 86–94). London: Tavistock.

Winnicott, D. W. (1971b). *Playing and Reality*. London: Tavistock.

CHAPTER THREE

The intersubjective matrix: influences on the Independents' growth from "object relations" to "subject relations"*

Joan Raphael-Leff

M apping beliefs and empirical findings across womb, cradle, and couch, this chapter traces the transition within the British Group of Independents towards intersubjectivity in psychoanalytic theorising. Focusing on both psychoanalytical modifications and social trends in mothering, I argue that recognition of the m/other "object" as *subject* spearheads a paradigmatic shift both within the clinical process and the parent–infant exchange, now conceptualised as a *bilateral meeting of minds*. Psychoanalytic models are supplemented by models of parental orientations.

Origins

For over half-a-century, the British Psychoanalytical Society was unusual in containing three different schools of thought under one roof. This diversity stems from the 1918 Budapest congress decree that

* A version of this chapter was presented at the Group of Independents' Cambridge Conference in 2006. My gratitude to historians and scholars (such as Professor Riccardo Steiner) on whose research I have drawn.

personal analysis was essential for practice. Consequently, founding members of the British Society chose to have analyses with Freud in Vienna, Abraham or Hans Sachs in Berlin, or Ferenczi in Budapest. The differing theoretical approaches they imbibed laid a seedbed of plurality, awareness of which further crystallised in the wake of the 1941–1945 "Controversial Discussions" (see King & Steiner, 1991, pp. 1–36). Over the years, the (uneasy) coexistence of Anna Freudian, Kleinian, and "Middle" group schools of thought revealed a multi-faceted picture of primary experience as viewed from differing perspectives. This was hallmarked by Anna Freudian ego evolution to mediate between conflictual internal structures and accommodation to external ones, Kleinian notions of an innate ego, internally gener-ated unconscious phantasy and narcissistic projections, and "Middle Group" focus on emergence of the subject from symbiosis to inter-nalised self-object relations. In addition to specifically British influ-ences, these also reflected differences between the Viennese baby's primary narcissism and anaclitic attachment, the Berlin baby instinc-tually driven by oral eroticism, sadism, envy (an innate hatred later ascribed to outward deflection of the "inarticulate" death drive) in the formation of primitive object-relationships, and initiation of the Budapest school's innately loving baby in a "dual unit", with aggres-sion seen as a secondary reaction to frustration and separation. These differences were passionately upheld. As Michael Balint quipped in 1949:

> We must not forget that we are arguing here about theoretical constructions. For we all agree that the earliest state of the human mind is not essentially different in London from what it is in Vienna or in Budapest. (1949, p. 30)

However, such agreement was sparse, and the babies of the three groups continued to differ. Paradoxically, this spectrum of models consisted of offshoots of different, even contradictory, developmental hypotheses about formation of psychic reality that Freud himself proposed at various times: the baby as a self-absorbed isolate, or a in a state of non-differentiated merger, or, as he stated in a footnote, part of a mother–infant system.

Similarly, mothers were presented as either "object" of the baby's desires or as a containing/transformative function. I argue here that the consequences of such maternal de-subjectivisation are that it negates personal experience of mothers. Idealised notions of mothering exclude necessary ambivalence and distort the psychoanalytic view of early family exchanges, thereby setting false standards if the mother–infant exchange is the paradigm for therapeutic treatment. Similarly, "abjectifying" the archaic mother as non-representable assumes the child's point of view. On the other hand, exploration of the variety of clustering beliefs, needs, wishes, and defensive patternings underpinning maternal subjectivity (Baraitser, 2006; Dinnerstein, 1976; Kraemer, 1996; Raphael-Leff, 1993, 2002) not only exposes some meanings real mothers give to their lived experiences while mothering, but throws some light on our own countertransferential experience as psychoanalysts.

I am aware that generalisations tend to overlook subtle distinctions within and between schools of thought. My depiction here reflects a somewhat artificial categorisation, denuding theories of their overlap. However, my point is that over time, as self-designations altered to "Contemporary Freudians", "Neo-Kleinians", and a looser "Group of Independents", each of these theoretical schools retained a distinctive stance, respectively focusing on the *interstructural, intrapsychic,* or *interpsychic.*

I will argue here that over the decades, cross-fertilisation within the British Society led to greater within-group heterogeneity, and, conversely, to more convergence among groups (especially regarding psychoanalytic process as intersubjective—spearheaded by the Independents). In addition to cross-group clinical meetings, scientific exchanges and political exigencies, theoretical revisions occurred as a result of new realities and a multiplicity of influences from related epistemologies, such as analytical philosophy, feminist theory, and developmental research (in particular, studies of procedural sub-symbolic modes of intersubjectivity).

In addition to a "two-person psychology" and the belief in psychosocial *actualities* as foundational to psychic reality, Independents were seen to practise selective eclecticism, to have a respect for empiricism, and a predilection for playfulness, paradox, and illusion, combining spontaneity with disciplined clinical restraint (see Kohon, 1986; Rayner, 1991). Recently, the British Psychoanalytical Society has taken measures to abolish the formal group structures in the name of "pluralism". None the less, signature modes of thinking abide. I suggest a key feature of the Independents is treatment of the psychoanalytic process as *dialogical*, and, hence, commitment to open-minded examination of both sides of the *interpsychic exchange*, including its bilateral ambiguity. Delineating some milestones in this group's theoretical shift from object-relations to "subject-relations" I note four early influences which paved the way towards intersubjectivity:

- Ferenczi's emphasis on reciprocal unconscious influences between carer and child (in "Confusion of tongues", 1933);
- Fairbairn's groundbreaking depiction of the infant's mind as inherently dyadic. In "The repression and the return of bad objects" (1943), internal relations are presented as *tandems*— endopsychic structuration through ego-splits each coupled with split-up exciting–tantalising or rejecting aspects of real object-relationships.
- In "Hate in the counter-transference" (1949), by highlighting the "good-enough" carer's (secret) *subjective* feelings, Winnicott ameliorates the idea of perfect unconditional care.
- Recognition that maternal resilience and survival of destructiveness enables the infant to discover her *alterity*. Paradoxically, "Use of the object" (1969) renders the mother a subject.

By posing *an interchange between two minds* as the foundation of intrapsychic awareness, these extraordinary papers expose the long-standing psychoanalytic resistance to recognising maternal subjectivity. And, since the treatment process came to be seen as isomorphic with baby-care, its redefinition as an *intersubjective matrix* now implicated the analyst's own subjectivity.[1]

Psychoanalytic models

My thesis is that at the root of all psychoanalytic theorising lies the question of how an infant's mind is humanised within the context of the nuclear family. Divergent approaches are underpinned by three interleaving registers:

- a specific *developmental model* based on beliefs about innate endowment and constitution of the self, which dictates *requirements for growth*;

- conceptualisation of *pathogenesis* resting on the particular developmental model held, which in turn defines *anamnesis*, the nature of illness and its treatment;
- finally, these two paradigms interlink to establish a presumed equation between *optimal parental care* and *analyst–patient therapeutic exchange*, informing psychoanalytic praxis within each school of thought.

Thus, in the UK, the Independents' conceptualisation of an inborn pristine ego, which will inevitably become divided, contrasts markedly with both the idea of a non-differentiated, fragmented, yet gradually cohering, ego, as postulated by the Freudians, and with the Kleinian idea of an innately solipsistic schizoid ego which will achieve depressive position integration. *These distinctions underpin fundamentally discrepant views of babies*: from an intricate neonate whose intense interior life will diminish or be reduced over time, as opposed to a simpler form of life which will ultimately evolve into the complex autonomy of adulthood.

Similarly, "objects" differ: Klein's baby's involvement with a biologically determined preconceived object differs from Anna Freud's notion of learning to love anaclitically through provisions of care, which differs again from Ferenczi's infant benignly engaged in primitive loving relatedness towards the "found" object who (inevitably) will disappoint.

Thus, different conceptualisations of early developmental processes dictate requisite care-giving. And the nature of pathogenesis will rest on causal assumptions and beliefs about conflicts or deficits of care in the aetiology of illness. Finally, building on a presumed equation between baby–carer and patient–therapist, each paradigm will indicate treatment procedures, therapeutic process, and outcome goals of the analytic relationship.

- When pathology is ascribed to *internal factors* (e.g., unresolved conflicts between life and death instincts or between internecine internal urges and reality demands), treatment will focus on working-through.
- If it is ascribed to *constitutional/instinctual factors* (malevolent destructiveness, excessive constitutional envy or greed, etc.), treatment aims to promote depressive guilt and acceptance of one's culpability.

●   If dangers are ascribed to maternal deprivation, or external impingements—environmental failure—treatment aims to provide an opportunity for regression, offering new empathic relational experiences to undo the damage caused by the archaic care-givers.

In sum, each psychoanalytic school of thought can be seen to seek answers within its own framework to the crucial question: what is a mind, how does it come into being, and how best to treat it when it is in trouble?

Across the Atlantic

Unlike the UK, in the USA, in its heyday, psychoanalysis enjoyed ubiquitous acceptance, with every psychiatrist analysed and trained in it. By contrast to British pluralism, a monolithic tradition evolved as a co-product of mostly Viennese psychoanalysts around Hartmann in the USA, affiliated with the group led by Anna Freud in London.[2] The American tendency towards breakaway secessionism left this mainstream hegemony of ego psychology largely unchallenged until the 1970s, when a scientific controversy erupted, of momentum akin to the British Controversial Discussions thirty years earlier. Significantly, the critique of ego psychology's "institutionalized blindness to the need for continued critical and original thought" (Schafer, 1970, p. 425) had its roots in Budapest. Those interrogating the "new orthodoxy"—Merton Gill, Roy Schafer, and George Klein—shared a mentor, Hungarian-born psychologist David Rapaport, who, although a staunch biological ego-psychologist, emphasised *relations*. This challenge also coincided with positive exposure in America of Ferenczi's ideas and those of British object-relations theorists.[3]

Like the Independents in the UK, the American dissidents challenged the unilateral paradigm with *a two-person psychology*, posing the session as a patient–analyst *co-creation*, a "complex of interacting transferences" imbued with "ambiguity and relativity of the interpersonal reality" (Gill, 1982).[4] Searching for alternatives to the mainstream monadic model of "psychic energy", and/or triadic Oedipal intrapsychic conflict, they focused on the early *dyadic process* of mental life. By analogy to the "nursing couple", they viewed emergent life history in sessions as *"a joint creation of patient and analyst ... subject* to a degree to the limitations, individualities and visions of the two participants in the analytic process" (Schafer, 1970, p. 495, my italics).

Another confrontation came from self-psychology, instigated by Heinz Kohut (1971), who posed an archaic merger with supportive idealised and idealising internal self-objects (based on the child's actual experience with external objects), and an affirming empathic psychoanalytic stance.

Interdisciplinary influences

In my reading, the shift away from an individual-centred approach and linear view of causality was also inspired in the USA by contemporaneous local developments in neonatal research, and in systems and field theories (e.g., von Bertalanffy and Kurt Lewin), emphasising both interactional and self-organisational properties. Similarly, in opting for hermeneutics, thinking was permeated by contributions of philosophers such as Binswanger, Sartre, Wittgenstein, Ryle, and Austin. Accepted dogma was questioned, bolstered by new findings in experimental developmental psychology and influenced by the challenge to authority of the Civil Rights movement and second-wave feminists, who critiqued Freud's phallocentric masculine model (on the grounds that it claimed the male body as standard, and privileged father–son, mother–son, and fraternal relations, with women deemed objects of exchange rather than subjects of patriarchal law. In time, the male-dominated domain of American psychoanalysis (so unlike the British Society) was accessed by more female candidates, who helped both to revoke the prerequisite medical degree, and the paternalistic institutional climate. Above all, treatment of a new group of patients with severe narcissistic, borderline, and psychotic disturbances provided a *clinical catalyst* for technical modifications. Ultimately, following the introduction of antipsychotic medication, a gradual cultural shift would occur in psychiatry, valorising science, biology, and psychopharmacology, with a simultaneous rapid rise of "quick-fix" therapies, including cognitive–behavioural interventions.

Within psychoanalysis itself, a schism was exposed between classical meta-psychology and clinical experience as the mode of investigation. A budding postmodernist approach led to radical theoretical revisions. Methodological critiques of the "objective" principles of interpretation began to undermine the psychoanalytical "grand schema", replacing the clinical aim of reconstructing a veridical historical "truth" with the idea of mutually generated "narratives" (Spence, 1982) as a product of interpersonal interactions, and of interpretations as subjectively formulated.

Consequently, where one theoretical perspective previously predominated in North American psychoanalysis, a proliferation now occurred, including contemporary Freudian, interpersonal, self-psychological, intersubjectivist, and, more recently, relational approaches. Here, too, I suggest that these various epistemologies (our "pluralistic psychoanalytic articles of faith", as Wallerstein called them (1988, p. 17)) are underpinned by divergent models about how the self is constituted in infancy (or even antenatally), which each promote a compatible paradigm of optimal primary care in the nursery, and, by extension, in the consulting room.

Womb

In common, influenced by Ferenczi, many early British object relationists shared a notion of intrauterine existence as *blissful plenitude shattered by the caesura of birth*. Loss of this primordial "fusion" was regarded as a causal factor in moulding the human condition. By contrast to Freud's notion of continuity across "the caesura" (1926d, p. 138), and his personal disavowal of "oceanic feelings" (1930a, p. 72), the object relationists' group postulated womb-relatedness and expulsion as a universal constitutive factor. Longing for lost pre-natal communion and unity was seen exemplified by a sense of cosmic connection, recaptured in profound therapeutic regressions within the consulting room.

I propose that, in time, this conceptualisation led to a metaphorical shift relating to the therapeutic process itself, from the idea of psychoanalytic interpretation as a phallic penetration to one of *gestation within a relational matrix/womb* (a shift later to occur in the USA, too—see Aron, 1996). A spectrum of idealised notions of intrauterine occupancy ranged, with subtle variations of emphasis, some shared with colleagues across the continent.[5] None the less, already in 1936, dissention arose as that Middle Group "voice of reason", Marjorie Brierley, queried idealisation of the womb, introducing the possibility of "trouble in paradise", as did Winnicott in 1949. Many years later, Melanie Klein, who had described the death instinct as a desperate attempt to reach back to *unconflicted* prenatal life, acknowledged that indeed, "unpleasant" antenatal experiences might foreshadow bad birth and postnatal ones (1957, pp. 2–3). And Bowlby, with typical parsimony, dismissed all speculations about intrauterine life, declaring "the theory of Primary Return-to-Womb craving" as both "redundant and biologically improbable" (1958, p. 350).

Idealisation is not without consequences; inferentially, the newborn's love for the mother always already carries *negative transference* from the prenatal period of idealised "unconditional" connection. Concepts such as maternal "holding" (Winnicott), and "containment"/"metabolization" (Bion) may be seen to mimic not only the womb's embrace, but its *placental function*. This glorification prioritises the *biological mother* with implications for prescribed care. Assuming that *mothering is primed by pregnancy* (Winnicott's "primary maternal preoccupation") unquestioningly targets *the birth mother* as exclusive, primary carer, and treats mothering as *"instinctive"*: inevitable, nonconflictual, and "natural". This supposes that mother, like baby, is similarly "merged", and engaged in an involuntary *"symbiotic"reciprocity* (A. Balint/Benedek). Mothering must prolong womb-like conditions post-natally and, applying the unconscious paradigm of a *"placental mother"*, must be continuous and unobtrusive. This essentialises primary parenting, unquestioningly assigning post-natal nurture to females.

To accommodate the infants they depict, to these theorists the mother remains a human incubator, despite a substantial body of autobiographical and fictionalised accounts, and clinical and empirical psychoanalytic literature on mothers' positive and negative subjective experiences of pregnancy and mothering (Balsam, 2012; Bibring et al, 1961; Deutsch, 1945; Kestenberg, 1976; Pines, 1993; Raphael-Leff, 1980, 1991a,b, 1993).

Most importantly, it *denies the mother as a person/subject in her own right*. Decades of depicting mothers as "objects" in their baby's mind universalises the particular, overlooking the singular impact of the ripely pregnant maternal body, and the infant's relationship with her subjectivity: effects of her specific psychohistory, internal representations of mothering, circumstances of conception, and social matrices of ethnicity, class, race, etc.

The focus on the offspring's retrospective intrauterine fantasies neglects the extraordinary range of each pregnant woman's unconscious wishes, beliefs, depressive or persecutory anxieties, and emotional expectations of destruction or rebirth while two people occupy her body for the duration of ten lunar months.

A shift of orientation began from the late 1970s among perinatal professionals and expectant parents, with routine ultrasound scans and media popularisation of the competence and complex capacities of unborn babies. However, this recognition failed to permeate psychoanalytic theorising for a long while. I argue that adherence to myths of blissful intrauterine "fusion" and its postnatal corollary of "symbiotic merger" *delayed* appreciation of both the degree of early differentiation already evident in embryogenesis, and of neonatal individuality and maternal variability.

Womb: empirical research

Perinatal research from the 1980s onwards found fascinating evidence of the competence and complexity of intrauterine life. Heart rate monitors revealed foetal responsiveness to subtle changes in internal and external environments. Sonography and intrauterine fibre-optic cameras exposed the high level of volitional foetal activity (which, astonishingly, far exceeds that of the gravity-bound, post-natal baby). Genetic blueprints and epigenetic schedules unfolding long before birth demonstrate that already, *in utero*, each baby shows highly individualised somatic and temperamental patterns which continue to express themselves throughout the life cycle. Experiments show that long before conscious experience, by the second trimester, most senses are operative, including pain receptors, discriminatory hearing, and REM sleep patterns, and that unborn babies prefer human voices over other sounds, showing evidence of sophisticated pre-natal learning.[6]

New technology produced scientific evidence far from the blissful "harmonious fusion" between the body's two (or more) inhabitants, revealing, rather, ruthless *competition over resources* (Haig, 1993). This was supported by data demonstrating that embryos and foetuses actively manipulate their interaction with the expectant mother, that the placenta is not a one-way conduit, but involves *bi-directional influences*, with waste products from the baby affecting the expectant mother, inducing nausea, metabolic changes, and sleep disturbances. Conversely, ante-natal maternal nutrition, stress, depression, and, especially, chronic anxiety are now shown to have lasting effects on child development, evident in behavioural manifestations even at age seven years (see O'Connor, Heron, & Glover, 2002; Van den Bergh, Mulder, Mennes, & Glover, 2005) and long-term effects on adult physical and mental health of the intrauterine sojourn (Burton, Barker, Moffett, & Thornburg, 2011). Perinatal sensitivity of the developing brain to maternal influences and the inextricable interaction of genetic and environmental factors are now clearly demonstrable. But the point I wish to stress here is that *the unborn baby already exists within a bi-directional system.*

Cradle

Emphasis on the pre-Oedipal mother, which already featured in the 1930 London–Vienna divergences, gradually eclipsed both the solipsistic and Oedipal foci of classical analysis.

Once the Independents were established in November 1964, a *"two-person psychology"* (coined in 1951 by Ferenczi's British analysand, John Rickman) now took centre stage, spotlighting *real* external relationships as formative of internal relational configurations (*vs.* phantasy), invoking maternal culpability.[7]

Rejecting the death instinct and innate malevolence, they proclaimed aggression as a reaction to maternal deprivation. Hence, they increasingly foregrounded exclusive and continuous maternal devotion as essential in safeguarding well-being and the initial state of "symbiotic union". Bowlby's now notorious 1951 World Health Organisation monograph went so far as to unrealistically advocate the (western) mother's maintenance of connectedness to her baby "24 hours a day, 365 days a year".

At the risk of oversimplification, I propose to draw out differences in the conceptual representation of a baby, and the correspondingly divergent care-giving.

● Theories that depict the newborn as fundamentally *pre-social*, *asocial*, or innately *antisocial* treat the care-giver's ultimate task as inserting the self-centred child into the existing social (and, ultimately, linguistic) order. "Socialisation" is the designated means of instating societal conventions through internalisation. Training the growing child to relinquish culturally prohibited instinctual gratifications is a task associated with adaptation, repression, renunciation and paternal/juridical intervention against a potentially overwhelming desire to regress or transgress.[8]

- Conversely, theories regarding the infant as *vulnerable, receptive, and object-orientated* from the start place their emphasis on sensitive meeting of the sociable baby's *relational needs,* believing that early indulgence pre-empts later craving. If, in addition, perinatal life is regarded as a *continuum,* as noted, the mother of pregnancy is designated the unrivalled carer. Her vocation is to prolong intrauterine "fusion" by intuitively providing womb-like conditions post-natally and exclusive continuous nurture that ideally mimics the placental process.

This privileging of the biological mother differs considerably from Anna Freud's notion that "[T]he person of the object remains interchangeable so long as gratification remains the same" (1991[1943], p. 419). (A view she was to change on the basis of her experience in the War Nurseries (1949)). Later, she wrote that "the figure of the mother is for a certain time the sole important representative of the whole outer world" (see Sandler, 2012).) A contributory factor is that when a baby is regarded as unable to discriminate between caregivers in the first six months, they seem substitutable in meeting "his majesty's" physiological needs. Furthermore, in this regulatory paradigm, as "mothering" implies *a state of mind* rather than a "maternal instinct", transactions can be conducted by non-mothers: "In the first period when the baby has the urge for the satisfaction of its bodily wishes, *a routine undertaken by anyone* could fulfil this need" (Burlingham, 1991[1943], p. 336, my italics).

In Hartmann's "average expectable environment" (1939), primary bonds are seen to be formed experientially on the basis of pleasurable satisfaction of physiological needs, regulatory tension reduction and discharge of drive-derived excitations. The baby's self-absorbed *autoerotic* interest is seen to be located in his/her *own body* (rather than the recently vacated maternal one, in Klein's version, or autoerotism seen as a defensive technique ". . . both to provide for himself what he cannot obtain from the object" and "to provide for himself an object which he cannot obtain", in Fairbairn's view (1941, p. 255)).

As the ego psychochologist's neonate is assumed to be "at this time exclusively concerned with his own well-being", the function of primary carers is *preservative*: to maintain an external barrier against stimulus overload for the as yet undiscerning infant, serving as his auxiliary ego. "The mother is important so far as she serves or disturbs this well being. She is *an instrument* of satisfaction or denial, and as such of extreme importance in the child's narcissistic scheme of things" (A. Freud, 1991[1943], p. 418, my italics).

This formulation of an *initial phase of undifferentiation* was shared in the USA by Hartmann, Kris, and Loewenstein, who agreed with Freud that through repeated experiences of tension-reduction, attachment to the (exchangeable) mothering person would gradually arise as a template libidinal object, and representative of the outer world.[9] Primary bonds are, thus, seen to be formed experientially on the basis of pleasurable satisfaction of physiological needs, regulatory tension reduction, and discharge of drive-derived excitations. Relationships are seen to develop from the initial state of primary narcissistic "objectlessness" to ultimate pre-emptive rationality associated with language and paternal law. Where internal conflict is seen to predominate, internal integration is a goal. "Taming of instinct" (Freud, 1937c, p. 225) is advocated to foster resolution of conflict with external demands and to reduce internal id–ego–superego tensions and to meet "civilised" goals of social obedience shared by drive theorists, Lacanians, and ego psychologists (albeit, to Lacan, internal discord is inevitable, integration and ego self-mastery illusory).

The early relational dyad

Bifurcating considerably from this classical "Apollonian" cluster of axioms are those of "Dionysian" object relations, postulating an early ego and an *innate urge to relate*.

Both the British Middle Group and the American Interpersonal School drew on Ferenczi's ideas of primary "object love", emphasising the profound impact in infancy of *non-symmetrical relationships* (with ramifications of shifting the transference–countertransference towards the pre-Oedipal mother). As noted, on the American scene, the interactive approach complemented Lewin's "field theory" of interpenetrating dynamics (1935). Similarly, in the 1940s and 1950s, Spitz (also a product of Hungary) had long emphasised mutual exchanges of "receptive empathy" between mother and baby. But the *bi-directional* effects and *reciprocal* systemic nature in the chains of "action cycles" forming the "primal dialogue" were overlooked. American theorists highlighted early maternal functions as crucial; yet the direction of influence was treated as *unilateral*, and, increasingly, accompanied by blatant "mother blaming".[10]

Psychogenesis

Unlike Freud's formulation of hysteria as ideogenic, the early Independents ascribed pathology to exogenous causes (that is, inadequate maternal function *vs.* the baby's hostile predisposition or fantasies). Emotional disturbance in adulthood was retrospectively ascribed to infringements in infancy: affirmative appreciation during the critical preverbal period was deemed necessary for healthy development. To theorists emphasising early sociability, "recognition" confers personhood. But, ironically, they neglected to recognise the mother as a person in her own right.

In common, early independent theoreticians expressed disagreement with the notion of anaclitic attachments. While not addressing the paradox of how the "fused" neonate is also "object seeking" from the start, they focused on the needy neonate's innate expectancies of relations and his/her resourcefulness in seeking these. Bowlby's theory is a case in point. The infant is seen to actively instigate proximity, utilising smiling, crying, sucking, clinging, and following to procure the mother's emotional investment rather than her milk. "Monotropic" attachment to the biological mother[11] is postulated as an instinctual attempt to establish a secure base against dangers (1958). This vision of a proactive loving infant tallies with the externally orientated baby of Bowlby's British predecessors, Suttie, Fairbairn, Guntrip, and Winnicott—*seeking relation rather than self-absorption*. Michael and Alice Balint, also, emphasised the newborn's "markedly active tendencies" and, partially influenced by their fellow Hungarian Imré Hermann's work on the instinct to cling, substituted the concept of "primary object relation" for Ferenczi's idea of "passive" object love (A. Bálint, 1949, p. 259). Rather than valorising separateness and autonomy, all these theorists cited *separation anxiety* as fundamental—an urgent response to the threat of loss resulting in self-fragmentation or annihilation.

Henceforth, among British analysts, too, if optimal mothering leads to mental health, psycho-pathology now becomes linked to deficient nurture.[12]

Maternal subjectivity

Psychoanalytic descriptions of *the* mother are myriad. However, to paraphrase Winnicott, there is no such thing . . . Each woman approaches pregnancy and parenting in a subjective way that reflects her own unconscious configurations and conscious aspirations, her internal mother–daughter lineage, and moment to moment fluctuating feeling states and emotional experiences with this particular baby. Psychoanalytically orientated empirical studies of mothering over the past many decades have been sparse (i.e., Benedek, 1970; Bibring, Dwyer, Huntington, & Valerstein, 1961; Birksted-Breen, 1986; Chodorow, 1978; Deutsch, 1945; Kestenberg, 1976; Lester & Notman, 1986; Parker, 1995; Pines, 1993; Raphael-Leff, 1980, 1985a,b, 1986, 1987, 2001a), and some of these carried an essentialist biological and even evolutionary–teleological bias. My own research and independent cross-cultural explorations of my model reveal that, like theoreticians, expectant parents, too, hold a variety of beliefs which determine their orientation to postnatal care. Few generalisations are possible, other than that pregnancy tends to engender high accessibility of unconscious activity, especially linked to basic issues of formation, transformation, and preservation (Raphael-Leff, 1991a), and that early parenting has *a catalytic power* to retrigger presymbolic affects. This is because implicit expectancies of mothering are primordial, yet acquired through the specific experience of primary care in infancy and coloured by exposure to archaic care-givers' mental states, conveyed unconsciously through facial expression, gesture, vocal tone, and rhythm, in intimacy and emotional mirroring.

In addition to influences within one's family of origin, self–other relationships and expectations are also sub-culturally determined and intensely affected by each woman's current socio-economic status and the availability of emotional support. Thus, an expectant mother's relation to her baby will reflect the nature and circumstances of this particular conception (desired or unplanned, within a loving relationship or outside of one, etc.) as well as the status of her changing internal world. Updated configurations are socially primed in myriad ways, reflecting both preverbal primary dialogues and nurturing encounters since then, and, above all, incorporating her own experience of mothering a previous baby. *Hence, approaches to mothering differ both between women, and for each individual woman over her respective pregnancies.*

My research attempted to capture and notate elusive qualities of mothering and the personal underpinnings of patterns of care.[13] Eventually, a schema emerged, and I evolved a model of parental "orientations" based on in-depth (recorded) subjective experiences as reported by several different empirical and clinical samples of mothers, seen daily from pregnancy into the third year of the child's life. (Before models sub-dividing "drive structure" and "relational structure" models became popular, I gradually came to realise that these orientations paralleled explanatory frameworks of psychoanalytic theorising (Raphael-Leff, 1983).)

Broadly, I found that in transitional cultures such as our own which condone a variety of child-care practices, parents who have the internal and external resources to do so will make choices on the basis of a parental "orientation" which reflects a cluster of their own beliefs about babies and parenting. From my trans-cultural work with primary health carers, I propose that loss of traditional normative child-care patterns allows for greater variety, yet also imposes constraints on parenting, now determined as much by unconscious internal world factors as by external circumstances or prescriptive advice. Already in place during pregnancy, these personal orientations continue post-natally, although they might change, and often do so, with subsequent pregnancies.

Maternal orientations

The mid-1970s heralded a period of precipitous change. My research, which began then and continued for some decades, reflects these changes. Although the focus of this chapter is on mothers, many of the joys, anxieties, inherent tensions, and defences are shared by fathers, too, who are also found to have a similar range of orientations. Inevitably, in two parent families, the orientations of partners may dovetail or conflict within each couple.[14]

I termed the first orientation *Facilitators*. An expectant Facilitator feels uniquely privileged to share her body with her baby, treating pregnancy as the culmination of female identity. Relishing pregnancy, she willingly submits to its emotional demands, feeling identified with idealised aspects of both the mother who carried her and also with the unborn child she carries. Believing she is being primed through "communion" with her baby during pregnancy (and later in breastfeeding), she sees herself as uniquely and exclusively qualified to intuitively decipher and meet her infant's every need. To ease the baby's transition, she desires as "natural" a birth as possible, aiming to recreate a womblike "nest" and tranquil atmosphere post-natally. Her birth plan includes lowered lights and sounds immediately after the birth and having the baby placed in direct skin-to-skin contact on her chest (before the cord is cut) to facilitate suckling.

A "Facilitator" mother *adapts to her baby*, believing that his/her security is totally dependent on her own sensitive responsiveness. Regarding herself as the exclusive source of nurture means having to be ready to respond to her baby's every cry, which she interprets as a communication. Therefore, it necessitates constant proximity, even at night. To her, the prime unit is the *mother–baby pair*. She eschews activities or relations that will divide her attention and, feeling compelled to devote her life totally to mothering, she utilises identificatory capacities to meet the infant's desires (and, by association, vicariously gratifying her own).

Post-natal distress is related to medical, socioeconomic, or personal obstacles to fulfilling her own high standards in providing this exclusive, "perfect" form of mothering. Should complications arise ante- or post-natally, doubts about the sufficiency of her own contribution during gestation and while breastfeeding render this woman susceptible to depression. Guilt at having failed to give her baby optimal conditions at the crucial time might lead to withdrawal, or self-blame and masochistic compensatory activities (and what Winnicott defined as "therapeutic" mothering).

This facilitating orientation is at variance with that of a *Regulator*— a woman who treats mothering not as a vocation, but as one role among many in her life. Envying the physical ease with which men become fathers, she regards pregnancy as a necessary but uncomfortable means of producing a baby, experienced at times as an intruder invading her body and taking over her internal space and thoughts. To some expectant mothers, the baby seems a parasitic "succubus", a foreign occupation appropriating her internal resources. As noted, this is no fantasy, as in actuality the self-serving semi-alien foetus (50% chromosomally unrelated) taps into and feeds off her bloodstream, competitively manipulating their interchange. To preserve her identity as a "Person" (rather than "Madonna"), she is determined to savour her freedom before the birth. Addressing forebodings about her life being taken over by the baby's neediness and "primitive" emotions, she resolves to let rationality triumph, forgoing introspection during pregnancy and resisting the disturbing reappraisal of identity posed by child-bearing. Aiming to have as "civilised" a birth as possible, she plans to utilise medical intervention to minimise the pain and "damage" she preconsciously believes she and the baby might inflict on each other. Consciously, she sees her main role as "socialising" the pre-social (asocial or anti-social) infant, and, therefore, getting *the baby to adapt* to the household and the particular social order within which she herself is embedded. To her, the prime unit is her adult sexual relationship, and the baby must fit in to conserve its parameters.

To this end she decides to establish a regime that minimises confusion. *The routine* also enables shared care-giving, deemed possible since, in her view, mothering is a learnt skill. Believing that the very young baby does not differentiate between care-givers, she aims to introduce co-carers as early as possible. Shared mothering enables her to return to work, and reduces the burden of sole accountability. On a deeper level, it decreases depletion of her emotional resources, and the risk of "contagious arousal" of her own infantile experience through exposure to the infant's raw feelings. The routine provides security for the baby, and contributes to predictability in a situation that the mother experiences as potentially chaotic and disturbing. Clearly, a set regime also relieves the mother from having to identify with the infant to fathom his needs (like the Facilitator), thus reducing the threat of recognising aspects of her own repudiated or repressed dependence, and her "shameful" needy, greedy, or angry infantile needs.

Post-natal disturbance stems from breakdown of her defences through unremitting exposure to the baby, which might be due to unemployment, lack of practical support, life events, and unconscious obstacles to maintaining her view of herself as a competent adult. It tends to take *a persecutory* rather than depressive form—phobias, paranoia, obsessional disorders, intrusive breakthrough thoughts, or panic states (Raphael-Leff, 1991a, 2001b).

A third orientation is that of the *Reciprocator*, who approaches pregnancy with mixed feelings about the little human being growing inside her, and aware of the many changes mothering will bring to her life. Accommodating to living in a state of uncertainty, she tries to maintain a balance between the pull towards absorption in the pregnancy and determination to meet the demands and offerings of her daily world, as she contemplates future curtailment of her own activities and both the positive and negative conditions for bringing up her baby. She is concerned about the baby's effect on her emotional relationships with her partner and her other child/ren, her parents, siblings, friends, and colleagues. While planning the birth according to her own wishes, she is also very aware of the likelihood of unforeseen contingencies which she must face should they arise. Similarly, rather than anticipating a habitual mode of adaptation (by either carer or baby), post-natally each incident is *negotiated* on its own terms within an interactive situation.

Underpinning this complex pattern is recognition of the baby as a person—both alike in having human emotions, yet different in being an infant, with age-specific yet uniquely individual and fluctuating infantile mental states, needs, and capacities. Through the security of familiarity and reliability, she hopes to expose her child to a range of caring relationships with significant others as well as herself, at a time and to a degree which she deems appropriate. *The prime unit is the family* (elastically defined), and needs of other members must be individually considered, including other children. This type of interaction is based on empathy and ongoing reflective understanding rather than rules of ethical care, primary identification, or denial of similarities. Parenting involves tolerance of uncertainty and acceptance of mixed feelings and unknown forces in both herself and the baby (rather than the Facilitator's denial of any negative feelings or the Regulator's fear of falling in love). Similarly, the baby is seen as sociable, sentient, yet limited in understanding, as opposed to the Facilitator baby, who is seen as "wise" and all-knowing, or the Regulator's asocial fierce bundle of needs who must be socially trained.

A fourth *Conflicted* response is one in which preoccupation with unresolved past issues vies with current engagement with the baby, and/or divergent orientations compete. The current relationship with the infant pales by comparison to a deeply significant event or overwhelming relationship in the past. As well as experiencing reactivated painful and traumatic emotions, the mother's internal conflicts might unconsciously reflect a "live" replaying of unprocessed differences between several internalised parents/care-givers, or relentless conflict between unintegrated "feminine" and "masculine" facets of herself, or split ideological discrepancies between baby-care ideals and feminist or other aspirations. Some cultures foster not conflicted but *sequential orientations*: for instance, Japanese child-rearing mores of facilitatory "skinship" in the first year followed by intense maternal regulation thereafter.

Although the models evolved independently of each other, correspondences to Attachment categories have been demonstrated.[15] And again, although my model of orientations was formulated on the basis of empirical findings, the equivalences with psychoanalytic theories are self-evident (Raphael-Leff, 1983).

Interestingly, while consistent in any one gestation and the early post-natal years, maternal orientation can and does change in subsequent pregnancies, depending on a variety of inner world psychodynamic functions and representations and social factors, including the previous experience of parenting (Raphael-Leff, 1985a,b, 1986, 1987, 1991a). The proportions of specific orientations in a sample reflect influences of local child-care practices and socio-cultural changes over time. Thus, my in-depth longitudinal research in a community centre in London (conducted on successive cohorts of parents at eighteen-month intervals from 1977) found an increase in Reciprocators from the mid-1980s onwards, also influenced by widespread UK media depiction of foetal and neonatal capacities. I suggest that theorising within the group of Independents has similarly shifted from a Facilitator to a Reciprocator mode of thinking (and that of some other psychoanalytic groups from Regulator to more Reciprocatory patterns).

Contagious arousal

A crucial issue in parenting is how to survive having life and death responsibility for an unknown, preverbal and vulnerable baby. Exposure to the infant's wordless anxiety and urgent neediness has a profound effect of "contagious arousal", as I termed it (1991a), stimulating implicit schemas of sub-symbolic memory of their own archaic care in the carer. As psychoanalysts know from their own therapeutic experience with projective identification in disturbed patients, such contagion can be extremely disconcerting (Winnicott, 1949). However, in parenting, it involves unremitting night and day demands. Having to tolerate insistent crying, to fathom and physically meet elusive yet raw and intimate needs, while suffering themselves from sleep deprivation and hormonal fluctuations, thrusts the parent back into an emotional way of being that threatens to abolish safe boundaries of rationality. Moreover, I argue that physiological arousal due to direct contact with evocative primary substances (amniotic fluid, lochia, breast milk, baby faeces, urine, posset, and mucus) has an additional impact, as it actively retriggers the realm of archaic implicit experience. Depending on the specific unconscious fantasies it reactivates, defences come into operation as a stabilising mechanism to prevent the parent becoming overwhelmed by this process of emotional "contagious arousal" (Raphael-Leff, 2003).

Thus, in their state of *primary maternal preoccupation*, Facilitators utilise identificatory similarities to re-experience infantile connections. "Altruistic surrender", manic defences, and idealisation are activated to negotiate prediscursive states and the illusion of infantile "fusion". But, as archaic processes are sparked back into life, reactivation can feel excruciatingly painful. Reliance on intuitive understanding in order to decipher raw preverbal experience needs poses a risk to some women's sense of adult autonomy. In this alternative state, "primary maternal *persecution*" predominates and a threatened new mother might resort to disidentification, utilising regulatory defences concentrated on thinking (intellectualisation, rationalisation, denial, repression, reaction formation, isolation, undoing, and obsessional mechanisms) rather than feeling, to intensify distance and differences between herself and the baby, as a protection against the risk of regression. Feeling less anxious, mature or more experienced Reciprocators manage to remain receptive and to maintain interactive attunement through empathic matching of emotion (rather than facilitatory identification or regulatory disidentification) and improvisation. Their resilience enables playfulness, spontaneity, and discovery, but emotional overload and sleep deprivation could precipitate lapses in either direction by a jangling, transferential "raw nerve".

Love, hate, and the mothering figure

Back to theory: the numinous "maternal object" has many forms. The British Controversial Discussions re-examined previous divergences (a Kleinian assertion of the unconsciously driven imago of an internal phantasy mother as opposed to Burlingham's and Anna Freud's notion of a "memory image"—a mental representative of reality based (interchangeable) mothering figures), to which Middle Groupers added *particularity*: "The psychic object, inasmuch as it is a presentation of the external object, will naturally reflect its peculiarities" (Brierley, 1936, p. 173n). But the mother is still an "object". I argue that theorising of maternal qualities lies in inverse relation to emphasis on the infant's constitutional attributes and/or internally derived phantasies (at first for the child the mother is "only an object who satisfies all his desires" (Klein, 1937, p. 307)), and vice versa.

Not only was primary maternal preoccupation/reverie obligatory, but so was *perfect attunement*. Maternal responsiveness was gauged by exact commensurability between the savvy baby's requirements and the sensitive mother's fine-tuned adaptation, accurate mirroring feedback, and exquisitely timed "graduated failure". Impingements that negated the infant's "spontaneous gesture" were seen to prematurely endanger his "illusion of omnipotent control" (Winnicott, 1971), thereby promoting "false self" responses (Winnicott, 1960). Yet, if her untimely intervention or withdrawal could destroy the "magic" of archaic "harmonious interpenetrating mixup", as Balint termed it in 1968, the mother's overly "magical" response would pre-empt conditions for dis-illusion, necessary for "perception" and "use of the object" (Winnicott, 1969). However, it is with this paper that the Independent's theoretical transition to maternal subjectivity is paved.

Winnicott describes the infant's transition from relating to the mother as a subjectively conceived object shaped by fantasy and desire, as well as experience, to a relationship with an other who is objectively perceived as existing outside the self. This "object", who survives attack, becomes hailed ("Hello"), and recognised as a "subject"—a real, complex other existing outside oneself, with feelings and needs of her own.

In theorising, too, once the mother is no longer merely a reliable purveyor of supplies, her *authentic responsiveness* becomes significant. Coincidentally, by thus placing greater emphasis on the care-giving arm of the equation, the Independents opened up the gateway to examination not only of the mother, but also of the *analyst's* personal qualities and subjective experience.

Self–object coupling: influence and representations

Thus, a momentous transformation arose within the British Independent group when maternal subjectivity, including its negative underbelly, emerged. Winnicott's 1949 sympathetic acknowledgement of a mother's ambivalence towards her baby and its linkage to a psychoanalyst's countertransferential hatred towards particular patients had introduced an *inter*psychic dimension into the dyadic relational system. 1969 introduced intersubjectivity—*a dialectic of unconscious forces in both mothering and analysis, operating in both directions.*

Prefigured by Ferenczi's extraordinary, yet deprecated, ideas about ramifications of "confusion of tongues", a medley of voices now began to be heard in the nursery, as in the consulting room. Progressively, the infant (and, hence, the patient) was depicted as *a reciprocally interrelating partner*, rather than a passive recipient of goodies, vulnerable victim, or vicious attacker of the analytic/nurturing process. Imperceptibly, this awareness propelled a theoretical shift from the maternal carer as holding–recognising "object" towards a view of *reciprocal recognition* where, despite asymmetry, *both* participants are susceptible to being affected as well as affecting (and, hence, psychoanalytic exchange, too, as *interaction between subjects*).

Consequentially, in this primary dialogue, neither analyst nor mother could be regarded as a detached authority figure or blank screen, empty container, or even indulgent empathic cipher. S/he took shape as *real, influential*, and *fallible*—and with an inner life of his/her own subject to influence. As we shall see, this *bi-directionality* resulted in dramatic changes in the conceptualisation of countertransference.

In tandem, the infant's mind itself came to be seen as inherently dyadic. Fairbairn's 1944 ground-breaking principle of *coupled self–other representations*[16] was later echoed in the USA by Jacobson (1954), where, under the influence of both these theoreticians, Kernberg (1966) came to emphasise affective linkages between object- and self-representations. Loewald (trained by Sullivan) went further, stressing that what is internalised are not objects but *relationships* and their interactions (1970), and Lichtenberg described earliest internalisations as *specific self–other dyads* composed of a self-image, object-image, and "affective coloring" of the interaction (1979).

In parallel, appreciation of the *relational nature of early experience* spread in the British Society. A paradigm shift occurred, as those around Anna Freud progressively transformed their original conceptualisation into an object-relational perspective (albeit, without diminishing the powerful role of the drives). Akin to their American counterparts, the Sandlers stated that "every wish involves a self-representation, object-representation and a representation of the inter-action between these" (1978, p. 288). In addition, Joe Sandler described *interactional* forces in the consulting room, in the analyst's counter-transferential "role-responsiveness" (1976), as actualisation of the patient's desire for a relationship "as a vehicle of instinctual gratifi-cation".

Intersubjectivity was now in the air on both sides of the Atlantic. As noted, among North American psychoanalysts the traditional structural theory was being undermined. A shift occurred from the classic threesome—interpretation of intrapsychic conflict, reconstruc-tion, and working through—towards *relational forces* as mutative in psychoanalytic treatment. The new perspective received impetus from Kohut's *Analysis of the Self* (1971), building on the legacies of Fairbairn, Balint, Winnicott, and Sullivan (with little acknowledgment), and emphasising the structural significance of *empathy* in parental care-giving and the narcissistic "core deficiency" arising from early depri-vation and deficits. This new conceptualisation of an interactive mother–infant pair now posed serious competition to the self-possessed infant of establishment ego psychology. Increasingly, the idea of intersubjectivity took shape among both self-psychologists in the USA and Independents in Britain.[17]

The concept of intersubjectivity, first introduced into the psycho-analytic literature by Binswanger in 1963, and extending Habermas's influence in philosophy into infant developmental research by Trevar-then in 1974, was later defined by Atwood and Stolorow in their 1984 *Structures of Subjectivity* as designating the "inter-subjective fields" that are formed by the "intersections of two or more subjectivities". Recognition of meanings as co-created within the dialogical situation (in both primary relations and in the consulting room) committed analysts to examining their own impact (and that of their theories) on the analytic exchange, intersecting with the patient's contribution.

Late in the twentieth century, evidence of the sophistication of perinatal capacities eventually filtered into contemporary theory. Borne out by research findings, the idea that "dual unity" is *not* a given, but is achieved through an increasing sense of the self's subjec-tivity (Stern, 1985) (and awareness of the other's alterity) via growing capacities for empathy, connectedness, and appreciation of divergent perspectives that allow for *relatedness*. In time, also influenced by such findings in neonatal research and neuroscience, not only the Independents but contemporary Freudians such as Fonagy and Target (2007), too, come to emphasise the interpersonal process as crucial, the interaction with the minds of others as a prerequisite for self-recognition and internalised mental states laying foundations for the core sense of self.

Furthermore, modifications in theoretical conceptualisation of the neonatal psyche lead to differences in praxis. I argue, here, that this recognition of "merger" as *a post hoc wish* rather than a primitive reality led to greater appreciation of fantasy, and of the asymmetrical yet systemic fluctuations and subjective experiences in both mother and baby between communion and competition, desired closeness and differentiation. Ultimately, this engendered the Independents' unique consulting-room stance of alternating two-ness and one-ness.

Intersubjectivity: sociocultural and research influences

A complex web of forces led up to this major paradigmatic shift in psychoanalysis towards intersubjectivity. Among these I would count repercussions of the 1960s countercultural revolution, which augmented the Women's Movement's demand for equal recognition. Western mothers voiced their disillusionment with enforced post-war return to domesticity and expressed a newly articulated goal of liberated "self-individuation". In turn, these led to greater female involvement in the workplace, which, in nuclear families, forced corollary *participation of fathers in primary child-care.*

Coincidentally, advances in technology enabled neonatal research to take off as a male-dominated field.[18] I ascribe this sex bias to admission of fathers to the birth chamber and growing interest in the (undrugged) newborn, with dawning awareness of effects of maternal medication in childbirth and puerperal separation (Klaus & Kennell, 1976). Infancy research burgeoned following Wolff's (1966) delineation of six states of consciousness in neonates, ranging from highly attentive to less alert states of consciousness. From the 1970s onwards, a host of cleverly constructed studies selectively timed to coincide with periods of "alert inactivity" demonstrated the amazing capacities of even premature newborns. *These findings forced revision of the classical idea of blanket primary narcissism and the norm of perfect interaction.*

In my view, delineation of early states of consciousness also resolved the puzzle of multiple versions of primary experience that had long perplexed psychoanalysts. Freud's baby had been regarded as immersed in *primary narcissism*, while an infant closer to the Budapest school was seen as benignly engaged in *primitive relatedness*. Conversely, the neonate conceived more through Karl Abraham's lineage than Ferenczi's was deemed intensely driven by innate hatred to violent phantasies. Theoretical debate raged around "discovery" of the mother and accessibility of preverbal primary experience, with differing conceptual, explanatory, and clinical interpretations.[19]

Opposing models had seemed even more puzzling once disciplined infant observation became a curricular requirement of psychoanalytic training in many IPA societies. However, if we agree to regard states of consciousness as variable, the findings of perinatal cognitive capacities and learning can be juxtaposed with neonatal non-awareness of self and moments of merger. Even during the course of one observational hour, each baby can be seen to display a subtle variety of those six "states of alertness", ranging from sleep or self-absorption through receptivity to sociable extraversion or distress.

Clearly, notwithstanding the desire for objectivity, the particular developmental model in the mind of the observer pre-assigns attributes to the baby, and colours the inferences made about his/her psychic activity related to the observed spectrum of behaviours. Furthermore, seminar leaders, too, unconsciously home in on aspects syntonic with their own theoretical beliefs, which set the parameters for meanings ascribed to the observed behaviour.[20]

Empirical evidence on the nature of primary experience

Dissemination of the many findings from neonatal research caused a "foundation shaking" on all sides of the theoretical divide in psychoanalysis (see Emde's 1981 overview in the *Journal of the American Psychoanalytic Association* of six volumes of developmental studies).

- Studies of neonatal capacities provided evidence of *innate sociability* and demonstrated the *complexity* of early development and importance of *context* and *mental state* in mutual exchange, exploration, and play, confirming many of the Independents' beliefs.

- With growing substantiation of interactive responsiveness, developmental research now shifted from the previous mode of investigating the baby in isolation or studying the parent's influence on the child to a dyadic systems approach of reciprocal influence.

Evidence of the bi-directionality of influence in primary infant–parent exchanges supports an intersubjectivist view.[21]

Predictability

As a result, psychoanalytic notions of *optimal care and of psychogenesis* would have to be redefined. While confirming that cognitive and creative developmental competence is most related to a carer's continuing "contingent" responsiveness, myriad studies could not reveal one single care-giving mode or variable associated with an invariant effect on children. As Freud had foreseen, beyond the early months, *change becomes relatively unpredictable.* Longitudinal studies revealed multiple pathways to the same diagnosis, due to fluctuations in the stability of individual differences in what was termed "the enormous metamorphosis of mental behaviour" (Sameroff, 1978, p. 731).

Furthermore, studies showed that far from a smooth and stable progression, infant development is characterised by a series of *discontinuous spurts* and qualitative transitions towards higher levels of organised complexity. (Substantiating what Anna Freud had postulated in 1965a regarding her "developmental lines", that age-related sequences occur from endogenous control of physiological sensory motor arousal systems to exogenous control with greater emotional expression, yet uneven progress across modalities.)

Findings such as these compelled revision of those aspects of the psychoanalytic model treating development as a linear process with predictable pathological outcome to "fixation" points.

Sociability

New evidence of innate sociability corroborated an object relations view.

- From the 1970s, aided by frame-by-frame microanalysis of filmed observations, neonatal research demonstrated that even within hours of birth, a non-drugged, calm, and attentive newborn displayed a *preference for human faces and a capacity to imitate* facial expressions and simple vocal sounds.

- Even very young infants provide evidence of *proactively soliciting attention*, motivated to enhance their own organisation through dynamic processes with selected care-givers.
- Recall of familiar speech patterns (or music) heard pre-natally confirms *learning in the womb*. And post-natal learning is demonstrated with *purposeful discrimination* within days of birth, *recognition* of the primary carer's face and voice, and an *acquired preference* for smell of her breastmilk and/or body odour.
- From birth newborns can enact others' actions and communicative gestures (ascribed by neurobiologists to mirror neurons), initiating a process of imitations, affective attunement, and primitive identification.
- In the early post-natal weeks, infants voluntarily express a *range of emotions* in smiles and coos of recognition, frowns of annoyance, and delicate eye and hand movements that signal changing affects and states of alertness, distress, or interest.
- By ten weeks, babies clearly demonstrate intentionality and a capacity to *distinguish* various expressions of affect in others.

(These findings have since been replicated by studies in societies as diverse as France, Greece, Sweden, the UK, the USA, Hungary, and rural Nepal.)

Primary communication

Research focusing on *communicative interaction* within primary dyads confirmed what early object relationists had postulated: that presymbolic expectancies and self–other representations preceding thought and language are activated through intensely emotional interactions with attuned mirroring others.

- Micro-analytic techniques applied to audio recordings and filmed face-to-face interaction confirm that *mother–infant exchanges* achieve high levels of efficiency in co-ordination and precision of timing, pitch, and rhythmicity. (Fathers are rarely studied, but research on primary care fathers shows similar capacities.)

- The *collaborative* nature of primary "dialogues", demonstrated in Trevarthen's "Conversations with a two-month-old" (1974), disclosed the infant's innate *turn-taking capacity*, and differential ways of relating to people and to objects, later shown even in premature babies.
- However, most importantl, far from a perfect "dance", microanalytic research revealed *numerous misunderstandings.* Some 30% of primary proto-conversation involves misapprehensions, necessitating continuous reciprocal efforts to *repair mismatches* in order to achieve and maintain mutual states of affective matching and synchrony (Tronick, 1989).
- Cycles of affective match, mismatch, and repair between infant and care-giver occur with split-second co-ordination.

Inevitably, this revelation shattered idealised notions of synchrony between mother and infant, also affecting the ideal of a "perfect" psychoanalytic exchange.

Rules of relating

Most surprisingly, spontaneous forms of interchange are seen to operate according to *primal rules of engagement*, with a built-in predictable pace, a set of *action schemes*, and age-appropriate expectations of how sequences of interaction will unfold in time and space from moment to moment, with commensurate patterns of affect and arousal (see Beebe & Lachmann, 1988, 1994; Mandler, 1988).

- The infant's (learnt and/or innate?) expectancy of intuitive *sympathetic* responsiveness from care-givers can be demonstrated in his/her surprise, confusion, and distress when disappointed, as in "still face" experiments or when "rules" of social reciprocity were violated by perturbations or intrusive and discordant behaviours, which elicited the baby's withdrawal or avoidance
- *Mirroring* and shared affective states deemed essential to the process of differentiation, when studied micro-analytically, showed that, although contingent on the infant's affective displays, caregiver's responses were *marked* and *exaggerated* rather than exact replicas (Beebe, Lachmann, & Jaffe, 1997; Gergely & Watson, 1996; Stern, 1985; Tronick, 1989). This heightened response assists

differentiation between one's own and the other's emotions, and, hence, development of a "theory of mind".

- The idea of "monotropy" was dispelled, as even very young babies demonstrate a capacity to relate to more than one person from the beginning. In addition to a range of different dyadic relationships (including father and siblings), babies discriminate among, and respond differentially to, a variety of other formations, including negotiating complex *triadic relationships*. An international longitudinal study on the process of triadification and triangulation shows interactional, representational, and transgenerational dimensions (Fivaz-Depeursinge et al., 1994).

- Research on the rediscovered developmental concept of *regulation* confirmed Winnicott and Bion's ideas that maternal intervention (holding, containment, attunement) alter the young infant's disrupted psycho-physiological states of consciousness, eventually leading to *self-regulation* through internalisation and reflexive self-awareness. Regulation through parental "kangaroo" skin-to-skin contact is used to replace incubators for premature babies, to reduce heightened arousal.)

- In addition to parental affect matching, evidence emerges of *mutual regulation* of affect across various modalities, such as gaze, vocalisation, facial expression, timing, etc., and dynamic processes of reciprocal adjustments and influence at various stages across the first year, using diverse methods of coding and statistical procedures (see Beebe & Lachman, 1994). These point to an effect on the care-giver, too.

These observations provide an empirical basis for conceptualising innate expectancies and variations in the quality of interrelatedness, as well as defining emergent dyadic phenomena which could not be depicted on the basis of either partner alone.

Primary carer–infant relationship

- Notwithstanding many analysts' conviction that fathers are "unimportant" until the phallic–Oedipal phase of development, early psychoanalytic gender research (Chused 1986; Pruett, 1983) showed that when fathers are primary carers, with close, continuous, and intimate contact with their babies, their nurturing is what we have deemed "maternalistic".

- Diverse studies find that in nuclear families where men increasingly share baby care, far from stereotypical ascriptions (maternal empathic soothing *vs.* paternal stimulation/instrumentality), like mothers, pre-Oedipal fathers alternate between comforting, communicating, and "stretching", and, later, can be as affectively immersed in imaginative play, linguistic interpretation, responsive emotional processing, and/or limit-setting, according to the need of the moment (Field, 1978).
- Furthermore, recent research finds hormonal changes in co-habiting fathers during their partner's pregnancy, post-natal reduction of testosterone, heightened arousal in their interaction with infants, and an elevated rate of post-natal disorders in partners of disturbed mothers.
- Research methods focusing on variability demonstrate the uniqueness of each dyadic primary relationship, in which each partner learns to apprehend and incorporate the assemblages of essential meanings of *the other's state of consciousness* (resembling what Winnicott referred to as background "shared expectancies") continuously *co-creating* age-appropriate new ways of being together (Stern, 1985; Tronick, 2003).
- Significant relationships thus grow, changing through recurrent elicitation, interactive communication and work of repair, and the effect of other relationships.[22]

These findings on multiple "unique" dyads negate psychoanalytic views of the mother–infant relationship as *prototype.* This has implications for psychoanalytic theories of parental roles and for praxis, given our preconceived ideas on "maternal" or "paternal" modes of relating with patients. Also dispelled is the romanticised notion of perfection (thus confirming Winnicott's notion of a "good-enough" mother). In Tronick's words, ". . . there is no perfect or perfectible form of a relationship (e.g., the ideal mother–infant relationship) nor would one want one, because it would not change" (2003, p. 476).

Developmental trajectory

Empirical findings of alert social responsiveness from birth posed a challenge to the basic tenets of separation–individuation theory. Summarising the evidence, Stern proposed that the earliest developmental thrust progresses from initial differentiation (and separateness) towards increasing capacities for union and connectedness, in contrast to Mahler's conceptual trajectory from "primary narcissism" and objectless "normal autism" (later retracted), followed by pre-objectal symbiosis, out of which differentiation then occurs.

Once again, this discrepancy indicates different observational foci at different levels of alertness. Also, potential conflation between *actual* neonatal experience and later fantasies of unboundaried fusion and omnipotence (now suggested to require language, self-reflexivity, and a capacity to recognise one's own separateness—achievements of the second year of life). Some analysts see the two models as complementary, not mutually exclusive, stressing the simultaneity of connection and separation. Following Hegel's thesis on conflict between the wish for absolute independence and the need for recognition, Benjamin (1990) asserts that human subjectivity evolves out of a dynamic tension between connection and separation: self assertion (being recognised) and recognising the other on the one hand, and Winnicott's tension between negation/denial of the other, and his/her affirmation ("use of the object"). Similarly, two fundamental developmental lines are demarcated: the need for *relatedness* and for *self-definition* (Blass & Blatt, 1996).[23] These are relevant to the Independent Group's view of the clinical process.

Memory and plasticity

In recent years, neuroscience has accorded with psychoanalytic interest, granting *interpersonal transmission of emotion* a regulatory role not only in the mind and cognitive mastery of experience, but in growth of the brain itself, reflecting proliferation or pruning of synapses in the ongoing experience with specific care-givers.[24] Here, too, a spurt in research potentialities was fostered by technological advances such as fMRI, enabling investigation of brain functions of the alert and interacting infant.

- Neuro-imaging reveals evidence of minimal brain anomalies and delimiting birth defects on the one hand, and of the neonatal brain's neuro-plasticity on the other.
- Neural networks (proliferating at the extraordinary rate of 1.8 million new synapses per second until two years after birth) are

shown to be activated, reinforced, or "pruned" within primary relationships. *Connectivity patterns of the neonate's brain circuits are modulated by the critical organising function of care-givers.*

- Darwin's basic emotions of sadness, anger happiness, disgust, fear, and surprise were redefined as universal, innate, "hard-wired" affective centres, delineated as *Seeking, Rage, Fear,* and *Panic,* activated by need, frustration, anxiety, and separation/ loss, respectively (Panksepp, 1998), confirming the Middle Group view of *aggression (vs.* anger/rage) as a *defensive reaction to frustration,* and of the *centrality of separation qnxiety.* This evolutionary heritage embedded in our procedural memories is clearly linked to survival of the species, and shared with all other mammals (validating Bowlby's assertions and Freud's delineation of self-preservative and other instincts).

- In 1980, Bowlby noted findings that information is stored in two distinct forms—*preverbal "episodic" and semantic.* Recent neuroscientific evidence elaborates on this distinction between *subcortically stored implicit schemas of sub-symbolic memory* ("memories in feeling"), in contrast to later accessible *"auto-biographical" memory* (Bucci, 1985; Damasio, 1999). The former is found to be revoked in states of high arousal, and through "mimicry", possibly aided by "mirror-neurone" resonance (Scalzone, 2005). (It is in this area that my finding of "contagious arousal" seems to operate.)[25]

Interim summary

Early on, Freud noted, "it is a very remarkable thing that the Ucs. of one human being can react upon that of another, without passing through the Cs" (1915e, p. 194).

Many of the findings presented above provide an empirical basis for conceptualising not merely the unconscious transmission Freud noted, but its dialectical nature and influence in the development of intersubjectivity between two minds, beginning in infancy. Research explicated parameters for variations in the quality of interrelatedness, defining emergent dyadic phenomenon: thus, procedural mutual regulation between care-giver and baby was shown to occur by means of innate expectancies, intuitive affect-matching, mirror neurones, contagious arousal, moments of disruption and attempted repair, mutual regulation, and attunement. Habitual forms of meaning from one individual's state of consciousness come to be co-ordinated with the meanings of another's (in terms of affects, relational intentions, and representations) (Lyons-Ruth, 1999), from which a "dyadic state of consciousness" emerges, unique to that relationship (and although claimed to be "untransferrable" to other relationships (Tronick, 2003), there clearly are instances of heightened transference).[26]

In my view, the most exciting empirical evidence has come from researchers who are also psychoanalysts (Beebe and Lachman; Emde; Fonagy and Target; Hobson; Stern; Solms and Kaplan; Tronick, etc). Their work has highlighted *a systemic model* of early relating, emphasising that each primary relationship is *both singular and co-dynamically transformative*. Yet, even within this bi-directional system, a baby-orientated focus has left the caring arm of the equation under-theorised. In my view, there is still insufficient enquiry into the emotional impact of care-giving *on the carer*, and the effect of each parent's subjective experience of parenting on the relationship with the baby and between carers—an imbalance that my own work has systematically attempted to redress.

Finally, more than 100 years on, evidence of the *inextricability of the brain and the inner world* (in terms of subjective experience of emotion, motivation, memory, phantasy, dreams, and hallucinations) provides confirmation of many of the conscious and unconscious processes proposed by Freud in his 1895 *Project* and elsewhere (see Solms & Turnbull, 2002). *These findings influence therapeutic approaches to issues of resistance, memory reconstruction, interactive patterns, and even use of the couch.*

Couch

Aetiology and treatment

I have argued here that, depending on their own frame of reference, psychoanalysts of different persuasions each hold a particular view of *pathogenesis*, which, in turn, determines their form of *treatment* and its specified aims. Divergent paradigms disagree about the nature of *therapeutic change*, but all concur that symptom remission is secondary to a more permanent alteration in the inner world "mental economy". Similarly, a common aim across theoretical positions is the goal of enhancing a patient's awareness of his/her own contributions to difficulties and engendering "responsibility", as expressed by a sense of agency accompanied by healthy anxiety and concern. However, as I stated at the start, what these changes consist of, and the psychical work involved in their achievement, vary according to underpinning conceptualisations of aetiology in each psychoanalytic model.

A prime distinction is *source of pathology*. As noted, when the infant is deemed "merged", yet receptive and vulnerable, dangers are ascribed to influences/impingements of *the external emotional environment*. Pathogenesis is assumed to be age related, differentially stemming from adversity at critical stages of development. In general, psychotic illness is attributed to early preverbal impingements, with borderline disturbances attributed to privation in toddlerhood, as opposed to neurotic disorders ascribed to Oedipal phase disturbance.[27]

"Cure" is then seen to reside in *new relational experiences* that undo the damage caused by failure of archaic care-givers. Provision of a more sensitive form of primary care facilitates reworking of old deficits, thereby changing internal representations. The level of inducement or tolerance of therapeutic regression matches the critical phase delineated by each theoretician.

This position revitalises the original Freud–Ferenczi controversy— whether insight–interpretation or a new corrective relation constitutes the mutative factor. Originally, the very nature of the therapeutic action of psychoanalysis seemed at stake; however, a synthesis posed by Gill (1982) modified the stakes by suggesting that most mutative of all is the patient's insight into his/her patterns of interpersonal relationship while also exposed to a new pattern of interpersonal relationship.

None the less, a major reconceptualisation is involved, as the relational model held by Independents is now embedded in a complex interactive field of *bi-directional affective transmissions*, counterposed to the classical model of an objective, neutral analyst acting as a "blank screen" for the patient's projections. The latter paradigm turns on ascription of pathology to *internal factors*, especially unresolved conflicts between life and death instincts (as in the classical drive model) or between internecine internal urges and reality demands (in ego psychology). Treatment, predicated on the analyst remaining detached and the setting invariable, is aimed to stimulate retrieval of veridical memories of traumatic events (or the original phantasy). Interpretations of intrapsychic vicissitudes of instinctual strivings and defences aim to foster insight in order to increase ego hegemony by reinforcing instinct control and renunciation of drive derivatives. While "making the unconscious conscious" remains central, today emphasis is on the interpretative *process* itself, and experiential know-ledge leading to more than mere intellectual understanding.

A third view attributes pathology to *both internal and external contri-butions*: a preponderance of innate aggression and derivative sadistic fantasies (attacking the "bad" breast or primal scene), as well as anni-hilatory and persecutory anxieties due to internalised frustrating bad objects, which lead to neurotic or psychotic disturbance.[28] Since, in this view, understanding the *distorted* aspect of early relations is central, the essential therapeutic tool of "mutative transference inter-pretations" was directed at impulses and primitive defences (splitting and projective identification) against instinctual forces and internal objects falsified by projection. While somewhat modified today, neo-Kleinians still regard psychic change as effected by tackling the "point of urgency" of current transference emotions ("memories in feeling") in the here-and-now analytic situation, chased up by the difference between the projected archaic object and the analyst. Within this system, intense and prolonged resistances leading to negative thera-peutic reactions are ascribed to the workings of pathological destruc-tive envy, a vicissitude of the death instinct (see Joseph, 1982; Klein, 1957; Rosenfeld, 1987). Reversibility of projective identification is seen to depend on the patient's capacity to face psychic reality and, in particular, to confront the reality of loss and to go through "the mourning process that results from this confrontation" (Steiner, 1996, p. 1075). The therapeutic alliance and analytic success depend on the patient's ability to identify with basic concepts that organise the analyst's observations and interpretations, leading to a modification in the patient's ego and superego.

Today, while among extremists the debate still rages about perni-cious or curative factors (also see Schafer, 1994), there is a growing trend towards *multiple modes of therapeutic action*: seeing supportive and interpretive strategies as operating synergistically, and dosed according to each patient's needs at any one point in time (Gabbard & Westen, 2003). Clearly, calibrating these depends on the degree of *match* between each individual patient's required quality of care and what a particular psychoanalyst brings to the encounter from his/her own personal history. His/her theoretical stance and chosen therapeutic style, will contribute to strengths and vulnerabilities within that pair's evolving patterns of relating.

Praxis

Given the many changes of the past decades, across the board, the therapeutic medium has switched from an authoritative paternal ideal within a triadic Oedipal axis to that of a formative dyadic matrix.

One catalyst of this change is psychoanalytic work with deeply disturbed patients. As noted, when psychosis was ascribed to pathological splitting in the face of unthinkable anxieties due to deficiencies of maternal care, analysis was deemed analogous to (corrective) early mothering. Ironically, for most Kleinians working with psychotic patients, the analyst's undeniable experience on the receiving end of "primitive" projective identifications confirmed the baby's capacity to project disowned split-off fragments in a bid for control and possession, rather than heightening awareness of the other arm of the equation, *maternal subjectivity* and increasing empathy for the primary carer's unconscious responses to primal experience.[29]

I have argued here that psychoanalytic treatment was also affected by empirical evidence from neonatal research. Once infant proactivity was confirmed, the next step was recognising the baby as *co-constructor* (and co-regulator) of joint experience within his or her uniquely refracted reality. Ultimately, highlighting the contributions of *both* partners in a primary relationship will sensitise analysts not only to issues of *mutual influence* in analysis, but to correspondences and dissimilarities in the parenting interrelation.

Once the human mind is seen as constituted interactively, and psychoanalysis is regarded as intersubjective, the analyst can no longer be regarded as an aloof neutral "arbiter" of the patient's reality (Gill, 1982; Schwaber, 1983) and analysis must include some examination of the analyst's subjectivity and the patient's experience of it. The *specificity* of the carer's qualities and beliefs pose expectations and theory-biased organisation of the patient's material.

Bidirectional regulation and how both patient and analyst generate data is at the crux of contemporary intersubjectivists' explorations of the analyst's conscious and unconscious contributions and the patient's countertransference in experiencing these. This emphasis, long held by Ferenczi and upheld by British Independents, has now burgeoned in the USA, especially among self-psychologists, intersubjectivists, and, more recently, relational therapists.

With these developments, if the metaphoric equation with infancy is to hold, the patient on the couch can no longer represent a self-centred solipsistic mind preoccupied with internally provoked conflicts between the ego's inter-systemic and intra-systemic relations. S/he has to be recognised as a subject who has evolved through experience with other minds, and continues to do so on the couch, in internalised exchanges, and even in solitude.

Among contemporary Freudians, clinical repercussions of the new research findings has led to combining *re*-constructive interpretations of the past and concern about inner state organisation with acknowledgement of ongoing relationships outside the consulting room as well as here-and-now interaction/*co*-construction within it (see Couch, 2002). The work of Fonagy and Target (2007) within the contemporary Freudian group has increased awareness of primary relations, parental "reflective function", mentalisation, and intersubjectivity.

Alvarez (1999) maintans that, surprisingly, despite their preoccupation with infantile phantasy, most Kleinian clinicians have been "strongly resistant" to findings from neo-natal studies.But modern post-Bionian theory holds "a third option" between the one-person psychology of drive theory and the two-person psychology of the intersubjectivists, relational analysts, and attachment theorists. This option of "an internal two-person psychology" is one where the analyst addresses the patient's psychic world to "explore and disentangle all of his internal objects, good and bad" (Alvarez 1999, pp. 213–214). None the less, growing awareness among Kleinians of co-created originary meanings has filtered through to awareness of a similar process within the psychoanalytic exchange, as O'Shaughnessy testifies:

> Over the past fifty years . . . psychoanalysts have changed their view of their own method. It is now widely held that, instead of being about the patient's intrapsychic dynamics, interpretations should be about the interaction of patient and analyst at an *intrapsychic* level. (1983, p. 281, my italics)

Finally, when both the patient and analyst are seen to evoke, respond to, and generate reciprocal communications in the conjoint analytic experience, the analyst as subject is subject to idiosyncratic fallibility. Ferenczi deemed "hypocritical" the analyst's alleged abstention from affective involvement within the consulting room. Arguing that patients often have an intuitive awareness, he advocated that analysts should acknowledge their mistakes and subjective experiences (1916, 1932, 1933). Post-Ferenczi, the thorny issues of deliberate and inadvertent self-revelation were debated by Michael and Alice Balint in 1939, and have resurfaced today within a psychoanalytic culture that still continues "to cast great suspicion on any deliberate self-disclosure" (Stolorow, Atwood, & Brandchaft, 1994).[30]

Although theorists argue that there is no single hegemonic discourse or technical practice that defines current relational theory or intersubjective "turn" (Aron, 1996; Mitchell, 1993), in general, when the analyst believes that a "new beginning" occurs in an intersubjective psychoanalytic context, with undeniable conscious and unconscious participation of the analyst, a self-reflexive utilisation of countertransference experience is a vital component within the therapeutic action. Practice and clinical understanding alters dramatically with replacement of a unidirectional model (previously emphasising the influence of the therapist on the patient) with a *bidirectional* one of mutual modification (including the influence of the patient on the therapist). (For an example of an old clinical case reworked using the new model, see Beebe & Lachman, 2003.)

In sum, when the human mind is seen as interactive (rather than monadic), inner and relational processes are given equal importance and treated as co-constructed.

Countertransference as bidirectional interpsychic processes

It may be argued that the catalyst for recognising the disputed concept of *unconscious dialogical forces* within the consulting room originated in Freud's 1915 statement about shared unconscious communication (quoted above). His other observation that "no psychoanalyst goes farther than his own complexes and resistances permit" (1910d, pp. 141–142) seems to lay the foundations for *redefinition* of countertransference.

Historically, a keystone of the Independents was the concept of repetition of patterns of *primary interactive relating* in the consulting room. An "interplay" of forces akin to the "interpenetrating mixup" of mother–infant interchange (as Michael and Alice Balint put it in 1939). Yet, the full significance of *analytical reciprocity* was yet to be realised. (Ten years later, Balint still had cause to comment, "what distortions happen and how much we miss while describing Two-Body experiences (analytical technique) in a language belonging to One-Body situations" (M. Balint, 1950, p. 124).) Therapeutic permeability to the patient's unconscious communications was rendered a crucial asset when Heimann declared that "[T]he analyst's counter-transference is an instrument of research into the patient's unconscious" (1950, p. 81). This idea of our emotional sensitivity as one of the most important tools of analysis, rather than an impediment or pathological interference, paved the way to acceptance of "contagious arousal" between two subjectivities in the consulting room.

The seeds of this paradigm shift to seeing human minds as constituted interactively is apparent in the Balints' re-description of analytical forces as the result of "an interplay between the patient's transference and the analyst's counter-transference, complicated by the *reactions* released in each by the other's transference on to him" (1939, p. 228, my italics). Recognition that this "interplay" constitutes "an inter-relation between two individuals, in a constantly changing and developing object-relation" (Balint, 1950, p. 123) led to conceding that both patient and analyst have "libidinal investments" in each other and in the analysis.

Thus, by the early 1950s, many Independents were citing counter-transference as a *joint product of interweaving unconscious forces*, with the analyst's hovering attention as *dialectical* counterpart to the patient's (interactive) free association. In time, analysts from other groups elaborated on this ever-present (necessary) dynamism in analytic work, albeit focusing on externalisation of the patient's internal self-object representations in the analyst's sensorium.[31]

The London Klein group long persisted in a view of countertransference as a *one-way* projective identification from the patient *into* the analyst (see Segal, 1977) despite Racker's view of the analyst's participation (including his/her countertransference) as a *constant co-determinant* of the patient's experience. However, by the 1980s, some shifts did occur and transference-induced countertransference, regarded as the patient's attempt to evoke feelings, came to be seen as an "invaluable" form of communication. Henceforth, Kleinian clinical practice changed, too.

Elaborating on Klein's (1952) account of transferring "total situations" from the past, Joseph now described this as transference of "a *living relationship* in which there is constant movement and change" (1985, p. 454, my italics). And, while not yet voicing the contribution of an analyst's *own* unconscious dynamics, a further breakthrough came with consideration of the unconscious dovetailing of patient communications with the analyst's vulnerabilities (Brenman Pick, 1985). Rosenfeld (1987) took it further, noting that the constant, principally unconscious interplay between analyst and analysand involved their *mutual introjection* of the other's projective identifications. With the recent convergence of ego psychologists and contemporary Kleinians, countertransference could now be conceptualised as "involving a gradient or continuum" as Gabbard (1995) noted, with projective identification on one end, enactment on the other, and considerable overlap in between. (Also see Schafer, 1994.)

Historically, in the USA, an interactive view had been actively negated by a series of influential papers by Annie Reich, beginning in 1951, reinforcing ego-psychology's view of countertransference as a *disturbance* related to the analysts' unresolved neurotic conflicts. In a curious analogy, she declared that similar to the part "attachment to the mother plays in the normal object choice of the adult man" countertransference must remain "shadowy and in the background" (p. 31). It was during that scientific crisis towards the mid-1980s that this notion of countertransference as an "interference" was queried in the USA. Like transference, it was reframed as a normal (unconscious) ingredient of the psychoanalytic process: "two faces of the same dynamic, rooted in the inextricable intertwinings with others" (Loewald, 1986, p. 276), with the session as a patient–analyst "complex of interacting transferences" imbued with "ambiguity and relativity of the interpersonal reality" (Gill, 1982).

Exploration among self-psychologists of the "lived" emotional experiences of both patient and analyst within the consulting room led to some intersubjectivists defining *all* relationships as subjective interactional systems. However, within the specificity of the analytic process, the analyst is clearly not only an enabler, but also a *delimiting factor* (see Freud's 1910 comment above) in determining and shaping the very field of clinical interchange. (This has led to a suggestion of distinguishing "co-transference" feelings empathically understood by the analyst from "countertransference" as interference in the analytical work (Orange, 1995).)

Finally, some relational psychoanalysts (e.g., Aron, 1996; Renik, 1993) and social constructivists (e.g., Hoffman, 1983) point to the "inescapability" of the analyst's subjectivity in understanding the patient's inner world due to unconscious personal motivations.

While clearly reducing the analyst's "authority", the shift towards intersubjectivity might be seen to grant the analyst a position of great responsibility. It entails awareness of the asymmetry of the analytic situation, and the inevitability of bringing conscious and unconscious organising principles and biographical vestiges that affect the patient. Conversely, like the Reciprocator mother, by recognising self and other as similar subjects the analyst can also more fully experience his or her own subjectivity in the presence of the patient's.

Summary: neonatal research and intersubjective dialectics

I have argued here that emanating from infant research and dyadic systems theory, the psychoanalytic process has come to be formulated by independents, intersubjectivists and relationalists as *interaction between two minds*: two different subjectivities/realities in the room, both of whom are transmitting, receiving, and co-constructing non-conscious communications. An ingenious statistical study confirms that between them, each pair evolves unique patterns of interaction within the consulting room (Ablon & Jones, 2005). Furthermore, since the advent of relativity and quantum theories, even diehard Kleinian psychoanalysts have now accepted that as an interpretative discipline, psychoanalysis offers no escape from the *mutual* influence of observer and observed (see Segal, 2006).

Most influential in this shift have been neonatal studies revealing the baby's innate need for emotional engagement and growing capacity for understanding interpersonal motives. Seen to enable ascription of a "mind" to self and other, this understanding ultimately entails recognising one's own image in the mind of the other and learning that different perspectives might exist about the same experience.[32]

Finally, I propose that these interactive factors, regarded as the primary organisers of mental growth in infancy, are tacitly accepted by intersubjectivists as instigators of *change in psychoanalysis.*

Contemporary Independents have come to recognise opacity—the inevitable influence of the analyst even on "free" association, the patient's right to privacy, and the ineffable unknowability within the alterity of the other. Thus, selectivity within associative narratives and their interactive corollary of "evenly suspended attention" can merely offer temporary postulates rather than "truths". *Interpretations become tentative hypotheses.* Furthermore, some analysts accept a postmodern premise of a composite and fluid organisation of self, patterned around different intersubjective self and object representations, all derived from different relational contexts and perspectives (see Mitchell, 1993). Here, the idea of a continuously evolving shifting plurality of a sense of "selfhood" replaces notions of a singular "True Self".

Like the mothers described earlier, as a complex subject, the analyst, too, inevitably brings to the dialogic encounter a personal frame of reference, with experiential legacies and myriad identificatory and implicit facets of his/her inner world. A "multivocality" of voices is now heard within the consulting room (Kennedy, 2007; Raphael-Leff, 1997) as each participant in the analytic relationship operates a complex interplay of conscious and unconscious spoken, silent, and non-verbally expressed implicit and conscious intrapsychic and interpersonal "voices". All of these can be fostered or inhibited in either of the participants, who engage in various permutations with the "voices" of the other within the psychoanalytic dialogue.

Therefore, in accordance with neonatal research findings from proto-communication, psychoanalysis has had to reconsider the idealised notion of a perfectly synchronised single voiced communicatory "dance". The question we must now ask is not only Heimann's (1956, p. 305) "why is the patient doing what now and to whom?", but which of the many voices within the patient is speaking now and to whom the analyst chooses to respond and in which voice? . . .

Beginning with neonatal proto-conversations, communication itself is now treated as a complex reciprocal exchange oscillating between misunderstanding and corrective reparation a great deal of the time. Indeed, some researchers suggest that "sloppiness" exists in all dyadic interaction: "[p]ervasive, inescapable and inherent", it is part of the unpredictability, indeterminacy, redundancy and

"fuzzy intentionalizing" that reflects both implicit relational representations and affective valences (Boston Change Process Study Group,
2007).

In addition, like early parenting, at times, psychoanalytic treatment renders both partners reciprocally susceptible to what I have
termed "contagious arousal" (Raphael-Leff, 1991a, 2003)—the pressures of unconscious evocation of implicit sub-symbolic emotions,
leading to transferential actualisations and countertransferential
enactments by both analyst and patient. This despite the analyst's
conscious striving to achieve and maintain that trilogy of "unattainable" and "illusory" goals, neutrality, anonymity, and abstinence (see
Panel Report, Stolorow, 1997), a failure possibly attributable to the
analyst's own "irreducible" subjectivity (Renik, 1993) and the multi-
faceted network of reciprocal associations within a dialogue.

In sum, it is as well to remember that the situations of analysis and
parenting are analogous, but not isomorphic. They are similar in that
both deal with *an asymmetrical relation* in which the more vulnerable
partner is to be safeguarded against inappropriate affects and/or
appropriation by the other. And in psychotherapy, as in pregnancy,
from the moment of first contact, expulsion from the womb/consult-
ing room is in sight, which in analysis, too, might come at term,
prematurely, or long over the "due date".

However, the situations differ in that, unlike mothering, analysis
is, by definition, *a time-bound "therapeutic" experience*. As Winnicott
noted, there is an end to each hour. Other than in parent–infant treatment, the patient is not a baby, and, as Tronick (2003) reminds us, each
older patient and therapist engage in age-possible meanings and ways
of being together that are *qualitatively different* from those of the infant,
including use of language, symbols, explicit knowing, different forms
of representation, self-regulation, and analytic capacities, some of
which are explicit, and many implicit.

I have argued that, like mothers, analysts, too, vary in their orientations. Some analysts veer towards believing they "know best" in
determining the "truth" and, like Regulator mothers, keep an invariable, routinised setting and frame, a "prescriptive mode" for coping
with resistance and potential attacks. Others, who, like Winnicott,
believe that "[T]he principle is that it is the patient and only the
patient who has the answers" (1969, p. 711) utilise primary process in
the service of providing identificatory facilitation and nurture. In this

case, the analytic situation could be construed as comparable to mothering a regressed baby/patient. A third orientation sees two people in interaction within the consulting room's transitional space, co-creating the multi-layered cumulative emotional and verbal fabric of a session, with both attempting to surrender to the process, rather than occupying a submission–dominance situation.

Like the "Reciprocator" mother, in this asymmetrical yet "subject-to-subject" position, while aware of his/her own subjectivity, the analyst utilises receptivity and unconscious processes to facilitate *the patient's discovery/articulation of self-experience.* Clearly, this varies at different times in each session and over the course of a particular patient's analysis, in terms of the degree of abstinence, self-disclosure, playful spontaneity, or more formulaic responses. *It is this complex admixture of subjectivity, intersubjectivity and intrasubjectivity in the service of the patient that I regard as the hallmark of the Independents.*

Finally, I contend that in recent years there has been an *intersubjective convergence.* Contemporary Freudians have moved away from classical objectivism, and a stance of the authoritative, knowing analyst. Likewise, Independents have moved on from the early object relation view of seeing the patient as the knowing subject, and the analyst as munificent purveyor of reparative provisions. Today, many assume primacy of a relationship in which neither analyst nor patient "know", but, from differing perspectives (i.e., ways of organising the shared "field"), *both participate in a journey of discovery* in which each, at times, occupies the "third position" (Britton, 1998; Ogden, 1994) of observation in the service of the patient's discovery.[33] Interestingly, among second—and subsequent—time round mature parents, a similar convergence tends to occur, with both Facilitators and Regulators modifying their stance towards greater reciprocation.

Conclusion

In this chapter, I have proposed that the intersubjective psychoanalytic approach spearheaded by the Independents has gained momentum over the past fifty years, influenced by developmental research, feminist critiques, and philosophical expositions on the human subject, ranging from Hegel, through the existentialists and humanists, to Habermas, Davidson, and Derrida. Historicism and new epistemologies have resulted in dramatic conceptual shifts from "one-person" intrapsychic conceptions to "two-person" intersubjective psychology, and from *intra-* to *inter*-psychic emphases; from positivist to constructivist and perspectivist approaches, with an exploration of meaning as interpretative, contextual, and culturally specific, all necessitating awareness of multiple theoretical models, and awareness of those as precisely that—just "models", rather than truths or prescriptions.

In my view, a still further shift is occurring. While acknowledging two reciprocally interacting subjectivities and a co-created psychic reality within the consulting room, some analysts now conceptualise *the clinical process itself as dialectical*. In other words, not only interpsychic, but a balance between intrapsychic and intersubjective dimensions in the psychoanalytic process that *sustains* rather than eliminates contradictions, alternately or concomitantly shifting focus between co-constructed intersubjective meanings and discovery of the patient as subject's pre-existing self-experience.

Therapeutic change is then regarded as emotional freeing of a spectrum of coexistent processes that enable healthy dynamic exchanges to happen in the present, both in the consulting room and outside it. It is this *dynamic tension* between interactive two-ness and introspective one-ness—of both the patient–analyst intersubjective dyad, and each within their individual separateness and different perspective—that forges an encounter through which *both are changed*. Once again spearheaded by British Independents (e.g., Bollas[34]), this dual-track mode of thinking is now shared by psychoanalysts as varied as Berman in Israel, Beebe, Benjamin, Cavell, Chodorow, Gabbard, Gill, Jacobs, Ogden, Polland, and Wallerstein. For the analyst, as for the parent, intersubjective relating that involves investing his/her own subjectivity in interaction, offers transformative opportunities to alter one's internal affective configurations as a result. When intersubjectivity forms a core concept of our theoretical understanding, we offer the patient clinically not merely a new model of being/working, but an understanding that there can be *many models*. And, as in parenting, the analyst is not merely the "growth promoting" agent but one who *grows* within the intersubjective encounter.

Postscript

Editing this manuscript on the Great Barrier Reef, I am struck by coral colonies as a metaphor for the unconscious—immerse oneself in them and teeming life is there. Raise your face and all you see is the bland ocean surface. Below the thriving diversity is sedimentation from the past, with camouflaged and ossified organisms, and ravages of time acting as bedrock to new growth. Diving partners potentially share experience, albeit with discrepant perspectives even on the same reef, and the need for a third point of reference for anchorage.

Not being co-constructed, the analogy falters here. Yet, each diver does cause counter-current disruptions. If repaired by non-threatening hovering, one is gradually rewarded by shoals of fish going back to their business: contracted tentacles extend from shells and shy creatures emerge from hiding places, giant clams reopen to expose their extravagant purple innards, and sensitive anemones unfurl and hungrily wave their fronds in the undertow ... Yet, in the clinical tension between "swimming" and patiently waiting for flurries to subside, all too often we are reminded of Ernest Jones' comment that "analysts, like fish, escape from the depths" ...

Notes

1. The Independent analyst's willingness for self-examination has long been the case: "The effort to understand in order to help is also a continuous process of learning from the patient" (Brierley, 1943). Others have elaborated in the same vein, stressing the need for the analyst's authenticity, flexibility, and imaginative creativity in relating to the patient: the Balints, Coltart, Fairbairn, Guntrip, Klauber, Khan, King, Heimann, Milner, Sharpe, Stewart, and Winnicott. Latter-day writings of Bierley, Bollas, Casement, Hopper, Kennedy, Parsons, Mitchell, Symington, and many others continue to examine the analyst's awareness of his/her influence on the exchange.
2. Some, like Lowenfeld, had hailed from Berlin, and, joining centres of orthodox Freudianism (such as the New York Psychoanalytic Institute), rejected their radical past.
3. Unlike the previous "Ferenczi issue" of the *International Journal of Psychoanalysis*, edited in 1949 by Michael Balint and Rickman, which had backfired, leading not to rehabilitation as hoped, but to open rejection of

his ideas and hostility towards Ferenczi's American heirs. Ferenczi's British analysands included Ernest Jones, Melanie Klein, and David Eder. Michael Balint, who had been director of the Psychoanalytic Clinic of Budapest, and Alice Balint were active in pre-war dissemination of the Budapest relational approach in the UK. This was extended with diasporic scattering of Hungarian analysts as Nazi forces closed in. Emissaries in the USA included Imre Hermann, Margaret Mahler, and Theresa Benedek; Franz Alexander, founder of the Chicago Psychoanalytic Society in Chicago; Sándor Radó, who established the Psychoanalytic Clinic for Training and Research at Columbia University; and four of the presidents of the New York Psychoanalytic Society. Several members were Hungarian refugees (including Géza Róheim and David Rapaport, in Topeka). Although there is some evidence that Harry Stack Sullivan developed some of his ideas independently (see Grey, 1994), the Interpersonal school included his analyst, Clara Thompson, who had been one of Ferenczi's patients in his experiment with mutual analysis. The prominent group around Erich Fromm and Frieda Fromm-Reichmann, who had settled in New York where Karen Horney was at the New School for Social Research, together developed the study of interpersonal relations. Embracing pluralism, pragmatism, and empiricism, they were also influenced by American thinkers and psychosocial scholars such as William James, John Dewey, George Herbert Mead, Adolf Meyer, and William Alanson White. Ferenczi's widespread influence often went unacknowledged, probably due to Freud's censure of his emphasis on trauma theory and view of infantile sexuality and the Oedipus complex as the unconscious projection of the adult's sexuality on to the vulnerable child. However, many of his ideas filtered through, such as the focus on therapeutic regressions, empathy, and safety provisions in treatment, and his engagement with numerous defence mechanisms, including defensive identifications with an overpowering aggressor, of the creation of a "false self", and of fragmented ego states (splitting, fragmentation, and dissociation), which heralded both Anna Freud's formulations of "identification with the aggressor" and "altruistic surrender"; Winnicott's description of the "false self" and the analytic "holding environment", and Kohut's descriptions of fragmented "self-states" (see Hoffer, 1990).

4. Freudian concepts had already been reconceptualised in *interactive* terms by Edith Jacobson, and by Hans Loewald, initially trained by Sullivan, who, in turn, had been analysed by Ferenczi's analysand, Clara Thompson.

5. The intrauterine state was paradigmatic. Despite his protestations, Freud
    also noted "man's yearning" for the safety of "the mother's womb, the
    first lodging" (see 1930a, p. 91) while previously (1916a), illustrating two
    forms of temporal regression-primary narcissism and hallucinatory wish
    fulfilment—Freud had likened adult withdrawal into sleep to a womb-
    like prenatal state. Similarly, Ferenczi ascribed to sleep gratification of the
    wish to be in the "unborn state". In his prolific writings, he noted the
    newborn's tendency to slip back into re-occupation of gestational "non-
    being", described a "continuous regressive trend toward the re-estab-
    lishment of the intrauterine situation", the adult desire for the prenatal
    sense of hallucinatory omnipotence, and sex as an illusionary genital
    return to the womb (1913). To his champion Michael Balint, every child's
    negotiation of post-birth experience both acknowledges and attempts to
    deny loss of the original "harmony of limitless expanses" (Balint, 1968, p.
    67), a view similar to Fairbairn's description of primary identification as
    a defensive act against awareness of separateness, posing relatedness to
    the mother as linked to the womb (1943). Similarly, Ella Sharpe attributed
    the phantasied introjection of the breast as a refusal of separate exis-
    tence—an illusion/delusion denying the reality of birth during "the
    semiuterine existence of infancy"—by taking the mother's breast within
    the child in place of the child within her, as in pre-natal days (1943, p.
    338). Conversely, for Guntrip, agoraphobic fears and regressive yearning
    to retreat back into the womb indicate wish for a *pre-objectal state* (1961),
    akin to Ferenczi's prenatal sense of undisturbed "non-being". Klein
    (1957) presumed "longing for the pre-natal state" to be universal.
    Idealisation of the intrauterine state was not confined to the Hungarian or
    British views. In France, Grünberger ascribed the source of all the vari-
    ous forms of narcissism to "memory traces" of a pre-natal state of
    tension-free equilibrium, of blissful elation, timeless omnipotence, and
    self-sufficiency, from which man was "traumatically expelled and that he
    never ceases longing to recapture" (1979, p. 12). Similarly, Chasseguet-
    Smirgel attributed perversion and destruction of reality to the regressive
    wish to return to an idealised "smooth" unimpeded intrauterine life
    pertaining to "disappearance of the father principle" in a "world without
    obstacles" (2005). In Italy, Gaddini attributed our "protective defence-
    fantasy" of physical contact providing a "magical and repetitive" inte-
    grative experience to pre-natal life, when the foetus was surrounded by
    the "protective boundary" of the amniotic sac, fortified by the womb
    (1982).
6. The literature is vast, but, for example, pre-natal learning can be demon-
    strated as newborns recognise a particular (Dr Zeus) text read aloud by

the expectant mother ante-natally, as well as a post-natal discriminatory preference for that book over other Dr Zeus books read aloud by the mother (DeCasper & Fifer, 1980). For other indications of continuity from ultrasound to infant observation, see Piontelli, 1992, and a review of capacities by Trevarthen and Aitken, 2001.

7. Although Freud's system of thought was predicated on object-relationships, descriptively, his focus was upon the mental apparatus and its internal forces and psychic mechanisms. In addition to the influence of Ferenczi, in stressing primary relatedness Independent theoreticians partook of Ian Suttie, a Scottish psychiatrist who already, in 1935, proposed *an innate need for companionship*—to both receive love and also to give/reciprocate. The *dyadic* view was later promulgated by Rickman's close friend Michael Balint, and others. Similarly, categorically opposing Freud's idea of primary narcissism, Fairbairn redefined libido as "object seeking" rather than geared to hedonism (1941). Winnicott, too, paid close attention to the primacy of relations, famously stating that there can be "no such thing as an infant" (1960, p. 39) without a carer. To him, formation of the baby's self (his "basic ego-relatedness") is deemed constituted through the "good enough" mother: her face is his mirror (1971). She empowers his illusion of omnipotence and his well-being depends on her close adaptation and *capacity to facilitate his separateness* through her "graduated" failures. Paradoxically, the baby's sense of self depends upon her survival of his repudiation of her in the course of learning to *use* her as an object (Winnicott, 1969). If she is unattuned or impinging, her deficiencies are instated in his "false self" structures and defences, since acquisition of his sense of self as subject clearly rests on their interpenetrating subjectivities (although Winnicott does not use that term).

Alice Balint (1949), too, overtly challenged the idea of a one-person psychology and a one-way dependent connection between mother and child. On the basis of psychoanalytic and anthropological material, she postulated *a mutual "symbiotic" instinctual need* between mother and child, albeit asymmetrical:

> ... the essential difference ... between maternal love and love for the mother [is that] the mother is unique and irreplaceable, [but] the child can be replaced by another. We experience the repetition of this conflict in every transference neurosis. (p. 257)

(Similarly, Sullivan suggested reciprocally "integrating tendencies" of the needs of both infant and mother (1953, p. 40).) Michael Balint, too, focused on the early dyadic non-symbolic mode of relating, stressing the *pre-Oedipal "two-body"* as opposed to Oedipal-triangular. Like Alice, elaborating on Ferenczi's conceptualisation of passive yearning for a primitive prenatal fusion, he, too, postulated an initial state of "harmonious interpenetrating mix-up" at the beginning of life in which newborn and mother form a unit due to the "instinctual interdependence of mother and child" (1949). But, in his desire to heal the Ferenczi–Freud split, he introduced *a "dual track"* dimension featuring both "primary love" for the mother and narcissistic "self-love", and, hence, libido as both object *and* pleasure seeking.

8. Clearly, the more a theory is focused on "autonomy" as an end-goal, the greater the perceived threat of "re-engulfment". Rationality is seen to lessen the danger of surrender to powerful regressive forces. A stark contrast will be drawn between the milk-mother of primary process thinking, sensuality, and unbridled emotion (stereotypically, feminine "expressiveness") and intervention of the "rational" father as "third-term", providing boundaries to support the "paternal" ideals of separateness, agency, and moderation (masculine "instrumentality"). On a metaphorical level, rule of the "head" over bodily impulses is analogous to rule of the father as head of the family, thus commensurate with patriarchal politics (and primal horde compromise).

9. Although Freud holds another paradigm of an original reality-ego and primitive object relatedness within a "psychical system" with "an external agency" (1915c, p. 134) (regarding this, also see Cohen, 2007), within the classical paradigm, to the self-preoccupied baby, instinct and internal reality predominates so that the conjured-up "hallucinatory" breast will go some way towards satisfying hunger. Indeed, Freud declares that

> the phylogenetic foundation has so much the upper hand over personal accidental experience that it *makes no difference* whether a child has really suckled at the breast or has been brought up on the bottle and never really enjoyed the tenderness of a mother's care. (1940a[1938], p.188, my italics)

Anna Freud added,

> The infant's first love for the mother is directed towards material satisfaction. (Stomach love, cupboard love, egoistic love; "to be fed".) In a next stage object love is still egoistic but directed toward non-material satisfactions, i.e. to receive love, affection, approval from the mother; "to be loved". As the child progresses from the

oral and anal to the phallic level, object attachment loses its egois-
tic character; the qualities of the object increase in libidinal importance while the immediate benefit from the relationship becomes
less important. The next and highest stage of development is the
ability to love the object regardless of benefit (altruistic love) (A.
Freud, 1946, p. 125).

10. Spitz emphasised *reciprocity:* "a give and take of action and reaction . . .
which requires from each of them both active and passive responses"—a
series of chains of "action cycles" forming the precursor "primal dialogue" (1964, p. 775), and Benedek (originator of the concept "emotional
symbiosis") emphasised mobilisation of reciprocal infantile feelings in
the carer: "the post-partum symbiosis is oral, alimentary for both infant
and mother" (1956, p. 398). However, Frieda Fromm-Reichmann (1959)
ignored the infant's contribution and took a unilateral approach. In keeping with Ferenczi's portrayal of the patient as passive victim of the insen-
sitive parent (and analyst), she introduced the concept of the "schizo-
phrenogenic mother". During the 1960s, the aetiology of both schizophrenia and manic-depressive illness continued to be ascribed primarily
to early maternal failures during the first few years of life by analysts
from the Washington school of psychiatry who were treating psychotic
patients at Chestnut Lodge. Similarly, focusing on the Oedipal level, the
Yale group around Lidz treated parental schismatic or skewed marriages
as *causal* of schizophrenia in daughters and in sons respectively. In the
subsequent decades of ego psychology, psychoanalysts treating psychotic patients unquestioningly ascribed the aetiology of psychosis to
maternal over-protection or "pseudomutuality" during the early "symbiotic" phase, overlooking anomalies in the infant. Aetiological phase
specificity of maternal failure was designated to personality disorders,
depressive, borderline, and narcissistic conditions, as well. In other fields,
Bateson's redefinition of schizophrenia as not an illness of the mind, but
a defensive strategy to combat "double-bind" communication, reasserted
the *systemic* nature of interaction. In Britain, in the 1960s, an antipsychia-
try movement followed psychoanalyst Ronnie Laing's extension of
causality beyond the family to society at large, using both a conspiratory
theory and a "psychodelic" model (schizophrenia as breakthrough rather
than breakdown) to reject schizophrenia as an illness, as did Deleuze and
Guattari in France. (See Hirsh & Leff, 1975, for overview and subsequent
scientific evidence failing to confirm these assumptions; also Willick,
1990.)

11. Ironically, it was attachment research based on Bowlby's own theories that negated "monotropy" by exposing each baby's capacity for simultaneous multiple and varied primary relationships, including differing modes of attachment! Following Bowlby's early work, as evaluation of the child's security of attachment at one year proved relatively stable, a veritable industry of empirical research arose, beginning with Ainsworth's "strange situation" (1978), and foundational studies by Sroufe, Main, Kaplan, and Cassidy. Prediction of the unborn baby's attachment from the expectant mother's account of her own childhood attachments, using the Adult Attachment Inventory (Steele, Steele, & Fonagy, 1996) confirmed environmental influences (as did antenatal maternal orientations preceding the relationship (Hershlovitz & Harel, 1998; Raphael-Leff, 1985a; Scher, 2001)).

12. In general, psychopathology was attributed to violation of the infant's "primitive wholeness". Fairbairn (1941) ascribed this to maternal failure to recognise the baby and/or refusal to accept his/her love. Guntrip (1968) felt that with breakdown of the innate state of primitive relatedness, "the living heart" of the self takes flight, harking back to intrauterine solitude. The "regressed ego" stance of yearning for a pre-objectal state is the ultimate schizoid defence. Similarly, Winnicott attributed "false self" defensiveness to breaks in "going on being" due to maternal failures of "holding", but defined psychosis as an "environmental deficiency disease" rooted in catastrophic privations during the earliest phase of self-formation (1960) when primary failure confronts the infant with the total disintegration of "unthinkable anxiety". Enid Balint (1963) also stressed the critical importance of maternal "feed-back", the failure of which she linked to "being empty of oneself", a "void" during that very early era that Michael Balint had termed the irremediable "area of the *basic fault*" (Balint, 1968). A further review of these ideas about phase specificity in causality and aetiology may be seen in note 27.

13. In my specialist pychoanalytic practice I worked with over 200 pregnant mothers or couples seen 1–5 times a week antenatally and postnatally for 2–15 years in a practice devoted since 1975 to reproductive issues. I also drew on disciplined observation of primary interaction: for 2½ years I conducted weekly (filmed) observations of three mother–baby orangutang pairs from birth (to establish a primate baseline). And over a period of eight years conducted thrice weekly observations of a total of twenty-three parent–child pairs from their early months, selected from 200 families attending a large Community Play Centre with their babies and toddlers. Observations were followed by empirical studies using

both quantitative and qualitative measures, including weekly (tape-recorded) unstructured discussion groups with pregnant women, in-depth interviews with expectant couples over the transition to parenthood, and semi-structured questionnaires with parents sampled at one-and-a-half year intervals from the families attending the PACT (Parents and Children Together) Play Centre (of which I was founder, and participant with three of my own children). Thus, I evolved my model of parental orientations using mixed methodology on a relatively small middle-class sample. However, the model has been subsequently confirmed by large-scale quantitative, prospective, and longitudinal studies conducted independently by others in the UK, Australia, Belgium, Holland, Hong Kong, Israel, Mexico, Portugal, Sweden, and elsewhere finding similar clustering of maternal beliefs, vulnerabilities, and different precipitants and timing of postnatal disturbance in each group, along with maternal attributions of intentionality and infant security (e.g., de Castro, Amieva, & Hernandez, 2012; Roncolato & McMahon, 2012; Scher, 2001; Scher & Blumberg, 1992, 1999; Sharp & Bramwell, 2001, 2004; Van Bussel, Spitz, & Demyttenaere, 2009a,b, 2010). Finally, as both clinician and academic psychoanalyst and social psychologist, my work has incorporated workshops with over a thousand parents and primary health workers on six continents over the past 40 years. While mainly written up for professionals outside psychoanalysis, I have also published findings of parental orientations from a clinical/empirical perspective, in relation to correspondingly diverse psychoanalytic theories (Raphael-Leff, 1980, 1983, 1985a, 1986, 1991/2005, 2001a,b).

14. Paternal orientations comprise "Participators", "Renouncers" and "Reciprocators" (and a conflicted group). Ongoing research with fathers, especially in egalitarian Scandinavia and Nordic societies, with their generous 12–18 months long maternity/paternity leave, leads to increasing recognition of male capacities for primary nurturing and responsiveness to emotional cues. This evidence negates assumptions of "maternal instinct" and a "hormonal" basis of nurturing, proving that paternal capabilities can involve more than mere provision of "support" for the mother, or acting as "third term" intervener in the emotional intimacy of the dyadic nursing couple.

15. My first three orientations (in moderation) have been shown in independent studies conducted at Haifa University in Israel to coincide with "secure" attachments, with more extreme Facilitators' babies tending towards ambivalent insecurity and Regulators' towards avoidant. "Conflicted" preoccupied parenting corresponds to disorganised attachment

patterns (Hershlovitz & Harel, 1998). An independent study in Leuven, Belgium found a correlation between the maternal orientation and expectations of labour and delivery, and between these and ante-natal depression (Van Bussel, Spitz, & Demyttenaere, 2009a,b). Similarly, in a large scale prospective research project conducted in Liverpool, analysis confirmed my findings of different pathways to post-natal depression within sub-groups of pregnant women, with Regulator mothering conferring an increased and independent risk for post-natal depression after controlling for ante-natal depression, and Reciprocators proving comparatively resilient to effects of expectations–reality disparity (Sharp & Bramwell, 2004). Hierarchical logistic regression revealed that mothering orientation moderated the associations between expectation–reality discrepancy domains and post-natal (GHQ) depression in two ways: (1) the childbirth domain was salient for Regulators and Facilitators, but not for Reciprocators; (2) the motherhood domain was only salient for Facilitators, in line with theory. Statistical interactions were evident even after controlling for other known risks. Finally, mothering orientation appeared to moderate the link between ante-natal and post-natal GHQ-D; a far larger effect size was found for Reciprocator mothers (Sharp & Bramwell, 2004).

16. By contrast to Klein's phantasy world of internal objects and part-objects, or the Freudian one of intrapsychic drives, internal conflicts, and defences, Fairbairn's is composed of *relational configurations*, within a schema perpetuating both the poignancy of unrequited love and the cruel criticism of an "internal saboteur" (in severe cases constituting the archaic, vengeful superego characteristic of schizophrenia). In his dry language, Fairbairn postulated that when mother fails to meet infant's needs, internalisation of the bad "primary object" occurs in an attempt to control "it", defensively splitting its representations into a tantalisingly unavailable "exciting object" and a punitive "rejecting object"—coupled with (libidinal and antilibidinal) aspects of the split ego. Repression is primarily exercised not against impulses which have come to appear painful or "bad" (as in Freud's final view), or even against painful memories (as in Freud's earlier view), but against internalised objects and parts of the self which have come to be treated as bad (Fairbairn, 1944, p. 73). Similarly, separation anxiety (dread of loss of the other), is seen to continue operating on an unconscious level in the complex dynamic "endopsychic structure", with lost parts of the self invested in the internalised split object, which remains beyond control of the central ego.

17. During exchange visits between London and Chicago in the late 1980s and early 1990s, the British Independents and American self-psychologists discovered many commonalities in their respective views of infantile experience, especially the importance of psychic reality (as opposed to phantasy) and real experience with primary carers, rejection of drives and primary destructiveness, focus on intrapsychic defensive reactions and psychic disruption as *reactions to environmental failure* (and, hence, the necessity for the deprived patient to regress back to this early experience in therapy). The phase-appropriate responsive, "mirroring", empathic self-object mother of self psychology was found to have much in common with the "facilitating" mother of the Independents, one who empathically recognises and reflects the infant's genuine self, lending herself to affect regulation and, ultimately, "transmuting" internalisation. Kohut (1971) described "self–object" needs for acknowledgment and affirmation (mirroring), for an admired, protective other (idealising), and for a sense of essential alike-ness (twinship). Self–object forms of relatedness, involving the use of another person for development and regulation of a sense of self, are prominent during times of self-expansion or of stress and vulnerability. Both groups still held that the mother's responsibility for her baby's future mental health and the critical vulnerability of early dependency justified their demands for her continuous devotion. Here, too, psychopathology was attributed to "developmental deficits" acquired through under- or over-responsive mothering, to be rectified in nutritive empathic therapy. For the self-psychologists, an ongoing need for an unconditionally loving self-object was seen to persist across the life cycle, with self-enhancing narcissistic aims as opposed to the Independents' assumption that developmental and therapeutic experience could bring about "mature dependence" and recognition of, or true concern for, the object (see Bacal, 1987; Raphael-Leff, 1994 for a comparative analysis).

18. Extraordinarily, in the British Society from the early 1920s, developmental interest was *female* dominated, as Susan Isaacs instituted disciplined child-observation in her nursery school in Cambridge, Nina Searl and Sylvia Payne presented papers on child analysis in 1924, and Mary Chadwick, Barbara Low, Alix Strachey, Ella Sharpe, Sybille Yates, Karin Stephen, Merrell Middlemore, and others expressed particular interests in child development and analysis long before Melanie Klein's arrival. In Vienna, Hug-Helmuth influenced all child analytic thinking, and Anna Freud and Dorothy Burlingham conducted direct observations in the Jackson Nursery, together with Eva Rosenfeld, Erik Erikson, and Peter Blos, and later in the War Nurseries (Freud & Burlingham, 1943), in Essex (see Raphael-Leff, 2001c).

19. As noted, the Controversial Discussions exposed divergence between tradition and innovation, and between interpersonal and intrapsychic foci regarding the nature and origins of inner reality (also see Hayman, 1994; King & Steiner, 1991). Debated was the baby's innate predisposition: whether anxiety in very young babies is caused by internal unconscious conflict between instincts or between instinct and ego defence on the one hand, or innate preponderance of destructive instincts and anxieties about retaliation through reintrojected aggression, on the other. Consideration of the death instinct and the status of aggression in clinical theorising exposed a further divergence among object relation theorists themselves. Whereas Winnicott attributed discovery of the mother's specific capacities to her own playful responsiveness and psychological capacity to "survive", allowing the child to gradually relinquish his own imagined omnipotence (1969), to Klein, eventual recognition of the "whole" mother is predicated not on *her* capacities, but on depressive position retrieval of projective identification, and integration of congenital love and hate. Similarly, regarding aggression: for the Independents (whom disillusioned Paula Heimann ultimately joined), it is *frustration of relational needs* that spawns it. Indeed, to Suttie, hostility is a protesting appeal for recognition. A case of "love to hatred turned", when anxiety mounts unbearably due to separation, disappointment, or rejection of "an overture demanding a response" from the unresponsive (m)other (1935, pp. 29, 42). Aggression, anxiety, and insatiability are reactions to the mother's intolerable "claims", which disturb their harmony. Narcissism, too, is treated as secondary, "always a protection against the bad or only reluctant object" (Balint, 1937, p. 82) arising out of the child's desperate need to re-establish the primary relationship.

20. That the significance of an observed manifestation can be interpreted variously depending on one's theoretical point of view was illustrated repeatedly in a comparative section I instigated in 1987 in the *British Journal of Psychotherapy*, with invited commentaries from authors of different theoretical persuasions on the same observational material.

21. Exploration of neonatal characteristics was enhanced by development of research instruments such as the Brazelton NBAS (Neonatal Behavioral Assessment Scale), (Brazelton et al., 1975). Used internationally, it revealed the individual variability of very early behaviour (as predicted by Balint in 1949) and its reciprocal nature, providing proof of innate human intersubjectivity. As psychoanalytically informed researchers such as Emde, Stern, and Beebe disseminated their findings, these ideas began to permeate the consulting room.

22. Over the following years, these researchers realised that their initial model failed to appreciate a crucial issue: the process of mutual regulation is a *co-creative process* rather than an exchange of *preformed* messages. Because it builds on an ongoing relationship rather than an interactive conversation, this process generates a unique way in which each primary pair are together. This view of the differentiation of relationships contrasts with notions of abstracted interactive regulatory patterns: Stern's RIGS (representations of interactions as generalised) or "depersonified" modes of expectations (Beebe & Lachmann, 1994). It also differs from Freud, and Fairbairn's view of the originary mother–infant relationship as *prototype* of other later-developing relationships, also shared by attachment theory (Bowlby; Ainsworth; Cassidy; Main; Sroufe, etc). Tronick's work contrasts the development of relationships with the development of cognition, stating that the latter becomes increasingly abstract, de-contextualised, schematised, and transferable. By contrast, relationships become more detailed; concrete; increasingly personified, tied to an individual; increasingly specific; and rather than universally applicable, they become less and less transferable (Tronick, 2003).

24. Developmental theory had long held that *contingent responsiveness* within the parent–infant expressive–receptive exchange has a special importance for an infant's psychological development, which is jeopardised when the intuitive process is faulty in *either* infant or adult care-giver (as noted by researchers such as Field; Fraiberg; Hobson; Stern; Tronick; Trevarthen; Murray and Cooper; Papousek and Papousek). This now has become demonstrable through fMRI confirming the belief of Independents that during the period of prolonged dependence, the susceptible infant's malleability calls for protective care and robust emotional responsiveness from others in order to promote healthy flexible connectedness, and to prevent "false self" distortive reactions to deprivation and/or parental unattunement. Studies demonstrate permanent maladaptive "wiring" of neural response patterns associated with emotionally damaging effects of parental depression, abuse, and neglect, and trauma-induced functional interferences with memory storage and retrieval (see Balbernie, 2001; Karmiloff-Smith, 1995; Schore, 2001; Trevarthen & Aitken, 2001). These "hard-wired" established patterns of hyper-arousal and super-vigilance are persistent and extremely resistant to change, as attested by work with adult patients suffering from early trauma or borderline conditions.

25. Theses findings in neuro-psychology pertain to debates during the Controversial Discussions: when countering Klein's view of the neonate engaged in complex and *retrievable* phantasy ("memory in feeling" drawn

from "phylogenetic" sources of knowledge with an *a priori* object), Anna Freud and her followers insisted that preverbal factors could not become accessible until basic functions of the ego (control of perception, motility, memory, experience, and learning) were operational. Furthermore, claiming that unconscious phantasy could only exist once the ego was established with repression as its main defensive operation, and even then (due to childhood amnesia and the nature of the unconscious) it was never directly demonstrable, but only inferable. In time, the debate about accessibility of the presymbolic had crystallised into demarcation by the Freudians of an unknowable "non experiential realm", with the emergent ego as the crucial agent instating the internal world by accretion of successive mental representations of objects and self. Klein's "memory in feeling" (the mental representative and corollary of instinctual urges) was deemed unreliable due to intermingling of perception and phantasy, and designated by contemporary Freudians as "intrinsically unknowable, except insofar as it can become known through the creation or occurrence of a phenomenal event in the realm of subjective experience" (Sandler & Joffe, 1969, p. 82). More recently, in a gradual reconciliation of these divergent positions, as classical drive theory has integrated with an object relations perspective, many follow the Sandlers in distinguishing between the past unconscious of procedural experience (non-cognitive primal experience, unavailable to verbal recall, yet accessible through the transference), which is indeed irretrievable, compared to the time-elaborated present unconscious, with its access to declarative knowledge since "the present unconscious, contains present-day, here-and-now fantasies and thoughts that are after all current adaptations to the conflicts and anxieties evoked by the contents of the past unconscious" (Sandler, 1986, p. 191) as "metaphoric" reconstructions.

26. Effects of these findings on psychoanalytic praxis are elaborated in the "Couch" section, but suffice to say that although each primary pair evolves a uniquely hallmarked relational experience, we know that transferability *does* occur, and, for some of our patients (as Freud noted), "transference" expectations predominate with an intense conviction that aspects of the new relationship will repeat earlier patterns. My own explanation of the puzzle of transference when relationships are essentially "non-transferrable" assigns the impetus for transferability to *absence* within the archaic primary relationship of precisely those elements which produce *reciprocal and dyadic consciousness*. In my view, *impairments of dialogical partnership* occur when irreparable mismatching gulfs are maintained by parental disturbance and/or factors resulting in the infant's

hypersensitivity. Essential elements of spontaneity, flexibility, fluidity, and reparation are then inoperative in the original interchange. By definition, it is precisely interactional patterns signifying *non-recognition of singularity* that are habitually transferred on to new emotionally charged relationships. In addition, clinical experience shows us that these same patterns tend to *militate against co-creation* of meanings in new interactions upon which fixed past relational schemas are superimposed. In the "emotional hothouse" of the consulting room, the patient's compelling need to externalise fixed predominating patterns produces corollary systemic pressure on the therapist to replicate the archaic emotional atmosphere of non-co-creation, especially when the analyst loses the freedom to play, and when internal processes "hook into" and reproduce the patient's unresolved archaic mismatches.

27. Winnicott (1952) differentiates a variety of pathological manifestations (deemed "environmental deficiency diseases"), such as autism, childhood schizophrenia, false-self, and schizoid defences attributable to privation and initial maternal failures in the stage of absolute dependence before "me not-me" is established, as opposed to antisocial tendencies arising from deprivations the stage of "relative" dependency. Likewise, Balint (1968) specifies the irretrievable "basic fault" resulting from primary disturbance as opposed to milder psychopathology derived from "instinctual" conflict. Fairbairn (1941) is more specific in his dating, relating schizoid type phenomena (unacceptable love) to *early* oral phase disturbances as opposed to depressive illnesses (unacceptable hatred) to late oral phase. (He later (1943) extended this to distinguish types of psycho-pathologies based on the relative strength of ego by contrast to the repressed core.) Influenced by Fairbairn, Klein, and Jacobson, Kernberg (1980) developed a chronological timetable of various forms of psychopathology based on relative failures in the development of internalised object relations. He asserted that faulty development at the primary undifferentiated stage during the first month of life is characteristic of autistic psychosis. Pathological fixation in the second stage (2–8 months) is characteristic of symbiotic psychosis of childhood, most types of adult schizophrenia, and depressive psychosis. Failures during the third stage (eight months to three years) of differentiation of self- from object-representations lead to the syndrome of borderline personality organisation. The neuroses and higher-level character disorders represent the typical psychopathology of the fourth stage (Oedipal period).

28. Kleinians ascribed psychosis to primitive defences relating to very early disturbance, reality denial, and fragmentation through extreme splitting/

projection, and borderline disorders to preponderance of paranoid–schizoid defences activated to deal with perverted/distorted perceptions of reality, such as internal control by a Mafia-like "gang" (Rosenfeld, 1987), resulting in a "pathological organisation" of the personality (Steiner, 1993). Another such "mixed" model offered by Kernberg (1982) designated as pathogenic both maternal deprivation and excessive constitutional aggression, pathological splitting, and conflicts between drives and their derivatives. With the growth of interest in borderline disorders, Kernberg developed a specific chronological timetable, corresponding to four stages in childhood for the aetiology of various forms of psychopathology based on relative failures in the development of internalised object relations.

Similarly, Mahler, Pine, and Bergman's (1975) theory of separation–individuation is based on a mixture of ego psychology and object relations, offering an opportunity for "channelisation" of innate love/aggressive tendencies to bring about "psychological birth" out of a closed system "autistic" phase. (Influenced by relational assumptions, this "autistic" phase was eventually modified in Mahler's later work. However, the goal of adaptation and individuated "self-sufficiency" was not.) Pathology, childhood psychosis, and borderline failure to individuate are laid at the pre-Oedipal mother's door.

29. Those working with psychotic patients (including Alexander, Sechaye, Bion, Sullivan, and later Kohut, Rosenfeld, Lucas, Hinshelwood, Williams, etc.) have all noted the highly emotional countertransferential feelings this arouses. Such heightened responses to "primitive" anxieties and close contact with uncensored material are akin to what I have termed "contagious arousal" of implicit schemata in parents (Raphael-Leff, 2003). However, in cases of severe pathology, concomitant anxieties focus on irrationality and unrestrained adult violence/sexuality. Some early Independents treating patients with schizophrenia and clinical depression, including Fairbairn, Guntrip, Khan, and Sutherland, found it necessary to conduct controlled clinical experiments with *regression* resembling child analysis with deeply disturbed patients (see Winnicott regarding Margaret Little). Despite Ferenczi's fall from grace, regression (of the "benign" as opposed to "malignant" form) within a safe and interactive relationship was mooted as a mutative factor in analysis. Although Anna Freud declared such procedures as "non-psychoanalytic", none the less she instituted a modified developmental approach of structure building, reconstituting defences and ego-supportive efforts with some patients, saying, "Where the libido defect is due to severe early

deprivation in object relations, interpretation of the transferred repetition has no therapeutic results" (1965b, p. 231). Her position was in direct conflict with Kleinian views that borderline and psychotic patients could be treated by a regular analytic technique with interpretation of the mother-infant relations.

30. Reworking old ground from a new standpoint, relational psychoanalysis has made a major contribution to this topic of how and what of the analyst's feelings, defences, and relevant past are implicitly revealed or explicitly shared with patients. Concern with "democratisation" of the therapeutic relation and with the analyst's potential misuse of power necessitates establishing guiding principles to determine when self-disclosure is an essential facilitating aspect of the analytic dialogue or is deleterious to it. When it might serve to modify a treatment stalemate, impasse, or analytic "crunch" (seen as a relational crisis engendered by both participants), or when it is an enactment leading to potential loss of "therapeutic leverage" (e.g., Aron, 2006; Meissner, 2002).

    Although conceding that the analyst's behaviour might influence the patient's overt behaviour, some ego psychologists deny that such influence would have any effect on the analysand's intrapsychic structure. Many Kleinians continue to maintain that material should come exclusively from the patient. Within the group of Independents, bilateral interplay is recognised and analytic mistakes freely admitted. However, as revealed in a recent exchange during a joint conference with the relational school, for many Independent clinicians the focus seems more on the analyst's self-reflection and empathic authenticity, rather than verbal revelation in the consulting room.

31. Within the British Klein group, an interactional dimension was introduced with Bion's ideas about "container–contained" (1962), extending the concept of projective identification from an unconscious phantasy in the one-person model into a process involving *two* participants—albeit, one of whom (the mother or analyst) was merely *an introjective metabolising recipient*. Akin to Klein's ego-boundaried neonate, two *separate entities* resided in the consulting room, too. Countertransference interpretations would, thus, emphasise what the patient is doing in relation to the analyst or *to* the relation with the analyst, including how the patient is trying to get the analyst to act in ways that confirm phantasies: "The analyst feels he is being manipulated so as to be playing a part, no matter how difficult to recognize, in somebody else's phanta" (Bion, 1961, p. 149). However, among other analysts of a Kleinian persuasion, where countertransference had been pathologised, Money-Kyrle (1956)

suggested that empathic introjective identification allowed for exploration of transference–countertransference as an *interactional process.* Unusually defining the patient's transference as "all the responses to the analyst's *counter-transference*", Racker (1968) named projective identification as fuelling the *bipersonal reciprocity* in the treatment process. Later, Racker (1968) divided the analyst's reactions into concordant and complementary countertransferences, which Grinberg (1979) extended with the term "projective counteridentification", to signify the analyst's introjection of an affective state associated with the patient's object-representation.

Similarly, among British Freudians, recognition that failures of the archaic maternal object—her emotional withdrawal or neglect manifest in inadequate attunement—would be replayed in the transference led to acknowledgement of powerful countertransferential pressure towards "role responsive" actualisation of the patient's transferential attributions (Sandler, 1976), brought interactive influence into the consulting room (albeit, as one-sided reactivity), and, hence, back into infancy. Similarly, Glasser's "core complex" linked adult longing for "union", "merging", "at-one-ness" with a combination of infantile projection of all-consuming needs and "knowledge" of the possessive incorporative desires of the mother (1979). Finally, substantiated by attachment research, Fonagy and Target could ultimately raise the issue of reality formation as a product of two subjective minds: that is, interpersonal aspects of an experience of external reality, rooted in primary intersubjectivity (2007). (Needless to say, many other contributors to the theory of countertransference not referenced here included Enid Balint, Bleger, Bollas, Etchegoyen, Green, Grotstein, Jacobs, Little, Meltzer, Milner, Ogden, Searles, Steiner, Symington, Volkan, etc.) With discovery of "mirror neurones" the physiological underpinnings of emotional resonance is now being explored neuro-physiologically.

32. In fact, intersubjectivity theory holds that children cannot become independent subjects unless they are recognised as having a mind, and feelings of their own, by their care-givers (Benjamin, 1990; Fairbairn, 1952; Fonagy & Target, 2007; Ogden, 1994; Winnicott, 1971) and, in turn, appreciate the subjectivity of their carers, allowing for an interpersonal "meeting of minds" (Aron, 1996). The "theory of mind" has been formulated as a need for reciprocal recognition from a care-giver who "mentalises" the baby's feelings, unconsciously ascribing a mental state of beliefs and desires to the child, who internalises this, laying foundations for a core sense of self (Fonagy & Target, 2007). True to the tenets proposed at the

beginning of this chapter, formulation of developmental theory and pathogenic conditions dictate treatment parameters. Mentalisation theory attributes borderline conditions and developmental disorders to interferences in the parental capacity for holding the baby's mind in mind. Psychoanalytic interventions provide corrective developmental provisions by re-creating an "interactional matrix" analogous to early mentalising effects based on the analyst's non-judgemental curiosity, contingent mirroring, and identification of the patient's mental states, motives, beliefs, and fantasies—thereby providing the patient with an image of themselves in their analyst's mind.

33. In addition to "negative capability" that allows the patient's subjectivity to emerge, Independent awareness, going back to Ferenczi (1933), of the analyst as fallible allows for both humility in admitting mistakes and taking the risk of authentic spontaneity, accepting the inevitability of failing at times, and that these failures might have meaning for the patient, lending themselves to therapeutic use (see Winnicott, 1956, p. 388).

34. Christopher Bollas, who has examined the effect of the patient on the analyst's elaboration of his own unconscious phantasy, has coined felicitous phrases to name processes in which many of us engage: acting as "transformational object", striving to create and maintain conditions to foster the "unconscious as process", in the service of locating the patient's disavowed psychic material, the "unthought known", and receiving "news from within" both analyst and patient. All are seen to occur both through receptivity to processes of unconscious intersubjective communication (evocative projection and introjection), and through the analyst's focus in the act of making an interpretation on self-reflection, shared countertransference, and coalescence of "psychic fragments" (see Bollas, 1987 onwards).

References

Ablon, J. S., & Jones, E. E. (2005). On analytic process. *Journal of the American Psychoanalytic Association, 53*: 541–568.

Alvarez, A. (1999). Widening the bridge: commentary on papers by Stephen Seligman and by Robin C. Silverman and Alicia F. Lieberman. *Psychoanalytic Dialogue, 9*: 205–217

Aron, L. (1996). *A Meeting of Minds*. Hillsdale, NJ: Analytic Press.

Aron, L. (2006). Analytic impasse and the third: clinical implications of intersubjectivity theory. *International Journal of Psychoanalysis, 87*: 349–368.

Atwood, G., & Stolorow, R. (1984). *Structures of Subjectivity*. Hillsdale, NJ: Analytic Press.

Balbernie, R. (2001). Circuits and circumstances: the neurobiological consequences of early relationship experiences and how they shape later behaviour. *Journal of Child Psychotherapy, 27*: 237–255.

Bálint, A. (1949). Love for the mother and mother-love. *International Journal of Psychoanalysis, 30*: 251–259.

Balint, A., & Balint, M. (1939). On transference and counter-transference. *International Journal of Psychoanalysis, 20*: 223–230.

Balint, E. (1963). On being empty of oneself. *International Journal of Psychoanalysis, 44*: 470–480.

Balint, M. (1937). Early developmental states of the ego. Primary object love. *Imago, 23*: 270–288. English version (abbreviated), *International Journal of Psychoanalysis, 30*: 265–273, 1949.

Balint, M. (1949). Early developmental states of the ego. Primary object love. *International Journal of Psychoanalysis, 30*: 265–273.

Balint, M. (1950). Changing therapeutical aims and techniques in psychoanalysis. *International Journal of Psychoanalysis, 31*: 117–124.

Balint, M. (1968). *The Basic Fault*. London: Tavistock.

Balsam, R. (2012). *Women's Bodies in Psychoanalysis,* London: Routledge.

Baraitser, L. (2006). Oi Mother, keep ye hair on! Impossible transformations of maternal subjectivity. *Studies on Gender & Sexuality, 7*: 217–238.

Beebe, B., & Lachmann, F. (1988). Mother–infant mutual influence and precursors of psychic structure. In: A. Goldberg (Ed.), *Frontiers in Self Psychology: Progress in Self Psychology* (Vol. 3, pp. 3–26). Hillsdale, NJ: Analytic Press.

Beebe, B., & Lachmann, F. (1994). Representation and internalization in infancy. *Psychoanalytic Psychology, 11*: 127–165.

Beebe, B., & Lachmann, F. (2003). The relational turn in psychoanalysis: a dyadic systems view from infant research. *Contemporary Psychoanalysis, 39*: 379–409.

Beebe, B., Lachmann, F., & Jaffe, J. (1997). Mother–infant interaction structures and presymbolic self and object representations. *Psychoanalytic Dialogues, 7*: 133–192.

Benedek, T. (1970). The psychobiologic approach to parenthood during the life cycle. In: E. J. Anthony & T. Benedek (Eds.), *Parenthood: Its Psychology and Psychopathology* (pp. 109–206). Boston: Little, Brown.

Benjamin, J. (1990). An outline of intersubjectivity: the development of recognition. *Psychoanalytic Psychology, 7*: 33–46.

Bibring, G. L., Dwyer, T. F., Huntington, D. S., & Valerstein, A. F. (1961). A study of the psychological process in pregnancy and of the earliest mother–child relationship. *Psychoanalytic Study of the Child, 16*: 9–72.

Bion, W. R. (1961). *Experiences in Groups*. London: Tavistock.

Bion, W. R. (1962). A theory of thinking. *International Journal of Psychoanalysis, 43*: 306–310.

Binswanger, L. (1963). *Being-in-the-World*. New York: Basic Books.

Birksted-Breen, D. (1986). The experience of having a baby: a developmental view. *Free Associations, 4*: 22–35.

Blass, R. B., & Blatt, S. J. (1996). Attachment and separateness in the experience of symbiotic relatedness. *Psychoanalytic Quarterly, 65*: 711–746.

Bollas, C. (1987). *The Shadow of the Object: Psychoanalysis and the Unthought Known*. London: Free Association Books.

Bollas, C. (1989). *Forces of Destiny*. London: Free Association Books.

Boston Change Process Study Group (BCPSG) (2007). The foundational level of psychodynamic meaning: implicit process in relaton to conflict, defense and the dynamic unconscious. *International Journal of Psychoanalysis, 88*: 843–860.

Bowlby, J. (1951). *Maternal Care and Mental Health*. Geneva: WHO, Monograph No. 2.

Bowlby, J. (1958). The nature of the child's tie to his mother. *International Journal of Psychoanalysis, 39*: 350–373.

Bowlby, J. (1980). *Attachment and Loss* (Vol. 3). *Loss: Sadness and Depression*. New York: Basic Books.

Brenman Pick, I. (1985). Working through in the countertransference. *International Journal of Psychoanalysis, 66*: 157–166.

Brierley, M. (1936). Specific determinants in feminine development. *International Journal of Psychoanalysis, 17*: 163–180.

Brierley, M. (1943). Theory, practice and public relations. *International Journal of Psychoanalysis, 24*: 119–125.

Britton, R. (1998). *Belief and Imagination: Explorations in Psychoanalysis*. London: Routledege & Institute of Psychoanalysis.

Bucci, W. (1985). Dual coding: a cognitive model for psychoanalytic research. *Journal of the American Psychoanalytic Association, 33*: 571–607.

Burlingham, D. (1991)[1943]. In the first discussion of scientific controversies: on Mrs Susan Isaacs' paper 'The nature and function of phantasy'. In: P. King & R. Steiner (Eds.), *The Freud–Klein Controversies 1941–45* (pp. 322–356). London: Routledge.

Burton, G. J., Barker, D. J. P., Moffett, A., & Thornburg, K. (Eds.) (2011). *The Placenta and Developmental Programming*. Cambridge: Cambridge University Press.

Chasseguet-Smirgel, J. (2005). *The Body as Mirror of the World*, S. Leighton (Trans.). London: Free Association Books.

Chodorow, N. (1978). *The Reproduction of Mothering*. Berkeley, CA: University of California Press.

Chused, J. F. (1986). Consequences of paternal nurturing. *Psychoanalytic Study of the Child, 41*: 419–438.

Cohen, D. W. (2007). Freud's baby: beyond autoerotism and narcissism. *International Journal of Psychoanalysis, 88*: 883–893.

Couch, A. S. (2002). Extra-transference interpretation: a defense of classical technique. *Psychoanalytic Study of the Child, 57*: 63–92.

Damasio, A. (1999). *The Feeling of What Happens: Body, Emotion and the Making of Consciousness*. London: Heinemann.

DeCasper, A., & Fifer, W. (1980). Of human bonding: newborns prefer their mothers' voices. *Science, 208*: 1174–1176.

de Castro, F., Amieva, C., & Hernandez, G. (2012). Factors associated with maternal orientations in early infancy: an empirical study. Poster APSA conference, New York.Deutsch, H. (1945). *The Psychology of Women*, Vol. II (Motherhood). New York: Grune & Stratton.

Dinnerstein, D. (1976). *The Mermaid and the Minotaur*. New York: Harper & Row.

Emde, R. N. (1981). Changing models of infancy and the nature of early development: remodeling the foundation. *Journal of the American Psychoanalytic Association, 29*: 179–219.

Fairbairn, W. R. D. (1941). A revised psychopathology of the psychoses and psychoneuroses. *International Journal of Psychoanalysis, 22*: 250–279.

Fairbairn, W. R. D. (1943). The war neuroses—their nature and significance. In: *Psycho-Analytic Studies of the Personality*. London: Tavistock, 1952.

Fairbairn, W. R. D. (1944). Endopsychic structure considered in terms of object relationships. *International Journal of Psychoanalysis, 25*: 70–92.

Ferenczi, S. (1913). Stages in the development of the sense of reality. In: *First Contributions to Psycho-Analysis* (pp. 213–239). London: Maresfield Reprints, 1952.

Ferenczi, S. (1932). *The Clinical Diary of Sandor Ferenczi*, J. Dupont (Ed.), M. Balint & N. Z. Jackson (Trans.). Cambridge, MA: Harvard University Press, 1988.

Ferenczi, S. (1933). Confusion of tongues between adults and the child—the language of tenderness and of passion. *Contemporary Psychoanalysis, 24*: 196–206. Reprinted in: *Final Contributions to the Problems and Methods of Psychoanalysis* (pp. 156–167). London: Hogarth, 1955.

Field, T. (1978). Interactional behavior of primary versus secondary caretaker fathers. *Developmental Psychology, 14*: 83–184.

Fivaz-Depeursinge, E., Burgin, D., Corboz-Warnery, A., Lebovici, S., Stern, D. N., Byng-Hall, J., & Lamour, M. (1994). The dynamics of interfaces: seven authors in search of encounters across levels of description of an event involving a mother, father, and baby. *Infant Mental Health Journal, 15*: 69–89.

Fonagy, P., & Target, M. (2007). Playing with reality: IV. A theory of external reality rooted in intersubjectivity. *International Journal of Psychoanalysis, 88*: 917–937.

Freud, A. (1946). The psychoanalytic study of infantile feeding disturbances. *Psychoanalytic Study of the Child, 2*: 119–132.

Freud, A. (1965a). The concept of developmental lines. In: *The Writings of Anna Freud* (Vol. 6) (pp. 62–92). New York: International Universities Press.

Freud, A. (1965b). *Normality and Pathology in Childhood*. London: Hogarth Press.

Freud, A. (1991)[1943]. Contribution to the discussion of Susan Isaac's paper. In: P. King & R. Steiner (Eds.), *The Freud–Klein Controversies 1941–1945* (pp. 415–425). London: Routledge.

Freud, A., & Burlingham, D. (1943). *War and Children*. New York: Medical War Books.

Freud, S. (1895). *Project for a Scientific Psychology. S.E., 1*: 281–391. London: Hogarth.

Freud, S. (1910c). *Leonardo da Vinci and a Memory of his Childhood. S.E., 11*: 59–137. London: Hogarth.

Freud, S. (1910d). The future prospects of psycho-analytic therapy. *S.E., 11*: 139–152. London: Hogarth.

Freud, S. (1915c). Instincts and their vicissitudes. *S.E., 14*: 105–158. London: Hogarth.

Freud, S. (1915e). The unconscious. *S.E., 14*: 159–215. London: Hogarth.

Freud, S. (1916a). On transience. *S.E., 14*: 303–307. London: Hogarth.

Freud, S. (1926d). *Inhibitions, Symptoms and Anxiety. S.E., 20*: 77–174. London: Hogarth.

Freud, S. (1930a). *Civilization and its Discontents. S.E., 21*: 59–145. London: Hogarth.

Freud, S. (1937c). Analysis terminable and interminable. *S.E., 23*: 211–253. London: Hogarth.

Freud, S. (1940a[1938]). *An Outline of Psycho-Analysis. S.E., 23*: 141–207. London: Hogarth.

Gabbard, G. O. (1995). Countertransference: the emerging common ground. *International Journal of Psychoanalysis, 76*: 475–485.

Gabbard, G. O., & Westen, D (2003). Rethinking therapeutic acton. *International Journal of Psychoanalysis, 84*: 823–841.

Gaddini, E. (1982). Early defensive fantasies and the psychoanalytical process. *International Journal of Psychoanalysis, 63*: 379–388.

Gergely, G., & Watson, J. S. (1996). The social biofeedback theory of parental affect-mirroring. *International Journal of Psychoanalysis, 77*: 1181–1212.

Gill, M. M. (1982). *Analysis of the Transference* (Vol. 1). New York: International Universities Press.

Glasser, M. (1979). Some aspects of the role of aggression in the perversions. In: I. Rosen (Ed.), *Sexual Deviation* (pp. 278–305). London: Oxford University Press.

Grinberg, L. (1979). Countertransference and projective counteridentification. *Contemporary Psychoanalysis, 15*: 226–247.

Grey, A. (1994). Ferenczi and the International School. *International Forum of Psychoanalysis, 3*: 103–108.

Grünberger, B. (1979). *Narcissism*. New York: International Universities Press.

Guntrip, H. (1968). *Schizoid Phenomena, Object Relations and the Self.* London: Hogarth Press.

Haig, D. (1993). Genetic conflicts in human pregnancy. *Quarterly Review of Biology, 68*: 495–532.

Hartmann, H. (1939). *Ego Psychology and the Problem of Adaptation.* New York: International Universities Press, 1958.

Hayman, A. (1994). Some remarks about the 'Controversial Discussions'. *International Journal of Psychoanalysis, 75*: 343–358.

Heimann, P. (1950). On counter-transference. *International Journal of Psychoanalysis, 31*: 81–84.

Heimann, P. (1956). Dynamics of transference interpretations. *International Journal of Psychoanalysis, 37*: 303–310.

Heimann, P. (1991)[1943]. Some aspects of the role of introjection and projection in early development. In: P. King & R. Steiner (Eds.), *The Freud–Klein Controversies 1941–1945* (pp. 501–531). London: Routledge.

Hershlovitz, R., & Harel, J. (1998). Maternal separation anxiety: precursors and outcomes. *Child Psychiatry & Human Development, 71*: 1629–1639.

Hobson, P. (2002). The cradle of thought: exploring the origins of thinking. London: Macmillan.

Hoffer, A. (1990). The Clinical Diary of Sandor Ferenczi. *International Journal of Psychoanalysis, 71*: 723–727.

Hoffman, I. Z. (1983). The patient as interpreter of the analyst's experience. *Contemporary Psychoanalysis, 19*: 389–422.

Jacobson, E. (1954). The self and the object world—vicissitudes of their infantile cathexes and their influence on ideational and affective development. *Psychoanalytic Study of the Child, 9*: 75–127.

Joseph, B. (1982). Addiction to near death. *International Journal of Psychoanalysis, 63*: 449–456.

Joseph, B. (1985). Transference: the total situation. *International Journal of Psychoanalysis, 66*: 447–454.

Karmiloff-Smith, A. (1995). Annotation: the extraordinary cognitive journey from foetus through infancy. *Journal of Child Psychology and Psychiatry, 36*: 1293–1313.

Kennedy, R. (2007). *The Many Voices of Psychoanalysis*. London: Routledge.

Kernberg, O. (1966). Structural derivatives of object relationships. *International Journal of Psychoanalysis, 47*: 236–252.

Kernberg, O. (1982). Self, ego, affects and drives. *Journal of the American Psychoanalytic Association, 30*: 893–917.

Kestenberg, J. S. (1976). Regression and reintegration in pregnancy *Journal of the American Psychoanalytic Association, 24*(Suppl.): 213–250.

King P., & Steiner, R. (Eds.) (1991). *The Freud–Klein Controversies 1941–45* London: Routledge.

Klaus, M. H., & Kennell, J. H. (1976). *Maternal–Infant Bonding*. St. Louis, MO: Mosby.

Klein, M. (1937). Love, guilt, and reparation. In: *Love, Guilt, and Reparation, and Other Works* (pp. 306–343). New York: Free Press, 1975.

Klein, M. (1952). The origins of transference. *International Journal of Psychoanalysis, 33*: 433–438.

Klein, M. (1957). Envy and gratitude. In: *Envy and Gratitude and Other Works: 1946–1963* (pp. 176–235). New York: Delta

Kohon, G. (1986). *The British School of Psychoanalysis: The Independent Tradition*. New Haven, CT: Yale University Press.

Kohut, H. (1971). *The Analysis of the Self*. New York: International Universities Press.

Kraemer, S. B. (1996). 'Betwixt the dark and the daylight' of maternal subjectivity: meditations on the threshold. *Psychoanalytic Dialogue, 6*: 765–791.

Lester, E. P., & Notman, M. (1986). Pregnancy, developmental crisis and object relations: psychoanalytic considerations. *International Journal of Psychoanalysis, 67*: 357–366.

Lewin, K. (1935). *A Dynamic Theory of Personality*. New York: McGraw-Hill.

Lichtenberg, J. (1979). Factors in the development of the sense of the objects. *Journal of the American Psychoanalytic Association, 27*: 375–386.

Loewald, H. W. (1970). Psychoanalytic theory and the psychoanalytic process. *Psychoanalytic Study of the Child, 25*: 45–68.

Loewald, H. W. (1986). Transference–countertransference. *Journal of the American Psychoanalytic Association, 34*: 275–287.

Lyons-Ruth, K. (1999). The two-person unconscious. *Psychoanalytic Inquiry, 19*: 576–617.

Mahler, M., Pine, F., & Bergman, A. (1975). *The Psychological Birth of the Human Infant.* New York: Basic Books.

Mandler, J. (1988). How to build a baby: on the development of an accessible representation system. *Cognitive Development, 3*: 113–136.

Meissner, W. W. (2002). The problem of self-disclosure in psychoanalysis. *Journal of the American Psychoanalytic Association, 50*: 827–867.

Mitchell, S. (1993). *Hope and Dread in Psychoanalysis.* New York: Basic Books.

Money-Kyrle, R. E. (1956). Normal counter-transference and some of its deviations. *International Journal of Psychoanalysis, 37*: 360–366.

O'Connor, T. G., Heron, J., & Glover, V. (2002). Antenatal anxiety predicts child behavioural emotional problems independently of postnatal depression. *Journal of the American Academy Child & Adolescent Psychiatry, 41*: 1470–1477.

Ogden, T. (1994). *Subjects of Analysis.* Northvale, NJ: Jason Aronson.

O'Shaughnessy, E. (1983). Words and working through. *International Journal of Psychoanalysis, 64*: 281–289.

Orange, D. (1995). *Emotional Understanding: Studies in Psychoanalytic Epistemology.* New York: Guilford Press.

Panksepp, J. (1998). *Affective Neuroscience.* New York: Oxford University Press.

Parker, R. (1995). *Torn in Two: Experience of Maternal Ambivalence,* London: Virago.

Pines, D. (1993). *A Woman's Unconscious Use of her Body: A Psychoanalytical Perspective.* London: Virago.

Piontelli, A. (1992). *From Fetus to Child: An Observational and Psychoanalytical Study.* London: Routledge.

Pruett, K. D. (1983). Infants of primary nurturing fathers. *Psychoanalytic Study of the Child, 38*: 257–277.

Racker, H. (1968). *Transference and Countertransference.* New York: International Universities Press.

Raphael-Leff, J. (1980). Psychotherapy with pregnant women. In: B. Blum (Ed.), *Psychological Aspects of Pregnancy, Birthing & Bonding* (pp. 174–205). New York: Human Science Press.

Raphael-Leff, J. (1983). Facilitators and Regulators: two approaches to mothering. *British Journal of Medical Psychology*, 56: 379–390.

Raphael-Leff, J. (1985a). Facilitators and Regulators, participators and renouncers: mothers' and fathers' orientations towards pregnancy and parenthood. *Journal of Psychosomatic Obstetrics & Gynaecology*, 4: 169–184.

Raphael-Leff, J. (1985b). Facilitators and Regulators: vulnerability to post-natal disturbance. *Journal of Psychosomatic Obstetrics and Gynaecology*, 4: 151–168.

Raphael-Leff, J. (1986). Facilitators and Regulators: conscious and unconscious processes in pregnancy and early motherhood. *British Journal of Medical Psychology*, 59: 43–55.

Raphael-Leff, J. (1991a). *Psychological Processes of Childbearing* (4th edn). London: Anna Freud Centre, 2005.

Raphael-Leff, J. (1991b). The mother as container: placental process and inner space. *Feminism & Psychology*, 1: 393–408.

Raphael-Leff, J. (1993). *Pregnancy: The Inside Story*. London: Karnac [reprinted New York: Other Press, 2001].

Raphael-Leff, J. (1994). Shifts in theory, shifts in practice: an Independent's view. In: *Clinical & Theoretical Challenges: Progress in Self Psychology*. Hillsdale, NJ: Analytic Press.

Raphael-Leff, J. (1997). The casket and the key: thoughts on gender and generativity. In: J. Raphael-Leff & R. J. Perelberg (Eds.), *Female Experience: Four Generations of British Women Psychoanalysts on their Work with Female Patients* (pp. 237–257). London: Routledge. New edition, London: Anna Freud Centre, 2008.

Raphael-Leff, J. (2000). Behind the shut door: a psychoanalytical approach to premature menopause. In: D. Singer & M. Hunter (Eds.), *Premature Menopause: A Multidisciplinary Approach* (pp. 79–95). London: Whurr.

Raphael-Leff, J. (2001a). Climbing the walls: puerperal disturbance and perinatal therapy. In: J. Raphael-Leff (Ed.), *Spilt Milk: Perinatal Loss and Breakdown* (pp. 79–112). London: Routledge.

Raphael-Leff, J. (2001b). Primary maternal persecution. In: B. Kahr (Ed.), *Forensic Psychotherapy and Psychopathology: Winnicottian Perspectives* (pp. 27–41). London: Karnac.

Raphael-Leff, J. (2001c). Women in the history of psychoanalysis: issues of gender, generation and the genesis of COWAP. *Psychoanalysis & Psychotherapy*, Special Issue: 113–132.

Raphael-Leff, J. (2002). Presence of absence. In: F. Thomson Salo (Ed.), *Journey to Motherhood* (pp. 6–20). Melbourne: Stonington Press.

Raphael-Leff, J. (Ed.) (2003). *Parent–Infant Psychodynamics: Wild Things, Mirrors and Ghosts*. London: Whurr.

Raphael-Leff, J. (2007). Femininity and its unconscious 'shadows': gender and generative identity in the age of biotechnology. *British Journal of Psychotherapy, 23*: 497–515.

Rayner, E. (1991). *The Independent Mind in British Psychoanalysis*. Northvale, NJ: Jason Aronson.

Reich, A. (1951). On counter-transference. *International Journal of Psychoanalysis, 32*: 25–31.

Renik, O. (1993). Analytic interaction: conceptualizing technique in light of the analyst's irreducible subjectivity. *Psychoanalytic Quarterly, 62*: 553–571.

Rickman, J. (1951). Number and the human sciences. In: *Selected Contributions to Psycho-Analysis*. London: Hogarth Press, 1957.

Roncolato, W., & McMahon, C. (2012). Facilitators and regulators: psychometric properties of maternal orientation measures in pregnancy. *Journal of Reproductive & Infant Psychology, 30*: 1–19.

Rosenfeld, H. (1987). *Impasse and Interpretation: Therapeutic and Anti-therapeutic Factors in the Psychoanalytic Treatment of Psychotic, Borderline, and Neurotic Patients*. London: Tavistock.

Sameroff, A. (Ed.) (1978). Organization and stability of newborn behavior. *Monograph Society for Research into Child Development, 43*(5–6): 138.

Sandler, A.-M. (2012). Anna Freud's influence on contemporary thinking about the child. In: N. D. Malberg & J Raphael-Leff (Eds.), *The Anna Freud Tradition: Lines of Development—Evolution of Theory and Practice over the Decades* (pp. 47–53). London: Karnac.

Sandler, J. (1976). Countertransference and role-responsiveness. *International Review of Psychoanalysis, 3*: 43–47.

Sandler, J. (1986). Reality and the stabilizing function of unconscious fantasy. *Bulletin of the Anna Freud Centre, 9*: 177–194.

Sandler, J., & Joffe, W. G. (1969). Towards a basic psychoanalytic model. *International Journal of Psychoanalysis, 50*: 79–90.

Sandler, J., & Sandler, A.-M. (1978). On the development of object relationships and affects. *International Journal of Psychoanalysis, 59*: 285–296.

Scalzone, F. (2005). Notes for a dialogue between psychoanalysis and neuroscience. *International Journal of Psychoanalysis, 86*: 1405–1423.

Schafer, R. (1970). An overview of Heinz Hartmann's contributions to psychoanalysis. *International Journal of Psychoanalysis, 51*: 425–446.

Schafer, R. (1994). The contemporary Kleinians of London. *Psychoanalytic Quarterly, 63*: 409–432.

Scher, A. (2001). Facilitators and regulators: maternal orientation as an antecedent of attachment security. *Journal of Reproductive & Infant Psychology, 19*: 325–333.

Scher, A., & Blumberg, O. (1992). Facilitators and regulators: cross-cultural and methodological considerations. *British Journal of Medical Psychology, 65*: 327–331.

Scher, A., & Blumberg, O. (1999). Night waking among 1-year olds: a study of maternal separation anxiety. *Child Care, Health & Development, 25*: 323–334.

Schore, A. N. (2001). The effects of early relational trauma on right-brain development, affect regulation, and infant mental health. *Infant Mental Health Journal, 22*: 201–269.

Schwaber, E. (1983). Psychoanalytic listening and psychic reality. *International Review of Psycho-Analysis, 10*: 379–392.

Segal, H. (2006). Reflections on truth, tradition, and the psychoanalytic tradition of truth. *American Imago, 63*: 283–292.

Segal, H. M. (1977). Psychoanalytic dialogue: Kleinian theory today. *Journal of the American Psychoanalytic Association, 25*: 363–370.

Sharp, H., & Bramwell, R. (2001). An empirical evaluation of a psycho-analytic model of mothering orientation and the antenatal prediction of postnatal depression. *Archives of Women's Mental Health, 3*(Suppl. 2): 14–19.

Sharp, H., & Bramwell, R. (2004). An empirical evaluation of a psycho-analytic theory of mothering orientation: implications for the antenatal prediction of postnatal depression. *Journal of Reproduction & Infant Psychology, 22*(2): 71–89.

Sharpe, E. F. (1943). Response to Susan Isaacs. First discussion of scientific papers. In: P. King & R. Steiner (Eds.) *The Freud–Klein Controversies 1941–45* (pp. 336–340). London: Routledge, 1991.

Solms, M., & Turnbull, O. (2002). *The Brain and the Inner World*. London: Karnac.

Spence, D. P. (1982). *Narrative Truth and Historical Truth: Meaning and Interpretation in Psychoanalysis*. London: Norton.

Spitz, R. (1965). *The First Year of Life*. New York: International Universities Press.

Steele, H., Steele, M., & Fonagy, P. (1996). Associations among attachment classifications of mothers, fathers, and their infants. *Child Development, 67*: 541–555.

Steiner, J. (1993). *Psychic Retreats*. London: Routledge.

Steiner, J. (1996). The aim of psychoanalysis in theory and in practice. *International Journal of Psychoanalysis, 77*: 1073–1083.

Stern, D. N. (1985). *The Interpersonal World of the Infant: A View from Psychoanalysis and Developmental Psychology*. New York: Basic Books.

Stern, D. N. (1995). *The Motherhood Constellation*. New York: Basic Books.

Stolorow, R. (1997). Current conceptions of neutrality and abstinence: Panel Report. *Journal of the American Psychoanalytic Association, 45*: 1231–1239.

Stolorow, R., Atwood, G., & Brandchaft, B. (1994). Epilogue. In: R. Stolorow, G. Atwood, & B. Brandchaft (Eds.), *The Intersubjective Perspective* (pp. 203–209). Northvale, NJ: Jason Aronson.

Suttie, I. D. (1935). *The Origins of Love and Hate*. London: Kegan Paul.

Sullivan, H. S. (1953). *The Interpersonal Theory of Psychiatry*. New York: Norton.

Trevarthen, C. (1974). Conversations with a two-month-old. *New Scientist*, 2 May. Reprinted in: J. Raphael-Leff (Ed.), *Parent–Infant Psychodynamics: Wild Things, Mirrors and Ghosts* (pp. 25–34). London: Whurr.

Trevarthen, C., & Aitken, K. J. (2001). Infant intersubjectivity: research, theory and clinical applications. *Journal of Child Psychology and Psychiatry, 42*: 3–48.

Tronick, E. Z. (1989). Emotions and emotional communication in infants . *American Psychologist, 44*: 112–119. Updated and reprinted in: J. Raphael-Leff (Ed.), *Parent–Infant Psychodynamics: Wild Things, Mirrors and Ghosts* (pp. 35–53). London: Whurr.

Tronick, E. Z. (2003). 'Of course all relationships are unique': how co-creative processes generate unique mother–infant and patient–therapist relationships and change other relationships. *Psychoanalytic Inquiry, 23*: 473–491.

Van Bussel, J. C. H., Spitz, B., & Demyttenaere, K. (2009a). Anxiety in pregnant and postpartum women. An exploratory study of the role of maternal orientations. *Journal of Affective Disorders, 114*: 232–242.

Van Bussel, J. C. H., Spitz, B., & Demyttenaere, K. (2009b). Depressive symptomatology in pregnant and postpartum women An exploratory study of the role of maternal antenatal orientations. *Archive of Women's Mental Health, 12*:155–166.

Van Bussel, J. C. H., Spitz, B., & Demyttenaere, K. (2010). Childbirth expectations and experiences and associations with mothers' attitudes to pregnancy, the child and motherhood. *Journal of Reproduction & Infant Psychology, 28*: 143–160.

Van den Bergh, B. R., Mulder, E. J., Mennes, M., & Glover, V. (2005). Antenatal maternal anxiety and stress and the neurobehavioural development of the fetus and child: links and possible mechanisms. A review. *Neuroscience Biobehaviour Review, 29*: 237–258.

Wallerstein, R. S. (1988). One psychoanalysis or many? *International Journal of Psychoanalysis, 69*: 5–21.

Willick, M. S. (1990). Psychoanalytic concepts of the etiology of severe mental illness. *Journal of the American Psychoanalytic Association, 38*: 1049–1081.

Winnicott, D. W. (1949). Hate in the counter-transference. *International Journal of Psychoanalysis, 30*: 69–74. Reprinted in: *Through Pediatrics to Psycho-Analysis* (pp. 194–203). London: Hogarth, 1975.

Winnicott, D. W. (1952). Psychosis and child care. In: *Collected Papers* (pp. 148–156). London: Tavistock, 1958.

Winnicott, D. W. (1960). Ego distortions in terms of true and false self. In: *The Maturational Processes and the Facilitating Environment* (pp. 140–152). London: Hogarth, 1965.

Winnicott, D. W. (1969). The use of an object. *International Journal of Psychoanalysis, 50*: 711–716.

Winnicott, D. W. (1971). *Playing and Reality*. London: Penguin.

Winnicott, D. W. (1988). The birth experience. In: *Human Nature* (pp. 143–151). London: Free Association Books.

Wolff, P. (1966). *The Causes, Controls and Organization of Behavior in the Neonate. Monograph 17*. New York: International Universities Press.

CHAPTER FOUR

Psychoanalytic learning, training, teaching, and supervision in relation to the ego and especially the superego

Bernard Barnett

Initial remarks

I n psychoanalytic circles, the superego has generally had a bad press. This is a pity, because the concept, together with its close ally, the traditional "conscience", does indeed have some very important positive attributes. I have in mind the contribution that the superego and the accompanying sense of guilt make to a person's individual wellbeing and (as Freud himself emphasised) to civilisation in general. However, in this chapter, I, too, will treat the superego as the villain of the piece, whatever the piece is.

I begin my discussion on education in relation to the superego with some remarks made by Woody Allen concerning reading, a major skill needed in learning and education. In his stand-up comedy routine in the 1960s, Allen tells us that he has just completed a course on speed reading, which was popular at that time. He then says that he has now read Tolstoy's *War and Peace* and that he has done this in twenty minutes! He then adds, for the benefit of his listeners, "It is all about Russia!"

Allen's point here is that there is "reading" and that there is "reading", and in this chapter I wish to argue that "there is education" and "there is education". I make this observation after having spent a professional lifetime involved in the education of children, the teaching of mental health professionals, and the training of psychotherapists and psychoanalysts. In this pursuit, I have indeed learnt something about the problems of "education", but rather less about how we should go about the process. This means that I am able to say more about how we should *not* go about it. However, in the second part of the chapter, with Winnicott as my guide, I will move towards some tentative observations on educating the ego.

Introduction

> It is in fact nothing short of a miracle that the modern methods of instruction have not yet entirely strangled the holy curiosity of inquiry; for this delicate little plant, aside from stimulation, stands mainly in need of freedom; without this it goes to wrack and ruin without fail. It is a very grave mistake to think that the enjoyment of seeing and searching can be promoted by means of coercion and a sense of duty . . .

> Bodily exercise, when compulsory, does no harm to the body; but knowledge which is acquired under compulsion obtains no hold on the mind. (Einstein, 1940)

This quotation, then, by opposing the use of "coercion" and "compulsion" in education and promoting "curiosity of inquiry", "freedom", and "seeing and searching", neatly introduces the issues with which I am concerned.

Writing nearly sixty years ago, Michael Balint published a critique of psychotherapeutic training. In that period, he detected a certain dogmatism, a secretiveness, and the use of authoritarian techniques among the trainers. With regard to the trainees, he found them "far too respectful towards their training analysts", too willing to accept "exoteric fables", and "too submissive without protest" (Balint, 1947, 1953).

In describing the prevailing attitude in training institutes, he used the term "superego education". In his view, in the course of their analytic training, there tended to become established in trainees a strong, special kind of unconscious, an unfettered and long-lasting superego. (Notwithstanding effects of regression on all trainees in analysis, as stressed by Eglé Laufer (2007), I, however, would add especially "vulnerable" trainees.) Balint suggested that students tended to become easily overawed and dependent on their masters. In essence, they became over-identified with their own analysts' ideas, which led to a depletion in their ego/self. There was then a marked absence among the trainees of what Winnicott might have referred to as "the spontaneous gesture", and I will return to this issue later in this chapter. According to Balint, part and parcel of superego education was that the analysand tended to over-idealise the analyst, to introject this idealised image, and then project a fierce aggression on to the outside world. I want to emphasise his use of the metaphor that "the analyst had been swallowed whole". In his view, this process later led to such negative effects as intolerance, sectarianism, and what he called "apostolic fury". At its worse, he pointed to the possibility of a covert, unconscious collusion between the analyst and candidate, which resulted in what he termed the "superego intropression of the analyst", a concept first used by Sandor Ferenczi.

What is superego intropression?

Now, it is interesting to consider this notion of "superego intropression" in more detail. In *The New Shorter Oxford Dictionary*, we find the meaning of the verb "to impress" as "stamping a mark made by pressure"). Applying the prefix "intro", we arrive at "superego intropression" as "the quality of driving inwards".

In a further, psychoanalytically helpful elaboration, Balint writes of intropression as a communicative process in which "a rule or precept is forced into the mind of the person such that it produces an over-strong superego and a tendency to weaken the ego". We may note, here, his stress on how intropression has a reciprocal effect on the ego and superego. Ferenczi himself did not elaborate on his concept, but he did, nevertheless, provide an illustration of this incorporative process that had arisen from the life-long struggles that had taken place in his overall relationship (including his very brief periods of analysis) with Freud. Shortly before his death in 1933, he wrote the following in a diary note to himself:

> I was brave (and productive) only as long as I (unconsciously) relied for support on another power ... Is the only possibility for my

continued existence the renunciation of the largest part of one's own self, in order to carry out the will of the higher power to the end (as though it were my own)? . . . Is the choice here one between dying and 'rearranging myself'—and this at the age of fifty-nine? (Ferenczi, 1988[1932], p. 212)

It has been suggested that an internalised Freud persisted in Ferenzi's mind as a "hardly digested introject", an "idealised internal father" that could not be "worked through". His further comments support the idea that the total experience of his relationship to Freud was dominated by a superego intropression in such a way that, in his own words, Freud was "too big for him" and "too much of a father".

Now, Freud himself was certainly aware of the dangers of this problem of what might also be called a "primitive identification". As early as 1919, he wrote,

The patient should be educated to liberate and fulfil his own nature, not to resemble ourselves . . . We refused most emphatically to turn a patient into our own private property, to decide his fate for him, to force our own ideals upon him to form him in our own image and see that it is good . . . I have been able to help people . . . without affecting their individuality. (Freud, 1919a)

However, I doubt whether Freud, in his practice, and like many of us, was always able to keep to this principle of non-intrusion, especially in the matter of giving firm advice to Ferenczi, his close colleague and very occasional patient.

Wrestling in my mind with these issues in relation to the problems of psychotherapy training, I found myself thinking about some of the "Do's and Don'ts" of education more generally, including the education of children (especially as it was "then" and as it is "now"). With regard to "then", it was helpful to find something relevant to my theme in D. H. Lawrence's novel, *The Rainbow*, which was published in 1915. I would add that Lawrence had himself spent something like eight years (between 1902–1911) teaching primary-aged children, in classes of 50+. In the novel, Lawrence portrays Ursula, a seventeen-year-old woman who is a new and idealistic trainee-teacher, and who finds herself in a strictly authoritarian and very threatening educational environment, in which "power" and "force", from the head teacher downwards, were the ruling principles. Faced with this regime, Ursula's wish was to oppose this rigid system by becoming a "responsive" teacher who could provide her pupils with a "personal and vivid", individualised education. However, when confronted by a class of fifty-five boys and girls, she discovers "not children . . . but a squadron . . . not individual . . . but a collective inhuman thing" and this experience, she found, led to the feeling in her of being "utterly non-existent" (Lawrence, 2007, pp. 349–350).

Lawrence describes how, in this school atmosphere, it was assumed that teaching was a matter of "will", in that the will of the school, the head master and the teacher was to be imposed on the will of the children. This aim demanded "the abnegation of the teacher's 'personal self' and an application of a system of laws, for the purpose of achieving a certain calculable result, the imparting of certain knowledge" (ibid., p. 356).

That Lawrence's description of the dehumanising effects of this teaching–learning situation can be linked with superego intropression is made clear in his account of the head master's aim. This was, he says, "to crystallise the children into hard mute fragments fixed under his will: his brute will which fixed them by sheer force" (ibid., p. 360).

Keeping this fictional example of an extreme, superego-orientated education in mind, we can now turn to the training of psychotherapists in the present day.

What is wrong, and how can things be improved?

The central aim in training is, I think, uncontroversial, although it does not take us very far. That is to build up in the trainee an ego with a strong critical capacity and one suitable for bearing the considerable strains of analytic work. The problem then becomes one of how this can best be achieved.

One approach to this question is to consider the identification processes that are relevant to many types of learning and by making a distinction between "benign" and "malign" aspects of identification. If we assume "good-enough" analysis, supervision, and teaching, trainees will tend towards a positive identification with their analysts and supervisors, and this can be understood as a part of a healthy developmental stage on a long and tough path to a personal and professional identity. A path leading to a more pathological process would then be one in which the trainee had become stuck fast in an idealised, unreal and false identification with the other and under which was often hidden a painful sense of inferiority (Gill, 2001).

We can also consider these learning processes in terms of a continuum in which at the more benign end, the subject had internalised the
many inevitable partial identifications (the "building blocks" of
personality) with all persons with whom he/she has close connections. Then, at the more pathological end, we can envisage a pattern
of forceful and consuming identifications (for example, with aggres-
sors, abusers, etc., see Berman, 2002).

Since Balint's early critique of psychoanalytic training, in which he
complained of a lack of interest among analysts, there has accumulated a large literature on psychotherapeutic education, which has
expressed much concern with the many problems and has made a
number of suggestions as to how things might be improved. For
instance, Kernberg (1986, 1996, 2000, 2006, 2007) and others have
noted the development of a destructive, "utopian state of mind", and
one giving rise to some common idealisations. Examples are the
tendency among some colleagues of maintaining that there is one, and
only one, correct standard analytic technique, the belief that it is possible to become "fully analysed" and the assumption that a training
analyst is always a superior analyst (Werbert, 2007).

Another belief system, which, to say the least, has its dangers, is
the conscious–unconscious tendency present in the hidden assumption that "inner reality" is "good" (i.e., all-important) and outer reality
is "bad" (i.e., mostly irrelevant). Before turning to Winnicott and to
my own experiences as trainee and teacher, I want to mention briefly
another important, but somewhat neglected, contribution in the area
of training by Patrick Casement. Similarly to Lawrence's description
of problems in a class of fifty-five children, Casement (2005) has
drawn attention to the issue of "power" in the Institutes and the ensuing problems of abuse and the trainee's fear of failure. He describes
the effect of an "atmosphere" in which honesty is restricted and autonomy, spontaneity, and creativity inhibited. In some further comments
on the style of supervisors, he suggests the dangers of what trainees
might perceive as a too dogmatic, controlling, or punitive attitude. Of
course, this perception might be related to problems in the trainee, but
in situations in which it is also accurate, it could lead to an over-
compliance with the demands of the training programme and, thence,
to a "false-self" development. This concept is less comprehensive than
Winnicott's 1960 formulation, but it also has similarities in so far as it
might involve a reaction to environmental demands and a seduction

into compliance. Klauber (1983) seems to have coined the term "analytic false self" to describe at least the part-functioning of inexperienced analysts, including himself. Berman (2004) has also pointed to the danger of impingements during the training process, and of how "The allure of belonging, of being accepted, of being liked by our seniors is considerable and may have the upper hand in many instances" (p. 117).

Casement suggests various checks and balances, by means of which the negative effects of analytic power may be monitored and controlled, and he concludes as follows:

> When we have put on the Emperor's new clothes . . . we owe it to ourselves, our students and to psychoanalysis itself that we guard against the pitfalls inherent in this privileged position that psychoanalysis tempts us to claim as its own. (p. 1158)

Authenticity

I begin my discussion with Winnicott's central concepts of authenticity, not directly with his ideas, but with a conclusion of my own, which is a statement of the main finding of my eight years (very part-time) research into the theory of the superego/conscience. I think this can best be summed up by posing the following questions.

How do we ever come to develop and sustain an individual voice of our own, a person capable of choice (an "Ego", a "Self", an "I", or a "Me")? How, that is, is a state of relative independence and maturity achieved? The kind of person I have in mind is one who is "in health" and, therefore, capable of authenticity, spontaneity, creativity, playfulness, liveliness, etc. How, then, can such a state of human development and interdependence be achieved and sustained in the face of the many complex and durable influences and pressures upon us which originate in our background (i.e., our parents, family, teachers, culture, country, language, and society etc.) (Barnett, 2007)?

These questions lead me back to Winnicott's work and his view that "authenticity" and "originality" are among the hallmarks of a person's aliveness and mental health. Suppose now we imagine (though, of course, this kind of thing is not unknown in reality) a student faced with an essay assignment, who chooses to surf the

Internet and make a wholesale copy of the information that he finds there, an account, that is, that somebody else has written, and he then submits this as his own piece of work. We could think of this action as not only a kind of minor league plagiarism, but as an example of a dead, "false" learning process and product and, therefore, the very opposite of what Winnicott would have regarded as something personal, vitalised, and authentic.

However, particularly relevant to my discussion is that, in spite of his overall emphasis on originality and authenticity, there is also Winnicott's famous and honest comment on his working–writing method, about which he comments (perhaps tongue in cheek) as early as 1945, "What happens is that I gather this and that, here and there, settle down to clinical experience, form my own theories, and then *last of all, interest myself to see where I stole what*" (1945, p. 145. my italics).

This comment suggests, then, that authenticity and originality are unlikely to be absolute, and this brings me to the relevance of Winnicott's careful statement of how false/true self development is itself a matter of degree. Such development will clearly vary from person to person, in that one individual might display a truly pathological, split-off compliance, including feelings of futility, while another, and much healthier person, shows an ability, as Winnicott puts it, "to comply and compromise without exposure", and exhibit "a healthy social manner".

According to Winnicott, then, we all have a ratio of "false self to true self" development and a question of the balance between the two is always involved. I suggest that it is this balance that has to be borne in mind in our teaching activity and in our relationship to our students. This will, of course, as many colleagues have suggested, include the problem of monitoring our own countertransference and using it in the service of our students. It is interesting that Lawrence, in *The Rainbow*, quoted earlier, portrays the authoritarian, dictatorial headmaster also in true/false self terms. In Ursula's perception, the head master

> was imprisoned in a task too small and too petty for him . . . He did not believe in the least in the education he kept inflicting year after year . . . So he must bully, only bully while it tortured his strong, wholesome nature with shame like a spur always galling. (p. 360)

A return to our imaginary plagiarist raises another important question hinted at earlier: how far are the processes of superego education and superego intropression established and reinforced by the teachers and supervisors, and what might be contributed and sustained in this situation by the trainees and students themselves?

In thinking about this, I was reminded of what Winnicott's comment on the infant's "function of contributing-in", that is, the awareness of the part he/she can contribute to the mother's caring capacity. He says, "In health", the mother survives, and, as part of her survival, she is able to receive "the infant's spontaneous gesture". This enables the infant to grow towards a stage of concern and an awareness of growing responsibility for his impulses. A crucial part of this growth process is the presence and use of certain capacities in the infant (e.g., the capacity to search for the object, to find the object, and to search for the "sense of self"). We might say that these capacities *for whatever reason*, seem to be missing in our imaginary student.

Winnicott has also made some direct comments on the teaching process itself which are relevant to my theme. In these, he connects some of his important concepts together and also suggests what needs to be addressed in the educational enterprise. He says, "Teaching aims at enrichment. It is an insult to indocrinate people even for their own good unless they have the chance by being present to react, to express disapproval and to contribute" (quoted in Davis & Wallbridge, 1981, p. 65). And again,

> Teaching (is) not enough . . . each student must create what is there to be taught, and so arrive at each stage of learning in his own way . . . teachers [may neglect] the stultifying effect on the creative spirit of too great insistence on objectivity . . . creativity can be destroyed by the belief that in acting one must know beforehand what one is doing. (Winnicott, 1951, p. 392)

In a paper entitled "Contemporary concepts of adolescent development and their implications for higher education", published posthumously in *Playing and Reality*, Winnicott reflected on several elements of his own psychotherapeutic attitude. He writes that the individual must develop an "identification with social groupings and with society, without too great a loss of personal spontaneity". Reading this article, I noticed that Winnicott amazingly and amusingly comments that while imperfections are characteristic of the human being, "perfection belongs to machines"! We are left, then, with the important question of how analytic teachers can best promote and sustain a personal spontaneity in the trainee.

Spontaneity

The term "spontaneity" is complex, ambiguous, and, to some extent, controversial, and it can be understood on several levels. In a comprehensive discussion on the theme of spontaneity, Turner (2004) has connected Winnicott's ideas on spontaneity with the creative work of D. H. Lawrence and that writer's interest in "living spontaneously from the living real self". In brief, he points to Lawrence's awareness of the paradox that is involved in the impossible task of "trying" to be "spontaneous" and quotes Winnicott's theory of relationship: "Spontaneity only makes sense in a controlled setting. Content is of no meaning without form". In this paper, Turner also refers to the work of Newman, who stressed the "non-compliance" in Winnicott's thought and what he calls the celebration of risk, danger, and "ruthlessness" in the service of "feeling alive" and "feeling real". He, Newman, also points to the paradox in Winnicott of what he calls "learned spontaneity". (In reading about spontaneity and risk-taking, I was reminded of an incident when I found my father, at the age of ninety, climbing up a ladder, a task which he had, at times, carried out all his life. At that time I yelled and screamed at him to get down, but, looking back on this now, I can at least see his point, which was his continuing need, in extreme old age, to feel alive and spontaneous.)

Finally, I would add that Winnicott's view of spontaneity only makes sense for him in connection with his other central idea of "environmental holding". That is that "the truly spontaneous gesture, the revelation of the self to the self", can only arise in a safe environment (Davis & Wallbridge, 1981, p. 24). Winnicott's approach to the clinician, as a perceived authority figure, is also useful as a guide for the analytic teacher. He says that the clinician should respect the dignity of the patient and that, like the mother, should seek *not* to dominate. He was well aware of the negative effects of the power ratio (the asymmetrical relationship) in the clinical situation and speaks of encouraging the patient to feel "on equal terms with the doctor" and again, he says, "we are reduced to two human beings of equal status. Hierarchies drop away" (Winnicott, 1950, 1970). This power issue can also be applied to the specific case of supervision in psychotherapy. In this respect, we can note that the very word "super"-vision evokes associations with the "super" ego, and that the word "super" has resounding echoes with direction, control, oversight, and superintendence, all these actions being performed by a powerful and omniscient, superior authority (c/p "superman"). Such notions, might, of course, feed the fantasies of both parties to the learning situation, and many writers have noted that these might reinforce the trainees' submissiveness and compliance and, thus, also contribute to a powerful inhibition on the development of their own creativity.

Living creatively and its relationship to playing

With this in mind, and before turning to my own work, I would like to mention briefly Winnicott's important idea of "living creatively". This concept is not easy to summarise, but, in essence, it concerns a person's way of life and style of living. Here, he considers what it means for the particular individual to be alive, to feel alive, and, especially, to feel that life is worth living. He traces the roots of such feelings to the primitive love impulse, the illusion of omnipotence and "ruthlessness", always assuming a good-enough environment for healthy development. He also celebrates a theory of primary psychic creativity and connects this with an innate drive towards health. In thinking further about the playing, it is valuable to mention his idea of "unintegration" and its value (he describes this as having something to do with "periods of restfulness" and "feeling one with people" (see Milner, 1957 for a further elaboration). He applies this directly to the teaching–learning situation, in which he says there is a need for the teacher's tolerance, which would include allowing the learner to "flounder, to be in a state in which there is no orientation . . ." and *not* always having to be "an active person with a direction of interest or movement" (E. Balint, personal communication, 1990). In this respect, I am reminded of Michael Balint's work with discussion groups of doctors. While in no way encouraging the participants to indulge in "wild analysis", he does speak of encouraging them to "have the courage of their own stupidity" and the kind of tolerance in teaching that has also been much emphasised by the eminent American analyst, Thomas Ogden (Ogden, 2005).

In conclusion, we may note the value of the teacher's role in creating, sustaining, and protecting "the play space", nurturing the trainee's capacity to play and offering mutual playing, and I shall try to illustrate this quest in the case material which follows.

Case study

Some years after completing supervisory work with a number of trainees, I asked each of them for a brief written account of their experience of supervision, which paid due attention to its merits and defects. What follows is based on one of these responses, which I have selected to illustrate the emergence, at an early stage, of what I consider to be "a spontaneous gesture" on the part of the trainee. I now describe a summarised version of this supervisee's written account. Mrs K presented a male patient in his thirties who was intensely anxious from the start of therapy and remained so throughout the period of attendance. This patient's terror resulted in a sustained and unrelenting verbal attack on his therapist, amounting at times to near abuse. Ideas of trust, hope, associative processes, negotiation with the therapist, and insightful use of the therapy were all consistently attacked, negated, and destroyed by the patient. Each analytic session seemed to be wiped out, so that, at its end, the patient could return to a zero situation. After six weeks, he commented bitterly, "I don't know where to start, nothing has changed, nothing is achieved; I still feel full of negative thoughts." After eighteen months, the patient stopped abruptly, after a session in which he had commented with horror that, like his alcoholic, bullying father, the therapy had turned him into an abuser.

In her written account of her supervisory experience, Mrs K commented that she was relieved to find that, among other characteristics, the supervisor was pragmatic, authentic, and respectful. However, she *also* reported that at the beginning of her presentations, she had been so "flooded by anxiety" that she had dreaded the supervisory sessions. She felt that, at that time, she had invested the supervisor with power and authority, while she had become inept and without resources. Gradually, however, with time, *the superego tyranny* (her words) of the supervisory experience lifted, although in her sessions with the patient, she says "a sick anxiety" remained.

For the purpose of this discussion, I will now focus on the experience near the beginning of the supervision, about which Mrs K wrote as follows.

"After six weeks or so I realised that I needed to take myself in hand [and] to talk with BB about the parallel process . . . I described how the patient's paranoia seemed to be spilling over into the supervision [in that] I became paranoid and inadequate . . . I found BB receptive [and] I felt trusted and respected by him. This for me was the turning point. I felt reconstructed as a therapist having escaped the tyranny of my harsh superego and I never again felt tyrannised by the supervision."

Now, the point about what I am choosing to call "the spontaneous gesture" ("to take myself in hand [and] to talk . . . about the parallel process") has to do with the nature of the teaching–learning climate in which it had occurred. Mrs K's response stimulated me to think back to my own experience at the time of the supervision. I certainly had been aware of an intense anxiety in the room and, painfully, that we had seemed to be on different wavelengths. This led me to query in my own mind whether or not the supervision was really going to work. There was also the more specific problem of how adequately to deal with Mrs K's intense and, for her, painful countertransference. What I actually remembered was my attempt to try to maintain a holding situation and to wait for an appropriate time to discuss the so-called parallel process (see Berman, 2004). However, in retrospect, what I now think I might have done was to have intervened much earlier. I could have offered a more definite acknowledgment of what was going on (i.e., the parallel process between therapist and patient, supervisee and supervisor) and how this might then have been tackled with the patient from an interpretative point of view.

Weaving thoughts

I want to end by referring to a teaching method in relation to clinical seminars that aims to promote ego education and minimise the influence of the superego. I have been experimenting with this Bion–Winnicott inspired method for some years. It has been called "weaving thoughts", and I have tried it with both experienced practitioners and with trainees. In essence, the presenter offers the group some brief background material and some written-up clinical material from two recent sessions. Having done this, she remains present, but in a non-participating role, while the group (including the leader) wrestles with the material, makes observations on it, and discusses what they think is going on in the analytic encounter. The presenter is then, usually some twenty minutes before the end of the meeting, invited to participate and respond to the discussion and inform the group about what she has gained (and perhaps, less often, what she has not gained) from their observations and comments. This method has an important advantage over the more traditional clinical seminar, in that it seeks to avoid the problems that arise from the more direct supervision of the presenter by the seminar leader. This method can sometimes lead to brow-beating or persecutory feelings in the trainee. The "weaving thoughts" approach seeks to monitor and use the dynamics of the group and facilitate the work opportunity for imaginative, "uninte-grative" thinking among the participants (Norman & Salomonsson, 2005; Salomonsson & Badoni, 2002).

I have selected the reports of two participants of their experience in the seminar. The first is from a few years ago, and I quote briefly and selectively from her written account of the seminar.

"... the method stimulated creative thought ... multiple levels of acuity and perceptiveness were stirred-up in this free associative process ... (that is we were) free to attend in a more alive way to the present analytic relationship. ... There was developed (in the group) a new authentically reflective space ... the process was energising and we could feel more awake than when we arrived ... there was a deeper capacity to absorb new thinking. The emotional thinking that became possible felt liberating. The presenters were less anxious and inhibited."

The second report is from a clinical seminar which ended in 2009, and this emphasises the viewpoint of the presenter in the seminar.

"The method allowed the presenter to take in a different way the comments, thoughts, ideas in the group about her patient since there was no pressure on the presenter to respond. Likewise, there was no possibility for colleagues to defensively ask the presenter many questions, which could be a bit persecuting for the presenter and could also prevent other group members from thinking. If the focus is on seeking more and more information about the patient, as can happen, this in turn could add more pressure on the presenter.

"The method avoids the presenter providing a detailed history to the group so that the participants feel freed up from 'having to get it right'. This allows them to entertain all sorts of ideas about the patient and I think that was just the kind of thing that we should be doing with the material.

"I really enjoyed the group and the material. Thank you very much!"

Last, I would consider that the "weaving thoughts" method at least seeks to minimise what is probably the inevitable presence of persecutory anxiety in the trainee, student, or other experienced colleague in the training or other learning situation in which there is an evaluation process.

Conclusion

In this chapter, I have described some of the problems of psychotherapeutic training and education. I have suggested that a central aim is to promote ego strength and minimise adverse superego influence and, more specifically, to seek to avoid "superego intropression". In doing this, I have suggested that, in approaching these dilemmas, it is helpful to bear in mind and apply a few of Winnicott's central and interrelated ideas and especially his stress on authenticity, spontaneity, living creatively, and playing. Finally, I have attempted to illustrate my use of his ideas with examples from my work as supervisor and teacher.

References

Balint, E. (1990). Personal communication.

Balint, M. (1947). On the psychoanalytic training system. In: *Primary Love and Psycho-analytic Technique* (2nd edn) (pp. 253–274). London: Tavistock.

Balint, M. (1953). *Analytic Training and Training Analysis* (2nd edn). London: Tavistock. 275–286

Barnett, B. R. (2007). *You Ought To! A Psychoanalytic Study of the Superego and Conscience*. London: Karnac.

Berman, E. (2002). Identifying with the other—a conflictual vital necessity: commentary on paper by Jay Frankel. *Psychoanalytic Dialogues, 12*: 141–151.

Berman, E. (2004). *Impossible Training: A Relational View of Psychoanalytic Education*. Hillsdale, NJ: Analytic Press.

Casement, P. (2005). The emperor's clothes: some serious problems in psychoanalytic training. *International Journal of Psychoanalysis, 86*(4): 1143–1609.

Davis, M., & Wallbridge, D. (1981). *Boundary and Space: An Introduction to the Work of D. W. Winnicott*. London: Karnac.

Einstein, A. (1940). *The World As I See It*. London: Watts.

Falzeder, E. (1997). Dreaming of Freud: Freud, and an analysis without end. *Psychoanalytic Inquiry, 17*: 416–427.

Ferenczi, S. (1932). *The Clinical Diary of Sandor Ferenczi*, J. Dupont (Ed.), M. Balint & N. Z. Jackson (Trans.). Cambridge, MA: Harvard University Press, 1988.

Freud, S. (1919a). Lines of advance in psycho-analytic therapy. *S.E., 17*: 157–167.

Gill, S. (2001). Narcissistic vulnerability in supervisees: ego ideals, self-exposure, and narcissistic character defenses. In: S. Gill (Ed.), *The Supervisory Alliance* (pp. 19–34). Northvale, NJ: Jason Aronson.

Kernberg, O. F. (1986). Institutional problems of psychoanalytic education. *Journal of the American Psychoanalytic Association, 34*: 799–834.

Kernberg, O. F. (1996). Thirty methods to destroy the creativity of psychoanalytic candidates. *International Journal of Psychoanalysis, 77*(5): 1031–1040.

Kernberg, O. F. (2000). A concerned critique of psychoanalytic education. *International Journal of Psychoanalysis, 81*: 97–120.

Kernberg, O. F. (2006). The coming changes in psychoanalytic education, Part I. *International Journal of Psychoanalysis, 87*(6): 1649–1674.

Kernberg, O. F. (2007). The coming changes in psychoanalytic education, Part II. *International Journal of Psychoanalysis, 88*(1): 183–202.

Klauber, J. (1983). The identity of the psychoanalyst. In: E. D. Joseph & D. Widlocher (Eds.), *The Identity of the Psychoanalyst* (pp. 41–50). New York: International Universities Press.

Laufer, E. (2007). Personal communication.

Lawrence, D. H. (2007). *The Rainbow*. Harmondsworth: Penguin Classics.

Milner, M. (1957). *On Not Being Able to Paint* (2nd edn). London, Heinemann, 1971.

Norman, J., & Salomonsson, B. (2005). 'Weaving thoughts': a method for presenting and commenting on psychoanalytic case material in peer group. *International Journal of Psychoanalysis, 86*(5): 1281–1298.

Ogden, T. H. (2005). On psychoanalytic supervision. *International Journal of Psychoanalysis*, *86*(5): 1265–1280.

Salomonsson, B., & Badoni, M. (2002). Discussion paper. Conference of the European Psychoanalytical Federation, Prague, April.

Turner, J. (2004). In search of spontaneity. The Madeleine Davis Memorial Lecture, July, The Squiggle Foundation, unpublished.

Werbert, A. (2007). Utopic ideas of cure and joint exploration in psychoanalytic supervision. *International Journal of Psychoanalysis*, *88*: 1391–1408.

Winnicott, D. W. (1945). Primitive emotional development. In: *Collected Papers: Through Paediatrics to Psychoanalysis* (pp. 145–156). London: Tavistock, 1958.

Winnicott, D. W. (1950). Some thoughts on the meaning of the word democracy. In: *The Family and Individual Development* (pp. 218–250). London: Tavistock, 1965.

Winnicott, D. W. (1951). Marion Milner: critical notice of *On Not Being Able To Paint*. In: C. Winnicott, R. Shepherd, & M. Davis (Eds.), *Psychoanalytic Explorations* (pp. 390–392). London: Karnac, 1989).

Winnicott, D. W. (1958). The observation of infants in a set situation. In: *Collected Papers: Through Paediatrics To Psycho-Analysis* (pp. 52–69). London: Tavistock.

Winnicott, D. W. (1960). Ego distortion in terms of true and false self. In: *The Maturational Processes and the Facilitating Environment*. London: Hogarth and the Institute of Psychoanalysis.

Winnicott, D. W. (1970). Talk to doctors, given in St Lukes Church, Hatfield. Unpublished paper cited by Davis and Wallbridge in *Boundary and Space*, 1981.

PART II
INTERVENTIONS

CHAPTER FIVE

Incorporation of an invasive object

Paul Williams

Introduction

T his chapter addresses the experience of "being invaded" that is communicated by certain severely disturbed patients. The complaint can sometimes be couched in terms of bodily suffering and the patient might state that they have the experience of a "foreign body" inside them. It is suggested that these individuals have suffered severe early failure of containment of their projections, while simultaneously incorporating primitive characteristics of the object that have been projected violently into them. An object that invades in this way, it is suggested, experiences a compulsive need to expel unbearable states of mind using others as a repository. The infant incorporates these invasive projections as part of his own mental representational system, normal identification processes being impaired or disrupted. There occurs serious breakdown of processes leading to the development of a sense of self. Clinical examples of how the invasive experience manifests itself in the analytic setting, particularly in the transference and countertransference, are presented. It is argued that this highly complex form of early subject–object interaction (prior to the differentiation of psyche–soma) is more likely to be found in extremely disturbed individuals who are narcissistic or psychotic. Some reflections on the origins of invasive phenomena are provided.

The undermining of symbolic functioning

I shall try to sketch out a way in which symbolic functioning appears to be undermined in certain cases of severe disturbance. The failure I shall discuss reflects a developmental crisis, features of which became apparent to me during the analyses of three patients, two of whom I shall discuss here. Each of the patients, though very different in important respects and brought up in dissimilar circumstances, suffered serious narcissistic disturbances. A characteristic the patients shared was the experience of having incorporated an object with random, invasive tendencies, which, at times, could lead them to the brink of, or into, psychosis. By "incorporation of an invasive object", I wish to convey a primitive, violent introjection of aspects of an object that creates the experience of inundation by the object that can give rise to serious disturbance in the nascent personality. This form of pathological "proto-identification" takes place in early infancy and is consequent upon precocious interaction between infant and object, including , critically, failure of containment and maternal alpha-function (Bion, 1970).

Under normal circumstances, incorporation is the earliest mode of relating in which the infant feels himself to be at one with the other and is unaware of separation between the two personalities (Fenichel, 1945; Searles, 1951; Sterba, 1957). This experience decreases if development proceeds relatively unimpeded. If development is impeded, the experience can persist, leading to an equation between relatedness and engulfment, in which one personality is felt to be devouring the other (Searles, 1951, p. 39). The impulse to unite incorporatively with the other as a defence against separation anxiety has been widely discussed: cf. Freud (1900a, 1933a), Klein (1935), Heimann (1942), Fenichel (1945), Searles (1951), Federn (1952), Greenacre (1958), Segal (1981), Rey (1994), and others (Laplanche & Pontalis, 1972). All note how physical experiences are a characteristic of processes of incorporation, in contrast to the fantasy dimension of introjection into the ego, which assumed importance in Klein's (1935) thinking and which she discusses in the context of incorporative activity and the genesis of psychosis.

The patients I shall describe manifested incorporative self-states in the form of both bodily and psychological symptoms. I shall suggest that they underwent traumatic disruption to the psyche–soma at a time when their sense of self was barely formed and the psyche–soma had yet to undergo differentiation. A primitive introject appears to have been installed in their minds and their experience of their bodies that was held by them to belong to their own self-representational system. Contradictorily, at the same time, this introjected presence was experienced as a concrete presence of a disturbing "foreign body" inside them.

The experience of something that is not a part of the self, yet is confused with the self, can create not only psychic conflict but also incompatible or "heterogeneous" states of mind (Quinodoz, 2001). "Heterogeneity" is denoted as the product of a "heterogeneous constitution of the ego" (Green, 1993). This description reflects Bion's observation that "there is a psychotic personality concealed by neurosis as the psychotic personality is screened by psychosis in the psychotic, that has to be laid bare and dealt with" (1967, p. 63). Heterogeneous patients present for help because they suffer from their heterogeneity, unlike the majority (Quinodoz, 2001). This heterogeneous quality is implicated in the vulnerability and intrapsychic confusion of the patients I shall describe and seems to have affected not only for the way in which these patients related, but also how their thinking developed.

Clinical example 1: James

James, aged twenty-seven, entered analysis after a series of failed relationships culminating in depressive attacks with suicidal ideation. He possessed an unusually high IQ and was capable of abstract levels of thought beyond his years, and of grasping the nub of ideas and arguments. There was a paranoid tinge to many of his observations and his attention to others' motivation seemed compulsive. James was quintessentially a self-made man. He had failed at school, but as an adult had become successful in business. His father, an addict, died in his forties of a drugs overdose. James was a replacement child; a previous son had died, apparently unmourned, ten months before James's birth, his mother having been advised by her doctor to get pregnant again straight away. James's mother seems to have been an unstable woman consumed by hatred and grievances. He said his parents fought continuously during the marriage over affairs each accused the other of having. He recalled as a child sitting in horror in his pyjamas on the stairs while his parents brawled. He left home at sixteen and remained unreconciled to them. He saw his mother again once, when she was unconscious on her deathbed in hospital.

I was struck from the outset by the speed with which James seemed to reach the meaning of his fantasies and dreams. He would get there before me, with impressive intuitions, yet without making me feel excluded. He strove to be a "model" analysand. It became apparent that he needed to control the analysis, subtly and diplomatically, and that he suffered intense anxieties when he did not feel in control. He revealed that his controls were, in fantasy, controls over my thoughts. Why he needed to control my thoughts was not clear to him or me. His dream life provided evidence of a serious disturbance of the self. He dreamed repeatedly that he had murdered someone. The body, a male, lay buried under a road; it was a secret, but the police were piecing together clues and were on his trail. He developed insomnia to avoid the nightmares. James's compliant, controlling behaviour decreased as he became more depressed and nihilistic during the second year of analysis. In one session, he lay contemplating suicide, and said, with piercing dejection, "I came into analysis for consolation. I knew nothing could ever come of my life."

I was affected by his comment, which was said with no trace of defensiveness, and my response—an intense sadness—persisted after the session. I realised that I had been struck by, to paraphrase Marion Milner, a "thought too big for its concept".[1] I wondered whether analysis-as-consolation masked, for James, the site of an experience of annihilation anxiety. This phenomenon, which has been referred to as "a memorial space for psychic death" (Grand, 2000), denotes unspeakable, traumatic events that are felt always to be present, yet must remain absent. Metabolisation through language is the means we possess of approaching such catastrophe, yet this is disbarred, as language is experienced as unable to approximate the scale of the events involved.

I shall pass to a period in the third year, during which James decided he wanted to quit analysis and his suicidal feelings took a psychotic turn. He had become disillusioned and was prone to long, angry silences. "Is this all there is?", he would complain bitterly, following stretches of withdrawal. He could be abusive, accusing me of keeping him in analysis to maintain the vain illusion that I could help him.

If he felt I might be close to understanding what he was feeling, he would lash out contemptuously: for example, "This [analysis] is hypocrisy. It deceives, it lies, it's wanking. It's a middle-class fix: you haven't got the first idea about me or what people like me go through." He told me he felt burned out, disgusted by himself, and hopeless. The nightmare of having killed someone preoccupied him, including during the day, making it increasingly difficult for him to function in his work. As his condition worsened, I became anxious for his safety, as he was immersed in what appeared to be a developing transference psychosis. This situation continued for some weeks. I talked with him about his profound disillusion with me and the unmanageable feelings of despair and rage this engendered.

An event occurred in which James communicated his despair in a way that I felt revealed his having incorporated an object characterised specifically by invasiveness. James had spent most of this particular Wednesday session in tormented distraction at his inability to control his feelings of disdain towards his female partner, whom he was afraid would leave him. He described unpleasant scenes between them that left him confused and suicidal. The idea that there might be no change possible appalled him.

He twisted and turned on the couch, as though in bodily pain. I told him how afraid I thought he was of becoming more and more like his parents, at home and here with me, and how feelings of growing fear, resentment, and hatred of his partner and me pushed him into a terrible sense of failure. Feeling trapped in hate and fear, like his parents, destroyed his power and hope, turning him into a needy, hopeless child whom he hated. The only way out he could imagine, in the absence of anyone to help him, was to kill himself, but even this did not work as he still did not have anyone who understood what he was going through. James's writhing stopped and his body relaxed. He appeared to be relieved at having his confusion and fear acknowledged. However, he became more restless and what appeared to be a more thoughtful silence turned out to be not the case at all. He slowly and purposefully got off the couch, stared at me—or, rather, through me—and shouted with unbridled hatred, "Keep your platitudes to yourself, you stupid fucking moron!"

This outburst of violent, narcissistic rage seemed also to embody a psychotic effort to try to rid himself of an alien presence or state of mind, of which I appeared to have been the incarnation. He fell silent, walked unsteadily round the room, distracted, and eventually sat on the edge of the couch, trembling. I felt assaulted by the attack; fear and anger welled up inside me. I could not think of anything appropriate to say, only a wish to protect myself. I felt stripped of a capacity to contain the situation. James sat for some time holding his head in his hands. I recall the session ended with me asking him whether he felt able to manage getting home. The next day, James was in a distressed, confused state. "I don't understand. I can't remember it clearly . . . it is like a fog . . . something just came over me. I don't know how to explain it . . . I'm sorry. I feel a bit like it now, kind of stunned. My head feels full . . . there is so much going on that I can't think and my legs feel like lead . . . like my body wants to collapse. I don't quite know where I am in this. I don't know why I should scream at you like that . . ."

He continued in this bewildered, anxious way that seemed to combine guilt about what he felt he had done to me and confused feelings of dread and relief at having lost control of himself. I said to him that, although he felt a need to apologise, what was striking to me was that he had allowed me to see some of his deepest feelings, including those about me, without camouflage, something that I doubted he had done often, if ever, in his life. He said, "I don't think I had any choice; it doesn't feel like I did . . . it wasn't taking a risk. Something exploded. It was anger but there's something not right about that . . . it's not the whole feeling. Something in me could have killed you. I wasn't thinking this when it happened but it makes me think that something in me wanted to smash and smash you and shut you up so I didn't have to listen any more, ever again. As I say this it reminds me of my mother and how I couldn't stand the shouting but I couldn't do anything about it. Maybe I was fighting her . . . maybe being her— or being like her somehow—but in another way I was outside it, watching it going on . . . or rather, it was happening to me."

He talked about a "blizzard" having descended on him, pains in his head and a heavy sensation in his body. I was led to think that he had been in a psychotic transference. During the ensuing weeks,

James experienced much confusion and worsening bouts of with-drawal. Further attacks occurred, often when I least expected them. They seemed to be precipitated by contact with James's infantile self that he despised: that is, when he felt a childlike need for me or when I said something that made him feel understood, it roused an invol-untarily, psychotic sadism against both me and him. At times, his withdrawals took on what I thought was a narcissistic, even psycho-pathic quality: in these moments it was as though I ceased to exist for him; I had been obliterated from his internal world. Although each of James' attacks had seemed to free something in him initially, I became aware that his rages could be accompanied by a malignant, anti-life attitude that destroyed opportunities for his infantile needs to be met. What had been a form of letting go could, at times, resemble a sadis-tic, narcissistic defence. James's responses to his attacks varied from obliviousness to persecutory anxiety to acute paranoia. Yet, after one outburst, he commented, "I feel bad about what just happened. I hate you and you make me furious with the things you say, but I think just now it was out of proportion—my reaction, that is."

I queried his feelings, and he said, "I don't know how real my hatred of you is sometimes. It wells up . . . it is true. But when it happens it feels like an automatic thing . . . a gut reaction . . . some-times it doesn't matter what you're saying: it erupts and I have to silence you. You're somebody I have to keep out."

I felt that James was experiencing anxiety at feelings of frustration and rage towards me, but was also confused by a psychotic identifi-cation with an invasive object that was responsible for precipitating his attacks in order to try omnipotently to annihilate our relationship, in order to provide delusional protection against dependence on me. Non-psychotic and psychotic aspects of his personality seemed to vie for expression in this way. James's behaviour outside the session reflected this confusion, as seen in this example: at home, one Sunday, he heard a dog squealing in the street. He told me he had "no choice but to dash out to help it". He found a large dog belonging to some drunken youths pinning down a smaller dog by the throat. He dived between the dogs without thought for his own safety, prising open the jaws of the larger dog until the smaller one was freed and ran off. The youths turned on James, but James's unassailable resolve caused them to back off, without violence. In his session, he could not account for his impulsive behaviour, was not proud of it, and yet felt oddly better.

He showed little indication of excessive guilt or confusion. He simply had to separate the dogs, he said, and he could see that many people would think that what he did was dangerous and crazy. He wanted to know why he had been compelled to act. Later in the session, he remarked, "The thing with the dogs makes something clearer to me: it sounds obvious but it isn't. It does sound mad, but I think I thought that the fight that was going on was my fault, but it wasn't. Everything I did when I was a kid was wrong."

Although I did not say it to him, I had been struck by the desperate quality of his compulsive engagement in this conflict, as though only he could rescue the dog. I wondered about his omnipotence, about a child whose infant self was threatened with annihilation by savage attacks and about his witnessing repeatedly hate-filled fights between his parents. James's insight permitted work on feelings of "being intrinsically wrong", as he put it, in the eyes of his mother. He conceived of this as:

> Nothing I did was right. It wasn't only about making mistakes or doing things that annoyed her. I got everything wrong, as a matter of principle ... when I was small I thought I could please her and I tried to, but by the time I went to school I think I felt defeated. Nothing worked ... she couldn't bear to look at me ... not disapproval exactly, although there was a lot of that ... more that I was a terrible burden she'd had forced on her and couldn't stand.

> There were times when she could suddenly be nice but this lasted only for a few moments before she changed. I stayed out of her way, but I would forget and got screamed at. It took years for me to realise that the whole thing was impossible ... she was on a different planet. I know that by the time I was seven or eight, or earlier, I had thoughts that I'd be better off dead. I would feel relieved when I went to bed that I'd got through another day and pray that I wouldn't wake up. For years I went to bed early to blot things out.

Analyst (A):   You feel you died as a child.

Patient (P):   I do [cries] ... everything went wrong and I have been stuck with it all my life. I think my childhood was ruined ... now I am like her and I ruin it myself.

A: You feel you died and yet somehow you managed to go on; not only go on. but do well eventually.

P: I can't explain it. The only thing that comes to mind is that
                     I realised a few years ago talking to my grandmother that
                     my mother must have been delighted that I was born
                     healthy and lived. She must have been desperate not to lose
                     another child. My grandmother said I was doted on—given
                     special orange juice and supplements to build me up. But
                     she told me that the marriage was in trouble and my mother
                     started having affairs when I was born. I do recall different
                     men came to the house from as far back as I can remember.
                     I don't know . . . maybe I was made to feel special in some
                     way and that gave me a kind of good start. What I've
                     always felt is that my life wasn't my life. I felt I was some-
                     body because of what I did for others.

The analysis focused, in the transference, on his sense of having
died as a child, and how his attacks and withdrawals defended him
from the painful experience that his attempts to live felt unviable and
a lie, so damaged and confused was his sense of his own self. Gradually, he became more able to work at differentiating feelings of love
and hate, on the one hand, and a welling up of a psychotic rage
against me on the other, which represented an incorporation of a
narcissistic, invasive object. These eruptions were preceded by a vis-
ceral sensation, blood coursing through his veins or tinnitus-like ring-
ing in his ears; then came the outburst that bore a resemblance to
accounts of his mother's aggression. As these more extreme defences
came under more control (they ceased in the seventh year of the analysis) he told me he had always had a "wild side" to him of which he
was ashamed. He felt the same hatred of people his mother had
shown, with no justification. He did not evade responsibility for this,
but was concerned that it did not represent the complexity of his feelings, even at his most angry. He described it as a "default extremism"
or a "scorched-earth policy". James had indicated how frightened
he had been of his parents, but the scale of his intimidation at his
mother's mood changes (which lay behind his identification with
them) only now became apparent. Her attacks had left him profoundly disorientated as a child. He described how his mother's
violence was a part of his life from as early as he could remember, and
how he had been quite convinced that he had provoked it. He began
to engage in similar attacks from the age of about seven, he thought,
initially on his mother's dog, which he had tormented. The need to

attack others "when they got close" became something he was unable to be prevent.

After much work on the defacement of his personality and his primitive identification with invasiveness, his attacks on me receded and he acquired greater tolerance for his emotions and their limitations. He also began a more articulated grieving process that was paralleled by a reluctance to comply with others' demands. His relationship with his female partner improved and they began a family. The love between him and his baby daughter, though sometimes painful, afforded him awareness of his value to another person, something he had not previously experienced. This helped to offset his sense of loss at what he had missed in his life because of his behaviour. In the eighth year of his analysis he said, "I feel I have to pay attention every day to that child I was. It's like visiting someone in hospital or a grave. If I don't think of him or hold his hand, I can feel lost. I will never let him go again."

I felt that James had buried his childhood identity and evolved an impenetrable, seamless second skin that afforded him a false sense of integration (cf. Symington, 1985; Winnicott, 1960). Within this illusory maturity lay an experience of being unrecognised for himself and uncontained in his feelings. When James's true, alive self stirred, he was susceptible to fears of abandonment and disintegration, triggering, among other things, a defensive, imitative introject of an object that could not bear loss (and, hence, life) and which reacted invasively, generating narcissistic rage and masochistic compliance in an attempt to preserve an illusory sense of coherent selfhood.

Clinical example 2: Ms B

Ms B, aged forty-nine, was diagnosed in her thirties with a paranoid psychosis, although I came to think that she suffered from a borderline personality disorder. She came into analysis thirteen years ago. The middle child of a working-class family, Ms B complained she had had no relationship with her mother, who passed her from birth on to her father because her mother favoured the first child, a boy (her other sibling is also male). Her rage at her mother's rejection of her was unremitting—"she never showed any sign of wanting me—never" was her refrain. The father appears to have been paranoid and periodically incapacitated by his difficulties. Ms B said that at around two or three years of age, she had retreated into a fantasy world, becoming friendly with creatures from outer space who promised to take her away. She also came to believe that she was a famous actress. She maintained that she and her father had had an incestuous relationship up to her fourteenth year. She told me she had acquired a manager, a pimp-like figure called the "Director", who controlled many of her actions, feelings, and thoughts. "He" was to emerge in the analysis as a pseudo-hallucination. After four months of analysis, Ms B reported the following dream:

> "I am being fed. A hand slaps me across the face hard. Then I am on a terrorist exercise, rolling down a hill clutching a male officer. We fall off a cliff or shelf."

I interpreted that she was letting me know of a catastrophe, a loss in her life that she felt could never be made up, and that she had turned to men and sex to try to compensate. I rapidly became an object of idealisation, while her violent, perverse pathology was acted out, mainly sexually. By the second year, Ms B had begun to cut herself; she took a non-fatal overdose and jumped from a moving train, injuring herself. A psychosis asserted itself. This is a dream from that time.

> "A minibus crashes through the front of a food store. There is a huge explosion. My older brother helpfully leads people away. There are many dead pregnant women. I touch the stomach of one but there is no life. Tins of food are embedded in people's faces. They are missing arms and legs. The manager says, 'We carry on, we stay open.' I try to stop him but I can't."

She was unable to consider the themes of murder or dead mothers and babies in this or other dreams. Her behaviour became more disturbed and she was hospitalised following attempts to swallow a lethal dose of lithium medication. After a two-year period in which there was a good deal of extreme disturbance (which I do not have space to describe here), the direction of the analysis began to shift towards a more verbalised, transference-orientated hatred of her dependence on me. The patient moved from a predominantly paranoid position and acting out to one of sadistic, abusive attacks. From having complained of abuse, she became an abuser, of me and the analysis. For the purposes of this paper, I want to illustrate how the patient seems to have incorporated an invasive object that combines characteristics of the patient's projective activity with features of both parents.

In a Monday session during the second year of her analysis, Ms B complained at length that she was no good because girls do not get love. Love from mothers is "lesbian", she said, and this, she felt, was the most awful thing in the world. The way to get love was to be a boy like her older brother, or like her father. She was a boy, really, she suggested: so she could do anything boys could. She recounted how when she masturbated she fantasised that she was a man and that women queued up to have sex with her. She sometimes strapped a dildo to her waist when she went out to make her feel like a man. She talked further about childhood fantasies of being a powerful boy and how she had changed her sex (although the patient was talking about her fantasies, I was unsure whether she actually believed she was male as she spoke).

> A: I can see what you mean about the advantages you felt boys had, but I'm wondering about and remembering that you were born a girl; where is she? What has happened to the longing for love you wanted from your mother that you have told me about? You often tell me how lonely you feel and how much you want to talk to me, especially during weekends. That person seems to me like a little girl who feels her needs are being ignored.
>
> P: (becoming agitated and shouting): Keep out! Lock the doors ... the walls are moving. Lock the doors, shut up, lock them! Keep them out!
>
> A: Something I have said has alarmed you. Can you tell me what's happening?
>
> P: It's the Director ... he's telling me somebody is coming in. They're coming in and they're going to get me ... they're going to kill me!

This intrusion of the psychotic "Director" figure was to happen frequently and exerted enormous influence over the patient. The technical problems associated with interpreting these paradoxical "influencing machines", which purportedly protect, but in practice subvert and deny the patient good experiences of objects, are obviously considerable. What I wish to stress here is that these paranoid outbursts

revealed, in my view, not only Ms B's deep-seated fears of the consequences of her own projected destructiveness and invasiveness, but
also evidence of miscarriage of early introjective processes. The invasive narrative of Ms B's "Director" (which always involved accusations of people getting in, breaking in, stealing and attacking, when
not maniacally advocating sex) displayed elements of concordance
with the patient's accounts of her father's powerful paranoid anxieties
and of the rejections and indifference she attributed to her mother,
which she countered by intensifying her own projective activity.
Observations by her about her father and mother over several years
of analysis, often inadvertent and spontaneous, were consistent in
these respects and were paralleled by ways in which she herself could
respond compulsively when in the grip of a psychotic transference
characterised by invasive fantasies that defended her against feelings
of fragmentation. The "Director" seemed to afford her an illusory
sense of agency and ego-coherence when in crisis. "His" underlying
objective was, as I have suggested, to influence the patient's ego to
reject human contact and pursue a course of pathological, narcissistic
withdrawal, reflecting her primary narcissistic crisis, felt (delusion-
ally) to be more reliable.

Invasive experiences and the self

To avoid misunderstanding, I want to underscore that I do not propose in this paper a concordance between this patient's and her
father's or mother's personalities, or a linear causality between the
external object's influence and the patient's fantasy life. There
appeared to be no direct equivalence between her father's projective
activity and her identification with invasiveness—or, for that matter,
between the patient's narcissism and the mother's own psychopathology. The same applies to James and to any patient with this kind of
invasive disorder, I believe. The intrapsychic situation is likely to be
complex, involving aspects of the patient's infantile sense of self
becoming confused with the sequelae of uncontained projections
and with the introjection of projective activity of the object. This is
commonplace in many severely disturbed individuals. Identification
with the aggressor might be evident, but the impact of the processes
I am describing has a primitive, fragmentating outcome linked, I

suggest, to threats of annihilation of the core sense of self. Inadequately contained and violently projected part-objects are forcibly installed in the psyche of the infant, generating psycho-physical pain, confusion and chronic anxiety. The process involved comprises massive splitting and projection by the object into the infant, which has the effect not only of repudiating the infant's own projections, but also of overwhelming the psychic reality of the infant by extreme external stimulation. Gaddini (1992, p. 4) offers an account of how such a crisis could evolve. He reports on how normal imitation or mimicry—an oral introjective activity which takes place prior to identification—might miscarry under precocious conditions of oral frustration which cause disturbance to the psycho–oral area and, therefore, introjective mechanisms. Imitative introjections, instead of acting as precursors to normal introjections, might substitute for true introjections and cause internalisation processes to fail. Imitation could be used defensively to avoid subsequent introjective conflicts. The child's fragmented personality develops on the basis of these failed identification processes, imitation being substituted for object relating. Weiss (1960) distinguished imitation from identification, stressing that "no simple imitation" takes place in the infant's mind. There is, he suggests, a form of "reproduction" or "autoplastic duplication" (following Ferenczi) in which the organism acquires and modifies its shape and functional parts. A defensive use of autoplastic duplication probably gives rise to the seeming concordance between primitive elements of the patient's disturbed personality and invasive projections. Failure of containment and breach of the "contact barrier" (Bion, 1962), having rendered the individual vulnerable to excessive permeability, sets the condition for impairment of the development of the self through mimetic introjection.

Such disturbed early attachment processes can create, as in my patients, a backcloth for an amalgam of projections and introjected elements, expressed both corporeally and mentally. There is no space here to discuss the relationships between phantasy, projection, and introjection in these states, especially the influence of unconscious sexual phantasies. However, the organising roles of unconscious phantasy and memory, the impact of deferred action (*après coup*) and the re-elaboration of psychic reality that follows, would need to be taken into account to properly clarify the complex amalgam of projected and introjected elements. The intricacy of these early object-relations experiences—what might be termed metaphorically as encounters with "fractal objects"[2]—is identifiable through attention to a range of transference communications, through which it becomes possible to identify, *a posteriori*, introjective patterns that underlie the failures in identification. Such investigation is analogous to identifying the "sensitivity to initial conditions" in deterministic chaos theory, through which one or more variables can come to have an enduring, disproportionately perturbing effect on a complex system.[3]

If we think of the self as a developmental achievement deriving from the infant's need to mentally represent internal states, using the mind of another, then recognition of the intentionality of the care-giver's mind permits the infant to establish an internal representation of himself as a truly separate, intentional being. The quality of the care-giver's image of the infant as an intentional being is critical for the formation of this representation. If care-giving fails to contain and reflect the infant's experiences and anxieties, a misrepresentation of the infant will be internalised, corresponding to the partial or distorted representational capacity of the other infiltrating the fantasy life of the infant. The patients I have described experienced, during this early developmental phase, a pronounced failure to have their projections contained and metabolised, leading to an experience of emotional violence. Assailed by invasive projective activity, the trauma was an amalgam of inchoate external and internal experiences, the residuum or precipitate of which corresponded to the "foreign body" experience lodged in the unconscious and in the body, and which lacks mental representational status. Attempts to repel invasiveness through the counter-use of projective identification would be likely to heighten the intensity of the pathological interaction, as it is the identification with invasiveness (associated with projections by infant and object) that is employed defensively.

The infant's body is implicated in the trauma, in that it carries the status of a primary object to which the infant relates and which can become installed as an internal object. Laufer (2002) has discussed how uncontained bodily states, due to poor handling of the infant by the care-giver, can create adverse developmental conditions. I think that such deprived conditions pertain to incidences of invasiveness. Indeed, extremely deprived infants might "invite" invasion, or, at least, incorporate avidly powerful projections as a consequence of extreme need. Those who are compelled to expel unbearable mental states force the mind of the other to deal with what the invasive object's mind cannot. I became aware that, in my patients, once an offending mental state has been expelled, an invasive object ceases to have use for the subject as an object and reverts to a position of narcissism. Perhaps it is more accurate to say that the invasive object returns to a narcissistic state of unconscious fusion with an idealised internal part-object. Developmentally, managing a foreign body inside destroys mental space allocated to symbolising activity by the ego. Identification with characteristics of invasiveness disrupts processes of integration of experiences necessary for secondary-process thinking. The individual who has incorporated an invasive object is likely to feel unstable, depleted of personal meaning, and occupied or haunted by unidentifiable bodily perceptions. Complaints of feeling controlled, alienated, possessed, ill, or diseased could accompany these self-states. During analysis, the transference neurosis can come to resemble a psychosis, with the patient able to think only intermittently and prone to interaction that reflects the dynamics of invasion. The patient might employ stereotypical ideas and language displaying power without conviction, and, if pressed, might become disorganised. Identity diffusion can occur and there could be acting out. Such patients are unsure of who they are, and, under severe stress, communicate by proxy through their bodies.

Intrusion and invasion

Although, by definition, invasive objects intrude, I have found it useful in my clinical work to distinguish between intrusive and invasive objects. Intrusive objects, at least in my experience, tend to be motivated by a need to occupy or become a feature of the subject for reasons that can include parasitism and sadism. Invasive objects seek to expel unbearable, infantile conflicts using, for the most part, excessive projective mechanisms. Expulsion is compulsive and violent, and they do not appear to strive to colonise or become a feature of the subject in the same way, as their aim is to mould a repository for evacuation prior to retreat to a pathological narcissistic position. The identity of the recipient of the projected state is unimportant: securing a mind into which the state can be indiscriminately jammed is the goal. I think of invasive projections as akin to "psychosomatic missiles" that are expelled or "fired" into the other. The dream of Ms B, in which tins of food are embedded in faces and unborn foetuses are killed, is a vivid image that reflects oral invasiveness. Ms B's failure to internalise benign representations of her mother induced a developmental crisis of critical proportions at the oral stage, exposing her to uncontrolled envy and murderous feelings towards her mother and brother. Perhaps her gender confusion even contained a wish to *be* her brother, as a way, in phantasy, of attempting to resolve her identification problems. She seems to have violently rejected her mother, incorporated aspects of her mother's rejecting attitude, and become consumed by fantasies of invasion, also echoing themes in her account of her father's paranoid personality. I thought that a claustro-agoraphobic dilemma in relation to her mother (Rey, 1994) had forced her to turn to her father and assume a phallically omnipotent stance in relation to her objects. Her abnormal superego (O'Shaughnessy, 1999) usurped central ego functions, directing her thinking predominantly around the theme of invasiveness via the psychotic figure of the "Director". The fluidity and confusion of identificatory processes in Ms B's early life seem to have rendered her vulnerable to feeling inundated and overwhelmed, and, subsequently, she experienced herself as having little or no core personality of her own. Fonagy and Target (1998a) have discussed how violence in certain patients might be employed in an attempt to establish a sense of who they are, and I think the advent of Ms B's "Director" probably reflects such a process. Interestingly, after twelve years of treatment, Ms B reported that she was no longer sure whether sexual intercourse had occurred between her and her father. How true this statement is I do not know, but it made me wonder to what extent it is possible that incorporation of aggressive, sexualised part-objects of the type I have described readily lead a disturbed infant's mind to phantasise, via the somatic dimension of the incorporative process and confusion between inner and outer reality, that sexual contact has taken place.

James, in contrast to Ms B, incorporated the impact of a refusal to acknowledge his very personality. This derived from what appears to have been projections by a narcissistically disordered mother unable to mourn the death of her first child and who became, in André Green's words, "centrally phobic" to the experience of loss (Williams, 2000). James's feelings of authenticity were destroyed and he consigned himself to living out a counterfeit, shame-filled life in identification with this denial of his own existence and his brother's death. It is possible that there are different forms of incorporation of invasive objects. For example, the impact of a projectively invasive mother, as experienced by bulimic patients, might point to how projected "missiles" can later be reprojected physically as well as mentally (Williams, 1997). Invasion fantasies also feature in the psychodynamics of anorexia (Lawrence, 2002).

In certain psychoses, auditory or command hallucinations can reflect incorporated aspects of objects, drawing on unsymbolised sexual and aggressive impulses (cf. Jackson & Williams, 1994). Perhaps the dynamics of rape and the implications for the types of personalities involved merit study from the perspective of experiences of invasion by an object. It seems that invasive experiences can occur under a variety of circumstances and are linked to faulty or over-fluid identificatory processes. What they have in common is forcible introjection and embodiment of pathological internal part-objects that disrupt ego functioning and the evolution of a sense of self. The confusion with which the subject lives reflects multiple axes of relatedness (projective and introjective) to these part-objects—a subject about which we still know relatively little.

The literature on severe early object-relations conflicts touches on issues raised in this paper. Sterba (1957) and Anna Freud (1951) studied the impact of oral invasion that leads to overwhelming identification with a rejecting object. Heimann (1942) described miscarriages of sublimation linked to experiences of intrusiveness. Rosenfeld (1975) depicted the clinical consequences of introjected part-objects, particularly their "mafia-like" qualities that purport to protect the ego through intimidation while countermanding opportunities for recovery and development. Sohn (1985) identified in sudden, unprovoked assaults a form of primitive identification with a violent, invasive, uncontaining object he terms the "identificate". Gaddini (1992), Winnicott (1960), and others have made the observation that the primitive self of the infant that reverts to a pathological use of mimesis can experience attempts at integration as a threat to the self if a fragmented history of identification has come to be relied upon defensively, a defence that perpetuates developmental arrest. Bion (1962, 1963, 1977), above all, identified the consequences of failure to contain an infant's projections and how this gives rise to states of terrifying persecution. There is consensus, irrespective of theoretical persuasion, that, without the establishment of a "third" position based on a capacity to incorporate the "mother-as-environment" (Winnicott, 1967), leading to the acquisition of "reflective function" (Fonagy & Target, 1998b), "binocularity" (Bion, 1967), or "intersubjectivity" (Trevarthen, 1993), ego capacity is consigned to managing psychic trauma. The examples I give indicate that no "third" position had been established. If characterological disturbances within the parents are projected into the offspring throughout development, leaving no stage of childhood untouched, a third position is probably unattainable. Object-relations disturbances are lifelong, starting in infancy and having an impact on each unfolding developmental stage (Martindale, 2004, personal communication). The appearance of invasive objects in treatment is often seen as unpredictable and based on disorganised patterns of attachment (cf. Fonagy, 2000). I think that these invasive assaults, on examination, are often more predictable than they appear, being patterned according to the ego's phobic responses to particular constellations of primitive affect (Green, 2000) that result in the body–ego consequences described. Developments in neuroscience confirm that assaults on the psyche–soma of infants during the first year of life can indicate loss of cortical function in the fronto-temporal areas (Perry, 1997). It seems clear that the long-term neurological and psychological impact of invasive experiences may be significant in understanding serious disturbance in infant development.

To conclude, I suggest that incorporated aspects of an invasive object become confused with the nascent infant's self and are subject to idealisation. In psychoanalysis, the prospect of relinquishment of a mimetically constructed, incorporative relationship for one with an ambivalently cathected, separate object can be experienced as a catastrophe, as this is equated with loss of the ongoing sense of self. It might be necessary for the patient to endure a period of psychotic confusion as the process of unincorporation and dis-identification takes place. Without this, the invasive object remains an active object in the unconscious. The patient might attack the therapeutic process in order to prevent the experience of catastrophic change (Bion, 1965). This defensive activity is, in my view, a response to the confusion that derives from experiencing a "foreign body" inside, which must be got rid of if disruption to psychic functioning is to be halted and personality development restored, but which the patient feels cannot be forsaken as it is experienced as a part of the self.

Notes

1. The title of an abstract picture painted by Marion Milner.
2. A "fractal object" is a structure that repeats itself infinitely and remains identical whatever its scale.
3. I am grateful to Jean-Michel Quinodoz for the observation that "sensitivity to initial conditions" refers to one variable among many being responsible for modifying an entire course of events. It is possible to predict only the short-term evolution of such a system; however, it is also possible, *a posteriori*, to go back to initial events and to determine one or more factors that might have triggered the perturbation of the system. Quinodoz (1997) has discussed this analogical model in the context of psychic change.

References

Bion, W. R. (1962). The psycho-analytic study of thinking. II—A theory of thinking. *International Journal of Psychoanalysis, 43*: 306–310 [reprinted in *Second Thoughts*, 1967].

Bion, W. R. (1963). *Elements of Psycho-analysis*. London: William Heinemann [reprinted London: Karnac, 1977].

Bion, W. R. (1965). *Transformations*. London: Karnac, 1984.

Bion, W. R. (1967). *Second Thoughts: Selected Papers on Psycho-analysis*. London: Karnac.

Bion, W. R. (1970). *Attention and Interpretation*. London: Tavistock.

Bion, W. R. (1977). *Seven Servants*. New York: Jason Aronson.

Federn, P. (1952). *Ego Psychology and the Psychoses*. London: Imago, 1953.

Fenichel, O. (1945). *The Psychoanalytic Theory of Neurosis*. London: Routledge & Kegan Paul.

Fonagy, P. (2000). Attachment and borderline personality disorder. *Journal of the American Psychoanalytic Association, 48*:1129–1146.

Fonagy, P., & Target, M. (1998a). Towards understanding violence: the use of the body and the role of the father. In: R. Perelberg (Ed.), *Psychoanalytic Understanding of Violence and Suicide*. London: Routledge.

Fonagy, P., & Target, M. (1998b). Mentalization and the changing aims of child psychoanalysis. *Psychoanalytic Dialogue, 8*: 87–114.

Freud, A. (1951). Negativism and emotional surrender. Paper presented to the International Congress, Amsterdam.

Freud, S. (1900a). *The Interpretation of Dreams. S.E.*, 4–5. London: Hogarth.

Freud, S. (1933a). *New Introductory Lectures on Psycho-analysis. S.E., 22.* London: Hogarth.

Gaddini, E. (1992). *A Psychoanalytic Theory of Infantile Experience.* London: New Library of Psychoanalysis.

Grand, S. (2000). *The Reproduction of Evil: A Clinical and Cultural Perspective.* Hillsdale, NJ: Analytic Press.

Green, A. (1993). *The Work of the Negative,* A. Weller (Trans.). London: Free Association Books, 1999. [Le travail du négatif. Paris: Editions de Minuit.]

Green, A. (2000). The central phobic position: a new formulation of the free association method. *International Journal of Psychoanalysis, 81:* 429–451.

Greenacre, P. (1958). Early psychical determinants in the development of the sense of identity. *Journal of the American Psychoanalytic Association,* 6: 612–627.

Heimann, P. (1942). A contribution to the problem of sublimation and its relation to processes of internalization. *International Journal of Psycho-analysis, 23:* 8–17.

Jackson, M., & Williams, P. (1994). Unimaginable storms: a search for meaning in psychosis. London: Karnac.

Klein, M. (1935). A contribution to the psychogenesis of manic-depressive states. In: *Love, Guilt and Reparation and Other Works.* London: Hogarth.

Laplanche, J., & Pontalis, J.-B. (1972). *Dictionary of Psychoanalysis.* London: Hogarth.

Laufer, E. (2002). The body as an internal object. Paper presented as the Spring Lecture for the Centre for the Advancement of Psychoanalytic Studies, London.

Lawrence, M. (2002). Body, mother, mind, anorexia, femininity and the intrusive object. *International Journal of Psychoanalysis, 83:* 837–850.

O'Shaughnessy, E. (1999). Relating to the superego. *International Journal of Psychoanalysis, 80:* 861–870.

Perry, B. (1997). Incubated in terror: neuro-developmental factors in the cycle of violence. In: J. Osofsky (Ed.), *Children in a Violent Society* (pp. 124–149). New York: Guilford Press.

Quinodoz, D. (2001). The psychoanalyst of the future: wise enough to dare to be mad at times. *International Journal of Psychoanalysis, 82:* 235–248.

Quinodoz, J.-M. (1997). Transitions in psychic structures in the light of deterministic chaos theory. *International Journal of Psychoanalysis, 78:* 699–718.

Rey, H. (1994). Universals of psychoanalysis in the treatment of psychotic and borderline states. London: Free Association Books.

Rosenfeld, H. (1975). *Impasse and Interpretation*. London: Tavistock.

Searles, H. (1951). Data concerning certain manifestations of incorporation. In: *Collected Papers on Schizophrenia and Related Subjects*. New York: International Universities Press, 1965.

Segal, H. (1981). *The Work of Hanna Segal: A Kleinian Approach to Clinical Practice*. Northvale, NJ: Jason Aronson.

Sohn, L. (1985). Narcissistic organization, projective identification, and the formation of the identificate. *International Journal of Psychoanalysis, 66*: 201–213 [reprinted in E. B. Spillius (Ed.). *Melanie Klein Today: Developments in Theory and Practice. Vol. 1: Mainly Theory* (pp. 271–292. London: Tavistock/Routledge,1988].

Sterba, R. (1957). Oral invasion and self defence. *International Journal of Psychoanalysis, 38*: 204–208.

Symington, J. (1985). The survival function of primitive omnipotence. *International Journal of Psychoanalysis, 66*: 481–487.

Trevarthen, C. (1993). The self born in intersubjectivity: the psychology of an infant communicating. In: U. Neisser (Ed.), *The Perceived Self* (pp. 121–173). Cambridge: Cambridge University Press.

Weiss, E. (1960). *The Structure and Dynamics of the Human Mind*. New York: Grune and Stratton.

Williams, G. (1997). Reflections on some dynamics of eating disorders: 'No entry' defences and foreign bodies. *International Journal of Psychoanalysis, 78*: 927–941.

Williams, P. (2000). The central phobic position. A new formulation of *The Free Association Method* by André Green. *International Journal of Psychoanalysis, 81*(5): 1045–1060.

Winnicott, D. W. (1960). Ego distortion in terms of true and false self. In: *The Maturational Process and the Facilitating Environment* (pp. 140–152). London: Hogarth, 1964.

Winnicott, D. W. (1967). The location of cultural experience. *International Journal of Psychoanalysis, 48*: 368–372.

CHAPTER SIX

Boundary issues in the recovery from trauma and abuse

John Keene

Introduction

This paper describes the evolution of the author's perception that his patient's move from passive acceptance to taking control of boundaries both of her body and its symbolic equivalents, and accepting responsibility for her states of mind were aspects of the patient's psychological functioning which had been badly disrupted in her history of early trauma and abuse. The acting out of the determining issues in and around the analytic frame can be seen to be crucial issues in her recovery. Some patients stretch our technique and our thinking more than others. David Riley (2005), among others, has written about the variations between analysts as to the degree to which the patient is required to fit the analyst's technique or the analyst to find a way to relate to a particular patient. Marjorie Brierley put her characteristically Independent view of this dilemma in 1943.

> Naturally I approach every patient with a full quota of implicit rather than explicit theoretical and technical preconceptions. On the whole it seems to me that these pre-conceptions are of the nature of a chart on

which the patient plots his own pattern. They don't force any shape on the pattern itself but they certainly influence the ways in which I apprehend the pattern and the terms in which I describe it to him. But I am more inclined to alter my pre-conceived notions to fit the patient's new pattern than to cut the pattern to fit my notions. The effort to understand in order to help is also a continuous process of learning from the patient. (King & Steiner, 1991, p. 620)

I shall discuss three key episodes in an analysis where my flexibility was much valued by the patient, although she was also threatened by it. In analysing this challenging patient, I was encouraged both by colleagues and by Sandler's (1983) account of the importance and prevalence of analyst's "unofficial theories". Sandler observed that psychoanalytic theory is by no means a complete and integrated system, so that, alongside our official theories, we often have to develop our own co-existing idiosyncratic theories to understand individual patients. These *might* be clear to us, but equally, or more often, are preconscious and closely related to the analyst's character. They might remain out of awareness, particularly where they challenge "official" models of theory and technique, but we might gradually become aware of them through noting what we find ourselves saying to our patients. In the case I shall discuss, the patient experienced helplessness in certain aspects of her being, and particularly over "ownership" of her body and her feelings. Gradually, the question of "boundary control" featured more and more in my thinking until it became the focus of a piece of acting out in the transference which led to major changes in her relationships in the outside world.

The analysis

After failing in her inititative to repair some key relationships, Ms A sought analysis as a final attempt to find a life for herself that would be worth living and to keep her from suicide. She had turned down several analysts whom she had found too frightening to talk to. During the consultation, there was a repeated oscillation between approach and avoidance, with every move towards closer engagement or distancing herself causing an outburst of anxiety. She said that she feared "falling apart" between sessions. Then she became frightened at the idea of five times a week analysis and asked if I could see her once or twice only, because she could not bear for me to become too important to her; she knew she would feel too dependent. A healthy, life-seeking part of her became dominant when she quickly agreed to analysis after I pointed out that she would have to face her fear of "falling apart" alone for much longer in a non-intensive therapy.

To start with, neither the suicidal feelings nor the fear of falling apart could be spoken about directly. I found I had a responsive patient for whom work in the transference made immediate sense and who was co-operative and artistic, with a vivid mental life. However, I was quickly aware of puzzling incongruities between what she said, her behaviour in the session, and the feelings (or, more often, the lack of feelings) about what she was describing. Towards the end of the first session, I said that I sensed she was much more distressed than she showed. She responded amiably by mentioning, in the manner of an aside, a conversation with a friend who felt life was not worth living and was contemplating suicide. She left the session cheerily remarking that the analysis felt very sexual and she thought it was going to be a rough ride. When I pointed out a similar mismatch the following day, she acknowledged enormous confusions in her feelings and made some powerful and prescient comments. She realised that she never knew what she really thought. She was always doing what other people wanted. She felt she had never met herself.

I was rapidly aware that, as described by Freud in "Constructions in analysis" (1937d), it was only through oblique methods that I could piece together her history and her defences against disturbing aspects of it. This included mental illness in the family, violence, domestic discord, separations, and sexual assault, and a rather cruel and exploitative culture in the surrounding society. I would notice an absence of feeling about something vividly described, such as suicide, or cruel behaviour, or an oddity in the material that seemed to me to be immediately and obviously relevant to her, whether in the present or in the past, as I came to learn about it. If I referred to it, there would mostly be a sense of relief and usually some clearer further disclosure, often including the bringing of dream material that anticipated the issues of the session. Dreams seemed to be her preparation for the session, but she seemed to be unaware of them as she started a session. On some issues, there was an immediate and enduring positive response. When

I pointed out that her translation of everything into Oedipal and sexual terms was a disguise for her much greater needs for more basic maternal comfort and security, part of her seductiveness stopped immediately. She was relieved, too, when I showed her how a number of dreams revealed a complex mixture of adoration and murderousness towards a younger brother.

I learnt, over time, how the patient had grown up in a rural community in a former British colony with a rather macho, frontier spirit. The town had a veneer of sophistication, but the impression was of a culture in which toughness was a frequent cover for cruelty. Her mother had told her a story about her father's mother. When she wanted him to stay in one place while she was away, she stood him on a chair by a door, put a noose around his neck, and made as if to secure the rope on the other side of the door. She left him, saying that if he moved while she was away, he would hang himself. Ms A greatly feared this sort of attitude in me, feeling that my concern for her was part of a cruel trick. Her father was a scientist and, as a child under five, she was frequently expected, on visits to a family farm, to watch while he slaughtered animals, castrated them, or carried out vivisections. According to mother, father had hit Ms A a lot when she was a baby, and mother did when she was older. Mother comes over as insecure, hypochondriacal, and prone to dramatic mood swings. When the patient was two and a half, she had been left unsupervised and she was seriously injured on some unguarded machinery. She was hospitalised for several weeks, out of contact with her parents, and she had to be held or tied down while her injuries were treated.

After a couple of months, it became clear to me that, in her eagerness and co-operation, Ms A had been anxiously trying to be the perfect patient she believed that I required to avert my becoming cruel. This need to please brought to the fore an unwanted interaction between technique and compliance. Because Ms A worked readily in the transference, it had seemed appropriate to link material to me whenever possible. I recognised a problem with this when she tacked on to an account of somebody behaving very unlike me, some reference to me. When I asked her what that was about, she said, "Oh no, you're not like that at all but I felt that everything had to refer to you so I did it anyway." This increased my concern about compliance and engendered a very cautious approach to her material. It seemed that much of the repetition in and around the transference had to do with the exploration of what from her past was felt to be knowable by me, and whether she could allow herself to experience it with the associated feelings.

Enactment and counter transference enactment: the trap

In the ninth week of the analysis, the early sense of a straightforward working relationship with the patient gave way to something considerably more complex. In a Wednesday session a few weeks before the first summer break, I had to announce a cancellation without being able to give her much notice. I was struck by her apparent indifference to this announcement, considering her frequently expressed dependence on the sessions. She wondered, without irony, whether I did things to give her something to talk about, and she went on to speak chattily about how she was going to occupy herself in the summer break, before continuing in the same tone to refer to a film about a handicapped child who wanted to commit suicide.

I commented on the chatty style that she adopted, while making it clear that my announcement had brought up thoughts of suicide in her.

She contemplated a pattern in the paint on the ceiling, and said, "It looks like a little girl being examined by a doctor. The girl is lying over a table and looking down at the floor. She senses that something nasty is about to happen. Either he would give her an injection or rape her. The little girl is quite happy with this; she knows she'll get him any way."

Then she felt awful to think this had been so. She said that she had not realised she had felt it all along. I checked out what I had heard, ". . . that whatever I do to her, her little girl self has got it all sewn up. Whatever happens she is pleased that she can find some pretext for saying that I am the doctor giving something painful to her or raping her."

"Absolutely," she said. "I feel bad that I hadn't realised I felt that from the moment I saw you. I thought, 'Hi you, I want to kill you, or castrate you.'"

I thought here that the most powerful emotion was her shame that she could not be honest with herself and with me, rather than the overt aggressive content. I said that it might have been difficult for her to make that sort of feeling clear right at the start, as I wanted to highlight the internal attack on her striking capacity for honesty.

She then said, with much more feeling, that she felt *terribly* criticised by me; that I was *forcing* ideas into her.

I suggested that this drama had just been enacted: that she says she can find ways to feel triumphant whatever happens, and when I clarify what she means, she makes out she is an innocent whom I have raped and forced all these ideas into her.

She replied, "How very strange it all is", and we had to stop there.

On the following day, I sensed that she was warding off powerful anxieties about the impending summer break by various exciting distractions as she freely compared the satisfactions—gratitude, but mixed with embarrassment—which she got from being found out by me with those of controlling me and a sense of triumph. She agreed with my comment that the triumphant feelings and this conversation were her ways of trying to distance herself from the painful discoveries of yesterday and the lonely period that was coming up. Then she became giddy and frightened. She felt she had been criticised for having thoughts of her own and must not upset me.

In the Friday session, she spoke in a way that reminded me of a dream in which she was terrified of giving a performance. This became all right when she realised that the audience were just a band of monkeys. There was some material that seemed ripe for making rather obvious "psychoanalytic responses", and then the patient said that the shapes in the plaster on the ceiling looked like eggs in a nest, and she had to see if they were warm; perhaps she was the pregnant chick, but then she added, "God, I feel ridiculous."

The question of ridicule felt powerful to me at that moment, rather than the underlying anxiety about tenderness and maternal feelings in the transference. The imagery also seemed rather commonplace for my patient's well-developed and sophisticated aesthetic sense. I said that it was not clear whether she was laughing at me or felt I was laughing at her. If I saw through *her* she felt ridiculous, if I did not, then *I* seemed to be the ridiculous one. On the other hand, if I spoke about the part that is trying to outwit me, then she feels I am cruel for ignoring the hurt little girl. Her response seemed to confirm the interpretation. She explained that she feels quite invulnerable to things one minute, then totally vulnerable the next—terrible extremes. "That's part of the trap—you never know which me you're going to be dealing with from moment to moment. *I feel like an infant, not really in control.*"

I said how painful that was for her, and how difficult it must make being in analysis. At this, I sensed real emotional contact, and she went back to the bird's nest, and, feeling quite pleased with where we had got to, I said, without thinking too much why I was saying it, that *for her*, as an artist, this was quite a "twee" image and I wondered what that meant. She was mortified and hurt by this and believed that I obviously wanted to get rid of her, did not want to see her any more.

I felt that I had committed the most callous and heartless misunderstanding of her, and I worried that I had completely ruined the analysis and she would leave. I found it hard to think. As I recovered some capacity, I saw that this was the trap she had warned me about. I realised that, among the other things were going on, I had missed her hurt self, which needed acknowledging. I also remembered that, the previous day, a piece of understanding had been *followed* immediately by its dramatisation, and this could be linked with an earlier remark about *needing to bring things to life*.

I said that I could see that my missing where she was in this had hurt her, and added that I thought she had been expecting me to do this since the beginning of the analysis. I said I thought this could include a need of hers to bring it about, to see if she can find out what *had* happened to her in the past and what *can* happen here and in the future. She responded immediately with some more very painful details of her history, which connected to her anxieties about fertility. It was the end of the session and she said wistfully as she left that she wondered what would happen.

On her return after the weekend, she provided an important clue about relationships in her internal world. After further berating me over my use of the word "twee", she confessed that she had written down the session as best she could, but it had been several hours before she noticed what she had written: that I had actually said, "*She* must find analysis very difficult", meaning that I understood her difficulty, and not what she had chosen to have me say, a complaint against her, that "I was finding the analysis very difficult."

This sequence suggests the presence of two quite dissociated parts of herself, one of whom could perceive and remember events truthfully, and another or others who distorted things. I felt that her first version was also a reflection of her wish to make life difficult for me, and a perception that she had actually done so. Two of Freud's concepts, over-determination and instinctual fusion, could be used to understand such situations. I would suggest that over-determination is more helpful, as it indicates that the behaviour that is actually performed is the behaviour that satisfies the requirements of a hierarchy of schemas representing object relationships, each including a set of need-/impulse-meeting strategies and sets of anxiety-driven inhibiting stategies. (In mathematical terms, it is the resultant of a number of combined forces.) This seems to me to be richer and more susceptible to further analysis than the idea that each behaviour will be a combination of libidinal and destructive elements.

I would argue that, for similar reasons, the presence of dissociation between parts of the self limits the relevance for this situation of Bion's observation that where a patient gives material in such a way that whatever the analyst chooses to interpret he can be shown to be wrong, then this is an attack on the analyst's potency. This understanding fitted superficially with the patient's declaration about killing me or castrating me, but depends on an integrated ego to co-ordinate the manoeuvre . On the other hand, my immediate emotional response was not to be convinced by this statement. At the time, I had thought "Where on earth is that coming from?" and, actually, at no time had I felt under murderous or castrating attack from her as, for example, I have experienced with psychotic patients. As the pattern was repeated, it seemed mainly that Ms A wanted to be able to represent me as callous and overwhelmed by her to protect her self from the consequences if she found me truly sympathetic and helpful.

As we recovered in subsequent sessions from the sudden threat of a catastrophic breakdown of the analysis, I became more convinced of the importance of her statement that she felt powerless to know who she was from moment to moment. In fact, this phrase perfectly captures her sense of vulnerability to a largely unconscious internal organisation. The phrase "to bring things to life, to see what happened and what can happen" was also prescient. For some reason, Ms A could not think about her experiences without reliving them and bringing them to my attention through dramatisation.

After the sessions in which the traps for me were disclosed, there was an increase in a pattern that had been present occasionally from the start. In sessions in which we had gone beyond her trying to be pleasing and had made straightforward emotional contact, sessions could be turned bad towards the end in two different ways. One was that she would either become panicky, helpless, and unable to think, which left me feeling cruel and anxious for sending her away, and the other was to find some pretext for becoming suspicious of me and finding something to complain about. This seemed mainly to ensure that she did not have to miss me between sessions, and controlled what was, for her, the inevitable disappointment that I would cause her by not living up to her expectations.

In this period, it was difficult to decide from moment to moment how the patient was using me and why. Integrated ego functioning seemed transitory. For quite a while it was more like analysing a crowd, a gang, or a class of children than an integrated individual. I would seem to be talking to one person, then suddenly I could be attacked by someone else. I noted a curious pattern by which something would be described and then immediately enacted in the way that a dream can be repeated in action. The closest paradigm with Ms A is the classroom situation where someone tells teacher just as another child is about to be naughty.

In the first week of the analysis, Ms A had described enormous confusion in her feelings and stated that she never knew what she really thought because she was always doing what other people wanted, so she felt she had never met herself. It took me some time to crystallise the view that this lack of a clear sense of herself could be seen as resulting from a psychic structure in which *several* care-taker "selves" (Winnicott, 1960) organised a variety of self-protective strategies. These included massive compliance, seductiveness, unknowing, lack of will, and disconnection from the body. The net effect of these defensive operations was what Kernberg, among others, would describe as "identity diffusion".

It seemed that Ms A felt menaced at two levels. At times, she would completely disown, deny, or obliterate something she had clearly "known" a few moments earlier. I noticed tiny flashes of terror, under which many of these confusing mental operations were taking place. There were moments of frozen panic if there was a noise outside the door of the consulting room, and, at times, she would flinch and cower on the couch if I moved or hesitated before speaking. Any retreat from total vigilance left her feeling utterly exposed to the danger that if she were not a pleasing and responsive patient, I would hit her, or abuse her in some unspecified way. In a similar way, the earlier eager pleasing behaviour had been driven by powerful fears that I would lose interest in her, and terminate the analysis. She also feared that if she were too emotional and did not show continuous improvement, I would feel she was too mad to treat.

The self that could be truthful and have a good relationship with me also felt bullied and intimidated by a band of internal characters, whom we came to call, variously, "the spies", as they appeared in her dreams, "saboteurs" (after Fairbairn), the Mafia (after Rosenfeld), or "the terrorists". She experienced them as sadistic, lurking in the shadows, always out to mock and undermine any good feelings she might have about me, as had happened over the use of the word "twee", which the spy self had seized upon to cut short the developing understanding. Away from my presence, she felt completely at the mercy of this internal organisation. For this reason, many of the communications from her truthful self came as disguised messages smuggled out. If I understood the communication, well and good, if not, it could be disowned.

I believe that the pattern of action in the sessions that I noted from the beginning of the analysis followed from this. I would usually have been turned bad by the spy self by the end of the previous session or in the interim, so she was always unsure what kind of analyst she would find on her return. One way or another, the material would be presented as something detached from her. For example, she would talk about a story she was writing, some drawing she had made, something she read or watched. If I did not understand its more intimate significance, she felt that I was one of the Mafia, and she was better off keeping her hopes and her shame at thinking well of me to her self.

There appeared to be several parts of her with an interest in the omnipotent control of perceptions, including, particularly, the allocation of blame and causality. A desperate, frightened child was driven by terror to comply with whatever seemed immediately necessary for survival, including taking the blame for things she had not done. To cope with this, she would become panicky and confused, not knowing or remembering anything; or she could zoom off, withdraw, anaesthetise herself, or be what the other required by appeasement or seduction. The distortion of truth could be used in two contrasting ways. It could be readily adapted for triumph, expedience, or trickery to feel powerful and independent in relation to others. Alternatively, as Fairbairn described in the "moral defence", she could distort in the other direction by seeing herself as in the wrong to sustain hope that if she could learn to be good she would find she had good parents. This seemed to be behind her frequent failure to perceive cruelty in the outside world, or else to make excuses for it. The consequence for herself was, cumulatively, to feel bad, cruel, stupid, and useless instead of the other people. "Not knowing" and "not feeling" were essential to her survival, but they left her vulnerable to the feeling that I could get into her mind and control it, in order to exploit her. Collectively, these undermined her capacity to make any stable sense of her history or her relationships in the present.

"The floor session" and reconnection to the body

It took a long time for Ms A to accept the possibility that the analysis could be a transitional space where the causes and meanings of things could remain undecided and different viewpoints could be considered. Slowly, she came to see that I believed that her dreams, daydreams, stories, and art works might have worth as evidence rather than being merely fanciful. The process was accelerated by a sequence of sessions in the fourth year of her analysis. Dreams from this period give a vivid picture of her inner world.

> It was night and she had been crossing an arid desert area towards an ocean liner, which was ready to sail to a beautiful new land. She had got as far as the boundary of the port facility and could see the floodlit gangplank leading on to the vessel, but felt that the spies were all around her in the dark and that if she tried to get on board she would be dragged back or shot.

I understood this to be a description of her longing to escape from from the arid internal landscape and its menacing presences in which she felt trapped. It showed that as she approached in her analysis the possibility of moving to somewhere more luxurious and beautiful, she was aware of all the parts of herself that opposed it and would destroy her rather than allow her to get better.

The following day she brought another dream

> She was visiting a castle and there was a cart with a white cage on top of it offering rides, which she was very frightened of. There was a man in a suit who was organising this and seemed to own the castle. She was sure this man stood for me. She immediately became anxious that this thing which

had promised to be a pleasure ride was really a secret way of capturing her and other visitors, possibly to torture them and kill them She felt very unsure about how she should get help about this without arousing suspicion. There was a woman running the concession shop, but she was rather strange as she seemed to be someone, perhaps a man, wearing a wig, and she certainly could not trust her—she too was employed by the castle and too much of a danger. She got away and thought of going to the police, but then immediately felt terrified because she thought that they too would be in league with the powerful owner of the castle. She then had the added burden of trying to behave as normally as possible so that nobody would sense she had discovered what was going on.

It seems to me that I am felt to be the omnipotent and omnipresent representatives of her internal oppressive organisation. I am the castle owner, and also the woman in the wig, masquerading as a maternal figure offering her something exciting but only in order to trap her and torture her. All are in collusion with the police, so she can find no external authority who believes in justice and truth.

Three weeks later she tells me another dream.

An investigating officer (like the television detective Columbo) is trying to put a film of her past together but couldn't find the right equipment for viewing, editing, and putting it together. She had broken bits of film in her hand but couldn't do anything with them. Then she was suddenly in Asia, Malaya? Or Indonesia, on this exotic river called Sue Big or Sue Bic.[1] But any space to work was not really safe because the place was being invaded by the Japanese and there were spies everywhere—she didn't know who was who.

It seemed she was trying to find the right equipment in her mind, with her shabby but astute analyst detective, with which to view herself and her history. But as soon as she started to assemble a coherent and truthful account, she was transported to somewhere alien and threatened by invading forces and their undercover spies. A dream a few days later repeated this theme, with images of a clock, half dissolved, with the numbers in a jumbled heap, to which she is connected by a fragile umbilical wire. This seemed to me to use the image of the early accident to her to represent the destruction of her cognitive functions and temporality, caused by the mental operations that were being unveiled. The connection between her baby self and her mother–analyst is felt to be just a fragile wire.

A few days later she mentioned that she had attended a lecture on Ferenczi's "Confusion of tongues" paper. She had taken from this the possibility that analysts retraumatise their patients through their technique. This was not directed straight at me, but contained warning of a confrontation, highlighted by her account of the stand-off that her brother was in with his therapist. The following day, she came in clutching some things and lay on the couch.

> "I wanted to look at you yesterday but I was too scared—scared of looking at you and hating you so much. I don't want to use the couch, it never feels comfortable. It feels like a straitjacket. I just feel observed. [Then, assertively, as though making a speech] If I've been traumatised then you should make some effort to come towards me. I've been talking to my brother. He says that if I can't trust you then this whole thing is pointless. I'm so frightened I want to be able to see you. This needs to be on the floor on the same level or you'll tower over me—I thought you wouldn't—you wear a suit. The chairs look too far apart—I couldn't sit that far away. It's a test like my brother says—he has given his therapist a book and demanded she reads it—to see if he should go to somebody else."

She goes on to say that she has brought things to show me: some art work, poems she wrote for me two years ago, some photos . . . Then she cries.

> "It's my big break and I don't know what to do—it's absurd."

I said that it seemed far from absurd. The poems are about attachment and love for me and here she wants to find out if I deserve those feelings or if I will get it wrong for her and be a big disappointment. She was torn by the feeling that she did not want to do analysis my way and wanting me to adapt to her, at the same time as wanting to show me things that are very personal and important to her.

She is quiet and thoughtful, and after a while she says,

> "Can we sit on the floor?"

I asked, "Is it necessary?"

> "Yes" (with the implication that I was stupid to even have to ask).

I sat down promptly and made myself comfortable in front of my chair. She became very anxious and shy, and sat down on the floor in front of me, tears streaming down her face in an absolute panic.

"I don't know what to do next. I was certain you wouldn't sit on the floor—This was supposed to show me you weren't flexible enough for me—which was most important. Then I could just say—You wouldn't do it! Now I am just frightened of having to be myself."

I waited, and after a while she gathered herself and showed me some photos of her and her grandfather, and then the book of a recent presentation she had given. Then she says she has not shown me the most controversial stuff.

I said that I think she is afraid that I will be conservative and judgemental.

She brought out some flowers and, after a lengthy pause, I asked her to tell me about them.

"They were collected at the farm."

She says she does not know why, but she puts the flowers from the farm alongside little casts of herself that she had planted in the garden. She calls them her fossils.

I remembered that the farm was called "Hope Farm", and suggested she was putting the symbols of life and hope against the dark earth and the bones of her deadened child self that were becoming exposed.

There was a deep pause

"It's not just me you know." [Indicating that she fears being blamed for everything.] But I feel so stupid for taking three years for this. It's so stupid. It's my fault."

I wondered who was telling her these things and why. Was it her sense of a cultural demand she frequently experienced to continuously achieve and get better that was felt as completely persecuting—the part of herself that sees everything in terms of fault? If it was not me it was her—somebody has to be to blame.

She replied, "It's difficult for something just to be."

I said that she had thought the straitjacket was for my benefit, but now she finds she had chosen one for herself that had been useful to her. She nodded, and then we had to stop.

In the following sessions, the tensions remained very great. She felt my behaviour in agreeing to her request was not genuine after all, but just another technique, "a cheating trick" to turn her into a domesticated puppy. She was frightened of both sitting on the floor and lying down. Some days she did one thing, sometimes the other. Having understood some of the significance of the pressure to act, I stayed in my chair. She described being torn between the longing to relax and her need for total vigilance. She said that whenever she relaxed she felt terrified. She is afraid I am trying to take over her mind. Eventually, she says she feels great love for me, but fears that it will go wrong, just like it did with father and with a boyfriend of her mother's who was too sexual with her. One day, just before the break, she said in a most heart-rending way, "I wish you could *really adopt* me."

As I became clearer about the aggressive elements in Ms A's behaviour, this immediately revealed a connection to the breaking down of boundaries. On her return from the summer break, she started by expressing appreciation of what we had done and then launched an attack on my many shortcomings. When I pointed out her change in attitude, she finally acknowledged how abusive she could be to me and how destructive this was of our work together. She felt sorry for how much she had hurt me in the past and concluded that she might need to control herself. Afterwards, she dreamt of a man breaking down the toilet door of her apartment when she was inside. She equated the toilet door with the consulting room, and compared my showing her how aggressive she could be to a rape. Later, she said she had lived all her life with the windows to the outside world covered by her own pictures. I had broken in and was substituting windows for these static pictures of hers. This is a powerful image of the opening up of a rigid boundary with the outside world, which had largely been viewed in terms of repetitions of her inner dramas, conscious and unconscious.

She began to distinguish between a difficult interpretation and a rape. These events brought her right in touch with her fears about what she called "an unscripted life". This expresses perfectly Fairbairn's (1958) description of the chief aim of psychoanalytic treatment as being to promote, in the setting of a therapeutic relationship with the analyst, a maximum synthesis of the structures into which the original ego has split, and, thus, to effect breaches in the closed system which constitutes the patient's inner world. As a result, this inner world can become accessible and responsive to the influence of outer reality.

Striking changes followed this understanding. Ms A reported the beginnings of sensation in her genitals. She realised that for all the years that she had been sexually active, seeking the feelings of closeness and affection represented by the men's desire, she had been self-anaesthetised. Crucially, she acknowledged the value of *keeping things distinct in her mind*, rather than letting go and collapsing into confusion. She recognised what an active process this had to be, and she completely stopped spoiling the ends of sessions. She had some dreams about killing that suggested she might enjoy it, although the content was confused by her feeling that a man had got inside her and was teasing her with his gun. For her, this brought her traumatic experiences with men together with the seductiveness of suicide as an escape from pain and suffering.

As she began to put into action her new relationship to her body and its *interior/exterior boundary*, a number of other situations began to change, reflecting changes in her relation to the internal organisation. She found herself increasingly irritated that her lodger used the whole of the flat, including Ms A's room, as if it were her own. However, she believed that setting any limit to this would result in a violent assault. To take charge of things was fraught with anxiety if she did it, and furious resentment if she did not. She talked to her mother about whether she was sexually abused. Mother did not deny it, but would like it to have been while Ms A was in hospital, but mother did admit that her daughter was quite changed after spending time at her father's house with his new family. A further psychic conflict appeared as a boundary issue. She had to organise an exhibition as part of a course she was taking. She was utterly bewildered when the staff of the venue asked her how much space she wanted for her exhibit, and could not answer. Her associations showed her belief that other people were able to exercise absolute control over her boundaries. She equated their control with the expression of their hatred and murderous intent. In the session, she became very regressed for a while, and was convinced that if she said she wanted to die, I would kill her there and then. She was convinced that I was just waiting for her to ask to be killed in order to make *her* responsible. She believed I would starve her, suffocate her, or poison her. I connected this with her frequent complaint that the sessions were always too short for her, and yet I continued to torment her by starving her. She complained that I just do not give her enough to stay alive, so she had better get in first.

I said that I thought she had no idea what to do with the question about the space she needed because it was an invitation *to mark some-*

thing out positively, whereas, for much of her life, she had been pre-occupied with her childhood powerlessness, and had clung on to the possibility of dying at her own hand as being preferable to suffering the humiliation of being at the mercy of a hateful other. I saw this as a missing link between her suicidal urges, her sudden outburst—"I want to kill you or castrate you", and the turning on me in the sessions to destroy the analytic progress. In her mind, these were pre-emptive strikes, killing precious things—her achievements or her life—rather than waiting for me to do it. This understanding gained credibility, as she told me in the following session that she would mark out her exhibit by drawing a line right around it, establishing what belonged to her and what did not. Previously, she believed her work would have to be merged with everyone else's.

This development, in which she reclaimed her previously split-off power, brought forth a renewed attack from the superego, as she immediately felt responsible for everything she had "allowed" herself to suffer. Power and potency were felt to be all or nothing capacities. She berated herself, believing that if she has any power at all, then she should have known about and prevented all the painful things that had happened to her. That meant that she was bad. Matters were further complicated because she also accused herself for her heinous mistrust of adults, which should be punished, so she had to be both passive and wholly trusting, regardless of evidence to the contrary.

Consolidation

The third episode that I wish to discuss took place six months later, and proved to be something of a turning point. The patterns that had become familiar to us were given a surprising new twist. It was the Friday session of a week in which she had been thinking about babies and why she believed she could never have any. She was puzzled as to why she was thinking of giving up a kind boyfriend, because, in spite of herself, she still felt attached to a rather perverse and cruel one. She thought that she might be staying with the cruel one in order *not* to have babies. She could not bear the thought of having them with him. So, by staying with him, she protected herself from something that she feared for reasons related to her phantasies about her insides and the vulnerability of her body openings. She thought a baby would tear her apart and prove to be some foul product of her insides.

She started the session by telling me how stressed she was on her college course and because of some awful dreams. Although she was exhausted, she had had a reassuring tutorial with a lecturer who seemed not to be part of the dominant staff group, whom she experienced as very politically correct and intolerant. The lecturer had praised her work and suggested he supervised her project to protect her from her main tutor who, he believed, was unreasonably prejudiced against my patient. The lecturer's attitude felt good to her but she was not sure how much to trust him, as it seemed a bit conspiratorial. I took this to refer to me as a good and reassuring presence, but of uncertain power in relation to the "Mafia", represented by the dominant college staff whom she did not want to provoke. She talked about the way the course denied the existence of the subjective and the personal. When she speaks about the importance of history in her project, she is always being reminded that there is no *personal* history—only histories—either as a lesbian, as a gay, as a black, as a woman. She says, "What they mean is, there aren't allowed to be *people* in it; only ideas and objects, nothing human. It's crazy, isn't it?"

I had heard much about the ideas and behaviour of the staff of this course, and a lot of it had a rather perverse quality to it, although, as with conspicuous cruelty, Ms A was often reluctant to see or name it. I took the material to be a statement that, under internal and external pressure, she felt in danger of abandoning her belief in her own perceptions, and in need of an ally.

I said that it was clear how under attack she felt in her striving to understand and know her own personal history. She wanted confirmation that she was faced with a crazy set of ideas, and not have to make out that she is the crazy one.

Without commenting directly, she told me about scary dreams that had woken her up.

> She was watching two men playing by a pool and was with her cruel boyfriend or someone like him. The men were enjoying themselves, and one jumped in making comic gestures. She laughed, and the man she was with was furious.

> Then she was in a group of people rather close together. There were some crumbs down her shirt, like flaky pie crust. After a while, she registered that someone was touching her breast, but she hadn't noticed it before although it had been going on for some time. Because of the crowd, she could not work out who it was.

In the third dream, there seemed to be lots of pictures of vaginas, but they were more lifelike than pictures; perhaps more like three-dimensional models, but out of some horrible textbook, as they had warts and growths on them. In one, the genitals seemed to be merged with the earth and she could see holes where the worms had been burrowing through the flesh. It was revolting.

The first part of the dream seemed to me to be about her feeling that the cruel people always demanded proper respect. The second part showed how she desensitised herself to what happened to her, and this made her crumbly mentally, so she could not follow what had happened to her. I did not think I had been "touching her up" in any way in the recent work, although I realised that the talk about babies earlier in the week might have been arousing. The reference to something going on for a long time without her noticing I took as referring to some continuing issue that came from her past or from outside the room that she was trying to bring to my attention. The manifest content of the third dream showed how her genitals felt disgusting to her and burrowed into, turned into part objects for others to look at. I thought the dream linked to previous material where she had talked about feeling her vagina did not belong to her: that it was a public thing for others to use as they pleased.

She was clearly anxious, so I expected she would want to talk about it, but she moved straight away from it. She was so tired and she needed time on her own to feel better. She wondered whether to see the kind boyfriend. She thought not. I took this to be both working with the dream and also a transference statement that solitude seemed safer then even kind boyfriend–analyst, either because we were suspect, insufficiently powerful, or could touch her in intimate ways without her realising it. I decided not to say the last bit because of the risk of being experienced as sexually provocative.

I said that she had doubts about even approaching the kind people, including myself, because she is afraid it will go wrong. She feels the only truly safe way to preserve her boundaries is to find a place, on her own, where she can repair herself. She seemed to agree with this, and said warmly that she was worried about giving too much away to the college staff of her rejection of their ideology, but it was nice to think she might be able to work with the helpful tutor and another concerned colleague. This did not sound like a merely compliant statement and suggested the presence in her mind, and in external reality, of allies in the struggle to see things clearly, rather than according to need or ideology. There seemed no evidence from the material or my emotional responses to the material to suggest that it was my ideology she was rejecting. I found myself replaying internally what I had said, and I was struck by the fact that I had framed it to her as a boundary problem. But I also noticed that I was now feeling full of anxiety about the content of the dreams while she seemed empty of it, with the descriptions of the vaginas the most dramatic and emotionally disturbing aspects.

I said to her that I thought she was hopeful of finding a me who could work with her on the dreams, but that her fears of giving too much away meant she had to keep those very painful things to herself. She responded with unexpected vehemence. "You're accusing me of not exposing things and showing you everything."

This reaction surprised me much as her reaction to "twee" had done several years earlier. This time, I felt confident that it had been said with concern for her and understanding of her predicament. I felt I needed to say something, and just commented that there was something familiar in this way of hearing what I had said. She agreed, and said she might just be anxious about me. After a period of silence, I decided to take the material from the beginning of the session about the different sorts of lecturer and how much she could be truthful as portraying her anxieties about me in relation to the dream.

I said that I felt she was afraid that if she showed me what the dream really meant for her, she would discover that I was like the college in treating her as a thing, not as a person with a history of personal feelings and meanings. By keeping things from me, she tried to keep alive the idea that I was her ally and not like that. There was an immediate reduction in tension.

She said she wanted to go with her kind boyfriend to see an exhibition in another town. Against that idea was the fact that they would have to stay with friends and be sociable. Then she remembered she had promised to go and visit their friend's child again, a lonely child who was always expected to be older than he was. She had promised to bring him something to keep his secrets in. "He hasn't got anywhere for them, so I told him I would bring a box and perhaps inscribe it for him to make it special." She supposed I would think it was silly—she should not encourage people to keep secrets.

This was the point at which I became convinced of the connections that lay behind her different problems in *taking charge of things*, whether it was her body, her flat, her exhibit, her impulses, or, ultimately, her choice of life or death. She had been able to take charge *negatively* by isolation or by self-destructively assuming the worst. Could she now take charge and set limits positively? I felt she had demonstrated the mental equivalence of her body space and her mental space, and how the keeping of secrets was an important example of the presence of a real boundary between what is inside and what is outside—what people can get to touch and what they cannot.

I said that I felt she was very in touch with the need of a child for privacy, for a place to keep secrets that she can control. I felt this was one thing her dreams were about, about her feeling that people could touch her intimately without her even noticing. This made her feel fragile and she felt that she was only safe when she was alone. She had tried to show me, through keeping her thoughts about the dreams to herself, how she could now manage to protect herself from invasions of her body and mind that had left her feeling rotten, interfered with, and exposed, like the vaginas on display. She knew how she wanted the secret places in her body to be treasure boxes that she could control and keep private.

As I spoke, she became obviously upset, but in a sad rather than a tense, anxious way. She wistfully linked it to her wish that she could have a period with her boyfriend of just being loving friends and not feeling obliged to act as though she were already married to him. She left the session in a considerable panic, but she came back after the weekend delighted that she had been able to say "No" to sex for the first time in her life. This accelerated her recovery of bodily awareness and the sense, weakly established at first, that it was possible to preserve boundaries and protect things of value. This in turn led, through much working through, to a considerable stabilising of her view of herself, particularly her sense of what is truly her. In terms of the transference, she was able to draw her line much more clearly around our work and cherish that, too, giving up her sabotage. While it might be argued that saying "No" to sex with the kind boyfriend was evidence of a continuing rejection of a good object in favour of her continuing attachment to perverse and cruel objects, my own view remains that her experiment in saying "No" needed to be tried out first with a benign object as a safer first step than frustrating someone cruel and dangerous.

She was able to get a good qualification without sacrificing her integrity. She made a relationship with a man and has a baby with him. To her joy, she has found that her womb and breasts are treasure boxes that can grow and nourish a baby, rather than being the rotten useless objects of the dream.

Discussion

In Churchill's words, we had come "not to the end, not even the beginning of the end, but at least to the end of the beginning" of the analysis. In this first four and a half years of analysis, a pattern of action was established in and around the transference in which could be discerned three important features. The first was the emergence of different layers of defensive operations in the patient, each of which diminished her capacity to sustain good relationships and take care of herself. Over time, there was a change in the balance between her different care-taking systems. At their heart throughout was the wariness of a child who has received unpredictable and, at times, painful handling by her parents, who have unsuccessfully functioned as a protective shield during infancy and later (Freud, 1937d; Khan, 1974). The dangers in exposing her true or libidinal self could be contained for a time by various ways of keeping things apart in her mind and becoming a false self for the object. Beyond this, after two months of analysis, she revealed how she felt at the mercy of an internal organisation of superego figures who felt like a powerful Mafia (cf. Fairbairn, 1944; Rosenfeld, 1971, 1987; Steiner, 1993). These internal figures offered gratifications and a sense of security based on identification with the aggressor and a sense of invulnerability (A. Freud, 1937). This could not be a stable solution, because she could not eliminate her powerful need for good objects and her wish to feel innocently good about herself. This was directly in conflict with her belief that she had to accept that she was bad in order to keep alive the hope that if she could be better her parents would be loving towards her. Under pressure of anxiety, these incompatible requirements led to the secondary sacrifice of many perceptual and discriminating ego functions, including her sense of time and historical memory. As a consequence, she was left feeling as unbounded mentally as she did physically, and she lived with a phenomenologically unstable sense of her self and her agency.

Ms A was very aware, as I was, of her acute sensitivity to changes in her surroundings. Freud's description of the importance of a "protective shield" (Freud, 1920g) between the self and the outside world seems pertinent here, and informed my sense of Ms A as psychically and physically skinless, or, at least, without an intact skin. Ms A's statement that she felt like an infant at the mercy of things that took her over could have come straight from Heimann's (1958) description of the way that painful attacks and penetrations of the body leave the patient feeling that there is no barrier at all, so that things get inside where they roam around at will, alien and persecuting. Heimann and Winnicott discuss invasions or impingements in early infancy, and serious later invasions, whether medical procedures or penetrative abuse, must massively revive these infantile anxieties. I believe that adaptations to invasive objects rank alongside projective identification as causing serious confusions of self and object. This lack of a clear skin around the person at a physical level is augmented, rather than reduced, when parents have been prone to use the infant as a receptacle for their own uncontained feelings, which themselves can be felt as violent penetrations. Evaluating the contributions of early infant care and the later penetrations of her body is complex, but, in Ms A's case, was vitally important.

Freud's key paper, "Remembering, repeating and working-through" (1914g), establishes a vocabulary of acting out and enactment which is quite free of its later colouration with connotations of delinquency. This is implicit in Sandler's concept of the patient's need to "actualise" situations within the analysis, and in Limentani's important paper of 1966, "A re-evaluation of acting out in relation to working through". With Ms A's clinical picture, the actualisations, or dramatisations, play an essential part in both recovering the past and recovering from it. I am not here making a point in the debate over recovered *vs.* reconstructed memories, but about the Colombo-like piecing together of the clues in the fragments of her memory, which had been broken to avoid the pain of experiencing the full picture of her life. This could only be done in the presence of a trustworthy object with a functioning mind and a concern for the truth. Recovering her history under these circumstances required a very wide attention to the different modalities through which elements of the present and past are communicated. For example, in the first months, the apparently disinterested approach to feelings, followed by a false-self co-operation, seemed to combine an infant's wary approach to the breast after a separation with a wish to recreate a blissful union with me as mother, while simultaneously trying to achieve a loving relationship with a paternal experience of me. In the process, she repeated the precocious sexual behaviour of the abused child, wishing both that father can be seduced and should prove himself beyond seduction. In situations like this, the wish to please the analyst, coupled with an analyst's ready translation of the patient's utterances into statements about the analytic relationship, further compromises the patient's capacity to maintain her internal–external boundary. It easily reproduces an apparently omniscient parent and makes analysis potentially a violation, however well intentioned. Compliance, coupled with a repetitively "here and now" focus to interpreting the transference, can make it very difficult for such a patient to bring and explore something that is neither here nor now.

There was further over-determination in the second period, when the sudden spoiling of contact became a dominating feature. This had a defensive function in controlling the expected disappointment and so reduced one form of anxiety, but it also represented the triumph of the internalised gang over any libidinal strivings. In the process, it also transformed a passively endured experience into an active one and reversed the situation, giving the analyst the experience of being with a parent who turns on them without warning.

Recovery from the past brings me to the use by the patient of many different forms of representation through imagery, dreams, writings, artefacts, and action in the analytic setting to test out the validity of her pathogenic beliefs. In the last of the sessions that I have discussed, there is a final convergence of my conscious understanding of the situation with the patient's long-standing unconsciously prompted experiments with her beliefs that she has no intact mental or physical skin, and that any attempt to defend these boundaries would be untenable. On a larger scale than her micro-enactments within sessions, she had been concerned from the start to examine what kind of a space the analysis was and could become. She had to work out, through experiment, if it was a protected space free of invasions, in which she could bring out thoughts and the parts of herself attached to them without worrying about them. Here, both maternal and paternal aspects of the transference were important. The analyst's observance of boundaries and the making of distinctions were crucial to this process, in addition to collecting and holding in mind her fragmented experience, until both the images and the ego functions of thinking and memory could be restored by her. As she began to feel a little more trusting of the situation, she could show more of her true self and begin an unconsciously tolerated experiment with herself as active rather than passive, including by becoming a possible invader. Like many poorly protected children, she had created her own protective shield in the form of absolute rules, and she showed how she wished to be treated through the extreme sensitivity with which she respected the boundaries of the sessions and my privacy outside it. When she wanted to bring things to show me, this was terrifying, because she was experimenting with a transgression that was full of confused hope and provocation. My emotional response was in accord with this. I feared a disaster whichever way I responded. When we both survived, it gave her the confidence tentatively to play more freely

It is touching that the outcome of this experimental intrusion into my space was her acceptance of responsibility for her times of actual destructiveness towards our work. With this piece of mental integration, her body was present to be properly experienced, too. I think that the wished for, and feared breaking down of the toilet door, standing also for the inner barrier between her body and her mind, could only take place when she had a sense of an intact outer boundary to replace it. Once she had felt free to feel her sexual body boundary, she could take off and explore many different versions of territorial control, summed up in the revelatory phrase, "I can draw a line round my exhibit rather than having to have it merged in with everything else." With her exhibit, she envisaged herself as someone who could be in charge of her life. The turning point session was powerful because it was not as new as I thought on the day. It recapitulated and consolidated many of the central issues of the analysis to that point, and the boundary control problem reappeared symbolically as a transference issue. As I became preoccupied with the powerful and distressing sexual images from the manifest dreams, she could experience me as the prurient, invasive father and shut me out. In this new version, she could take an active protective role for her boxful of treasures, which are the latent content of the dreams. Here, she perhaps regained an archaic sense of herself as good, with the bad outside, that had been prematurely lost. With the establishment of a proper skin around herself, and a sense of a right to exist, she could assert herself more realistically in the world, rather than turn her rage on herself in destruction or suicidal thoughts. Once there is a boundary that can be defended, there is a chance to get the invaders outside, and from that position begin to discriminate between, and integrate, good and bad aspects of herself. My experience suggests that it is better initially to give the patient the benefit of the doubt that aggression is defensive (cf. Heimann, 1966). This is less likely to lead to an impasse over the patient's destructiveness and allows for something to be elaborated over time in which the gratifying aspects can be allocated their proper place. As a result, her difficulties with her own destructive wishes and the narcissistic threats and temptations of the internal organisation, which had been largely unanalysable in the first four years, were then available for consideration.

Note

1. Subic was the site of a major battle between US forces and the Japanese during the Second World War, but I was not aware of this at the time.

References

Brierley, M. (1991)[1943]. Memorandum on her technique for the training committee of the British Psychoanalytical Society. In: P. King & R. Steiner (Eds.), *The Freud–Klein Controversies 1941–45* (pp. 617–628). London: Routledge.

Fairbairn, W. R. D. (1944). Endopsychic structure considered in terms of object relationships. In: *Psychoanalytic Studies of the Personality*. London: Routledge, 1952.

Fairbairn, W. R. D. (1958). On the nature and aims of psychoanalytical treatment. *International Journal of Psychoanalysis, S39*: 374–385.

Freud, A. (1937). *The Ego and the Mechanisms of Defence*. London: Hogarth and the Institute of Psychoanalysis.

Freud, S. (1914g). Remembering, repeating and working-through. *S.E. 12*: 145–155. London: Hogarth.

Freud, S. (1920g). *Beyond the Pleasure Principle*. *S.E.*, *18*: 7–64. London: Hogarth.

Freud, S. (1937d). Constructions in analysis. *S.E.*, *23*: 257–269. London: Hogarth.

Heimann, P. (1958). Notes on early development. In : M. Tonnesman (Ed.), *About Children and Children-No-Longer. Collected Papers of Paula Heimann 1942–80*. London: Tavistock/Routledge, 1989.

Heimann, P. (1966). Comment on Dr Kernberg's paper on 'Structural derivatives of object relationships'. *International Journal of Psychoanalysis*, *47*: 254–260. Reprinted in: M. Tonnesman (Ed.), *About Children and Children-No-Longer. Collected Papers of Paula Heimann 1942–80*. London: Tavistock/Routledge, 1989.

Khan, M. M. R. (1974). The concept of cumulative trauma. In: *The Privacy of the Self*. London: Hogarth Press.

King, P. H. M., & Steiner, R. (Eds.) (1991). *The Freud–Klein Controversies 1941–45*. London: Tavistock/Routledge.

Limentani, A. (1966). A re-evaluation of acting out in relation to working through. *International Journal of Psychoanalysis*, *47*: 274–282. Reprinted in: *Between Freud and Klein: The Psychoanalytic Quest for Knowledge and Truth* (pp. 35–49). London: Free Association Books.

Riley, D. (2005). Two approaches to interpretation. In. S. Budd & R. Rusbridge (Eds.), *Introducing Psychoanalysis* (pp. 211–225). London: Routledge.

Rosenfeld, H. (1971). A clinical approach to the psychoanalytic theory of the life and death instincts: an investigation into the aggressive aspects of narcissism. *International Journal of Psychoanalysis*, *52*: 169–178.

Rosenfeld, H. (1987). *Impasse and Interpretation*. London: Tavistock.

Sandler, J. (1983). Reflections on some relations between psychoanalytic concepts and psychoanalytic practice. *International Journal of Psychoanalysis*, *64*: 35–46.

Steiner, J. (1993). *Psychic Retreats*. London: Routledge.

Winnicott, D. W. (1960). Ego distortions in terms of true and false self. In: *The Maturational Process and the Facilitating Environment*. London: Hogarth Press, 1982.

CHAPTER SEVEN

Endings and beginnings

Sira Dermen

Introduction: no ending without a beginning

In the seventh year of his weekly treatment at the Portman Clinic in London,[1] Mr A, a transvestite patient, ended his therapy as follows. In mid-session, he said, "I'm sorry, but I have to do this," got off the couch, and walked out of the consulting room.

It was not wholly out of the blue. We had been talking about ending for some two years, but when he ended in this singular manner—*doing this*, as he called it—I was dismayed, though I knew he was telling me he could not "end" in any other way.

After some weeks, Mr A contacted the clinic again, requesting to see me. In this last meeting, I commented that he had to come back to check that I was alive: ending his therapy had not killed me. I did not hear from Mr A for the next ten years. Then, in the very month that I was retiring from the Portman Clinic, he was referred back to the clinic by the same agency that had originally referred him eighteen years earlier.

* * *

Ms B was a private patient in five-times-per-week psychoanalysis, an accomplished professional woman, in a stable marriage, with two children. Yet, after ten years of analysis, an ending was nowhere in sight. She would, from time to time, raise the question of ending in the form of how much longer "this" would last. By contrast, my preoccupation was not with an ending, but with a beginning. Despite diminution of her psychosomatic symptoms, despite substantial improvements in family life, especially her relationship with her children, despite positive developments in her career, I felt little had changed in her mode of engagement with herself or with me. She remained dissatisfied and demanding, controlled and controlling, and there was a cold, calculating quality in her attitude toward me, as if her eye were constantly on a narcissistic balance sheet.

Beneath the veneer of psychological formulae she had acquired, Ms B remained untrusting, ever-vigilant, and un-free to associate. She felt she had been helped by her analysis, but it seemed that analytic engagement was still as alien to her as it had been at the start of our work together. True, needing analysis was now less of a narcissistic blow to her, so she felt less belittled and more tolerant of interpretation, but her attitude toward insight remained what I came to think of as *instrumental*.[2] In this, she had something in common with Mr A: they were both preoccupied with *how to do it*.

* * *

Mr A treated insight as a formula, a prescription. He told me that, as he was leaving a session in which he had been struck by an interpretation, he said to himself, "Do this and you will never feel anxious ever again." He had been bitterly disappointed because it had only worked for a few days. It took me some time to understand how he had turned the interpretation in question into a "do this"—a formula.

With all her sophistication, Ms B carried out a version of the same thing. It was only when I started addressing the *instrumentality* of her mode of engagement with me that an area of resistance came to light. To give an example: I had often interpreted her envy of those she saw as capable of *doing* whatever she felt she could not do, and this ranged from her husband's capacity to simply pick up the phone and make social arrangements to my capacity to analyse her. Ms B could now reveal that she felt entitled to dismiss any interpretation that made her feel "uncomfortable". Her hitherto silent, dismissive response of

"How is that supposed to help me?" could find voice. We could now put into words her belief that it was my job to give her the tools to get whatever she wanted while simultaneously relieving her of all "discomfort", especially any feelings remotely approaching depression or guilt.

This realisation paved the way to analysing the particular form of dependent relationship in which Ms B engaged with me, wherein she felt she owed me nothing, as well as the wishful fantasies sustaining it, which, up to then, she had silently gratified. Her certainty that she knew what constituted real help arose out of her need to obliterate any *emotional experience* of being helped by me. Reluctantly, she came to think that maybe she should "consider" some of the uncomfortable things I said because they *might* help her.

For my part, I could appreciate what uphill work analysis was for Ms B, as she had no natural bent toward inwardness, no acceptance of the necessity of learning from experience—the opposite of the instrumental approach—without which there is no true psychoanalytic engagement.

* * *

To follow up these opening remarks, I will state my theme in the present paper. There is no ending without a beginning. Patients who cannot end analysis are patients who, like Mr A and Ms B, have not begun, because their approach to analysis is to evade the give and take of *emotional experience*. Having managed to get by in external life, they are, thus, reinforced in the instrumentality of their approach to psychic life.

Of course, Ms B was doing better than merely getting by; viewed externally, she was far less disturbed than Mr A. Ms B had a richer life, except that her demands and complaints precluded her from inhabiting her life, and, equally, her analysis. It is telling that for years she referred to her analysis as "this". In short, psychoanalytically, both she and Mr A fell within the broad diagnostic category of narcissism.

Experience and its modes: reification

Emotional experience is the medium through which we apprehend the clinical situation. It is also the medium of self-awareness.

Whatever psychoanalytic understanding we have reached, our concern is to convey this to the patient in a way that will resonate with his emotional experience. The locution "the patient's experience of the analyst" is the commonest, the most natural, form of words in conveying the analyst's sense of the manifest transference.

But, unlike transference, *experience* is not a technical term, so it does not claim our attention. We are not inclined to say, "It depends on what you mean by *experience*," as we might of a theoretical term, which might have acquired different meanings with the development of psychoanalytic theory. It seems obvious that we all mean the same thing by *experience*, that *experiencing* itself—as opposed to its content—refers to one and the same phenomenon, that it is the inevitable and irreducible aspect of being a sentient creature. To have sense perceptions and feelings is to have the potentiality to have an experience.

Yet, my clinical work with perverse patients, and some narcissistic patients, has forced upon me the realisation that I cannot take for granted that experience is a unitary phenomenon. It appears to have modes, some of them pretty strange. I have already alluded to one such mode: an instrumental approach to psychic life. Instrumentality is entirely appropriate to acting upon an object, with behaviourism as its background theory. But acting is not the core of experiencing. Instrumentality is inimical to the enterprise of psychoanalysis.

The psychoanalytic setting enables the gradual unfolding of an experiential process, lived and meditated upon, all in the service of learning. Beyond instrumentality, there is a more extreme deformation of experience that defies our implicit understanding of the concept in that it is denuded of emotional qualities. The patient is always observing himself from a distance. He is never *in* his experience. He brings to his experience of himself a mode of apprehending more appropriate to an inanimate object. So, what kind of "experiencing" is this? Tentatively, I call it a *denuded experience*.

Characteristically, experience is a two-way process, active and passive, operational and receptive, with the emphasis on the passive and the receptive. Typically, the two directions are going on at the same time. Above all, it cannot be controlled. It is *given*, and one has to be open to it. For this reason, *undergoing an experience* is a better choice of words than *having an experience*. We could call this *ordinary, rich, saturated experience*, experience fully lived, in contrast to the denuded experience of a patient who is always at a distance, observing himself.

Patients who do not actually begin analysis, despite turning up five times a week, are trying to avoid the two-way movement of full experience. Acquiring knowledge from a book, or the analyst-as-book, is considered not only preferable to learning from the analyst-as-human being, but even the ideal kind of relation. The advantage of a book is that it does not talk back. But knowledge so acquired changes nothing, as we know. I propose that analytic engagement on this basis is a non-beginning. I also suggest that such a non-beginning can last for years.

Optimally, the psychoanalytic process has two components. On the one hand, the patient has to allow himself to be *in* his experience, yet, over time, he has to learn to stand back sufficiently to join the analyst in reflecting upon it. This is not easy, but managing this tension is one of the capacities that grow in an analysis in which growth is happening. This capacity for self-observation is an indicator in assessing the patient's readiness to end analysis. Where emotional experience itself is evaded, there can be no true self-observation either. Instead, there is a great deal of self-absorption, rumination, and vigilance that are believed to yield truths about self and object—convictions sometimes of a delusional quality—but there is no self-observation.

So far, I have put things in black and white, to indicate that experience is not a unitary phenomenon. However, it is more fruitful to consider deformations of experience as residing along a continuum. At one end, we have full experience, the capacity to be *in* one's experience. At the other end is what I shall describe as the *reification of experience*, a deformation so extreme that it moves into a different dimension.

Along this continuum, we can place patients who frequently gravitate toward *the observer* position. Clinically, it makes quite a difference whether or not the move to the observer position is a tendency only, a position to which a patient resorts defensively in identifiable emotional situations, while having the capacity for full experience. I would place Ms B somewhere about here.

However, when the observer position is essential to the patient's central defensive structure, and, therefore, has become the *only* mode of experiencing, we are in a qualitatively different situation. We encounter this situation with perverse patients, where we are confronted with the startling human capacity to treat not only the object and the body as inanimate, but also the mind. This extreme state of affairs is the most intractable obstacle I know of to psychoanalytic engagement, to initiating the psychoanalytic process. Every hint of a beginning is nullified through the reification of potentially full experience. The essence of the defence of reification is the turning of a live experience into a dead thing.[3]

Case presentation: Mr C

I turn now to a more detailed case presentation: that of Mr C, a perverse patient who was seen five times per week. In this analysis, after the well-known aspects of the perverse transference—sexualization, sadomasochistic relating, and deception—had been sufficiently analysed, there emerged a puzzle: something silently undermined every insight, every new beginning. I shall describe how the solution to this puzzle hinged upon identification of the defence of reification of experience. I shall then discuss the usefulness of this understanding in opening up the analytic process. I shall go on to examine how these openings led to a fuller appreciation of the power of this defence to nullify every potential beginning.

Mr C was a fifty-year-old, single man when he started analysis. The reason he gave for seeking analysis was that he wanted to get married and have children. But he had a problem: whenever he started a relationship with a woman, his eyes began hunting for another woman. This identified his perversion: voyeurism.

By the end of the consultation, Mr C was able to sum up his predicament as "I cannot love or be loved." He arrived for treatment with an arsenal of analytic jargon, a bastion against the analytic process. Any interpretation could contribute to pseudo-talk. If I took up what I *supposed* was his anxiety, he would go along with it, but the nature of engagement did not change. (He secretly believed himself to be immune to anxiety. It took us three years to reach the point where he could say, "I live outside the perimeter of anxiety.") Technically, here-and-now interpretations posed a particular danger: it was a game whose rules he thought he knew and could play with great skill. On the other hand, what I took to be a free association would turn out to be in reality a mental action—for example, taking himself out of the room, absenting himself. He believed he could use even his dreams to defeat and trick me.

Mr C was tall, lean, and muscular, yet came across as effeminate. He was tricky and passive, controlled and controlling, and expressed absolutely no affect. He would offer a well-scripted "thought" and then fall into a dead silence. On the couch, he lay like a corpse. His early communications were of himself as "neither dead nor alive", but leading the halfway existence of a "zombie". Nothing touched him; he existed "behind a glass wall".

The pathos of this state of affairs remained obscure to others and to Mr C himself, as he perpetually engaged in seduction—of everyone. The transference was sexualised, dominated by sadomasochistic dynamics, with the patient initially firmly entrenched in the masochistic position. Deception in the transference was ever present, a source of erotic and narcissistic gratification.

Mr C found extremely difficult his perception of me as someone whom he could not easily seduce, but he came to appreciate my efforts *not* to be seduced into pseudo-analysis. This meant I could stand not being appreciated, and I could bear to know his secret denigration of me. With time, he could be more honest, less dedicated to conscious deception. The relief he reported was one of feeling less fraudulent, less alone with his lifelong sense of being bad and/or mad.

He began to join me in attempting to discriminate pseudo-contact from real contact, and to articulate how impossible it was for him to be a patient on the couch. He could not say what was on his mind, as his mind was dominated by the part of his personality that he came to call *the observer*, the one who scrutinised my every move to find out what *I* required of *him*. Mr C could, thus, be in control of the proceedings by *appearing* to give me what he believed I wanted, while secretly withholding. Frustrating me was exciting. As *the observer*, he was in a superior, unaffected position; he watched and controlled all interactions between us, literally from a great height, wholly *dissociated* from his body, the seat of his emotions.

On those rare moments when the patient was actually *in* his body, when he was not the observer, he felt profoundly disturbed, on the edge of breakdown. Emerging from such a state, he said, "My whole life is organised around never feeling loss." I would add only that loss—to the extent that it can be represented—is always a betrayal; at a deeper level, it is bodily disintegration (what he later came to call "chaos").

During the first three years of Mr C's analysis, there were changes in two areas: his aggression, and the narcissism of the object. He began to own his hostility toward me and the whole analytic endeavour. His belief system could now be expressed. *The observer* was his true protector. The observer was all powerful and all knowing, antidependent and antianalysis. Without the observer, to be a patient was to be in my power. He began to ask why he came to analysis five times a week if he was so determined to defeat me. And how could I stand him, such an unrewarding patient?

Mr C could see a link between his punishment of me and his hatred of his mother. He began to take some interest in his dreams, which, at this stage, featured repetitive images of robbers, criminals, and terrorists. Something had changed. Nevertheless, I felt that something else, something not yet identified, quietly undermined every insight we reached. Every session started as if there had been no previous session: with lifeless statements, minimal, scripted offerings called "thoughts".

A change in the countertransference was that I no longer felt the same pressure of frustration. I felt, rather, that if something were to happen, the onus of creativity had to be entirely on me; I must be the sole bearer of the wish for meaningful contact. I must not count on any collaboration from the patient; I must keep alive the hope that, at some unpredictable moment in the session, I *might* get through to him in a way he *might* then appreciate. Which left me with a puzzle: what had happened to his experience of moments of real contact?

One day, there came a clue. Having done some productive work, Mr C said, with anguish in his voice, "I wish I could say that I have had an experience of being understood by you—which I have—and that this will make a difference. But I know it won't." There was masochistic defiance here. But what was *new* was the anguish. This alerted me to the fact that, during this moment of real contact, something was happening to the *experience of being understood*. That he routinely edited me out of the process, so that the understanding became his creation, was not new. Neither was it new that he fed his grandiosity and obliterated any awareness of dependence on me; such emotional stealing had been a familiar part of the work. The new insight concerned the silent dynamics of *reification* of his experience of being understood by me.

Mr C abstracted the *understanding* from the *experience of being understood*.[4] This is *the observer* in action: the patient removes understanding from its living context, which alone gives it meaning, gives it life. Denuded of the shared experiential context, understanding becomes a *thing* that can be possessed by the patient and stored in his mind. (This is Bion's (1962) knowledge as possession, as opposed to the emotional experience of coming to know and be known.) Reification transforms insight into artefact, understanding into information. Thus, instead of understanding living and growing in Mr C's mind, his mind came to possess a collection of things called *understandings*. These were filed, classified, reclassified: this was what he called *thinking*.

When this dawned on me and I could interpret it, Mr C's confirmation was unequivocal. He said, with unprecedented conviction and vehemence, "I don't want the living context! I don't want to experience!" The energy in his voice was singular: he had really come to life—at the very moment that he was rejecting life.

How does this help? First, the concept of reification illuminates the recalcitrance to internal transformation of perverse patients. Second, it is salutary to realise that the mere occurrence of emotional contact between patient and analyst can be overvalued in work with perverse patients. Not that emotional contact never occurs, but rather that, even as the analyst is moved, and is having an experience, and believes herself to be sharing the experience with her patient, the patient has already silently destroyed the moment of real give and take.

Clinically, this conceptualisation not only enabled me to analyse the reification in the moment, but also allowed access to the hitherto hidden, split-off, mad parts of Mr C's mind, an area ruled by delusional beliefs, such as, "I am the only boy–man in the world." Work could then follow on his confused gender identity: his overt passivity equated with femininity and his hidden masculinity equated with exciting delinquency and violence. His sense of himself was as everything: girl, boy, man, and yet as nothing: not-girl, not-boy, but a "zombie".

Mr C would occasionally express the hope of coming alive, or some concern over wasting his life and his analysis in the ceaseless vengeful triumph over his mother and me. Yet, what he called "hope" could now be seen to be a manic, omnipotent state of mind, and despair, when it emerged, was suicidal in quality. Moments arose when his terror of utter helplessness could be touched on. We now had a real word for anxiety—his word: *panic*. Any hint of dependence on me led to the panic of disorientation, the terror of leaving the consulting room and experiencing the world as *chaos*.

While the understanding of reification opened up the analysis and made for some movement, again, it felt as if nothing was changing. The old problem of *no experiential continuity* was still there, dressed in new clothes. At this point, I noticed something: although understanding was growing in *my* mind, something different was going on in *his* mind, an accumulation of disconnected pieces of knowledge, but no growth. I now felt the full force of the concept: reification precludes the growth of true understanding. *Things* cannot grow. They can only be put together into lifeless aggregates, or kept apart, assembled and disassembled, and all this with no effect upon the one in charge of the activity. My patient treated his mind as a cabinet of curiosities.

But what is it that reification defends against? What is so terrifying about being alive that live objects are treated as inanimate matter, and experience itself is treated as a thing that can be operated upon?

The tantalising mother: the genesis of reification

Over the years of Mr C's analysis, an unvarying situation changed in one respect only: it became more overt. Every time I gave the patient the dates of an incipient break, weeks of silent hostility were ushered in. The patient grew as dead as it was possible to be, essentially walking in and out of the consulting room and breathing on the couch. He spent considerable time sleeping on the couch. When awake, he lay absolutely still and silent.

In every session after my announcement of a break, Mr C uttered one or two carefully scripted sentences, never in response to anything I had said, but merely to prove that nothing I said had any impact on him. Even if occasionally there was contact, the following day it was as if there had been none. Over the years, I offered many interpretations at such times, including the dual aspect of his sleeping: to obliterate all awareness, and to be at one with me forever. In practice, I found interpretations of his sadism and his unquenchable thirst for revenge to be the most accessible to him; I had to realise that I had committed an unforgivable crime, for which my punishment was life-long torture. But interpretations that linked his revenge to the approaching break were not convincing—not to him, and increasingly not to me; the nature of my crime remained unknown.

On one particular occasion, after many weeks, there came an opening. Near the end of a session, out of the blue, the patient asked himself a question: "Why do I hate my mother so much? What she did to me was not *that* bad."

This led, in subsequent sessions, to work on identifying her original crime. I condense here the image of the *tantalising mother*, which emerged gradually as a result of collaborative work, but the words and phrases I use are his. She could not get enough of him; she fussed over him, could not leave him alone; he was all she wanted. He fitted in with her, gave her everything she wished for. He was not a child, he was a grown-up, the one whom Mother desired. Then, suddenly, she wanted to be with Father, and he was told to leave her alone. When she had her husband, she became haughty; she treated him like a child, to be seen and not heard, to be told off: "Stop being such a baby!"

This was the pivotal moment: the moment of betrayal. We had been there before, but never accompanied by a current of such strong affect. Mr C's violent rage now found words appropriate to the maddening frustration: *"You complain about the thing you made me into!"*

This was a deeply moving moment. And there was no question that the patient was reliving his unbearable experience. But, in subsequent work, I had to learn, yet again, that what *I* learned from my clinical experience with Mr C and what *he* made of it were discrepant. I felt he had been disinherited; his childhood had been taken away from him. I suspect it was the empathy he picked up from my tone of voice that he could not stand. Coldly, he disagreed with me and informed me that he *loved* being a grown-up, and that he looked down on children; what he hated was his mother's treating him like a child.

And, of course, this was timelessly true. In the analysis, he hated my treating him as a patient. Taking this up enabled him to spit out at me, "I'll tell you how it makes me feel! It makes me feel *profoundly unimportant!*" He could then acknowledge his conviction that, were he to allow himself to stay with his fury for more than a moment, I would be in danger of being murdered. To come alive was to kill me. Being in his experience was to plunge into a psychotic transference where I *was* his mother. He evaded the dilemma and settled for a war of attrition. The episode ended with his declaration to me, "If I am to be *real* with you, I will have to dispute *every single thing* you say."

Mr C kept his promise. He did dispute what I said. And this, of course, had the potential for a real beginning. Except that there was not one. Instead, I was told by the patient, "You have to understand that there is an ever-present background against which I hear everything you say. You are cold, harsh, and critical." There were variations on this theme (he "knew" that I hated him), and he could develop imagery suggesting that I was not so much hating of him as *indifferent* toward him: me the surgeon operating on him, me dedicated to psychoanalysis but not to *him*.

One might think these images to be full of potential—a surgeon operates on an anaesthetised patient, psychoanalysis and I as the parental couple—except that they proved not to be. The characteristic of all Mr C's statements about "the background" was that they were presented as unnegotiable reality, as dogma. It was in this new era of his freedom to be overtly critical of me and to tell me how he "experienced" me that the problem about the quality of his "experience" came to the fore. It became clear that, when the patient told me I was cold, harsh, and critical, he was not communicating his experience to me as a human analyst who might receive the communication and understand it. Rather, he was telling me who I was; he was telling me this was his reality, and even to allow for any other possibility was for him to comply with my requirements and, therefore, to be driven to deception, which he was no longer willing to do.

Thus, Mr C's newfound capacity to be more outspoken, which one might think he owed to the analysis, became an instrument to defeat the analysis. Quite a conundrum—but it did have the merit of putting centre stage the issue of deception.

I will return now to the tantalising mother. This material suggests a construction, a hypothetical moment in which the patient initiated and instituted the reification of experience, which, henceforth, became his main mode of psychic being. The image of the tantalising mother condensed the maddening emotional experience that could not be lived because it led to murder, yet it was re-enacted within the mode of reification. The solution (the defence) was for Mr C to vacate his experiencing, bodily self and become the observer of his own experiencing. The gain was to preserve the needed object. The fantasy was that, from the observer position, whatever was needed to sustain life could be extracted from the object, with no regard for what was being done to it. He, the observer, was entirely immune from being affected by it, a thing. Any emotional experience of give and take was dispensed with.

The catch in this solution was that an awareness remained that the object would *hate* being so treated, as a thing to be used, so that deception of the object was imperative. A pretence of caring was substituted for real caring. Deception was instituted at the same moment as reification. That the reification did not obliterate all awareness of feeling—hatred aroused by being treated as a thing—was the only tribute paid by this solution to the truth of the original experience. It lived on as the ever-present threat of the object's hatred of him, the subject, should she get to know what he was really doing under the façade of seductive care.

While such reification ensures survival, it does not obliterate guilt—in fact, guilt becomes a conviction of irremediable badness. There is a vicious circle here. By putting himself outside the human condition (through reification), the patient also puts himself beyond the reach of what he most comes to need, the mitigation of his guilt. Guilt cannot be mitigated without the intervention of a *live* object capable of offering him understanding of his predicament, which could lead to forgiveness, first and foremost of himself. But the only way he knows to make contact is through seduction and deception. The vicious circle is lived out in the analysis.

The model of reification is exactly that, a model, and not a historical reconstruction. The model hypothesises the experience of being tantalised and treated as a thing, as the central experience defended against through reification. I do not claim genetic primacy for this experience. Historically, a great deal had happened before the period from which this memory comes; it is not from infancy.

Interestingly, Bion (1962, Chapter Five) hypothesises a disturbed early feeding situation in which the infant's solution to irreconcilable fears—fear of aggression, his own or another's, on the one hand, and fear of death through starvation, on the other—is to create a distinctive form of splitting between "material and psychical satisfaction" (1962, p. 10). This enables the infant "to obtain what later in life would be called material comforts without acknowledging the existence of a live object on which these benefits depend" (ibid.). Bion also connects this "enforced splitting" with the destruction of alpha-function, and with the distinction between knowledge as possession and knowledge as a process of coming to know. With such patients, the paradigmatic psychoanalytic relationship of the analyst getting to know the patient, and the patient getting to be known by the analyst, cannot be realised. In Bion's words:

> The patient ... does not feel he is having interpretations, for that
> would involve an ability to establish with the analyst the counterpart
> of an infant's relationship with a breast that provides material wisdom
> and love. But he feels able only to establish the counterpart of a rela-
> tionship in which such sustenance can be had as inanimate objects can
> provide. ... The patient uses equipment suited for contact with the
> inanimate to establish contact with himself. (ibid., pp. 11–12)

It appears that Bion (at least in this text) is according ultimate
explanatory status to the split he postulates between material and
psychological/immaterial satisfaction, with its correlate in contact
with inanimate versus animate objects, a sort of bedrock of the
patient's being. Interestingly, though Bion's concern here is with
thought-disordered patients, in my experience, it is remarkably illuminating of something fundamentally intractable one comes up
against in the analysis of perverse patients.

That there might be a close link between what we call disorders of
thought, on the one hand, and perversion, on the other, raises many
questions. At the most abstract level, it raises questions of nosology/
classification: whether perversion can be placed on a continuum
extending from psychosis to neurosis. Glover grappled with this question and reached a negative conclusion. (For his alternative classification of a "parallel series," see Glover 1956, p. 226.)

I do not, as yet, feel in a position to grapple with the role of psychic
temporality and causality—the Freudian *deferred action*—in this material.[5] The model of reification brings together meaningful things Mr C
has said in seemingly unconnected contexts, separated by long periods of time. To take only two examples: in his view, there was a point
at which he stopped caring and started to pretend to care, the point at
which he said—in his mind—to his mother, "You are *nothing* to me!"
At another point, the patient said that the woman he had sexual intercourse with was not a person, but a "bundle of flesh". What I claim
for the model is that it addresses my persistent clinical puzzles and
struggles, as well as my failures to speak to the patient in a way that
ameliorated his underlying sense of isolation, despair, and guilt.

The model illuminates why Mr C's *experience* of his mother in the
transference remained so inaccessible to analysis. The purpose of reification is to render the self immune to being affected by the object—in
other words, to obviate the need to *experience* one's self as linked to
the object. It is this that was repeated in his analysis. The patient was

voicing the truth when he said to me, "Nothing you say will make any difference to me," and equally so when he said, "You are cold, harsh, and critical."

But the truth lay in the service of *doing* something to me—making me a thing, repeating and reinstating his defence. I might understand him to be saying, "Nothing you do will ever take me there, where I feel, where I am subject to the maddeningness of true experience." But the clinical problem remained: that is, how was I to convey this understanding to him?

Since he had to reinstate the defence, he could not allow my words to resonate with the needy, vulnerable, human part of himself. And even if there were a stirring of an emotional experience, within a matter of seconds, reification would occur. The situation was greatly complicated by sexualisation, so that there was triumph in this, and sadistic gratification. More than gratification, it was the only counter to Mr C's deadening reification; it was his only avenue to life—life as triumphant excitement. But the fact remained that, in doing it, he was halting the possibility of revisiting the maddening original situation in the presence of a new object, his analyst.

So, when I conveyed to the patient my understanding of what he was defending against, he might go along with me, but we ended up having a theoretical discussion about him. If I addressed his defence and took up his indifference to me, I had to address the fact that indifference was his ultimate revenge against me. At a certain point, he could acknowledge such interpretations intellectually, but this did not help his guilt. At best, it became a piece of dead knowledge, and at worst it became sexualised and experienced as my weapon to make him feel even more bad about himself than he already felt. His guilt could never be mitigated—he had placed himself outside human intercourse.

A model I have found *not* to illuminate clinical facts is one based on the assumption of the patient's identification with his mother. The clinical facts suggested, rather, that the mother was lodged and kept inside Mr C as an *introject*, an alien other who had to be kept *doubly alien*—she was a thing, and she was a not-him-thing. This was the only way he could say no to her (and to me). His whole being and energy were devoted to keeping her at arm's length, keeping her as a thing to be acted upon: imprisoned, punished, extracted from ("I force you to care for me"), and denied life, save for the bare minimum of sensual contact when the need arose ("All I know is to pleasure the woman, service her, and get pleasure back"); the need to deceive was unmitigated. This at least explained my conundrum that, even though *I* might think he had a sustained experience of me as someone whom he did not have to deceive, *his* psychic reality was that he had no such experience.

Another merit I claim for my chosen model is that it helped with my countertransference. Frustration ceased to be the main problem. The greater danger was my indifference, indifference born out of my repeated experiences of sheer outrage and disbelief as I listened to what Mr C did with the insights we had reached with such painstaking work, moments I found so moving. He rendered them lifeless things, which he himself learnt to call "just words", "empty words", "meaningless words", or "just theory". And not only this, he also took credit for the fact that, in saying they were meaningless, he was being honest. His capacity to turn any gain in the analysis into a weapon against me was limitless. The twists and turns of deception were extraordinary, and disentangling what was genuine from what was false, what was in the service of revenge, or what expressed his profound despair, could feel like an impossible task, and yet it was the main task. My countertransference problem was: how could I maintain empathy, rather than resort to interpretation as a mechanical procedure?

It was not difficult to attribute the function of deception to the patient's observing self. In a productive session, he was able to say, "Whenever I am approaching really feeling something . . . like now . . . it's like I am reaching out to put my hand into the fire. The observer says, 'It isn't real,' and I draw back . . . and then *it isn't real any more.*" We could then see that the observer, held in place as Mr C's true protector, was, in fact, a deceiver—he "protected" him by telling him that what was real was not real. In time, the observer became a bit less reified, became acknowledged as part of the patient himself, and with this came some capacity to own and to take the measure of his confusion about what was real and what was not.

Here is a brief excerpt from a session. The issue here was the ever-present me in "the background". On this occasion, the cold me was elaborated as *deaf to him.* This arose out of my taking up Mr C's habitual gesture of forcefully poking his ear with his index finger, as a communication of his experience of my emotional deafness to him.

The patient then talked as though he believed I had spoken to him in an unemotional tone of voice. Since this was not convincing to me, I addressed his defence.

> *Analyst*: "I think you edit out any emotion you hear in my voice because it's dangerous. It could affect you."
>
> *Mr C*: (immediately). "I don't think you have any emotions."

He stopped and fell into a dead silence. He was not to be contradicted. By this point, I had learnt that when he made such a statement in such a tone, he was not communicating his experience of me in any ordinary sense of that word. But he was doing something very familiar—making me into a thing. I chose not to interpret this, as it felt repetitious and mechanical. As the silence continued, I associated to words we had recently got to in a tiny opening, after his sustained indifference upon returning from the break, and after he had sufficiently impressed upon me the fact that the problem was not the break itself because, break or no break, the situation was always the same for him—he felt "incredibly bad, ugly, and frozen out". If anything, he had said, the break was a relief for him because he could at least distract himself. Now, "frozen out" was pretty close to what *I* was feeling. Having got to this point, I no longer felt frozen, and it felt all right to remain silent.

> *Mr C*: "You are emotionally deaf to me." (This was my interpretation of his experience of me—now issued as his, and as fact! I felt that directly interpreting this was likely to draw me into an all-too-familiar sadomasochistic enactment—would close rather than open a space for experience. I remained silent.)
>
> *Mr C*: (After a long silence, he spoke in a different, more reflective tone.) "Maybe *I'm* emotionally deaf." (Silence.)
>
> *Mr C*: (with a hint of distress) "Maybe I'm deaf to my own emotions."

(Another long silence followed. He started rubbing his forehead with his fist; there was a sense of struggle.)

> *Mr C*: "I'm confused. I can't work it out . . . I can't work out whether I am really emotionally deaf and pretend to be hearing . . . or whether I pretend to be emotionally deaf and I can really hear . . ."
>
> *Analyst*: "You can't work it out without help from me, an analyst able to hear you emotionally. You did away with that analyst the moment you said, 'You have no emotions.' You made it real for yourself that I am emotionally deaf to you."

Conclusion

I hope I have illustrated the problem of interminability with a patient with whom what it is to have an emotional experience cannot be taken for granted, and also that the problem of interminability is one of how to begin. At least, it was so in this case. It is said that, in the legal arena, hard cases make bad law; in psychoanalysis, by contrast, hard cases are revelatory. What we learn from hard cases illuminates dynamics with a wider range of patients.

I will end with a further clinical vignette from the analysis of Mr C. It occurred at the end of a week in which he had given evidence of having derived some benefit from a session, and then proceeded to show me that he could not tolerate this being acknowledged. On Friday, there was a surprising development. He said, "As you were talking, my thoughts went to yesterday's session . . . and I thought, *you accept* that there are *some* sessions I benefit from, and others I *don't* benefit from."

This was offered as a revelation. He went on, "You are not trying to control all the time. . . . It felt like . . . I don't know how to describe it. . . . It felt like a very grown-up position."

I found myself saying, "I accept my limitations." His revelation was matched by my own; I felt I had spoken out of a sense of my own fallibility and mortality.

After a silence, the patient said, "So much of my thinking is done from the observer position that when I begin to think from another place . . . inside . . . it is freeing, but frightening, because there is chaos."

*   *   *

In sum, we all have to face our terrors. We believe analysis offers the patient the opportunity to face them in the presence of an analyst who is prepared to accompany him on a journey, wherever it leads, and who can, over time, transform such stuff of raw experience sufficiently to make it bearable. For some patients, their defences obliterate any awareness that there is a journey to be undertaken—in psychoanalysis as in life. And so they do not begin.

Perhaps we continue working with such recalcitrant patients not only because of what we learn about the complexity of the human mind, but also because they teach us to realise our limitations—and our mortality. It is paradoxical that being confronted with an interminable analysis should connect us with the unalterable fact of life: that it ends. If we do not believe in forced terminations of analysis, the option of giving up is not available. This may sound like an excess of therapeutic zeal, but for some considerable time, I have grounded myself in Bion's (1965) dictum: "Psychoanalysts do not aim to run the patient's life but to enable him to run it according to his lights and therefore to know what his lights are" (p. 37).

I discovered that working with Mr C made me more deeply alive to the pain and the beauty of Shakespeare's (1623) couplet:

> Golden lads and girls all must,
> As chimney-sweepers come to dust.
>   (IV:2: 325–326)

The lights by which Mr C lived his life rendered him immune to pain, but, sadly, also to beauty. For him, everything was merely as dull as dust. It was this, his ultimate sense of isolation in his reified world, that I had to stay with for as long as it took.

Notes

1. The Portman Clinic is a public sector outpatient clinic in London which specialises in offering psychoanalytic psychotherapy to patients who suffer from perversion, delinquency and violence. It is part of the Tavistock and Portman NHS Foundation Trust.

    I would like to acknowledge my debt to my colleagues at the Portman Clinic, with whom I have discussed perversion dynamics over a seventeen-year period. Glasser (1979, 1986) and Campbell (1995, 2008), in particular, have been seminal influences.
2. Roth (2009) addresses a recognisably similar clinical phenomenon from a different angle. She conceptualises it as the *commodification* of the object.
3. *Reification* comes from the Latin *res*, a thing.
4. Joseph (1989) makes the identical distinction between the experience of being understood and "getting understanding" (p. 79).
5. Perelberg (2008) suggested an answer to this question: in killing experience, the patient is killing time and space. With the collapse of time, there is no *après-coup*.

References

Bion, W. R. (1962). *Learning from Experience.* London: Heinemann.

Bion, W. R. (1965). *Transformations: Change from Learning to Growth.* London: Tavistock.

Campbell, D. (1995). The role of the father in a pre-suicide state. *International Journal of Psychoanalysis, 76*: 325–323.

Campbell, D. (2008). The shame shield in child sexual abuse. In: C. Pajaczkowska & I. Ward (Eds.), *Shame and Sexuality* (pp. 75–91). London: Routledge.

Glasser, M. (1979). Some aspects of the role of aggression in the perversions. In: I. Rosen (Ed.). *Sexual Deviation,* 2nd ed. Oxford University Press.

Glasser, M. (1986). Identification and its vicissitudes as observed in the perversions. *International Journal of Psychoanalysis, 67*: 9–17.

Glover, E. (1956). *On the Early Development of Mind.* London: Imago.

Joseph, B. (1989). *Psychic Equilibrium and Psychic Change: Selected Papers of Betty Joseph,* M. Feldman & E. Spillius (Eds.). London: Routledge.

Perelberg, R. (2008). Personal communication.

Roth, P. (2009). Where else? Considering the here and now. *Bulletin of the British Psychoanalytic Society, 45*(3): 13–22.

Shakespeare, W. (1623). *Cymbeline.* London: Penguin, 2005.

CHAPTER EIGHT

The Oedipus complex

Gregorio Kohon

I n spite of its many contradictions, inconsistencies, paradoxes, and ambiguities, psychoanalytic theory has a certain definite structure; within it, one single aspect of the theory cannot be understood without taking into consideration the rest of the metapsychological structure. The Oedipus complex would not make sense unless put in the context of the psychoanalytic understanding of the unconscious. At the same time, the concept of the unconscious cannot make any sense without understanding the meaning given to sexuality in psychoanalysis. The psychoanalytic concepts of sexuality and the dynamics of the unconscious cannot be understood without reference to the Oedipus complex and its corollaries, the castration complex and the concept of penis envy. Yet, castration would not make much sense without its theoretical connection to the primal scene and the phantasies of seduction. The theory is intricate and comprises a multiplicity of meanings, which are all interlocked and interconnected.

At the same time (and to complicate things a bit further), the use of common, already known, and frequently employed concepts in everyday language have been transformed and changed by psychoanalytic theory in such a way as to make them unrecognisable. Psychoanalysis should be understood as a theoretically and clinically distinct discipline, with its own specific paradigms. In trying to comprehend psychoanalysis, we are constantly taking the risk of sliding back to more familiar paradigms, which distorts the endeavour. For example, the understanding of the body in psychoanalysis does not follow the same laws that biology does. The body in psychoanalysis is a sexual body, it is organised and structured in a different manner to the "natural" one, as studied by biology and physiology. The same applies to other concepts, like sexuality, or the distinction between sex and gender; or the debate between nature and culture; or the question of time, etc. With the discovery of the unconscious, Freud produced an epistemological jump, a rupture that turned psychoanalysis into something different from any other psychological theory of the mind.

Psychoanalysis and tragedy

From its beginnings, psychoanalysis was as much a therapeutic method of treating the neuroses as it was a theory of the mind. And, as such, it was concerned with the destiny of human beings as tragic subjects. In this respect, psychoanalytic ideas address the same fundamental questions posed by literature and other forms of thought across the centuries:

> . . . how to live in a world in which justice and power, right and might, often seem to have nothing to do with each other? how to deal with the fear that my own aggression and violence will overflow and violate all that I care about? how to confront my own death, and the deaths of those I love? how to act responsibly in the absence of freedom? how to make this inhumane world a more human place, and so comfort myself, and offer comfort to others? (Alford, 1992, p. ix)

The interest and passion that Freud showed for Greek tragedy and the great myths of literature were motivated not only by a wish to explain or justify his theories. Freud found in Oedipus the representation of universal unconscious incestuous wishes, the interplay of transgression and punishment implied in the actions of a literary character who appeared to be both innocent and guilty, and the impact and significance of the basic laws presiding over our morality in somebody who "knows and does not know a thing at the same time" (Freud & Breuer, 1895d, p. 117).

The core of Freudian psychoanalytic ideas rests, in fact, upon a double tragic model: not only on Oedipus's unconscious predicament of incest and crime, but also on the repressed symbolic reproduction of this drama in the guilty consciousness of Hamlet. In *The Interpretation of Dreams*, Freud says,

> Shakespeare's *Hamlet* has its roots in the same soil as *Oedipus Rex* . . . In the Oedipus the child's wishful phantasy that underlies it is brought into the open and realised as it would in a dream. In Hamlet it remains repressed . . . we only learn of its existence from its inhibiting consequences . . . Hamlet is able to do anything – except take vengeance on the man who did away with his father and took that father's place with his mother, the man who shows him the repressed wishes of his own childhood realised. (Freud, 1900a, pp. 263–264)

As neurotic patients, we are closer to Hamlet than to Oedipus.

When we search for the concept of the Oedipus complex in the psychoanalytic literature, we might become confused by the multiple, at times rather subtle and sophisticated, interpretations of the myth. Yet, the interpretations are impossible to systematise. Freud himself refused to, or could not give a systematic account of the complex. Nevertheless, while the meaning of Hamlet's drama, as popular as it has been, has remained relatively obscure in the imagination of the general public, Oedipus's tragedy has, rather mystifyingly, become a commonplace. The simplistic understanding of the Oedipus complex, its distortions and simplifications (including those that have been produced by psychoanalysts themselves), hide its rejection.

Freud commented in a footnote to *The Interpretation of Dreams*,

> None of the findings of psychoanalytic research has provoked such embittered denials, such fierce opposition – or such amusing contortions – on the part of critics as this indication of the childhood impulses towards incest which persist in the unconscious. (ibid., p. 263).

Freud believed that the Oedipus complex defined psychoanalysis. No psychoanalytic theory could be accepted as such unless, according to him, it admitted the universality of this complex, and the importance of the incest theme. The Oedipal drama represents for him the fate of all of us (ibid., p. 262). In this, Freud followed the classics: in making the Chorus describe Oedipus as the paradigm of the human condition, Sophocles gave the same recognition to Oedipus. Aristotle too, in his *Poetics*, considered the drama of Oedipus Rex the prime example, the archetype, of all tragedies. For Freud, it was perfectly understandable that many people would disagree with his views, but then, he argued, their theories should be called something else, not psychoanalysis. It seems a fair request. In the *New Introductory Lectures on Psycho-analysis*, ironically referring to the theories of the dissident followers, Rank and Jung, he says,

> Suppose, for instance, that an analyst attaches little value to the influence of the patient's personal past and looks for the causation of neuroses exclusively in present-day motives and in expectations of the future ... We for our part will then say: 'This may be a school of wisdom; but it is no longer analysis.' (Freud, 1933a, p. 143)

In psychoanalysis, the Oedipus complex plays a central role in the structuring of the personality of each individual. The vicissitudes of its resolution will define the sexual orientation of the person. The concept helps us to understand and to explain the psychopathological presentations of the self as well as the variations and changes of the individual's identification processes.

Oedipus Rex was written around 320BC. After twenty-three centuries, we are still deeply struck by the themes of love, hate, guilt, incest, desire, and death which are explored in Sophocles' play. The Oedipus myth is, in many ways, a relatively simple story. At one level of interpretation, it describes an incestuous sexual love for the parent of the opposite sex and a murderous impulse towards the rival, the parent of the same sex. This is what Freud described as the positive form of the Oedipus complex. In its negative form, we find the reverse picture: love for the parent of the same sex, and murderous hatred of the opposite one. In fact, these two different forms do not exclude each other; they always co-exist in every individual, complementing and supplementing each other, surviving in a dynamic tension, in an ever-changing, permanent conflict. In any case, in presenting us with this distinction, Freud was simplifying things a bit too much: the love of a child (whether male or female) towards his or her mother cannot be simply put side by side with the love for the father; the two forms of love fulfil a different structuring function in the development of the subject. As we will see later, there is no actual symmetry that would allow us to make this comparison possible.

Universal phantasies

In *The Interpretation of Dreams*, Freud commented,

> Like Oedipus, we live in ignorance of these wishes, repugnant to morality, which has been forced upon us by Nature, and after their revelation we may all of us well seek to close our eyes to the scenes of our childhood. There is an unmistakable indication that the legend of Oedipus sprang from some primaeval dream-material ... (Freud, 1900a, p. 263)

In this view, Freud speaks of a myth that transcends the individual history of a person (Laplanche & Pontalis, 1967, p. 283). He suggests that there is, in the unconscious of each and every individual, the same complex of instinctual impulses dominated by the Oedipal drama. It tells the universal story of how each of us resolves the unavoidable challenge of how to become a man or a woman. In psychoanalysis, the Oedipus complex is there from the beginning of life, giving expression in an imaginary form to our instinctual sexual life. It is what makes the sexuality of human beings human.

It is a notion very closely connected to another difficult Freudian concept: primal phantasies, patterns—if you wish—which structure the imaginative life of the subject. They are scenarios that provide a form of representation to the enigmas of childhood: where do I come from? How are babies made? Am I a boy or a girl? The structures cannot be reduced, or explained just by the individual's lived experience, and yet, "it is against the backdrop of these given scenarios that the individual's own story develops, a story marked by psychic and bodily inscriptions that are both uniquely personal and socially shared" (Kohon, 1999, p. 67).

The themes present in primal phantasies are limited. In the first place, there is the phantasy of a primal scene, which describes the sexual intercourse between the parents. This, of course, could have been actually observed by the child, but it seems to have been more frequently inferred on the basis of certain details picked up by him or her. In any case, it is not a question of "empirical evidence" which would demonstrate the existence of the event. It has to be understood that Freud came to the conclusion of its existence through the analysis of adults, through the material provided by the patients in the actual psychoanalytic situation. It was something arrived at through interpretation and speculation. Phantasised or perceived, the relevant aspect of this primal scene is that it is always imagined by the child as an aggressive act on the part of the father, who is pictured as having anal intercourse with the mother in the context of a sado-masochistic relationship. The scene itself is both frightening and exciting for the child, and provides the background to castration anxieties.

Another primal phantasy is constituted by the phantasy of seduction, which describes the imaginary scene in which a child has been passively subjected to the sexual advances or manipulations of an adult. This concept has been greatly misunderstood. Freud did not deny the actual existence of sexual abuse in childhood, or ever doubted that it could play a significant part in the creation of the neuroses. The sexual abuse of children, as any other form of violence in childhood, is a serious, traumatic event. But Freud was rather shocked to discover that some of the accounts offered by his patients had been imagined or phantasised; therefore, he had to admit that an infantile sexual trauma was not always the cause of hysteria.

Finally, another central primal phantasy worth mentioning here is that of *castration*, which is produced "in response to the child's puzzlement over the anatomical difference between the sexes (presence or absence of the penis): the child attributes this difference to the fact of the girl's penis having been cut off" (Laplanche & Pontalis, 1967, p. 56).

The phantasies of castration play an important part in the scenario of the Oedipus complex: the threat of castration will put an end to the boy's attachment to the mother, while penis envy will motivate the girl to look for something other than the mother. We will come back to these controversial issues later.

As Laplanche and Pontalis point out, all these unconscious, primal phantasies have something in common; they are all related to the question of origins, played out in the realm of sexuality. In the primal scene, it is the origin of the subject that is represented; in seduction phantasies, it is the origin or emergence of sexuality; in the phantasy of castration, the origin of the distinction between the sexes (ibid., p. 332).

Klein and Oedipus

For Melanie Klein, primal phantasies were also very important. In her case, she believed that one could see, through the child's play, the presence of multiple identifications with each of the parents from very early on. In this context, she believed that there were pregenital phantasies connected with the primal scene. This primal scene, she suggested, was understood by the child (who was ignorant of the facts) in terms of his own oral and anal impulses and needs. She said that "intercourse comes to mean to the child a performance in which eating, cooking, exchange of faeces and sadistic acts of every kind (beating, cutting up, and so on) play the principal part" (Klein, 1927, pp. 175–176).

While Freud had also understood the primal scene in terms of an attack by the father against the mother (which, as we saw, took the form of a sadistic anal intercourse), Klein kept the idea of a sadistic attack, but changed it in a radical way. First of all, the parents were seen as part-objects; the early Oedipal parents were not people, they were individual organs: the penis in the vagina, the nipple in the breast. The mother's breast engages with the father's penis, the father's penis inhabits the mother's vagina. The parents became, in her concept of an "early" Oedipus complex, a combined parental figure. The central characteristic of this combined parental figure at this early stage was, for her, that of a fearful couple locked in violent intercourse that would destroy each other and the infant (Klein, 1932):

> [the] combined parents (or their organs) destroy each other in a world disaster for the infant that leaves nothing for him; at the same time the figure turns on him because of his own omnipotent phantasies against the parents and subjects him to the same destructive forces that he believes they wreak upon each other . . . (Hinshelwood, 1989, p. 60)

To this terrifying world one has to add the phantasised babies who (the child believes, according to Klein) live in the mother's creative body, arousing in the infant intense aggressive feelings and phantasies. In Klein's view, there were at least two important consequences for the infant: (a) the sadistic phantasies provoked great anxieties, fear for the parents, fear of a retaliation, and a sense of remorse; (b) in the early stages, the "positive" and the "inverted" Oedipus complexes are combined, co-existing at one and the same time; this creates intense mixed and ambivalent feelings towards each parent (*ibid.*, pp. 58–59).

Castration anxiety and penis envy according to Klein became different concepts to those expounded by Freud. In terms of the castration complex, for Klein the fear of castration was reinforced in the boy by the phantasised attacks on the mother's body, in order to destroy the father's penis. In the case of penis envy, it was connected in the girl with her attacks on the mother; she wished to destroy not only the father's penis contained in the mother's body, but the babies the mother was creating. As a consequence of the theoretical modifications introduced by Klein, the anxieties that she described were then of a different sort to those described by Freud. As Hinshelwood says, "Klein in the 1920s had described a new anxiety – that of violently invading mother's body, and the fear of a comparable retaliation on the child's own body" (*ibid.*, p. 62).

Furthermore, the very nature of the complex is essentially changed. In the words of Hanna Segal,

Klein considered that the Oedipus complex starts in the first year of life and is fundamentally affected by the child's relation to the breast. *It is the frustration at the breast, and crucially the weaning, that makes the infant turn to the father's penis and become aware of the triangular situation* ... (Steiner, 1989, p. 2, my italics)

We can see how, in changing the understanding of psychoanalytic concepts, we inevitably then change the theory and its structure; it becomes a different metapsychology. In replacing castration by the process of weaning as the decisive moment of the structuring of subjectivity, Klein radically changed the Freudian concept of the Oedipus complex. In her account, the father's penis is an alternative to the mother's breast. The theoretical changes are inevitably reflected in the clinical practice of psychoanalysis. For many Kleinian analysts,

if weaning is the fundamental moment in the relationship with the primary object, it follows than that separation should be considered as central to the task of interpretation. This would explain the disproportionate emphasis given to the effect of weekends and holidays. (Kohon, 1999, p. 13)

In addition, if these changes introduced in the metapsychology of psychoanalysis are not well kept in mind, they can become the locus of multiple misunderstandings, errors, misapprehensions, and confusion among psychoanalytic colleagues, let alone among those outside the psychoanalytic field.

Oedipus and language

More recently, Laplanche offered an alternative view of primitive unconscious phantasies. He described a primitive situation, which he calls the *fundamental anthropological situation* of the human infant; he argues that, whatever the individual circumstances of the child, it is not possible for the baby to survive without encountering an adult world. This encounter takes place between an adult and the newborn child in a relationship in which, together with the necessary care provided by the adult, there is an unconscious implantation of enigmatic messages in the unconscious body-ego of the infant. These messages are traumatic for the child because they are derived from the unconscious sexuality of the adult in what then becomes inevitably a situation of seduction (Laplanche, 1999).

The adult world is a world full of meanings, containing linguistic, proto-linguistic, and para-linguistic messages that a child might not understand but to which he or she has to respond. For better or worse, there is a "confusion of tongues" (Ferenczi, 1933, pp. 156–167). The relationship established between the infant and the adult takes place in two different registers at one and the same time. At one level, there is a loving and reciprocal relationship; at another, the relationship is implicitly sexual, where the two partners are not equal. The primal situation of seduction describes a fundamental scenario in which "an adult proffers to a child verbal, non-verbal and even behavioural signifiers which are pregnant with unconscious sexual significations" (Laplanche, 1987, p. 126). For example, the breast offered to the child by the mother is not only an object that satisfies a need, it also contains a double message, explicit and implicit; the mother gives the breast to the child while she is also having positive, or (at worst) negative sexual unconscious feelings. If the feelings are positive, she communicates pleasure; if they are negative, she might communicate disgust. This cannot be ignored by the infant, who will have to respond in some way even if the message signified is a mystery to him. Laplanche has, in this way, argued against the Freudian notion of a pre-given reality, mysteriously and genetically inherited, as suggested by the concept of primal phantasies. The response of the child consists of the attribution of meaning to a specific message coming from the adult. Therefore, the phantasy conveyed by the primal scene becomes, in Laplanche's view, an attempt to translate the enigma for the child of his or her parents' sexuality.

Let us try to develop further some of the ideas described above. Given the fact that human beings are born prematurely, the baby only survives because there is a physical and psychological environment that will protect him, look after him, feed him, and, in general terms, help him to survive and develop for a relatively long time. Freud described the human baby as being born in a state of helplessness. The baby is completely dependent on other people for the satisfaction of his most basic needs. In *Inhibitions, Symptoms and Anxiety* (1926d), Freud used the concept of helplessness as the prototype of all traumatic situations.

This extreme situation, of having to have his or her biological needs satisfied if the baby is to survive, applies to both sexes. They both depend completely on a mother, their first love object, with whom they cannot communicate through language. In the context of the infant's initial dependency, it is specifically the mother's breast which plays a decisive, fundamental role in the development of the mental, physical, and emotional life of the child. The breast is the infant's first object of desire; the physical relationship with mother (nursing, touching, cuddles, and caressing) necessarily includes sexual and erotic feelings. It provides the necessary milk for the baby's survival but, at the same time, in doing so, it will also come to represent the lost union with the mother which the baby once had inside her body. It should be noted that one of the most important aspects of the relationship with the breast is the ongoing process of comings and goings, of the presence and absence of the mother. One could argue that, with each absence, the desire for her presence is established more clearly.

The need for nourishment provides the first experience of satisfaction, one that will determine all future experiences of satisfaction. The baby is hungry and he screams. The timely intervention of the mother provides relief. Freud says,

> An essential component of this experience of satisfaction is a particular perception (that of nourishment, in our example) the mnemic

image of which remains associated thenceforward with the memory
trace of the excitation produced by the need (Freud 1900a, p. 565)

What does this mean? First, that there is an original situation of satisfaction of a biological need; the baby is hungry and he gets the milk
provided by the breast. In the second place, that there is a mnemic
image of this experience, a particular perception which remains linked
to a memory trace of the excitation produced by the need. Every time
that the need emerges (hunger) this will be accompanied by the
mnemic image, the memory of the original perception of the breast.
This, in psychoanalysis, we call a wish. Perhaps the best example is
thumb-sucking: that which was once present (the breast) is now hallucinated and replaced by something else. At this precise moment, when
this hallucination appears, we find ourselves in the realm of the
unconscious. It is here that psychology turns into psychoanalysis.

Need, then, is different from wish. Need derives from a state of
internal tension (hunger), and achieves satisfaction through the
specific action which is offered by the adequate object (breast, milk).
From then on, wishes will always be associated to memory traces. In
the unconscious, wishes will be fulfilled through the hallucinatory
experiences that have become the signs of the satisfaction.

In one example taken from literature, this hallucinatory experience
and its dynamic interplay with reality is expressed thus,

> I touch your mouth, I touch the edge of your mouth with my finger, I
> am drawing it as if it were something my hand was sketching, as if for
> the first time your mouth opened a little, and all I have to do is close
> my eyes to erase it and start all over again, every time I can make the
> mouth I want appear, the mouth which my hand chooses and sketches
> on your face, and which by some chance that I do not seek to under-
> stand coincides exactly with your mouth which smiles beneath the one
> my hand is sketching on you. (Cortázar, 1998[1963], p. 32)

The search for a love-object in the real world is a symbolic venture,
entirely governed by a relationship to signs. Wishes are related to the
real objects only through the mediation of the phantasies that form
part of them. Wish fulfilment could be said to be an illusion: the wish
appears to the human imagination to have been realised. The tendency of the primary process is towards reinvesting the ideas attached
to the original experiences of satisfaction (primitive hallucination) by
establishing a perceptual identity.

It is not difficult to see that all this constitutes a mythical, retroactive structure, which is the effect of a symbolisation of a past that never really was. This is also clearly reflected in literature as well as in language. Alberto Manguel makes Robert Louis Stevenson say,

> The word 'nostalgia' . . . had been invented in the seventeenth century by an Alsatian student in a medical thesis, to describe the malady that afflicted Swiss soldiers when far from their native mountains. For [Stevenson] it was the contrary: nostalgia was the pain of missing places that he had never seen before. (Manguel, 2004, p. 40)

Equivalent forms of understanding nostalgia have specific, untranslatable words in other languages, one example being the word *saudade* in Brazilian Portuguese. The fact that these words cannot be properly translated into other languages might justify the claim that language, after all, refers to something that knowledge cannot properly apprehend (Kertész, 2002[1997], p. 116).

There is another important consequence of the total dependence of the human infant on its environment: "the state of helplessness implies the mother's omnipotence" (Laplanche & Pontalis, 1967, p. 190). This first object of love, what is known as the pre-Oedipal mother, is an omnipotent mother, who could do anything and who possesses everything. How could she not, if she is the one who saves the baby from total destruction and allows him to survive? This omnipotent, pre-Oedipal mother does not need anybody else. The baby's fixation to the primary relationship with her, in the initial phase of exclusive and equally intense lasting attachment, will be at the source, or at the origin, of psychotic states and of the perversions.

In time, the mother's breast will become the mother as a whole person. She was believed to have it all, but soon the love object will be discovered to be not perfect after all; mother is not omnipotent. In Freudian language, mother was believed to have a phallus. Now she is seen *not* to have everything, she needs something else for her completeness; she demands some kind of satisfaction from the baby; she wants to be loved, and cared for. The form that this question takes in the unconscious is, "Do I have that which mother needs? Do I have what it takes to satisfy mother?" And both boys and girls are forced to recognise that *no* is the answer to this question. I have previously put forward the idea that,

It is the realisation that boys and girls do not and cannot have what it takes to satisfy mother fully which creates the logical moment in the structure of the unconscious that allows the subject to separate from her. It is as if the boy has to acknowledge that 'he hasn't got that which mother needs (for procreating) and desires (for her sexual satisfaction); and even if he were to pretend that he's got it, it is too small, too inefficient, and it can be cut off (in other words, it's only a penis and not a phallus); so he'd better give mother up, he'll renounce his phallic narcissistic identification, acknowledge that which he does have, and use it as best as he can somewhere else, with somebody else at the appropriate time'. There is a similar (although not the same) challenge for the girl: 'she is not (and she hasn't got) that which mother needs and desires; she'll renounce her phallic narcissism, accept what she does have, and look for somebody to give her satisfaction, the baby that she wants (or might not want)'. This relinquishing of the primary object, of course, is never completely achieved. On the one hand, from the point of view of the mother, she will never stop hoping for something beyond the baby, which might take the form of an implicit demand addressed to all children, boys and girls, for the rest of their lives: 'Why don't you do as I wish? Why aren't you as I wish you to be? Why don't you do as I tell you?' On the other hand, from the point of view of the subject, he or she will never sufficiently forego the identification with the imaginary object, the phallus (or with a primary object that is believed to possess it). But if the subject does not face this necessary disappointment, then narcissism, omnipotence and envy will prevail in the subject's love life.

It is impossible not to take a position in relation to the desire of the mother, not to decide who (what sexual being) we are for her. First, we desperately need to believe that we are the object of her desire, and then we have to go through the disillusion and the painful realisation that we are not it. This moving away from the primary object is overdetermined, not free, but this does not necessarily mean that it is prescriptive of heterosexuality ... The resolution of the oedipal conflict is never dictated by social norms alone, nor can it be exclusively determined by biological forces. The psychoanalytic explanation of the differentiation of the sexes through the resolution of the phallic position in the context of the oedipal conflict seems to be the only theory that describes this predicament mainly in terms of an unconscious process (Kohon, 1999, pp. 8–10)

From a psychoanalytic point of view, it is not possible to appeal to biology to explain the difference between the sexes. As I have previously argued,

> There is in the unconscious a danger and a threat for the man, and a desire and envy for the woman. There is not (as it is at times assumed) an over-valued penis and an under-valued vagina. A penis, just as much as a vagina, does not secure or guarantee anything for the subject in becoming a sexual human being (Masotta, 1976). If nothing else, the idea of bisexuality in psychoanalysis denotes precisely the uncertainty of the process and the struggle through which all human beings become either a woman or a man. (ibid., p. 10)

It is not a question of an actual penis or a real vagina—the concern has nothing to do with anatomical reality. It is only the presence or the absence of *that which the infant imagines mother wanting* (see also Kohon, 1986, pp. 362–380).

The father and not-I

What is the place of the father in all this? The father is there to reveal the desire of the mother, a desire not exhausted by her wish to have a baby. This is the condition: a father who is desired by the mother, and, one should add, a mother who wants to be, and accepts being, desired by a father, which will liberate the child from the illusion that he or she is the sole object of his or her mother's wishes. The mother, after all, desires somebody else . . . children are forced to confront, sooner or later, the fact that their mother's desires extend beyond them.

Described as the father of the individual prehistory (Freud), the imaginary father (Lacan), the non-mother (Le Guen), the absence of the mother, the stranger, or the phallus, this place has been aptly named as *not I* (Kristeva, 1983). The imaginary father would, thus, be the indication that the mother is not complete but that she wants, "Who? What? The question has no answer other than the one that uncovers narcissistic emptiness: 'At any rate, not I'" (Kristeva, 1983, translated for this edition). *Not I* denotes a recognition of the subject's radical separation from the original object, the giving up of an omnipotent dream of a blessed harmony with the world.

If there is a father (imaginary or real) who fulfils this function in the mind of the mother, the child will have to accept that he or she cannot be what the mother wants. The child will be able to recognise himself or herself as a son or a daughter, as a testimony and a consequence of the parents' intercourse, not as the cause of such an intercourse.

All this, in the last resort, is inevitably condensed, and extremely reductive. By necessity, an "introduction" would tend to simplify, misrepresent, perhaps, thus, even distort the complexity of psychoanalytic theory. The question concerning the father is certainly one of the most difficult to summarise. In Freud, there is a very specific and clear theoretical movement from the original conceptualisation of the father according to the interpretation of *Oedipus Rex* to the myth of the terrifying and perverse father of *Totem and Taboo* (Freud, 1912–1913), not to mention the later vision of the father in "Moses and monotheism" (Freud, 1939a). Nevertheless, in the context of this chapter, what we need to emphasise is the importance and relevance of the paternal function as a structuring figure: how his word is (or should be) present in the mother's discourse as a third agency. The father, as this third party, is not merely a rival to be defeated and killed, but an irrevocable law, a principle which mediates and establishes difference: difference between mother and child, between boys and girls, between incest and exogamy, between biological origins and identity. The paternal function, in psychoanalysis, is not a sociological role but a symbolic principle.

The most important aspect of this triangular structure is that it forces the child into a specific, definite place within the family. The structure regulates desire, introducing a repetitive process of substitution of symbolic objects. There is a radical asymmetry between being caught in the imaginary relationship with the mother (which is narcissistic and specular) and the symbolic participation in a triangular structure with access to language, the acknowledgment of sexual difference, the need for recognition by the other and the difference between generations, and the acceptance of death.

Many critics of Freud have insisted that, in focusing his attention on the character of Oedipus, he neglected or ignored the other elements in Sophocles' play. For example, it has been claimed that the murder of Laius by Oedipus is only one aspect of the different dramas taking place in the Oedipus cycle. What about the abduction of Chrysippus, some critics protested, and the homosexual seduction that is the source of the original curse? What about the consequent important "original" crime of the father wanting to get rid of the son, the filicidal wishes of Laius against Oedipus? And what about Jocasta's complicity? According to some authors, this would explain, if not justify, Oedipus's crime as a true act of self-defence.

We should remind ourselves once and again that Freud was talking about the unconscious mind of the child, not about the real events that take place in the life of an individual. Freud's genius resided in seeing Sophocles' play in terms of a dramatisation of unconscious wishes. In fact, it can be argued that this was Sophocles' own originality: he also ignored the previous "history" of the characters and did not offer any "explanation". That which is critically "explained" in the play (by a considerable number of authors and commentators) comes from other sources, not from the play itself (Rudnytsky, 1987, p. 255). Sophocles himself had made a creative choice: the play is not about the culpability of Laius, but about the tragedy of Oedipus in his search for his origins.

Many of the criticisms perennially addressed to Freud originate from a basic misunderstanding: the unconscious and its laws are ignored, and the primary process is denied. Another important psychoanalytic concept, primary process, describes a type of mental functioning completely different to the thought processes traditionally understood by psychology. It has its own mechanisms and its own laws; for example, it functions within a different concept of time; in fact, there is no time. The model of the primary process would be the dream, where past and present are mixed. The criticisms, then, are based on phenomena which belong to the secondary process, in other words, to the conscious part of our minds. Some of these attacks are not so much anti-Freudian but—as Mitchell clearly showed— pre-Freudian (1974, p. 9); they predate the discovery of the unconscious.

We are expected here to make a very special effort of imagination in order to understand that the Oedipus complex is not the actual history of a family constellation; it is not the account of the conscious desires involved in a social situation. Furthermore, it does not originate in the mindful acceptance of incestuous wishes, or murderous phantasies. The Oedipus complex is the "nucleus of neuroses" because it shows the repression of all these wishes and phantasies. These things can only be deduced, interpreted, speculated upon. The specificity of psychoanalysis as a theory of the mind consists in its attempt to describe unconscious psychic reality. We infer and construe the Oedipal infantile sexual organisation from what we hear from adults in the consulting room. It is a process that works retroactively, from the present to the past.

The question forced upon each subject by the Oedipus drama is not only the triangular tragedy of rivalry, jealousy, and love but the misrecognition (*méconnaissance*) of the subject's own history: Oedipus is the son of Jocasta and Laius but he does not know it. Or, perhaps, he does not want to know it. According to Freud, one can be afflicted by a "blindness of the seeing eye". From this point of view, we could say that the Oedipal drama describes "the strange state of mind (as I have quoted above) in which one knows and does not know a thing at the same time" (Freud & Breuer, 1895d, p. 117; see also Steiner, 1993).

As in the world of law, not knowing does not make human beings less responsible. This is what inevitably turns every single human destiny *tragic*. "Tragedy means, above all else" Alford argues, "that people are responsible without being free" (1992, p. 115).

We might become more insightful through psychoanalysis but this would not make us necessarily any wiser.

References

Alford, C. F. (1992). *The Psychoanalytic Theory of Greek Tragedy*. New Haven, CT: Yale University Press.

Cortázar, J. (1998)[1963]. *Hopscotch*. London: Harvill Press.

Ferenczi, S. (1933). Confusion of tongues between adults and the child. In: *Final Contributions to the Problems and Methods of Psychoanalysis*. London: Hogarth Press [reprinted London: Karnac, 1980].

Freud, S., with Breuer, J. (1895d). *Studies on Hysteria. S.E.*, 2. London: Hogarth.

Freud, S. (1900a). *The Interpretation of Dreams. S.E.*, 4–5. London: Hogarth.

Freud, S. (1912–1913). *Totem and Taboo. S.E.*, *13*: 1–161. London: Hogarth.

Freud, S. (1926d). *Inhibitions, Symptoms and Anxiety. S.E.*, 20: 77–174. London: Hogarth.

Freud, S. (1933a). *New Introductory Lectures on Psycho-analysis. S.E.*, 22. London: Hogarth.

Hinshelwood, R. D. (1989). *A Dictionary of Kleinian Thought*. London: Free Association Books.

Kertész, I. (2002)[1997]. *Yo, otro – Crónica del Cambio*. Barcelona: Acantilado.

Klein, M. (1927). Criminal tendencies in normal children. *British Journal of Medical Psychology*, 7: 177–192. Reprinted in: *The Writings of Melanie Klein Vol. III: Love, Guilt and Reparation, and Other Works*. London: Karnac, 1993.

Klein, M. (1932). *The Psychoanalysis of Children*. London: Hogarth. Reprinted in: *The Writings of Melanie Klein Vol. II: The Psychoanalysis of Children*. London: Karnac, 1998.

Kohon, G. (Ed.) (1986). *The British School of Psychoanalysis: The Independent Tradition*. London: Free Association Books.

Kohon, G. (Ed.) (1999). *No Lost Certainties to be Recovered*. London: Karnac.

Kristeva, J. (1983). *Histories d'amour*. Paris: Denoel. English edition (1987): *Tales of Love*. New York: Columbia University Press.

Laplanche, J. (1987). *New Foundations in Psychoanalysis*. Oxford: Blackwell.

Laplanche, J. (1999). *Essays on Otherness*, J. Fletcher (Ed.). London: Routledge.

Laplanche, J., & Pontalis, J.-B. (1967). *The Language of Psychoanalysis*. London: Hogarth Press, 1973.

Manguel, A. (2004). *Stevenson under the Palm Trees*. Edinburgh: Canongate.

Mitchell, J. (1974). *Psychoanalysis and Feminism*. London: Allen Lane.

Rudnytsky, P. L. (1987). *Freud and Oedipus*. New York: Columbia University Press.

Steiner, J. (Ed.) (1989). *The Oedipus Complex: Clinical Implications*. London: Karnac.

Steiner, J. (Ed.) (1993). *Psychic Retreats: Pathological Organizations in Psychotic, Neurotic and Borderline Patients*. London: Routledge.

CHAPTER NINE

Embodied language

Kenneth Wright

T he psychoanalytic relationship offers a unique kind of intimacy. Although asymmetric, it demands intense involvement from both parties, and a willingness to share thinking and feeling to a degree unparalleled in other kinds of relationship. Such unprecedented sharing is mediated principally, though not exclusively, through language, and while analytic debate considers every aspect of this curious engagement, I shall focus on talking, in particular the way the analyst talks to his patient.

Historically speaking, this is a relatively neglected topic. Clinical discussions have usually focused on the *content* of the patient's communications and the way these are understood by the analyst. The emphasis has been on whether, when, and why the analyst makes an interpretation and which aspect of the material he "takes up": for example, whether he focuses solely on the here and now of the transference or whether he also includes reconstructions of the past.

Discussions of this kind make two assumptions: first, that the analyst's main task is to make sense of the analytic material, including the analyst's countertransference; second, that interpretation, however defined, is the most important analytic intervention. These assumptions underpin an approach to analysis in which the primary aim is to draw the patient's unconscious organisations of experience into the realm of conscious thought, and, within this view, interpretation is the analyst's main tool.

This way of thinking reaches back to the beginning of psychoanalysis, when Freud discovered that hysterical symptoms had unconscious meaning. The approach flourished unchecked for more than fifty years and threw light on every aspect of mental functioning, from dreams and neurotic symptoms to religious practices and artistic creativity. In every case, the analyst sought out the unconscious content of the structure in question, and attempted to make this conscious and explicit. Interpretation was the principal tool of this endeavour and, at least implicitly, the major factor in promoting psychic change. Within this framework, discussions of technique (interpretation) aimed to clarify different kinds of interpretation in terms of content (anxiety, defence, transference, extra-transference, reconstruction, etc.) in order to pinpoint those that most reliably led to mutative insight. The *way* the analyst delivered his interpretations—his tone of voice, use of words and images, the resonance of what he said with the utterance of the patient—found little place in such accounts.

Finding a voice

From a present day perspective, this view of analysis is simplistic because theory and practice, especially in recent decades, have evolved in complex ways, and, *parri passu* with the realisation that insight on its own is often insufficient, the emphasis has shifted from explicit interpretation to more subtle background factors, such as holding (Winnicott) and containment (Bion). But whereas theories of *interpretation* are relatively detailed and coherent, operational accounts of *holding and containing* are harder to come by. Constituting an unobtrusive background to the analytic frame, they seem to have eluded clear description.

It can be argued that the analyst's way of speaking to the patient is part of this background holding. I refer to this as the analyst's voice, meaning both the voice and words with which he speaks and his inner relation to what he says. For example, it would include whether the analyst speaks with his own voice or that of someone else, perhaps his own analyst or supervisor, and whether his utterances are professional and safely distanced, or more recognisably personal, and issuing from his own affective core.

At some time or another, every analyst has to confront such questions in relation to his own work, and, arguably, the passage from professional to personal voice is interwoven with achieving an integrated analytic identity.[1] Beyond this, however, the issue has interpersonal dimensions, it being mainly through his voice that the analyst makes affective engagement with the patient, and equally through his voice that the patient gauges his analyst's integrity

Finding a personal voice is not the exclusive concern of the psychoanalyst; it is an issue for any creative person, not least for the patient who frequently discovers an authentic voice during the course of an analysis. It is certainly an issue for the poet. "Finding a voice", writes Seamus Heaney, "means that you can get your own feeling into your own words and that your words have the feel of you about them" (Heaney, 2002, p. 16). Heaney refers to the poet's voice, but his statement has relevance for analysis, for it indicates maturity in the analyst when his words develop his own personal stamp, and equally in the patient when he finds a voice that genuinely expresses his inner being.

How, then, does the poet find his voice? Heaney tells us that

> in practice, you hear it coming back from someone else, you hear something in another('s) . . . sounds that . . . enters the echo chamber of your heart and excites your whole nervous system . . . In fact . . . this other writer *has spoken something essential (that) you recognise . . . as a true sounding of aspects of yourself and your experience.* (2002, p. 16, my italics)

The notion of finding oneself in another's speech is clearly pertinent to the psychoanalytic enterprise which also involves a sense of being profoundly recognised by another person (the analyst) who makes 'a true sounding of aspects of (oneself) and (one's) experience.' Heaney implies that through such recognition a new ability is formed, the ability to make "true soundings" of *oneself* and to capture these in authentic, personal language. We could, thus, surmise that the analysand, too, develops an authentic voice through being first "spoken" by the analyst. This would be a further form of the general truth that we only become fully ourselves through first being "recognised" in an authentic way by another person.

In Heaney's account, this process is far from intellectual: the other's words enter one's heart and excite the whole nervous system. Not all words have this ability, however; only some have the capacity to "carry truth alive into the heart", as Wordsworth put it in his Preface to the Lyrical Ballads (2005[1802], p. 301). If we transfer this insight to analysis, which depends equally on words, we can see how the analyst's words and the way he uses them could be centrally important to the analytic process. Thus, it becomes meaningful to consider different ways of speaking and to ask which forms of speech might best convey the analyst's "true soundings" of the patient's states of mind, and, hence, offer a transforming "recognition".

Creating a language

I do not want to explore the complicated process through which an analyst becomes more truly himself when he works with patients in an authentic way. There might, however, be a direct relationship between his capacity to do this and that of the patient to find his or her own identity; as Searles (1973) first described, there must be a therapeutic symbiosis before there can be separation with enhanced maturity. I believe that such symbiosis involves, among other things, the creation of a joint and living language within which the pulse and feel of the patient's experience can be shared. If, in Heaney's account, we substitute "analyst" for "this other writer"—the *analyst* "has spoken something essential . . . that you recognise as a true sounding of . . . your experience . . ." (Heaney, 2002, p. 16)—it is possible to glimpse the interpenetration of language and experience that genuine analytic discourse requires. For, while it is true that *explanatory* interpretation might enlarge a patient's understanding, it frequently fails to "excite the whole nervous system". The ability of words to "enter the echo chamber of [the patient's] heart" depends on some other quality. As Ogden writes:

> The analytic discourse requires of the analytic pair the development of *a metaphorical language* adequate to the creation of sounds and meanings that *reflect what it feels like* to think, feel, and physically experience (in short to be alive as a human being to the extent that one is capable) at a given moment. (Ogden, 1997, p. 3, my italics)

Inevitably, the analyst must be prepared to lead in this process, but, unless he can find his own analytic voice and learn to speak in his own embodied and metaphorical way, he will hardly be a useful guide.

Discursive and metaphorical language

In suggesting that the analyst should cultivate the art of metaphorical speech (a language of images), I am adopting a view that goes beyond the classical idea of interpretation as explanation. As I have already described, the task of the interpreting analyst was to make the unconscious dynamic explicit. His work was a process of explanation and clarification that gave sense to every psychic phenomenon, however bizarre or unintelligible. Classical interpretation had an explanatory form that aimed to create insight: "You are doing this, feeling that, because of *a, b, or c,* perhaps to avoid *x, y or z.*" An extreme statement of this position was that of Ezriel (1956), who believed that every interpretation should be able to show how the present behaviour (the required relationship) was a defensive avoidance of some other state of affairs (the avoided relationship), the occurrence of which would lead to specific consequences (the calamity). Indeed, he thought that the analyst should remain silent unless he could offer to the patient such a complete tripartite structure.

Ezriel's attitude was extreme, but softer forms of his position were endemic until the past few decades. As a position, it required a relatively silent analyst whose active participation was limited to occasional interpretative utterances (explanations). Characteristically, these would be delivered in a level and logical way which left little room for ambiguity. It was also perhaps part of this model that the analyst should be a blank screen (in terms of his behaviour, though not in terms of his countertransference receptivity), it making sense that the analyst should not disturb his professional façade or the development of the transference with lively, emotional contributions of his own. I am not suggesting that in practice analysts always behaved in such a distanced way, but describe a model that existed in the back of the analyst's mind that, in some degree, would have influenced his practice.

Whether or not this description strikes any chords, it can be argued that the *act* of interpretation necessarily incorporates distance.

Precisely because it offers a discursive survey of the patient's feelings and behaviour, it requires at least a temporary standing back from involvements based on identification, with consequent loss of vividness. As Spencer Brown (1969) put it in a different context, to "explain", to set things out in discursive form, is "to take a view away from its prime reality or royalty, or to gain knowledge and lose the kingdom". In this formal sense, knowledge inevitably implies loss of verisimilitude; formal relationships are grasped at the expense of living detail.

There could, therefore, be said to be two ways of knowing an object, which complement each other. The first is experiential, sensory, and engaged and includes identification with the object; the second involves standing back from the object in order to obtain a totalising, but more distant, view. We can think of the first as providing sensory, lived knowledge of the object (or subject), the second as yielding a more distanced external schema (Buber, 1937; MacMurray, 1957; Wright, 1991).

These forms of knowing can also be described in terms of relational structure. Thus, the engaged type of knowing is *dyadic*, knowledge being gained from identification and interacting with the object; the second is *triadic*, and involves locating oneself outside the dyad in the position of a third. From this more distanced observer position, the dyad can be seen as a totality; it acquires a coherent and more external form.[2]

If we think of interpretation in these terms, it clearly involves standing back from the dyad (e.g., the lived transference relationship), in order to "see" it (understand it) more clearly; the interpreting analyst is the third, the totalising, distanced observer. Through this operation, the dyadic relationship acquires an "objective", quasi-visual form through which it can be grasped and held in the mind. However, in making such an interpretation, the analyst is asking the patient to engage in a series of moves that shadow his own; in other words, it requires the patient also to separate and stand back from his lived experience and suffer the loss of its "prime reality or royalty". It is my contention that the way the patient negotiates this separation from sensory immersion will depend on his earlier experience of separation (i.e., from the mother) in the primary dyad.

A clinical example will illustrate this. Shortly after beginning my psychotherapy training, I inherited a near psychotic man who, over several years, had been seen in weekly sessions by a succession of psychotherapy registrars. I quickly decided that he lacked the capacity to use psychotherapy, and, with all the enthusiasm of a beginner, I broached the subject of termination. He did not appear to take much notice, so the next time I saw him, I again raised the topic in a more determined fashion. I said I thought we should have a good look at the situation and consider if it was really useful for him to continue. We might perhaps decide that working towards an ending was the best option. At this, the patient got up and left the room. The next thing I knew, he had returned and hurled a tea mug at my head, and before I could react, he had launched himself on me in what I am convinced was a homicidal attack. At the time, I literally did not know what had hit me and was too busy preserving my life to think about what was happening. Forty years later, I perhaps begin to understand. My omnipotent belief in my new-found powers as a psychotherapist had led me to make a poorly timed and, from his point of view, catastrophic interpretation that he was inherently ill-equipped to handle. It is probable that his visits to the department, with whom he had developed a kind of symbiotic relationship, were the only times in his life when he felt in any degree safe, if not alive. Thus, he experienced my asking him to "stand back" (in the observer position) and "look at" the possibility of stopping his therapy as a murderous attack, and his only way of dealing with this was to try to annihilate me.[3]

To summarise, my argument suggests that interpretation leads to a relatively distanced kind of knowledge contained in the totalising forms of experience-distant "viewing". These are coded in discursive language and offer an objectifying and explanatory account of behaviour. They utilise the generalised and shared language forms of the social world, which are poorly suited to capturing the uniqueness of individual experience. Some patients react to this interpretative process badly, feeling observed and dislocated from themselves in a way that transforms them into objects or specimens; they feel scrutinised and looked at, and robbed of their subjective individuality. In such cases, the observer/analyst is at best experienced as unempathic, at worst, as a mortal threat to the self.

Not all patients, perhaps relatively few, react in this way, and this implies that in "normal" scenarios, personal experience is felt to be less vulnerable. To account for this, I make the hypothesis that protection is afforded by pre-existing containing structures that offer a barrier to the analyst's objectifying gaze (interpretation). These would be transitional, non-verbal structures that "hold" and "resonate" with experience, thus keeping it alive. They would be related to, though not the same as, metaphorical language, and would constitute the source—the "image cellar" (Heaney, 2002)—from which metaphor and incipient understanding arise.

One of the most striking features of metaphorical language is its closeness to sensory experience; it is a form of embodied language. If I try to explain to another person what an experience is *like*, my only verbal recourse is metaphor. I might say: "I feel as though I'm in a dark tunnel", or "I feel broken", or "I feel as happy as a bird on a summer's day." In each case, I invite the other person to imagine himself into a certain situation (in other words, to occupy the metaphorical image) and trust that through creative extrapolation from that situation, he will gain some inkling of how I feel. Thus, I lead the other person to my feeling through an analogical, imagined structure which resonates in some crucial way with the "shape" of my own experience. This structure then acts as a bridge that evokes in him a feeling state that echoes my own.

Being able to use images in this way empowers me with a language through which I can communicate my feelings. It implies that, in some degree, I know what my feelings are, though I might not understand them or know what they are about. And it means that I can "have" feelings and experience them as "mine". In this sense, I am a person and a going concern, and I cannot easily be robbed of my feelings because I have at my disposal a means of holding on to, containing, and accessing them within myself. I think of this "holding" as mediated by *non-verbal*, perhaps transitional, symbolic structures that replicate the "shape" and/or quality of the relevant experience, and imagine that when I speak metaphorically in order to convey my feeling, I draw on this substratum of available symbolic forms. I shall not, at the moment, discuss this substratum, except to say that it seems to be a developmental achievement that depends on prior maternal provision. From this point of view, my ability to "speak" myself through images[4] depends on having first been 'spoken' in this way by another person (originally the mother).

If, as counterpoint, we think of the state of affairs in a psychotic patient, a critical difference becomes apparent: the power of using images to symbolise experience is severely impaired. For example, I once had a patient who informed me that his spinal cord was fused with that of another person. He suffered greatly because of this, as it gave "the other person" (his delusional figure) extraordinary power over him, so that he felt constantly controlled and influenced by him in a persecutory way. As I got to know him better, it became increasingly clear that this other person was a derivative of his mother, from whom he had never been able to separate sufficiently. Of course, when his medication "worked", his delusion would diminish its hold on him, but frequently he stopped taking it and his sense of persecution would then return. During one such period, he got a can of petrol, sprinkled it around the parental home, and set light to it. Fortunately, the parents were not killed, but his murderous intent was plain.

Clearly, this patient had divined in some degree what his difficulty was. There was rudimentary "knowledge" in his "image cellar", but he did not possess this in a form he could hold in his mind (i.e., in symbolic form). He had never learnt (or, perhaps, lost the capacity) to "speak" his experience to himself: that is, to tell himself in metaphorical mode "what his situation was like". Thus, he *suffered* the "sense" of his situation in a concrete way (i.e., in the realm of things), and tried to get rid of the problem in a similar concrete fashion. Thus, the only way he could rid himself of his "fused" mother was by killing her—presumably, he felt that his spinal cord (the core of his being) would then become free. It can be seen from this that his delusion contained a seed of knowledge, but he lacked the means to free it from the concrete experience; in other words, to speak it in metaphorical language. According to my thesis, this would have stemmed from his having been insufficiently "spoken" by another person during a formative stage of his development—presumably by the mother he had tried to kill.[5]

Learning to speak

Interpretation, in the sense I am using the term, is relevant and meaningful to a person who can already "speak" his feelings. It can then help him to understand and organise those feelings in a new way. If a patient is not able to "speak" his feelings, if he does not "have" them, or "know what they are like", the task of analysis, in my view, is to help him develop a way of "speaking" that will enable him to know them. In other words, he has to be helped to discover his feelings experientially and contain them,[6] *before* they can be discussed and interpreted. This requires that the analyst discover ways of speaking to the patient that are markedly different from traditional interpretation. As Quinodoz (2003) says, the analyst himself must "learn to speak", by which she means to speak in a sensory and metaphorical language.[7] This view is close to Winnicott's teaching that interpretation in the absence of a capacity for play is indoctrination, because it pressures the patient to inhabit a set of external forms that have little connection with his own experience. In such circumstances, analytic "insight" can only create a "false self" structure.

To link this with what I said earlier, if the language of interpretation is a post-separation language that takes for granted what is sometimes termed "triangular space" (Britton, 1998), the new language that the analyst must learn is a language of "dyadic space". In this language, embodied imagery is the prime symbolic currency and identification the main tool of "knowledge". With such dyadic patients, the primary aim is not so much to understand what everything is about; it is more a question of making room for something to be there, and helping it to find a voice (i.e., a language). This voice will not, in the first place, be centred on talking *about* the self, but will use words and images *to bring the self to life* and *foster the development of* feeling and experience. In this process, image and metaphor will be more important than ideas, and enrichment and development of images more important than explanation.

Approaching the patient's material from this perspective is likely to bring the analyst into conflict with everything he has been taught. In this arena, attunement and spontaneous response are more important than "correct" behaviour, and explanatory interpretation will often be counterproductive. Thus, while conventional teaching urges the analyst to *use* his countertransference in the making of interpretations, but not to express it, the new perspective would argue for greater spontaneity and some sharing of one's responses directly with the patient. There is probably no way of arguing this point that would convince its opponents; its justification lies in the "feeling" of the session, the need to respond freely to evolving imagery, and the evidently beneficial effects of behaving in a less constrained fashion. For example, if a patient's material evokes in me an image or a line of poetry, I will *sometimes* offer this as a more or less un-vetted response. I might do this quite literally, or preface it with something like "listening to you talking makes me think of this . . ." (line of poetry, image, etc.). This form of response, which could be seen as a verbal equivalent of Winnicott's squiggle game, involves both trust in one's intuitive reactions and a relative freedom from paranoid anxiety in relation to the patient; in other words, the analyst has to feel reasonably "safe" with the patient, *as well as* the patient feeling reasonably safe in relation to the analyst. I suspect, in fact, that such activity would not normally suggest itself unless the ambience of the session was sufficiently relaxed and mutually trusting.

As a way of responding, this could be seen as deriving from early forms of relatedness between mother and baby, in particular mirroring (Winnicott, 1967) and attunement (Stern, 1985). In both these processes, the mother's response is shaped by her identification with the infant's affective "experience" (as sensed by her) and offers the infant a resonating "form" that portrays (embodies) its essence. Such responses may be similar to what Ogden had in mind when he spoke of the necessity for the analytic pair to develop

> *a metaphorical language* adequate to the creation of sounds and meanings that reflect *what it feels like to think, feel, and physically experience* (in short to be alive as a human being to the extent that one is capable) at a given moment. (Ogden, 1997, p. 3, my italics)

Winnicott (1967) believed that maternal reflections (e.g., the expression the infant sees in the mother's face) give experiential reality to the infant's spontaneous gestures. He saw them as consolidating the sense of agency and the feeling of being an "I" who can influence (create) the outside world.[8] From this point of view, such forms can be seen as the mother's way of "speaking" her child into existence by providing images that contain his emerging experience. These would provide a first counterpart of the process described by Heaney, in which the other person's words are experienced as a "true sounding" of oneself—the mother's sounding would, thus, "create" the infant's experience and make it feel "real" and fully alive. Eventually, such forms would be internalised as containers of experience— incipient non-verbal symbols that capture its unique patterns and provide a "place" for it within the developing inner world.[9]

It is probable that patients with fragile self structures have suffered a deficiency in such maternal responses, and it seems appropriate that analysis should address this deficit through a comparable reflective process. *Discussing* with a child or patient their inability to imagine is unlikely to have much effect; *showing* the child or patient *how* to imagine is more likely to be effective. I will illustrate this idea with a clinical vignette.

Clinical illustration

This patient, who taught me a great deal, was important in crystallising the thoughts and feelings I explore in this paper. She was a woman in her fifties, divorced, lonely, and unhappy. I saw her three, sometimes four, times a week for several years. She was emotional and volatile, with extremely limited capacity for reflection, and she often taxed me to the limit. She saw things in stark terms as "black" or "white", "good" or "bad", and, for much of the time, I was "bad", at least on the surface. On the other hand, she came to sessions regularly and found breaks extremely difficult. She lay on the couch in sporadic and sometimes unconventional ways; at times she lay on her stomach, and fixed me with her eyes at point-blank range. She would pace the room or move from chair to chair. She made extensive use of the cushions (she called them "*my* cushions"), taking them away during breaks and sometimes throwing them when she was angry. Usually, she held "her cushion" close to her and sometimes hid her face in it.

In the very early stages of therapy, she was polite and compliant, even at times seductive, but, as we got into the therapy, she reacted negatively and contemptuously to practically everything I said. I felt this was not so much because she thought I was wrong; it was more the fact that she experienced all my interpretations as a form of control that threatened her very existence. She often tried to shut out my words by putting put her hands over her ears and telling me to stop talking.

I suffered her onslaughts for a year or more and tried to interpret what she was doing in a more or less conventional transference way. She was the youngest of three siblings with an older brother and sister, and always felt she was an afterthought who was not really wanted. Her life was ruled by a strict and overbearing mother, who continually told her off, while her weak and gentle father stayed out of trouble in the background. These "facts" provided ample material for my interpretative efforts, but eventually, in the face of her unabated hostility and a sense of complete stalemate between us, I began to change my way of working.

At the time, this was largely an intuitive response, and I could not have formulated very clearly what I was doing or why. However, I gradually found myself becoming less interpretative in a formal sense, and more responsive and interactive. No doubt I was reacting to the frustration and sense of helplessness she induced in me, a feeling that seemed to reflect what she had felt with her authoritarian mother. However, having tried every way of interpreting to no avail, I felt that *any* improvement in our relationship would be more therapeutic than the unremitting repetition and destructiveness.

The changes that slipped into what I did were largely non-verbal: the way I sat forward in my chair, the amount of eye contact, and the frequency of my interventions. I became more genuinely involved and perhaps my voice became more responsive to the tenor and tempo of her moods (i.e., less the level interpreter in the observer position). The pattern of the interaction became more conversational and I found myself laughing, and probably sighing, more freely. In short, I think I came down from my analytic "high horse" and, as a result, felt more "human". This also certainly meant that she saw my exasperation with her more clearly as well.

Inevitably, I felt worried about my change of stance, and my analytic superego tried to chastise me for acting out; but, in spite of this, I continued what I was doing and gradually became more confident that the change was beneficial. I seemed to be discovering ways of being with the patient that enabled the therapy to move forwards.

Until this point, my struggles often left me exhausted at the end of sessions. There was intense pressure to react to her outbursts, though mostly I resisted, and hoped in this way to provide some point of constancy in the midst of her emotional storms. Sometimes, I felt like an instrument on which she was playing her tunes, and, while I knew that I did not have to dance (in the sense of doing what she wanted me to do), it took me longer to realise that interpretation was not my only option and a different kind of "dancing" might be possible. It was this different way of responding that gradually evolved.

The main idea that supported me was Winnicott's distinction between holding and interpretation and his growing emphasis on holding.[10] At this time, I did not really know what holding involved, but it seemed to me that this patient was pushing me, in the only way she knew, towards a different approach.[11] I can now see more clearly that this meant my allowing, and, at times, fostering, a more transitional form of relating.[12] I have already mentioned how she made use of the cushions to help her cope with unmanageable feelings at breaks and weekends, but, in similar vein, she would sometimes fax me to ask me if I was there. This, too, I "allowed" and would briefly answer her messages when I found them: "Yes, I *am* here, and I'll see you on such and such a day" (her next appointment). Because I intuitively felt that such token actions and responses helped her survive the breaks without falling apart, I went along with what was happening without trying to interpret it.

I will give just one example of an intervention that illustrates in some degree the shift from ordinary interpretation to something more transitional and containing. It revolved around my introducing a different chair into the consulting room. The patient arrived at a session one morning to find that I had replaced a large upholstered Victorian armchair with one of lighter weight with black wooden arms. Always sensitive to changes in the setting, and scrutinising things closely as she came into the room, she asked immediately where the chair had gone. At first I did not answer. Then she said, "I don't like *that* chair (the replacement chair)! It's horrible!" I could have remained silent, as previously I would have done, but knew from experience how unproductive this could be. So I said, "What don't you like about it?" She repeated, "It's just horrible", but eventually elaborated further: what she most disliked were the black wooden arms. The session at this moment felt interactive and emotionally engaged.

During this exchange, the thought came to me that the large armchair I had moved out of the room was somehow connected with her father (the more approachable and containing parent). This suggested that the armchair with black arms might be connected with her mother, a figure of hatred, even a kind of witch. Earlier in the therapy, I would probably have made a formal interpretation, but, having learnt from experience, I merely nodded towards the new armchair (which was black like a witch) and said, "That must be your mother's chair then!" She said nothing, but screwed up her eyes and looked at it closely; she then shrank back, at the same time covering her eyes with her hands in dramatic fashion. It was almost as though the chair in question *was* her mother. So I said to her, "Maybe the other chair was your father's, then?" She considered this in the same quizzical way, neither confirming nor contradicting my surmise. This in itself was unusual, as disagreement was standard. She then said, in a light and livelier tone, "Whose chair is *that*, then?", pointing to a smaller armchair sitting in its normal place. Quite spontaneously, she then exclaimed, "Maybe that's *my* chair! It's small, like a child's!" To which I replied, "Yes! That's what I was thinking! Did you have one like that at home?" She now became reflective and hesitant—extremely unusual for her: "No . . ." she said, then added excitedly, "Yes I did! It was a little wicker chair!" She then went on to tell me further memories from childhood in a lively way, the more engaged, at times playful mood continuing for much of the session.

Discussion

From a content point of view, the exchange over the chairs is hardly momentous, but, in spite of this, it marked an important change in the work. The interaction was light and playful and I was drawn into her experience. Although my thinking continued, at least in the background, I responded spontaneously; I stayed close to her feelings about the change of chairs and she responded in a different and lively way. The transformation was striking for someone who usually complained.

I felt that her difference depended on the different way I had responded. Whereas previously I would have made an interpretation about the "black" and "horrible" mother/analyst, I had made a more playful remark: "That must be your mother's chair then!" She responded by *playacting* her horror at this "mother" (embodied in the chair), her playful reaction being in contrast to the unmodulated hatred she normally expressed towards her mother and, frequently, towards me. Our "game" then developed to include "her chair", and through this we moved further into her experience. There was a genuine moment of sharing and trust.

If I had made a more formal interpretation about her blackening attacks on her black and horrible mother/analyst/black chair, we would soon have been back in the old pattern. She would have felt I was attacking her, and *I* would again have *been* this horrible mother, locked in a transference enactment from which there was no escape.

By responding playfully and staying close to the immediacy of her experience, it was possible to avoid this unproductive *cul de sac*. Measured against interpretation in the formal sense, my intervention was incomplete and possibly collusive. I could be seen as avoiding a negative transference (being the hated mother) and colluding with the patient to keep things sweet (being the nice father). There were things we did not talk about (on this occasion the analyst–mother link) and we sidestepped things that were still too difficult. All this may be true, but it misses the main point: *that reacting as I did facilitated the work and allowed me to engage with the patient's experience.* It enabled her to handle the sudden change without being overwhelmed by it, and to stay with her experience rather than getting rid of it in her usual manner. This benign development was linked with a more flexible use of objects (the three armchairs) which, in this exchange, both embodied her experience and remained separate from it. She was beginning to make use of illusion and transitional space.

I believe it was integral to what happened that I encouraged her to use objects in this way. My spontaneous questions and comments deepened her experience without dislocating her from it, and reflected what she felt without fully explaining it.

Transference interpretation

I suggested earlier that classical interpretation is a divisive process. By encouraging the move to an external (third) position (Wright 1991), it separates the patient from the immediacy of their experience and the correlative sense of being one with it. In this sense it is like a "subtle knife" (Pullman, 1997) that divides the patient from their own self. In its zealousness to create a structure of thought, it creates a gap in the fabric of being. The patterns of thought are then offered in place of the felt shapes of living (cf. Bion's (1962a) idea that a thought is a "no-breast") (Bion, 1962a).

When we speak of containment in analysis (Bion, 1962b, 1965), we imply a more maternal function, and, just as containment precedes symbolisation in development, so might a similar sequence be necessary in analysis. In assessing a patient's response to interpretation, it is, thus, necessary to consider his early experience of separation and, crucially, whether this emerged from a background of adequate containment or was arbitrarily imposed without regard for his ability to cope with it. If it was smoothly negotiated, in a way that safeguarded the continuity of experience, we might expect that interpretation would be tolerated. If, on the other hand, it was harshly imposed, with trauma to experience and the self, we might expect interpretation to revive that trauma.

In discussing the fate of the transitional object, Winnicott (1953) says that it normally fades away, gradually losing its emotional investment. The need for a near delusory sense of the mother's body becomes unnecessary, and is replaced by newly developing symbolic capacities that enable the mother to be kept alive internally. The concrete external object (the transitional object) is replaced by mental structures ("internal images") that hold her memory in more attenuated form. In the normal situation, this would take place under the mother's coverage (Winnicott, 1960), while she herself was sufficiently available to meet the baby's continuing need, and her absences were mitigated by continuing use of the transitional object. In this normal "journey" towards symbols (i.e., mental structures) (Winnicott 1971[1953], p. 6), the potentially traumatic loss of bodily possession is hardly noticed *provided* the mother furnishes the right conditions. The loss of the object is cushioned by intermediate and illusory forms of possession (transitional forms).

Interpretation can be thought of in a similar way. When the experience being interpreted can be "held" within transitional forms, the potential trauma of loss does not materialise (see footnote 6). The separated symbol (interpretation) can then be experienced in a helpful way as *completing* a pre-existing psychic structure, not as a "cold" and distanced substitute for it.

Containment and maternal forms

The maternal contribution runs through every aspect of Winnicott's theory of development, and in order to understand my position, it is necessary to recall the nature of this contribution. Essentially, it involves the provision of containing forms that realise or complete an infant need. In the beginning, such forms are embodied and sensual, but, as development proceeds, this quality becomes less marked. There is, thus, a sequence, beginning with the maternal "breast", that realises a concrete infant anticipation ("primary creativity", Winnicott,

1953); then the mother's facial expression, which mirrors and reflects an infant emotional state (Winnicott, 1967); a little later, her attuned enactments that provide perceptual analogues of infant "vitality affect" (Stern, 1985); and, finally, words that complete and name specific segments of experience, *at least in those situations where the mother is closely in touch with it*. Within this sequence, there is progressive attenuation of maternal response in an overall context of accurate attunement.

For Winnicott, the importance of such maternal forms has little to do with wish-fulfilment or instinctual satisfaction. His interest lies in the way the maternal response corresponds to an infant need or gesture in terms of formal similarity. From this point of view, it is not so much the *fact* of being fed, the fact of instinctual satisfaction, that is important, but the patterning and timing of the feed. Similarly, in relation to the infant's emotional state, it is not so much what the infant conveys in terms of specific need that catches his attention, but the patterning of the mother's response to it, and the way this portrays her identification with the infant's experience through its similarity of form.[13]

Winnicott's work, extended particularly by Stern (1985), highlights a form of mother–infant communication that depends on iconic resemblance of forms (pre-symbolic images) rather than conventional vehicles of meaning (fully fledged symbols, verbal or otherwise). Winnicott saw this as the primary mode of communication between mother and infant and realised that it played an essential part in laying the foundations of the self. He saw how the adaptive presentation of the breast allows there to be an experience of creative omnipotence (primary creativity), and how maternal mirroring draws the infant self from potential to actual being (i.e., your response gives "reality" to my experience). Stern's work on attunement can be viewed in a similar way, the mother's portrayal of an infant state providing an external "form" or dwelling place for nascent experience, which can then be internalised as a fitting container of it.

Fundamental to this way of thinking is the idea of *resonance* between forms. Resonance can be thought of in terms of primitive communication: it is based on the recognition of formal similarity and mediated intuitively (non-verbally) rather than intellectually (through words). Thus, in attunement, the mother's portrayal is similar in "shape" to the infant's embodied experience (Stern, 1985), and, in this sense, external form and *potentially* inner state could be said to "recognise" each other. Through such "recognition" ("true sounding"—Heaney) of the infant state, the *potentially* inner becomes an *actual* "experience" that the infant can recognise through the provided form. In this sense, the maternal form can be seen as a way stage in the development of symbols, the mother's "speaking" (singing, acting) of the infant providing the baby with a way of knowing and recognising himself.

Interpretation and image making

It follows from my argument that interpretation is only one form of analytic intervention and not necessarily the most important. Although the first to be described, and often regarded as defining the analyst's activity, it could be seen as a finishing tool rather than a basic implement. Its successful use depends on there being an "object" of experience that requires finishing. Work with narcissistic and borderline patients forces the realisation that this is not always the case—basic structures are often deficient. In such patients, there is a hole or gap where "experience" should be, and, as Enid Balint realised in the case of Susan, this is not so much the result of massive projection, but a consequence of deficient maternal recognition (E. Balint, 1993).

In the terms I am using, this hole in experience implies deficient containing structures. Elements of *potential* experience have never been matched to resonating forms (images) and, as a result, have failed to enter the (symbolic, or pre-symbolic) register of the self. The containing fabric of images is incomplete, leading to a sense of scarcely existing as a self and of living under constant threat of annihilation.[14] From this point of view, the annihilation that is feared by such patients is not physical extinction, but *experiential* death—the fear of subjectivity being overwhelmed by the other's objectifying "view". To such a person, the analyst's interpretation is a threatening structure of this kind.

In such situations, the analytic task differs from that in normal (neurotic) patients and requires different technical skills. For extended periods, interpretation might have little to offer, because the patient will tend to experience it in a traumatic way (as in the patient I have described). In these circumstances, a different approach is required: *a form of relating that fosters the development of personal experience.* I have given some indication of what this might be like. It involves, above all, the provision and drawing out of images that will strengthen and repair the containing fabric of experience and make a "place" for the emerging experience to "be". Whereas, with interpretation, the analyst's task is to draw together and explain the dispersed elements of the patient's material so as to make a coherent story ("I think this is what is going on at the moment: you are doing this, feeling that, because of such and such . . ."), the task of containment is to hold and foster growth of inner experience. The stance is one of identification; the need is to give back to the patient the embodied images engendered through this process.[15] The containing, as opposed to interpretative, model is one of pre-separation mother and infant, not of post-separation Oedipal child; the picture is of *conversation* between quasi-merged analyst and patient, not of overlapping *monologues* between separate individuals. I am thinking particularly of the rhythm of the interaction, which differs significantly in the two cases.

However, to speak of rhythm is again to evoke poetry, with its ability to make "deep soundings" of the self with containing imagery. Through this capacity, poetry can suggest the kinds of speech that best evoke and capture the deepest levels of feeling, and, while it cannot teach us how to speak as analysts, it can make us more sensitive to the way that feelings lie in the rhythm and cadence of words as much as their content, and in the concreteness of imagery rather than the logic of discursive description (see Ogden, 1997; Padel, 2002).[16] The poet Rilke, in his *Duino Elegies* (Rilke, 1960), described how the poet's task was to speak for the things of the world that had no voice, and, in so doing, to bring them into full existence. In a similar way, the analyst's speech must be impassioned (i.e., coming from his own feelings) and formative. Like the poet, he has to imagine experience into existence, for until he has done this, there is nothing to interpret.

Notes

1. I imagine that every analyst, at one time or another, finds himself speaking with someone else's voice. For a long time after I had qualified, there were occasions when I could hear my own analyst speaking as I made interpretations. These were probably times of increased anxiety, for, in

such circumstances, it is reassuring to be one's analyst rather than oneself. For an inexperienced analyst, the voice of one's own analyst offers a reassuring façade behind which he can hide his uncertainty and emotion.

2. Cf. Sartre (1976, p. 116): "The unity of a dyad can be *realised* only within a totalisation performed from outside by a third party".

3. An alternative explanation would simply be in terms of dyadic rupture— the threat of ending a dyadic symbiosis. The rupture of interpretation involves standing back from the dyad (i.e., becoming a third in relation to it), which recapitulates an earlier loss of dyadic closeness.

4. Dreams and metaphorical language are two ways in which a person may "speak himself" through images, but I also have in mind the great variety of artistic forms of expression: painting, sculpture, music, etc. I believe that the non-verbal forms employed in these different media are, in some degree, derivatives of, and dependent upon, an earlier experience of having been "spoken"/reflected by the mother or other caring figure through mirroring, and attunement. I discuss this more fully in Wright, 1998, 2000, 2006.

5. It could be argued that this patient lacked the capacity to "triangulate" experience, being unable to make the move to an observing third position. However, such a move is normally connected with the development of language, and it seems more likely that the psychotic defect is prelinguistic, and linked to failure in separation of pattern and experience at the dyadic level. It is part of my thesis that such separation is facilitated by maternal attunement, which minimises the sense of not having the object by recreating its illusory presence within a resonant form. When such a buffering of separation has been deficient, the loss of the object is experienced as a trauma to be avoided at all costs. In Bion's terms, it creates the pain and frustration of a "no-breast" (Bion, 1962a).

6. In a certain sense, "discovering" and "containing" are the same thing.

7. Quinodoz (2003) writes,

> Enabling a patient to relive personal experiences . . . and make links between the present moment and past emotional experiences . . . cannot be done with explanations or with purely logical language that appeals to the patient's rationality alone. [It] needs a form of language that evokes fantasies, that is close to poetry, and centred on affects . . . [It] is a form of language that resembles artistic and poetic discourse . . . that makes use of metaphors, images and analogies. (p. 1475)

8. The forms generated by maternal attunement (Stern, 1985) are probably even more effective in this regard.

9. I have discussed the notion of an internal maternal "place" (Wright, 1991) and compared it with a "no place" which is outside of maternal influence and "unconscious". I would now say that the notion of maternal "place" refers to experience that has been contained and "spoken" (i.e., reflected) by the mother.

10. This theme runs through Winnicott's work, making it difficult to pinpoint one source that is more important than another. It underpins the way he increasingly worked and he clearly describes the approach in Winnicott (1967).

11. "Holding" (Winnicott) and "containing" (Bion) are terms with distinct meanings given by the radically different theoretical matrices in which each is embedded. Ogden (2004) has provided a sensitive analysis of the terms from this perspective. His conclusion is worth quoting:

> Winnicott's holding and Bion's container–contained represent different analytic vertices from which to view the same analytic experience. Holding is concerned primarily with being and its relationship to time; the container–contained is centrally concerned with the processing (dreaming) of thoughts derived from lived emotional experience. Together they afford 'stereoscopic' depth to the understanding of the emotional experiences occurring in the analytic session. (p. 1362)

> I use the concepts in a more fluid and imprecise way that includes their ordinary meaning. This enables me to develop my thinking about such issues with less constraint from established theories. Nevertheless, I agree with Ogden that holding has a more generalised "feel" to it than Bion's containment (e.g., the way the setting "holds" the patient), while the latter concept more readily carries the sense of specific maternal (or analytic) operations, even though Bion himself was unforthcoming about their detail. Paradoxically, Winnicott's detailed accounts of maternal responsiveness give a better sense of what "containing" might actually involve.

12. I think of "transitional" in a Winnicottian way, as designating a state and/or time in which separation between self and other is not clearly established and illusory presences can be sufficiently vivid to soften the reality of absence.

13. Patterning, timing, and a resonant isomorphism are some of the characteristics of therapist response that I have tried to single out in attempting to describe what is meant by containing and mirroring.

14. I once had a patient who felt that her husband might come home one day and sit in the chair that she was occupying because he would no longer see her at all. Her sense of herself was so tenuous that she believed herself to be almost invisible.

15. Some readers might feel that this kind of responsive tracking and imaging is a major characteristic of how they work and a way of describing the analyst's countertransference. Ogden, for example, often describes in great detail the flow of his "dreamlike" responses to the patient. There are, however, two main differences in what I am describing. The first is an attitudinal set: when the analyst is engaged with the patient in a more containing way, he is, perhaps, less likely to be searching for material to interpret, and more "capable of being in uncertainties, mysteries, doubts, without any irritable reaching after fact and reason . . ." (Keats, 1954, Letter from Keats to his brothers, George and Thomas Keats, dated 21 December 1817). The second difference concerns the use the analyst makes of his responses. In the case of the interpreting analyst, such responses are merely the raw material that he ultimately processes into an interpretation. In the case of the containing analyst, they might be used in a more immediately reflecting way, with less concern about their part in the larger picture. This does not mean that such an analyst ignores the larger picture. He is merely less concerned about it at that moment and, in so far as he is thinking about it, he is more likely to keep it to himself.

16. Padel (2002, p. 13) writes, "[In a good poem] the sound becomes the meaning while it expresses it. [It is] a love affair of sound and sense". This is similar to Heaney's notion of "seek[ing] the contour of a meaning within the pattern of a rhythm" (Heaney, 2002, p. 34). Perhaps the same could be said of a containing intervention, that it evokes in its verbal form the experience of which it speaks.

References

Balint, E. (1993). *Before I was I: Psychoanalysis and the Imagination*, J. Mitchell & M. Parsons (Eds.). London: Free Association Books.

Bion, W. R. (1962a). A theory of thinking. *International Journal of Psychoanalysis, 43*: 306–310. Reprinted in: E. Spillius (Ed.), *Melanie Klein Today: Developments in Theory and Practice, Volume 1, Mainly Theory* (pp. 178–186). London: Routledge, New Library of Psychoanalysis, 1988.

Bion, W. R. (1962b). *Learning from Experience*. London: Heinemann [reprinted London: Karnac, 1984].

Bion, W. R. (1965). *Transformations*. London: Heinemann Medical Books [reprinted London: Karnac].

Britton, R. (1998). *Belief and Imagination: Explorations in Psychoanalysis*. London: Routledge.

Buber, M. (1937). *I and Thou*, R. Gregor Smith (Trans.). Edinburgh: T & T Clark.

Ezriel, H. (1956). Experimentation within the psychoanalytic session. *British Journal of Philosophical Sciences*, 7: 29–48.

Heaney, S. (2002). *Finder's Keeper: Selected Prose 1971–2001*. London: Faber and Faber.

Keats, J. (1954). *Letters of John Keats*. London: Oxford University Press. (Letter from Keats to his brothers George and Thomas Keats dated 21st December 1817.)

MacMurray, J. (1957). *The Self as Agent*. London: Faber and Faber.

Ogden, T. H. (1997). Some thoughts on the use of language in psychoanalysis. *Psychoanalytic Dialogues*, 7: 1–21.

Ogden, T. H. (2004). On holding and containing, being and dreaming. *International Journal of Psychoanalysis*, 85: 1349–1364.

Pullman, P. (1997). *His Dark Materials. Volume 2: The Subtle Knife*. London: Scholastic.

Quinodoz, D. (2003). Words that touch. *International Journal of Psychoanalysis*, 84: 1469–1485.

Rilke, R. M. (1960). *Selected Works, Volume 2, Poetry*, J. B. Leishman (Trans.). London: Hogarth.

Sartre. J.-P. (1976). *Critique of Dialectical Reason*. A. Sheridan-Smith (Trans.). London: New Left Books. First published as *Critique de la Raison Dialectique*. Paris: Gallimard, 1960.

Searles, H. F. (1973). Concerning therapeutic symbiosis. *Annual of Psychoanalysis*, 1: 247–262.

Spencer Brown, G. (1969). *The Laws of Form*. London: Allen and Unwin.

Stern, D. (1985). *The Interpersonal World of the Infant*. New York: Basic Books.

Winnicott, D. W. (1953). Transitional objects and transitional phenomena: a study of the first not-me possession. *International Journal of Psychoanalysis*, 34: 89–97. Reprinted in: *Collected Papers: Through Paediatrics to Psychoanalysis* (pp. 229–242). London: Tavistock, 1958, and in: *Playing and Reality* (pp. 1–25). London: Tavistock, 1971.

Winnicott, D. W. (1960). The theory of the parent–infant relationship. *International Journal of Psychoanalysis*, 41: 585–595. Reprinted in: *The Maturational Processes and the Facilitating Environment* (pp. 37–55). London: Hogarth Press, 1965 [reprinted London: Karnac, 1990].

Winnicott, D. W. (1967). Mirror role of mother and family in child development. In: *Playing and Reality* (pp. 111–118). London: Tavistock, 1971.

Winnicott, D. W. (1971). *Playing and Reality*. London: Tavistock.

Wordsworth, W. (1802). Preface to the Lyrical Ballads. In: R. L. Brett & A. R. Jones (Eds.), *Wordsworth and Coleridge: Lyrical Ballads*. London: Routledge, 2005.

Wright, K. (1991). *Vision and Separation: Between Mother and Baby*. London: Free Association Books.

Wright, K. (1998). Deep calling unto deep: artistic creativity and the maternal object. *British Journal of Psychotherapy, 14*: 453–67.

Wright, K. (2000). To make experience sing. In: L. Caldwell (Ed.), *Art, Creativity, Living* (pp. 75–96). London: Karnac.

Wright, K. (2006). Preverbal experience and the intuition of the sacred. In: D. Black (Ed.) *Psychoanalysis and Religion in the 21st Century: Competitors or Collaborators* (pp. 173–90). London: Routledge, New Library of Psychoanalysis.

Wright, K. (2009). *Mirroring and Attunement: Self-Realisation in Psychoanalysis and Art*. Hove: Routledge.

CHAPTER TEN

The illusion of belief: a not so uncommon misbelief

Leon Kleimberg

Introduction

I n this presentation, I shall describe a particular psychological journey and experience that I believe is present in normal psychic
development, but also in the several pathological deviations or
transformations that the life cycle challenge us with, when this journey can not be done or achieved. In order to do that, I shall quote first
an extract from the book of prayers for the Jewish festivity of the Day
of Atonement that I believe describes very well the journey I am trying
to describe.

The journey

There is a story that is told in every culture, in every Religion, in folk
tales, in legends and in our Dreams. It is the story of the journey of a
hero or heroine in search of a treasure. Every version of it is different,
yet every version is also really the same. The hero is called out of his
usual life—by seeing a burning bush, by hearing a voice saying: 'Lech
l' cha! Go! For your own sake, go!' Ahead lie many adventures and on
the way he meets an enemy who tries to stop him and a friend who

tries to help. At the end he reaches the entrance to the underworld, or the world of gods—Jonah entering the fish, Moses climbing to heaven to receive the Torah. With luck or skill or aid he crosses the threshold and enters this mysterious land, of darkness and beauty, where the treasure is to be found. It is a land where the usual rules no longer hold, where he discovers that the enemy and the friend he had met on his journey are really one and the same, and sometimes they turn out to be the guardian of the treasure that this mysterious world conceals. Whether the treasure is given, or it must be stolen, there begins the journey back to the familiar world again.

At the entrance there is a moment of reluctance—why return from paradise, or even the underworld, to a limited human reality? But something pushes or pulls him back through, for this treasure has to be given to mankind, this secret gained by such labour and courage. The hero's journey is completed and life begins again—somehow changed by the experience he has gone through. Whether it is sung as a mediaeval ballad, told as a Red Indian legend, re-enacted in a religious festival or pieced together from the Bible tales and midrash of our own tradition, it is in some way a tale about the journey of each one of us to discover who we are, what our life means" (Magonet, 1985, p. 264).

In a way, I think this metaphor communicates very well what I want to explore in this chapter, that is, the psychological journey that we all have to undertake in order to achieve some relative degree of mental health and some relative degree of psychic maturity and equilibrium.

In his "Autobiographical study" (1925d), Freud, in his own way, describes this process very movingly. He says,

The realm of imagination was seen to be a 'reservation' made during the painful transition from the pleasure principle to the reality principle in order to provide a substitute for instinctual satisfactions which had to be given up in real life. The artist, like the neurotic, had withdrawn from an unsatisfying reality into this world of imagination; but, unlike the neurotic, he knew how to find a way back from it and once more to get a firm foothold in reality. (p. 65)

In order to describe this journey of discovery and growth, I shall use the psychoanalytic concepts of unity or fusion between mother and baby (Freud, 1914c; Klein, 1957), illusion–disillusionment (Winnicott, 1951), transformational object (Bollas, 1986), and unconscious belief (Britton, 1995).

The psychological and emotional journey

But what is this journey really about? And why some people can successfully undertake it and some people cannot? I am sure there are many ways to understand and explain this journey. For example we could also describe this moment of change and revelation as a moment of insight or mourning, as described by Freud in in his paper "Mourning and melancholia" (1917e). Nevertheless, what I am trying to describe here is a psychological journey that, although carrying with it an experience of mourning and insight, means more than that; it means an experience that, in my view, happens constantly throughout the different critical points in our life cycle (Erikson, 1968), and throughout the different critical points at any particular given moment in our current and present life (Grinberg, 1978). But, specifically then, what is this experience about? Freud (1914c), Klein (1957), and Winnicott (1951), among many other writers, have made clear that the first critical moment in our lives as human beings is the abandonment of the state of partial or total fusion or unity between the baby and the mother. They go even further than this, and say that, in a way, during most of our lives, we keep struggling with the wish to return to such a lost blissful, psychic state of partial or total fusion or unity with the mother.

Klein (1957) says,

> Throughout my work I have attributed fundamental importance to the infant's first object relation—the relation to the mother's breast and to the mother—and have drawn the conclusion that if this primal object, which is introjected, takes root in the ego with relative security, the basis for a satisfactory development is laid. Innate factors contribute to this bond. Under the dominance of oral impulses, the breast is instinctively felt to be the source of nourishment and therefore in a deeper sense, of life itself. This mental and physical closeness to the gratifying breast in some measure restores, if things go well, the lost prenatal unity with the mother and the feeling of security that goes with it. (pp. 178–179)

Freud, in his paper "On narcissism" (1914c), when talking about beautiful narcissistic women, says, "It is as if we envied them for maintaining a blissful state of mind—an unassailable libidinal position which we ourselves have since abandoned" (p. 89). In the same paper, Freud goes on to say, "The development of the ego consists in a departure from primary narcissism and gives rise to a vigorous attempt to recover that state" (p. 100). Britton, in his paper, "Psychic reality and unconscious belief" (1995), exploring a similar psychological area of relating between mother and baby, adds to these views the notion that unconscious "believing" is something we do from birth, like breathing, and that we treat those initial beliefs as facts. He continues by saying that we only begin to emancipate ourselves from them when we first realise that they are beliefs and not facts, and then question their validity. It is relinquishment of these unconscious beliefs on the part of the individual that is necessary for fostering psychic change, he says, and that such a process takes time working through and involves mourning for a lost belief as if we are mourning for a lost object. This is a very important widening of the understanding of the original experience of blissful fusion, or unity, with the mother, and the mourning involved in the process of fostering psychic change in these early stages of life that Freud, Klein, and Winnicott, among other writers, talk about. But this very important experience of belief that Britton is talking about, in these early stages of psychic life comes also, in my view, with a very important emotional complementary part. The emotional complementary part to this unconscious cognitive function of belief that Britton talks about is, in my opinion, what Winnicott (1951) describes as the process of illusionment and disillusionment. Therefore, any emotional experience that any baby has to negotiate, from early on in the difficult process of separation and individuation from the mother in the journey towards psychic birth and growth, implies, in my view, some degree of emotional negotiation with illusion and disillusionment, as well as the cognitive intellectual ones between the misbeliefs and beliefs that Britton talks about. Yet, as Freud's and Klein's quotes suggest, any link between a self and the other, or, for that matter, the baby and his mother, cannot happen outside the context and the realm of the affective or emotional response, or only in the sphere of the cognitive and intellectual experience of belief. Affects are not only the vehicle of communication between the mother and the baby, but also between different parts of the internal world of the baby and the mother. The process of successfully separating from the object, and internalising it, facilitates the development of a symbolic function (Segal, 1991); such an important development is based on the different identifications that follow such an experience of separation and loss, which, ultimately, will constitute what we experience as the mind and the internal world. Being able to successfully separate from the object, in what Winnicott described as the process of disillusionment, can only happen if a relative period of sustaining an illusion of being one and the same with the object is allowed and tolerated (1951). Being successful in negotiating separation and disillusionment from the primary identification with the object will, one hopes, lead towards the development of the experience of the "transitional phenomena", a true cornerstone for psychological development and individuation. The psychic work done to negotiate this moving away from the mother in the process of separation from her, and the constant attempts to go back or re-find such fused, blissful states with her, is what, in my mind, constitutes ultimately the working through that helps to develop a mind in its most primary forms and helps to keep it healthy and expanding.

It is in this way, perhaps, that this dynamic and dialectic process is encapsulated in this "psychological journey" that I am talking about, and that, with its regressive and progressive urges, becomes the dialectic force of interaction between mother and baby and also between the experiences of illusion and belief that ultimately will give birth, in my opinion, to this virtual subjective experience that we call the mind and the internal world. I have the impression that on the whole, as Freud (1914c) says, we never really fully resolve this illusion of wanting to be reunited with the mother. Therefore, we are always in a constant state of dialectic turmoil or dynamic change. It is my opinion that unsuccessful negotiations in this area of separation–disillusionment and illusion–belief are what produces psychopathology in the personal and social arena (Kleimberg, 2006). In a sense, it is in this area of fusion and separation where illusion and belief are located and where, ultimately, I believe creativity and pathology operate. Fundamentally, what I am trying to say here is that in this emotional and intellectual journey we all have to do, of progression and regression and fusion and separation from the object in order to grow up to become individuals with our own identities, it is paramount to be aware of the continuous negotiations and workings through we need to do throughout our life cycles in this complicated area of illusion and belief. It is in this sense that I understand illusion as an emotional vision, which comes supported and reinforced by several intellectual systems of beliefs in the process of separation and individuation.

Grinberg (1978) has described these experiences as the turning point between mental health and pathological development. He says that mental health cannot develop if disillusionment is not allowed to happen. Patients with this type of problem will create a repetitive depressive vicious circle and will permanently retain a false state of illusion and a deceptive belief about their facts of life and their psychic reality.

> Depressive patients have often had early experiences of separation and loss which they have been unable to deal with and which are reactivated by every present loss bringing about increasingly more painful depressive feelings as well as a sensation of helplessness and inner emptiness. (p. 249)

Freud, in his paper "Some character-types met in psycho-analytic work" (1916d), when talking about Lady Macbeth crumbling after fulfilling her murderous wishes, says, "And now we ask ourselves what it was that broke this character which had seemed forged from the toughest metal? Is it only disillusionment" (1916d, p. 319). We must be aware of the fact that some people can attempt to make this journey in an intellectual way, or in a pseudo or false emotional way, but never really have a truthful emotional experience of disillusionment or of disintegration of a particular inadequate system of misbeliefs, and, therefore, never really achieve a true sense of integrity and fulfilment with themselves. In the life cycle, as much as in the analytic relationship, helped by the other person, the more we are able to allow healthy separateness from the object, the more able we are to internalise and identify with a mother or analyst that is experienced as helpful and transformational (Bollas, 1986). When this happens, our illusions and beliefs can be tested with internal and external reality and become more adaptive and integrative. (Britton, 1995). When separateness is not allowed or properly negotiated by the individual and the object, the person needs to construct systems of belief that do not correspond with the facts and with reality. Then an illusion becomes delusion, and belief becomes misbelief. This should be understood as the foundations for psychic deceit and pathological constructions. A good example of these are the different forms of false selves described by Winnicott (1952), or the psychotic pathological organisations described by Rosenfeld (1984) and Steiner (1993). Beliefs and illusions are the two psychological ingredients that consciously and unconsciously gel inside us the imago of ourselves and the imago of the object. It is the inability to negotiate properly these early experiences of disillusionment and change of beliefs that forces patients to hold on to illusions that become delusions and beliefs that become misbeliefs.

Clinical discussion

Alonso Cueto, a Peruvian writer, in his latest novel, *Grandes Miradas* (2003), describes very well this developmental journey, particularly in its creative moment of disillusionment, when a specific type of delusion is transformed into a realistic illusion and an intellectual misbelief is transformed into a particular system of adaptive beliefs. His main character, Gabriela Celaya, after taking revenge for the murder of her boyfriend, finds no more reason to live; she goes to the sea to commit suicide.

> I went into the sea. I was not thinking but started swimming until I was far out to sea, and there I wanted to let go. I was finally alone, far away, beyond the waves and the froth; everything was calm, I was alone and calm. I started to move my arms; I was full of energy that I did not know the source of, and thought that it would have been so easy to let go, to let it be, but, I do not know how, I realised that if I died, it would mean that I would lose Guido. Do you understand me? I thought about him when I was there alone in the water, I thought about him more than ever, and I realised that I am with him now because I am alive, and I have him with me, like you have him, because you feel his presence in your house or when you are in church. I had him, and I thought to find him in dying, but in the sea I suddenly realised that to die was to lose him. I realised he was here, everywhere, in his house, with you, and, I do not know, but I felt that I should live, to continue without him but at the same time with him. (p. 325)

Gabriela Celaya, being in the grip of the pain and grief that losing her boyfriend caused her, creates a system of misbeliefs and delusions that were designed to protected her from a very painful mental and existential state of mind. She constructed a system of misbeliefs and delusions that made her believe that by taking revenge on the murderer of her boyfriend and committing suicide afterwards, she would be reunited with him and be happy ever after again, so to speak. She was about to fulfil both misconstructions when the proximity of her own death made her realise that by taking her own life she was going to lose what was left of her boyfriend, an emotional and existential him that only existed in her internal psychological world. It was this insight and her capacity to tolerate pain and loss in disillusionment at the threshold of her own death that helped her to transform false delusions into healthy and hopeful illusions and misconceived and misleading misbeliefs into successful and adaptative beliefs.

A patient of mine, Mrs A, at a similar threshold of disillusionment to the one experienced by the fictional character Gabriela Celaya, presented this material to me at a time when she was in a state of emotional turmoil and suicidal belief, and, like Gabriela Celaya, was considering suicide as a way to stop her emotional agony. She became aware that her wasted life was mostly the painful result of having a very narcissistic and sadistic mother, who, up until then, she was trying to protect with unrealistic and false illusions and beliefs of being a wonderful friend and fantastic mother. To her horror, Mrs A also realised that the sadistic mother she was so disturbed by was now also part of her internal world, although in a split-off way. When this connection was made and these narcissistic illusions and beliefs partially desintegrated, Mrs A felt panic stricken, became persecuted by guilt, and was convinced that jumping in front of a train, after the session was over, was the only way out of this nightmare. For a while, it was very difficult to reach her during that session, and made me very concerned about the internal collapse that such partial dissolution of the illusion and beliefs was producing in her. After acknowledging the difficult situation for both of us, I decided to firmly interpret to Mrs A that in killing herself she would get rid of her internal sadistic mother, but that at the same time she would also lose me. Following my interpretation, there was a long and chilling silence, with a tense atmosphere, that was passionately and affectionately broken by her in trepidation with these words, "I am hearing a voice inside myself that is shouting 'Do not kill yourself because if you do kill yourself you will also die!'"

A second patient of mine, Mr D, a thirty-five year old nurse who comes from the West Indies, suffered from continuous physical ailments. He suffered from liver pain, stomach pain, bleeding from the digestive system, dermatitis, and various muscular twitching and aching, which were never shown to have a real medical justification. After a long period of five times a week analysis, he had, in the end, no choice but to accept that the problem was in his mind. Having to realise such a state of affairs was a very painful and disturbing experience to undergo. Years of not using his mind, or not having a mind to use, had left a trail of damage behind him, to himself and to his family, so that the pain and guilt he had to endure to own this knowledge was a very difficult thing to do for him and to watch for his analyst. An awful childhood background, with violent parents, father a drug dealer who abandoned a depressed wife early in the marriage, divorce with two boys of ten and fifteen who are also developing various psychological illnesses, and a big part of his life wasted in an unhappy marriage are among many of the different tragic events that this patient had to endure. In terms of Britton's systems of belief and misbelief (1995), Mr D's systems of belief and misbelief were all aimed at not letting him see the true situation, or, if he did see it, then to see only the positive. We had to struggle against all the emotional pain, guilt, and chaos that challenging the system of belief or misbelief he had constructed brought with it.

Mr D persisted with the illusion of being one and the same person with an idealised mother in phantasy, because the guilt, chaos, and psychic pain he felt when letting go of this misbelief when separating from this idealised mother was too overwhelming and disintegrating an experience for him. Such an experience was persistently repeated in the transference in analysis, by Mr D expecting, if not demanding, that I should take over his life, change it for him, and make everything good and harmonious. He would spend many sessions passively just waiting in silence for this to happen. Ultimately, what was felt for a long time in analysis as an insurmountable barrier between us, particularly for Mr D in the context of what is being discussed in this paper, was that he felt I was forcing him to develop a mind that would take and contain so much pain, guilt, anxiety, anger, and chaos. The emotional need to maintain the illusion or delusion of being fused in phantasy with a perfect mother or analyst who one day is going to make everything fine became a resilient defence and a deceitful system of belief and illusion that he found necessary to maintain in order to protect him from unbearable psychic pain. At times in the analysis, Mr D made his liver carry the pain in a psychosomatic form, because that somatic solution seemed a better and safer solution and belief for him than letting this pathological, protective, blissful illusion disintegrate and go. Ultimately, for Mr D, letting the idealised object go entailed having to endure the birth of a mind that came with a very painful burden. At times when disillusionment in analysis was possible for this patient, waiting was like an excruciating nine-month pregnancy. Another typical experience for Mr D during periods of disillusionment was that he would experience the separation from me as a psychotic breakdown that could only be contained by the sudden development of a physical illness.

Towards the end of six years of analysis, in one of those moments when I think true disillusionment and separation was beginning to take place, following a week of important analytic work, on returning from the weekend Mr D reported to me that he had a very difficult weekend. Initially, at the beginning of the weekend, he felt like breaking down because of the work done during the week and the waiting for me. He had a panic attack about becoming psychotic, and then he suddenly felt physically ill, but now he was feeling better and experienced relief in that he felt his problem was really that he had caught a virus and he was feeling much better now. I did try to take up the system of misbelief and delusion he created to stop the breakdown and protect himself from psychotic anxiety. Taking this anxiety up allowed Mr D partially to recover a portion of his symbolic thinking mind, and he remembered a dream he had that weekend:

> He went to his GP's surgery. When he arrived at the surgery, he tried to pretend to the doctor that in fact he was really fine. Suddendly, while he was talking to the GP, he had a panic attack and felt as if he was becoming psychotic. Then he went to the local hospital to look for me and realised that he had just had a baby. He forgot to feed the baby. He found me and asked me if he could feed the baby, and I said he coud. Then he fed the baby.

After telling me the dream, Mr D remembered that during that weekend he also felt lost, he could not find the keys of his house, and he had fantasies of being poisoned. Perhaps delivering his baby self symbolically in his dream, and being able to feed him even if this still had to be done with my permission, was an important indication that, at least in Mr D's unconscious, a shift is taking place, notwithstanding his psychotic anxieties about it.

Finally, a third patient of mine, Mrs R, presented a similar problem. She was depressed, and, at times in the consultation, she did not understand what was making her feel so unhappy. She was just trying to be a good wife and a good mother and could not understand her not having a purpose in life and the serious difficulty she had in committing herself to emotional relationships. She felt like an unwanted child, a child who was meant to save her parents' marriage. When therapy started, it became clear that a few years ago she had a severe breakdown that ended up with her spending a period in hospital with stomach related problems that almost killed her, although no cause was ever found for the illness.

After difficult analytic work, we finally discovered how neglected and abandoned by her mother she really was, and how much the patient covered this experience up during chilhood. She used to pretend to herself and others that "mummy was really there". She even filled in school forms for the mother so that teachers would not realise mother was not looking after her. In a session where some awareness of these painful memories was allowed to be experienced and the pain and depression was also felt, with tears in her eyes, Mrs R said to me, "I lived the illusion that my mother was there. That if I shone enough, I would reach her and she would reach me. What is the point in taking that mother away from my mind and leaving me with the real one? When I played with my friends, I pretended that my mother was like theirs. I did not want to admit who my mother was." The illusion that one day her "mummy" would "be there" made this patient construct the belief that if she waited long enough and that if she believed enough that her mother eventually would change, one day she would not have to suffer any more and would not be any different from the other children.

Three years into her therapy, I was beginning to understand that the breakdown that sent her to the hospital a few years ago with the severe stomach illness that almost killed her was the result of a partial breaking down of this illusion and those beliefs that mother one day was really going to change.

Discussion

Recent research in neuroscience has discovered that the immune system does not like grief (*Herald Tribune*, 27 April 2006). It is becoming apparent to me, from the clinical and literary examples I have given, that people and patients do not like grief either. Further recent research in psychology (*Herald Tribune*, 25 January 2007) has also discovered that we have an appetite for beliefs based in magical thinking, because, apparently, this sense of having special powers buoys people facing threatening situations and helps soothe everyday fears and ward off mental distress. Of course, the research also warns us that "in excess,this magical thinking can also lead to compulsive or delusional behaviour". We all seem to need illusions and beliefs in order to be able to integrate our inner worlds. Illusions and beliefs also seem to be able to organise our internal worlds in relation to ourselves and in relation to our objects. They do help us to have a reason to live and do help us to endure pain and disappointment. They must develop and adapt to new internal and external realities as we move on in our developmental life cycles to remain creative. But some of these illusions and beliefs will change and some will not. Apparently, the unconscious seems to be rather reluctant to let some of its archaic and primary illusions and beliefs be affected by time and relationships. These unconscious illusions and beliefs can be very useful in developmental terms, but when excessive magical thinking is used too much to ward off separation anxiety, pain, or object loss, it could easily lead to pathological states of mind, as I have described in this chapter and the psychological research has confirmed. It is because it is the capacity to bear grief that ultimately helps us to transform illusion into disillusion and misbeliefs into realistic beliefs that the working through of these experiences of separation and separateness from the object is so important for psychic growth (Kleimberg, 2002). As the Peruvian writer Alfredo Bryce Echenique says in his book, *Entre la Soledad y el Amor* (Between Solitude and Love) (2005),

> Complete blissful solitude is impossible. Nevertheless, in an individual and cultural maturational journey, solitude is positive. It is in itself a learning process that helps us to own our disillusions and to free ourselves from the obsessional presence of the other. (pp. 14–15)

Successful working through in this emotional and intellectual spectrum of the experience of separation and disillusionment with the object should eventually lead to the development of our inner world, or the world of the mind. It is my view that, in this sense, the birth of the mind and its continuous links with other people as separate human beings and the body as the starting point for all psychic life occurs in the primary area of illusion and belief.

Conclusion

In this chapter, I have tried to explore the connections between the need to develop unconscious illusions and beliefs as part of the normal process of life and the development of pathological structures following the inability to grieve for lost objects, in this way forcing the individual to create unconscious constructions based on misbeliefs and illusions in order to protect themselves from the psychic pain that accepting such losses would imply. Psychological manipulation in its emotional and behavioural forms, in my view, could also be understood as an unconscious response by the individual in the context of object relationships in order to try to protect himself or herself from the psychological collapse that challenging such delusions and misbeliefs would produce in their minds. Beliefs and illusions are like psychological binders to our inner world, but they can also have the opposite effect.

By becoming too rigid and too sticky, they can also prevent psychological development and growth. This process of creating and negotiating illusions and beliefs can be seen as a journey we all have to endure through our life cycles.

In this sense, analysis can also be understood as a journey towards the recovery of mourned or unmourned lost illusions and beliefs. Some people can manage this journey better than others, and some people cannot do it at all, perhaps because, like Lady Macbeth or some of my patients described here, they collapse in the process of disillusionment due to the vast waves of unbearable guilt and depression they experience in the attempt to separate from the object. For some people, dislocating, dislodging, and working through their internal pathological illusory unconscious collusions with their internal object is too dangerous to do, because they feel paranoid, guilty, anxious, or psychotic if these pathological illusions and certainties are really dislocated and dislodged. I should like to end this paper by quoting Freud again. In his paper, "Thoughts for the times on war and death" (1915b), he says,

Well may the citizen of the civilized world of whom I have spoken stand helpless in a world that has grown strange to him – his great fatherland disintegrated, its common estates laid waste, his fellow-citizens divided and debased! There is something to be said, however, in criticism of his disappointment. Strictly speaking it is not justified, for it consists in the destruction of an illusion. We welcome illusions because they spare us unpleasurable feelings, and enable us to enjoy satisfactions instead. We must not complain, then, if now and again they come into collision with some portion of reality, and are shattered against it. (p. 280)

References

Bollas, C. (1986). The transformational object. In: G. Kohon (Ed.), *The British School of Psychoanalysis: The Independent Tradition* (pp. 83–100). London: Free Association Books.

Britton, R. (1995). Psychic reality and unconscious belief. *International Journal of Psychoanalysis, 76*(1): 19–24.

Bryce Echenique, A. (2005). *Entre la Soledad y el Amor.* Lima, Peru: Peisa.

Cueto, A. (2003). *Grandes Miradas.* Lima, Peru: Peisa.

Erikson, E. (1968). *Identity, Youth and Crisis.* London: FF.

Freud, S. (1914c). On narcissism: an introduction. *S.E., 14*: 73–101. London: Hogarth.

Freud, S. (1915b). Thoughts for the times on war and death. *S.E., 14*: 275–300. London: Hogarth Press.

Freud, S. (1916d). Some character-types met with in psycho-analytic work. *S.E., 14*: 309–333. London: Hogarth.

Freud, S. (1917e). Mourning and melancholia. *S.E., 14*: 239–258. London: Hogarth.

Freud, S. (1925d). An autobiographical study. *S.E., 20*: 3–70. London: Hogarth.

Grinberg, L. (1978). The razor's edge: in depression and mourning *International Journal of Psychoanalysis, 59*: 245–254.

Kleimberg, L. (2002). Minding the gap: psychoanalysis and creativity . . . and what about the space in between? *Bulletin of the British Psychoanalytic Society, 38*(6): 45–52.

Kleimberg, L. (2006). Some reflections on the connections between aggression and depression. In: C. Harding (Ed.), *Aggression and Destructiveness* (pp. 181–193). London: Routledge.

Klein, M. (1957). *The Writings of Melanie Klein, Vol III: Envy and Gratitude*. London: Hogarth Press and The Institute of Psycho-Analysis, 1975.

Magonet, J. (1985). *Forms of Prayer for Jewish Worship* (8th edn), The Assembly of Rabbis of the Reform Synagogues of Great Britain (Eds.). London: Sternberg Centre for Judaism.

Rosenfeld, H. A. (1984). Psychotic states. A psychoanalytical approach. In: *On The Psychopathology of Narcissism: A Clinical Approach*. London: Maresfield Reprints.

Segal, H. (1991). *Dream, Phantasy and Art*. London: New Library of Psychoanalysis.

Steiner, J. (1993). Psychic retreats,pathological organizations. In: E. B. Spillius (Ed.), *Psychotic, Neurotic and Borderline Patients* (pp. 1–13). London: New Library Of Psychoanalysis.

Winnicott, D. W. (1951). Transitional objects and transitional phenomena. In: *Through Paediatrics to Psychoanalysis* (pp. 229–242). London: Hogarth Press, 1982.

Winnicott, D. W. (1952). Psychoses and child care. In: *Through Paediatrics to Psychoanalysis*. London: Hogarth Press, 1982.

CHAPTER ELEVEN

The interplay of identifications: violence, hysteria, and the repudiation of femininity

Rosine Jozef Perelberg

Introduction

In this chapter, I suggest that what lies at the basis of violence and hysteria in some patients is the repudiation of femininity. Whilst hysteria takes the person's own body as the vehicle for the expression of the drama of the conflict between masculine and feminine identifications, in violence there is an externalisation of the drama and an attack on the body of the other. In both, the "drama" is secondary to a primary conflict in relation to the maternal imago. Green has suggested that: "Manifestations of hatred and the following process of reparation are manifestations which are secondary to this central decathexis of the maternal primary object" (1986, p. 146). Both symptomatologies point to the limits of what can be expressed through representations. "A feeling of captivity ... dispossesses the ego of itself and alienates it to an unrepresentable figure" (1986, p. 152). Green suggests a crucial point of technique: "to interpret hatred in structures which take on depressive characteristics amounts to never approaching the primary core of this constellation" (ibid., p. 146).

In this chapter, I discuss violence with reference to a male patient who has been in analysis with me for many years.[1] My thinking about hysteria will centre on some thoughts about Anna O, the result of research I was able to undertake.[2] I would like to suggest that both violence and hysteria could be understood as attempts by the individual, overwhelmed by the fluidity of their identificatory processes, to repudiate their feminine, passive identification in the relationship to the mother. My patient's feminine identification is ultimately given representation in a dream, in the sixth year of analysis, of being buried inside a coffin in a state of sedation; Anna O's hysteria was expressed through an experience of void, paralysis, lapse of memory, and abolition of time: white, empty, blank, categories that Green has proposed and which point out to the links between the feminine and the subject of psychoanalytic investigations.

Identification as a mode of thinking

In his letter of May 1897 to Fliess, Freud described identification as *a mode of thinking* about objects (Masson, 1985). This mode of thinking lies at the origin of the constitution of the individual, through a series of modifications of the ego. It is an *unconscious* process, that takes place in *phantasy*. In the early modalities of identification, mental processes are experienced in bodily terms such as ingesting or devouring. It is through the process of internalisation and the progressive modification of the ego, through the differentiation between ego, superego, and id—each ruled by different timings—that the individual is constituted. These identifications, by definition unconscious, are in conflict with a sense of "I" as the centre of the subject, and this is one of the several revolutions introduced by psychoanalysis in terms of its thinking about the individual. The individual is not the "I". In the poet Rimbaud's formula, "I am another" (in Lacan, 1978, p. 17). The individual in psychoanalytic thinking is thus engaged in a process of *exchange* with the other.

Identification, as a mode of thinking, presupposes a fluidity between different positions and ideas and is present in all individuals. Freud's fundamental views about sexuality throughout his work concern the fluidity between masculinity and femininity:

psychoanalysis cannot elucidate the intrinsic nature of what in conventional or in biological phraseology is termed "masculine" and "feminine": it simply takes over these two concepts and makes them the foundation of its work. When we attempt to reduce them further, we find masculinity vanishing into activity and femininity into passivity, and that does not tell us enough. (Freud, 1920g, p. 171)

In this chapter, I discuss the interplay between "identification" and "identity", the "individual" and the "person", and outline the implications for the understanding of material derived from my clinical practice.

First, I have come to understand that in certain individuals the fluidity of identificatory processes becomes overwhelming for the mind, because of the lack of distinction between phantasy and reality. Such fluctuation is indeed common in borderline patients. I think that some violent patients attempt to immobilise a specific aspect of the whole range of identificatory attributes in order to establish a persona, an identity.

Second, I further suggest that violent behaviour might be an attempt to prevent the extreme fluidity between masculine and feminine identificatory processes and avoid the recognition of a profound sense of entrapment inside a female figure. The physical act of violence might be an attempt to create a mental space in relation to confusing internal primary objects, locked in a violent primal scene, particularly in relation to the mother.

Third, these ideas are to be understood in terms of the narcissistic structures of the violent patient, who attempts to evade the experience of relating. Green (1983) defines narcissism as fundamental resistance to analysis. "Doesn't the defence of the One imply the refusal of the Unconscious just as the Unconscious implies the existence of a part of the psychic apparatus which has a life of its own, which defeats the empire of the ego?" (p. 9).[3] This allows one to suggest that while most neurotic individuals might take their "identity" for granted, it becomes a major issue for the borderline and narcissistic personalities.

Fourth, it is my understanding that in the violent patient there seems to be a passage from an "unconscious phantasy" to a "delusional system" in response to a need to separate from internal objects through external violence. If we accept Freud's formulation that phantasies of violence in the primal scene are universal, in some violent patients these phantasies seem to acquire the status of actual beliefs.

Fifth, if violence, for some patients, is an attempt to immobilise the experience of an extreme mobility of internal identificatory processes, I would then suggest that a technical challenge in the analysis of these patients is to identify and keep in mind the shifts between the identificatory processes and formulate them in terms of interpretations to the patients.

Finally, I will try to indicate that as the analyst is progressively more able to identify the patient's internal movement between different states and identificatory processes and able to integrate these into interpretations to the patient, the patient is himself more able to tolerate the internal fluidity between identificatory processes.

I will now examine material from the five-times-a-week analysis of a violent young man, which has been the source of some of these thoughts.

A case of violence: clinical material

The main information Karl brought up about himself at his first consultation was his special relationship to his mother. Karl is in his early twenties; his father left his mother when she was pregnant with him. His mother married when he was still a baby, and this man adopted Karl as his son. Three years later, the couple had a baby girl. Karl feels, however, that his mother always let him know that he was the most important person in the family for her. At the same time, he experiences his mother as unable to tolerate his sexuality or, even less, him being a man. His father was violent towards him throughout his childhood, hitting him frequently about the head. He recalls being frightened of his father. When he was eighteen, Karl decided to study martial arts; he feels that his father then became frightened of him and stopped hitting him.

The analytic process: the patterns of the transference

At his first consultation, Karl presented me with a question that he felt had become an obsession for him and which expressed his concern about the nature of his parents' sexuality. He told me that his parents were involved in "sado-masochistic games". He had known this since childhood, because he and his sister had listened to them behind their bedroom door. During this same consultation, Karl started to let me know about the extent of the violence in which he had been engaged. At university, he had become involved in serious violent situations with other young men (an example was that of a fight where he and other youths had used broken bottles and which had left him in hospital with fifteen stitches in his head) and in escalating violence in his sexual relationship with a girlfriend. At that first consultation, I noted the possible unconscious association between his question about the nature of his parents' sexuality and his own relationships with male and female friends.

In tracking the way in which Karl related to me in his analysis, I progressively came to understand that each time his analyst understood him, he attempted to escape from an experience of having a mind. He then had to disappear by not coming to his sessions for a time. At the beginning of the analysis, this was expressed essentially in the states of sleep Karl would get into, from which he could not be awakened, neither by several alarm clocks nor by his mother shouting at him. He could disappear from the sessions for a week, for instance, without realising that so long had passed since his last session. The interpretations, during this period, consistently pointed to this complete retreat both from the encounter with the analyst and from the obstacles Karl inevitably experienced in his relationship with me. Karl's sleep was dreamless, and this was also interpreted as a flight, not only from me, but also from the experience of having a mind. Karl also spent a great deal of time compulsively playing computer games where violence was expressed in a robotic way against dehumanised enemies.

Karl gradually revealed how difficult it was for him to maintain contact with real living people, since this involved levels of frustration, violence, and terror that he simply could not tolerate. Yet, as his confidence in the analytic relationship grew, his thoughts and aggressive interactions outside the sessions became more vividly present in his accounts during the sessions. At times, he inundated me with accounts of extremely violent behaviour which left me disgusted, frightened, and hopeless about the possibility of my having any impact on him.

At this stage, I felt able to say no more than that his violence seemed to follow on from his fear of my intrusiveness in the transference. He responded by telling me that he possessed a gun and bullets, which he kept at home. As he talked about this, it seemed that he was keeping a part of both himself and myself hostage, terrorised by his potential destructiveness. At that point, I seriously considered terminating his analysis.

Inevitably, my interpretations were rooted in my countertransference: he needed to know that he could terrify me as a way of protecting himself from his own fear of me.[4] My interpretations allowed him to get rid of the gun, but this left him without the power to terrorise me; he felt lost, abandoned, and deeply depressed. To counteract his depression, he intensified his accounts of criminal activities. After a period in his analysis in which I consistently interpreted to him the function of his criminal activities as a means of creating a distance from me and the analysis, he was able to understand and acknowledge that it was easier for him to come to the sessions after dangerous criminal encounters, such as obtaining and selling stolen diamonds, which gave him a sense of omnipotence. I also suggested that this was because he felt less frightened of my power over him. His criminal activities, thus, served to distance him from me and, while they had many determinants, one transferential aspect was undoubtedly the wish to avoid a meaningful emotional relationship.

The alternation between presence and absence, life and death, love and hate

At the beginning of his analysis, Karl had many dreams that portrayed his experience of himself as inhuman, machine-like, deprived of feelings and thoughts. He dreamt that he was a computer, or different kinds of monsters; in one particular instance, he was a monster that was disintegrating. In the clinical material that follows, one can identify a trajectory whereby Karl was able to bring to the analysis images that express his terror of losing himself and becoming imprisoned, and of being manipulated by a lethal couple. I will indicate a progression in his analysis to a capacity to experience himself in a more humane way.

At the beginning of the third year of analysis, though, the image Karl spoke about most frequently was that of a disembodied head that did not belong to him. This image was derived from a television play by Dennis Potter, which had made a strong impression on him.

In one particular session, Karl came in and threw himself on the couch. He started telling me about watching *Cold Lazarus*, by Dennis Potter, on television. He said he was not sure what it was about the play that had caught his attention so much. Thinking about it had prevented him from sleeping at night. It was something to do with the language. He had watched it on both Sunday and Monday, and explained that the play was being shown on two channels. He told me the story, saying that it was science fiction and, thus, something to which he would immediately be attracted. In the story, a man has his brain cryogenically preserved in the hope that it could be revived 400 years into the future. In the play, the man's memory was being revived by two scientists. Karl said that it had been something in the quality of the language that had arrested his attention. It was like a language without a link with anything else, coming straight from the head. It reminded him of himself when his mental state was not good. The thing about this man was that he was just a head, so that, in a way, his memories did not belong to him. *He did not have an identity.* He was just what this couple of scientists did with him.

I said that he was describing a quality he could identify in himself when he was avoiding having any feelings and was talking from his head only. He then said that when he was in that state of mind—without feelings—*he felt that he did not have an identity.* His identity had then been taken over by another part of him, the "scientist", who he felt was in control. He said that there was a connection between that play and *Karaoke*, another play by Potter, in which a character who is an author feels that people around him are repeating lines from his plays, which are being fed back to him about his own life. I then spoke to Karl about his experience of relating to other people: he, too, feels that he can only re-find his own lines. Later in the session, I pointed out that there was also the issue of possession: is he a possession of mine or am I a possession of his? There is no one who can have a life of their own, a "real identity" (his term). Violence became Karl's solution to this dilemma.

Karl then told me about a dream:

> There were three men, a weak man, a bodyguard and a violent man, who was able to overcome the bodyguard.

In his associations, Karl spoke of "great men", such as Rabin or Kennedy, who were nevertheless in a fragile position. We understood this dream as expressing the various experiences he had of himself. Underneath the bodyguard, there was a fragile man, who was afraid of being hit by the violent aspect of himself.

A more three-dimensional experience of himself had, however, started to emerge in his analysis, as we also identified that it was the bodyguard—the man "in between"—who tended to come to the sessions. Karl was, however, afraid of being left with a perception of himself as a weak and unprotected man who was bound to be killed. In the transference, I was, at the time, acutely aware that I needed to keep all three aspects of him in mind.[5]

However, there was also an emphasis on the inevitability of death, as I could not avoid pointing out at the time. Karl then disappeared from a few sessions, and when he came back he brought another dream:

> Karl was inside a tomb and a panther was approaching him. He was terrified as the panther came closer and closer, and he woke up terrified.

In his associations, Karl remembered first seeing a panther during a trip to the West Indies with his mother, who had taken him on a visit to a friend who kept a panther as a pet. In the session, we were able to understand that the tomb was where he felt he had been for the week he had been absent from the sessions, and that he was now afraid of me, a panther, which posed a danger to him as a representative of the outside world. He was, however, also afraid that, like his mother's friend and his own mother, I would want to keep the panther in him as my pet.

This opened up his memory of a film called *The Vanishing*, which he told me was the most terrifying film he had ever seen in his life. In the film, a man called Hoffman had lost his girlfriend. She had vanished from a petrol station, and he had spent three years looking for her. Throughout this period, he kept getting letters from a man saying that he had made her disappear. This man tortured Hoffman in this way for three years; when they finally met, he told him that he, Hoffman, could take him to the police if he wanted, because there were no traces whatsoever of what he had done. The only way Hoffman could find out what had happened to his girlfriend was to go through the same thing as her. Hoffman thought long and hard; in the end he decided that he had to find out what had happened. He took the tranquilliser this man gave him, and at that moment he was sealing his fate. He fell asleep and woke up in a coffin, buried under the earth. It was the most terrifying experience anyone could think of, to be buried alive.

He then said that a scene that he could not forget took place in a car, when Hoffman became friendly with the fascist psychopathic kidnapper. Hoffman laughed with him and said that all his life he had done what was expected of him. He said that one knows that people who are kidnapped sometimes become friends with their kidnappers, like people who are kidnapped by Arabs and then come back to the West mad, holding the Koran and claiming that their kidnappers are, in fact, good people. Karl told me about an American version of the same story made by the same director, with Jeff Bridges in the leading role, and which had been a disaster. They had changed the ending so that Hoffman is saved by (Karl laughed) "John Wayne". Later, Karl added that in fact it had been this man's girlfriend who saved him, just as he was being buried.

I said to him, "You know, I think that it was terrifying for you to see in this film the way you bury yourself alive in your bed/coffin. You are terrified of experiencing yourself either like Hoffman, who takes the tranquilliser, or the psychopath/murderer who gets a kick out of it and of having killed the girlfriend three years ago [the analysis]. I also feel, however, that it is terrifying for you to wake up and find yourself in the coffin." (Equally, I thought that he was also terrified that trusting me was like taking the sedative that would lead him to feel buried in my couch and thus converted to the Koran, my mad version of things.) He was very struck by all this. He said that he could understand what I was saying, but he was not really afraid of me now. I added something about his misgivings about the ending. He thought that the version of the film with a happy ending had been a disaster, in contrast with the terrifying one. He had also pointed out the fact that it was the man's girlfriend who had saved him, not John Wayne. I felt that this showed his mixed feelings about the idea of a girlfriend/woman analyst saving him.

I thought this session was important. Karl had himself found a narrative and an image that referred to his own experience of his two states: being dead and the terrifying waking up, and the wish to be "saved", but also the terror of being saved by another entrapping/ dead/not birth-giving woman/mother/analyst; ultimately, the fear of a couple made up of the murderer and the coffin, a couple which was not life giving and which, ultimately, lived inside him. What I felt was so important in this session was the way in which we were able to identify these various positions within himself: the murderous couple and the victim who was being murdered.

Karl missed the next session, and on Friday he said that he had been unable to wake up on Thursday. He could not understand why. He talked about his relationship with his girlfriend, the first real relationship in his life, which he felt had changed him. Then he talked about a film called *A Matter of Life and Death*, which was one of the most beautiful films he had seen. David Niven plays an RAF pilot during the Second World War whose plane has been attacked. He falls through the air and Death comes to fetch him. It is, however, very foggy, so Death cannot find him. In the meantime, a woman hears David Niven on the radio when he is hit and she falls in love with him. She goes to find him in the hospital and they fall in love. Then, two days later, Death catches up with him and the rest of the film is about the trial at which David Niven defends himself. He says that because of these two days, he has fallen in love, and that it is not his fault they missed him, but now he needs his life extended. The judge has the power to decide whether to extend his life or not. In the end the judge decides to let him live. It was really a most striking film, Karl added. The title was most appropriate, truly "a matter of life and death".

I said that he felt that his analysis and his analyst had changed the course of his life, but that this put him, at the same time, in the hands of a judge who has to decide whether or not he can carry on living (or having his analysis). He is not sure if the judge is going to be benign or not. Karl said that he was not used to meeting benign people in his life. I pointed out the contrast between *A Matter of Life and Death* and *The Vanishing*, the former expressing the capacity for love, the latter the destructive/fascist forces inside him. I said that I thought it was difficult to find connections between these two films, these two experiences within himself. He was quiet for a moment (a rare experience). Later in the session, I said, "You know, I think that today you want me to know that there is a loving, devoted part of you as well." He said that this session had been really amazing.

Discussion

Phantasy and beliefs

Britton has proposed a distinction between phantasy, belief, and knowledge. He suggests that *"belief* is an ego activity which confers the status of psychic reality on to existing mental productions (phantasies) . . ."* (1995, pp. 19–20). I think these distinctions are useful in that, for my patient, his unconscious phantasies about the primal scene have the status of beliefs. In Karl's thinking, there is also a lack of differentiation between life and death and a terror of finding out that he is establishing an identity between the two.

While he is asleep in the coffin, Hoffman is not aware of his predicament, which I think includes the question of whether he is submitting to a man (an aspect of Hoffman that is a murderer) or to a woman (or a woman's womb, i.e., the coffin). It is only when he wakes up that he is terrified by the fact that he is trapped inside the coffin, which can ultimately be experienced as the combination of a parental couple which is not life-giving: the psychopathic father who commits murder by burying him, and the entrapping mother who does not allow him to be born or to live outside her body and her mind. The coffin was also the couch, the "bedrock" of his analysis, and where he was afraid of waking up to find out that he had submitted to a couple who had committed murder in the primal scene. In a state of ultimate sleep without any dreams, I think Karl attempted to remove all representations from his mind. The counterpart to that is the violence, where all this gains representation (as expressed in the derivatives of his unconscious phantasies in his analysis) and has to be expressed in action.

Hysteria: the case of Anna O

Anna O has fired the imagination of many psychoanalysts and a great deal has been written about her.[6] I will provide only minimal information, in order to outline some of my thoughts.

Anna O started her eighteen-month-long treatment with Breuer when she was twenty-one years old. Her parents had four children, three daughters (of whom she was the only survivor at the time she met Breuer) and a son, eighteen months younger than her. She had been looking after her father, who was ill with tuberculosis, for some five months, doing the night shifts while her mother looked after him during the day, when Breuer first saw her. Anna O initially started to suffer from coughing, sleepiness, and agitation in the afternoons. After the beginning of the treatment with Breuer, she developed a variety of other symptoms: ocular disturbances, paralyses, contractions, linguistic disorganisation (when she also spoke a mixture of five languages) and, later, mutism. She also had hallucinations of snakes. Once, while nursing her father, she had a hallucination of a black snake that was about to bite him. She tried to move her arm but was unable to do so, as it became paralysed. She tried to pray, but could only remember the lines of an old English nursery song (Humpty Dumpty). She looked at the fingers and each had become a little black snake, each nail a skull. After her father's death, four months later, Anna O suffered from a "negative instinct", recognising no one in her household and speaking only in English to Breuer. She also developed different personalities, at different times: initially a good one and a naughty one, later, one who lived in the present and another who lived 365 days earlier. It has been reported that on the day of the last day of her treatment with Breuer, Anna O displayed hysterical symptoms of a pregnancy, showing "contractions" and saying, "Here comes Dr Breuer's child".

Anna O herself designated her treatment with Breuer as her "talking cure" and referred to the cathartic method as "chimney sweeping". In 1953, Ernest Jones revealed the identity of Anna O. Her real name was Bertha Pappenheim, who, ten years after her treatment with Breuer, had become an important social worker and feminist in the Jewish community, saving the lives of many orphans from pogroms in Eastern Europe, and Jewish women who were being sold as slaves.

Hysteria, bisexuality, and primal scene

Hysteria and bisexuality have an essential link for Freud, who suggested that hysterical attacks express an experience of rape in which the hysteric plays both roles.[7] "In one case I observed, for instance, the patient pressed her dress up against her body with one hand (as a woman), while she tried to tear it off with the other (as a man)" (Freud, 1908a, p. 166).

It was in the discussion of the case of Katharina that Freud himself first related hysteria to the primal scene (Freud & Breuer, 1893a). Freud mentioned at least three further cases linking anxiety to the primal scene (in a letter to Fliess, in his paper on anxiety neurosis (1895), and in his analysis of Dora), although, throughout his work, he oscillated between regarding this as a "real event" and a "phantasy": "I maintained years ago that the dyspnoea and palpitations that occur in hysteria and anxiety neurosis are only detached fragments of the act of copulation . . ." (1905e, p. 80).

In a later letter to Jung in 1909, Freud wrote about Anna O's term "chimney sweeping": "The reason why a chimney sweep is supposed to bring good luck is that sweeping a chimney is an unconscious symbol of coitus, which is something of which Breuer certainly never dreamed" (McGuire, 1995, p. 161).

Freud attributed increasing importance to primal scene phantasies and, later in his work, he linked the origins of the function of phantasising itself to these primal phantasies. According to him, there is a specific, imaginary configuration to these primal scenes: they represent a scene of violence, where the father is inflicting pain on the mother (Laplanche & Pontalis, 1985). He later suggested that hysterical attacks represented phantasies about the sexual encounter as a scene of rape. In one of Bertha Pappenheim's plays, *Women's Rights*, the sexual act is represented as an aggressive act, a rape and a surrender to the enemy. A woman was raped and impregnated by her lover, who was already married and who then left her.

Anna O's symptoms started at her father's bedside when he became ill. She started to cough when he was dying of tuberculosis, revealing her unmistakable identification with her father: when she looked at herself in the mirror it was his skull that she saw.[8] At his bedside, the fingers in the shape of skulls, which Britton convincingly suggests refer to masturbation, are a reminder of Freud's text "A child is being beaten", according to which the wish to be loved by the father is transformed into the phantasy of "a child is being beaten" (where the individual disappears from the scene) (1919e). This central phantasy links masochism and femininity and expresses the guilt feelings for the incestuous desires towards the father. Breuer wrote, in his 1882 report, that Anna O had "truly passionate love" for her father (Ellenberger, 1972, p. 267). Freud, however, also suggested that, at its core, hysteria indicates a relationship with a hated object.

In his analysis of melancholia, Freud showed that the ego can treat itself as an object and is able to direct against itself the hostility that relates to an object. He suggested that in melancholia "the individual feels overwhelmed by guilt and hostility which become persecutory, demanding revenge and expiation" (1917e, p. 252). One could understand Anna O's symptoms as expressions of struggles with her melancholic state and as transformations of her mourning into sexual excitation (Braunschweig & Fain, 1975).[9]

The famous accounts of hysterical patients—Anna O, Lucy R, Elizabeth Von R, Dora—indicate that they have all been disappointed by their fathers through illness, impotence, weakness, and death. Coupled with this picture of disappointment with the father is the longing for another woman who becomes the personification of unattainable femininity, like Dora's longing for Mrs K. Is it that with the father's weakness, illness, impotence, or death, the daughter becomes frightened of being at the mercy of an internal imago of the mother?

In the years between 1920 and 1925, a new dimension appears in Freud's writings in relation to his understanding of female sexuality. The daughter's love for her father is an attempt to re-find a more fundamental and older love, related to the mother. In a letter to Stefan Zweig in 1932, Freud wrote about Breuer's flight from Anna O when he heard about her hysterical pregnancy: "At this moment he held in his hand the key that would have opened the doors to the 'Mothers', but he let it drop" (Freud, 1960). The reference to the "Mothers" is an allusion to Faust's mysterious researches (in Goethe's *Faust*, Part II, Act I). Is this Freud's intuitive view of what Anna O's father's death left her grappling with, her unconscious feelings towards her *mother*? Breuer himself made this reference at the end of the first section of the theoretical chapter of his book (Pollock, 1968). The mysterious mothers are goddesses who dwell below, in an internal void, without space, place, or time (Pollock, 1968). Are these not markedly similar to what Green (1993) describes as the expressions of the negative? Does this not, therefore, suggest a link between the negative and femininity?

One can link these ideas about the world of the "mothers" to the episodes of depersonalisation, mutism, paralysis, "time-missing", and gaps in memory that followed Anna O's hallucination of the snake. They are interruptions in the domain of a reality that is being disavowed, indicating, perhaps, what Britton has designated in his book as a "suspension of belief" (1998a, p. 15), when something is both known and not known at the same time. What is fundamentally known and not known is the fact of the division between the sexes (Chasseguet-Smirgel, 1985; Freud, 1927e, 1940e[1938]; Kohon, 1987). Sexuality is created through division and discontinuity (see Lacan, 1958, Mitchell, 1982; Rose, 1982), and these symptoms, paradoxically, seem to represent Anna O's identificatory struggles.

The literature on Anna O contains so little about her mother. It has been suggested that she had a negative relationship with her. We know that Anna O was between nine and ten months old when her mother became pregnant again, and that this would have had an unconscious impact on her libidinal and aggressive investment in the primal scene (Freeman, 1972, and also Riccardo Steiner (personal communication)). Breuer was oblivious to Anna O's reactions to his comings and goings, and we do not know if these were experienced by Anna O as a repetition of earlier infantile experiences of abandonment by her mother.

At the onset of her father's serious illness, Anna O lost her mother tongue and refused the nourishing environment representative of the mothering function which was taken over by Breuer. One could hypothesise that the erotic feelings towards a paternal analyst were defensive against both the risk of feeling paternal disappointment and of being left alone with a dangerous maternal imago. Through her rejection of her mother tongue, English became a language that she could share with Breuer, to the exclusion of everybody else. A phantasy of seduction indeed lies at the centre of Anna O's hysteria, and her treatment with Breuer indicates a confusion about who is the seducer.

If the hysteric is the feminine in the neurotic representation (Schaeffer), it is also the very repudiation of the feminine. Schaeffer (using an expression coined by Michel Cachoux) suggests, "The Ruby is a stone that has a horror of red. It absorbs and retains all the other colours ... (but) rejects and expels red ..." (Schaeffer, 1986, p. 925). Thus, the hysteric has a horror of the colour red, of sexuality, while at the same time displaying it. In her hysterical pregnancy, paradoxically, Anna O was rejecting a feminine identification, the woman who would produce babies as a result of intercourse. This pregnancy might also be understood as her attempt to deny separation and to hold Breuer inside her: that is, as a phantasy of incorporation. Denial and omnipotence constitute the first defences against the loss of the object, as Melanie Klein has suggested.

Some aspects of Bertha Pappenheim's later life represent transformations of Anna O's question, "Am I a man or a woman?" (see Kohon, 1986; Leclaire, 1971) albeit in a sublimated way. In her social work, she designated the social workers she trained as her daughters—products of an imaginary intercourse without a father or mother. The orphanage she built was known as "Papahome", the house of the father, in which she would fulfil the two parental roles.

Hysteria becomes, fundamentally, a mode of thinking about sexuality and the sexual object (Schaeffer, 1986).[10] Hysteria works by imitation; the difference between identification and imitation is that between "being like the object" and "being the object". Through her symptoms, Anna O seems to be *imitating* the sexual act. Her symptoms become like a theatre of the sexual act in an attempt to both deny and represent the primal scene and deny the mourning of her incestuous sexual desires. It is also displaying a body that cannot be experienced as sexual and feminine, but as bits and pieces that ache. The fracture of the mind (the Humpty Dumpty song she recited at her father's bedside) is mirrored in the fragmentation of the body through her symptoms.

Conclusions

Freud pointed out the fluidity that is the hallmark of identificatory processes. This fluidity contrasts with the individual quest for a *coherent* identity, a sense of cohesiveness that is denied him by the very nature of the psychic apparatus. It is, however, only the feelings of security engendered by attachments to objects of both sexes that prevent the individual from feeling overwhelmed by the pressure of the phantasies and desires, because they may then be anchored in a set of secure object relationships. Both Karl and Anna O might be seen as defending themselves against a wish for, and a terror of, fusion with the dangerous mother. In Anna O's case, the mother seems to be absent through bereavement; maybe she is more like the "dead mother" described by Green (1986), although one needs to emphasise the speculative nature of these ideas, as we do not have access to the here and now of an analytic process that would allow the material to unfold in the transference. In Karl's case, the mother provides the experience of death—the coffin, ultimately—in the sense that she is not psychically able to give life. Is it that Anna O attacks in her own body the body of her mother, whereas Karl has to find in the other the (m)other?

Violence and hysteria might be seen as attempts to give birth to another person who is disconnected from the lethal parental couple *and, at the same time,* a repetition of the relationship attributed to this couple. Violence and hysteria might be seen as attempts to create personas detached from the conflict of identifications.

Psychoanalysis is always characterised by an indeterminism, perhaps because phenomena are over-determined so that many different phantasies are necessarily attached to the patient's symptomatology. The psychoanalytic task is consistently that of "linking" affects, images, and words as they are expressed and experienced in the transference and countertransference, so that the preconscious may be constructed in this way.

The individual is, thus, placed in a chain of reciprocity in relation to his internal and external objects. I have previously suggested that Karl's fundamental concern in his analysis is to regulate his distance from his analyst (Perelberg, 1995).[11] I can now understand this as representing his conflict about entering a chain of reciprocity that is, ultimately, the force of the life instinct itself. It has been Karl's inability to take part in this system of exchange that has condemned him to death itself, to his coffin. In his analysis, we have been able to reach representations of this enclosure which, by definition, indicates his progressive entrance into the symbolic sphere.

Notes

1. This patient was seen as part of a subsidised scheme at the Anna Freud Centre in the Young Adults Research Group. This research group, whose clinical director was Mrs Anne-Marie Sandler, was composed of fifteen psychoanalysts who have undertaken analysis of young adults who suffered breakdown. I am grateful to the members of the group for helpful discussions of my patient. I am also grateful to André Green for his contribution when I presented a paper on this patient to the Paris Psychoanalytical Society in June 1998.

2. This research was presented on the occasion of the 1998 English Speaking Conference, held in London, when I was the discussant of Ronald Britton's paper "Getting in on the act: the hysterical solution" (1998b).

3. La défense de l'Un n'entraine-t-elle pas *ipso facto* le refus de l'inconsient, puisque celui-ci implique l'existence d'une part du psychisme qui agit pour son propre compte, mettant en échec l'empire du Moi? (Green, 1983, p. 9).

4. Being able to detect fear in me had the function of reassuring Karl that the fear was no longer in himself, so allowing him to feel safer. Sandler (1959) has suggested that in order to preserve its feelings of safety, the ego will make use of whatever techniques it has at its disposal. He gives examples of the way in which defence mechanisms can operate in the service of this "safety principle".

5. An important ingredient in Karl's analysis has been the accounts of films he has seen. At times, as in the sequence above, an account of a film, followed by an interpretation, was then followed by a dream. Money-Kyrle has suggested a theory of stages in representational thought that moves from a stage of concrete representation (where no distinction is made between the representation and the object represented), through a stage of ideographic representation, as in dreams, to a stage of conscious and predominantly verbal thought (1968, p. 422). I think that for Karl, films serve to contain projections of experiences before they can reach a stage of being able to be represented in dreams. The interpretations function as mediators in this process. This observation is in agreement with Sedlak's (1997) observation on the analyst's function in the transformation of the patient's dilemmas into ones that can be thought and dreamt about, although, in his paper, Sedlak is addressing the role of the countertransference in the process.

6. In my PEP (Psychoanalytic Electronic Publishing) CD ROM search I was able to identify 244 papers written on her between 1920 and 1994. For the present chapter, I have made use mainly of the following publications: Breuer & Freud (1893a, 1895d), Ellenberger (1972, 1984), Freeman (1972), Gay (1988), and Pollock (1986).

7. Leclaire has suggested that the question of the hysteric is "Am I a man or a woman?" (1971, also in Kohon, 1986). It is a question of shifting identifications in an attempt to retain one identification, which is phallic. This is also present in the violent patient.

8. Britton has suggested,

> If I were to schematise Anna O's case . . . I would see it beginning in the parental bedroom with her cough, starvation and progressive weakness; as a deadly union with a dying father; her cough was associated with dance music heard at the bedside and subsequently provoked by rhythmical music. The hallucination of the black snake then I take, to be death by intercourse and her death-

head fingers a deadly form of masturbaton. This was interrupted by her removal from the parental bedroom. Her subsequent paralysis expressed the infantile lack of locomotory power and the chaos of her movement and stiff limbed contractures a caricature of a primal couple in intercourse. Her speech mirrored her limb movement; infantile, dislocated and polysyllabic. (Britton 1998b)

9. Mourning has an extreme importance in the understanding of the development of the transference and countertransference in Anna O's treatment with Breuer. Bertha Pappenheim's maternal grandmother had died when her mother was ten. Her mother had three daughters, of whom Bertha was the only survivor in 1881. Her sister Flora died at the age of two, four years before Bertha's birth, in 1859 (the same year that Freud was born). Her older sister Henrietta died of tuberculosis in 1867, at the age of seventeen, when Anna O was eight years old. Wilhelm, the only boy in the family, was born when Bertha was eighteen months old. One can, therefore, imagine Bertha's mother as absorbed by bereavement as far back as her own childhood. Mourning had an important role for Breuer, too: his mother, *who had also been called Bertha*, had died giving birth to his brother, Adolf, four years younger than himself. This brother died of tuberculosis at the age of twenty. Breuer's own father died in 1872, when Breuer was thirty years old, eight years before he started treating Anna O. Breuer had himself five children, the eldest of whom, also called Bertha, was born in 1870.

10. Michel Fain has suggested that sexuality is a constant oscillation between hysteria and orgasm (in Schaeffer, 1986, p. 944).

11. In recent years, I have developed further thoughts about the role of the absent father in this analysis (see Perelberg, 2009, 2011).

References

Braunschweig, D., & Fain, M. (1975). *La nuit, le jour*. Paris: PUF.

Breuer, J., & Freud, S. (1895d). *Studies on Hysteria. S.E.*, 2: 1–251.

Britton, R. (1995). Psychic reality and unconscious belief. *International Journal of Psychoanalysis*, 76: 19–23.

Britton, R. (1998a). *Belief and Imagination*. London: Routledge, New Library of Psychoanalysis 31.

Britton, R. (1998b). Getting in on the act: the hysterical solution. Paper presented to the Weekend English Speaking Conference to European Members, October 9–11, London, British Psychoanalytical Society.

Chasseguet-Smirgel, J. (Ed.) (1985). Feminine guilt and the Oedipus complex. In: *Female Sexuality*. London: Maresfield, 1964.

Ellenberger, H. (1984). Anna O: insight, hindsight and foresight. In: M. Rosenbaum & M. Muroff (Eds.), *Anna O: 14 Contemporary Reinterpretations*. New York: Free Press.

Ellenberger, H. F. (1972). The story of "Anna O.": a critical review with new data. *Journal of the History of Behavioral Sciences, 8*: 267–279.

Freeman, L. (1972). *The Story of Anna O*. Northvale, NJ: Jason Aronson.

Freud, S., with Breuer, J. (1893a). On the psychical mechanism of hysterical phenomena: preliminary communication. *S.E., 2*: 1–19. London: Hogarth.

Freud, S. (1895). On the grounds for detaching a particular syndrome from neurasthenia under the description 'anxiety neurosis'. *S.E., 3*: 90–115. London: Hogarth.

Freud, S. (1905e). *Fragment of an Analysis of a Case of Hysteria. S.E., 7*: 1–122. London: Hogarth.

Freud, S. (1908a). Hysterical phantasies and their relation to bisexuality. *S.E., 9*: 159–166. London: Hogarth.

Freud, S. (1917e). Mourning and melancholia. *S.E. 14*: 243–258. London: Hogarth.

Freud, S. (1919e). 'A child is being beaten': a contribution to the study of the origin of sexual perversions. *S.E., 17*: 177–204. London: Hogarth.

Freud, S. (1920g). *Beyond the Pleasure Principle. S.E., 18*: 7–64. London: Hogarth.

Freud, S. (1927e). Fetishism. *S.E. 21*: 152–157. London: Hogarth.

Freud, S. (1940e[1938]). Splitting of the ego in the process of defence. *S.E., 23*: 275–278. London: Hogarth.

Freud, S. (1960). *Letters of Sigmund Freud*, E. L. Freud (Ed.). New York: Basic Books.

Gay, P. (1986). *Freud: A Life for our Time*. London: J. M. Dent and Sons.

Green, A. (1983). *Narcissism de Vie; Narcissism de Mort*. Paris: PUF.

Green, A. (1986). The dead mother. In: *Private Madness* (pp. 142–173). London: Hogarth Press and the Institute of Psychoanalysis.

Green, A. (1993). *Le Travail du Negatif*. Paris: Editions de Minuit.

Kohon, G. (Ed.) (1986). *The British School of Psychoanalysis: The Independent Tradition*. London: Free Association Books.

Kohon, G. (1987). Fetishism revisited. *International Journal of Psychoanalysis, 68*: 213–229.

Lacan, J. (1958). *Le Seminaire, Livre V. Les Formations de L'Inconscient*. Paris: Seuil, 1998.

Lacan, J. (1978). *Le Seminaire, Livre II. Le Moi Dans la theorie de Freud et dans la technique de la psychanalyse*. Paris: Seuil.

Laplanche, J., & Pontalis, J.-B. (1985). *The Language of Psychoanalysis*. London: Hogarth Press and the Institute of Psychoanalysis.

Leclaire, S. (1971). Jerome, or death in the life of the obsessional. In: S. Schneiderman (Ed.), *Returning to Freud*. New Haven, CT: Yale University Press, 1980.

Masson, J. M. (Ed.) (1985). *The Complete Letters of Sigmund Freud to Wilhem Fliess 1887–1904*. London: Belknap Press of Harvard University Press.

McGuire, W. (Ed.) (1991). *The Freud/Jung Letters: Correspondence between Sigmund Freud and C. G. Jung*, R. Manheim & R. F. C. Hull (Trans.). Harmondsworth: Penguin.

Mitchell, J. (1982). Introduction 1. In: J. Mitchell & J. Rose (Eds.), *Feminine Sexuality: Jacques Lacan and the Ecole Freudienne*. London: Macmillan.

Money-Kyrle, R. (1968). Cognitive development. *International Journal of Psychoanalysis, 49*. Reprinted in: D. Meltzer (Ed.), *The Collected Papers of Roger Money-Kyrle*. Strathtay, Perthshire: Clunie Press, 1978.

Perelberg, R. J. (1995). A core phantasy in violence. *International Journal of Psychoanalysis, 76*(6): 1215–1231. Also in R. J. Perelberg (Ed.), *Psychoanalytic Understanding of Violence and Suicide*. London: Routledge, 1998.

Perelberg, R. J. (1999). The interplay between identifications and identity in the analysis of a violent patient. *International Journal of Psychoanalysis, 80*: 31–45. Reprinted in: *Time, Space and Phantasy*. London: Routledge, 2006.

Perelberg, R. J. (2009). Murdered father, dead father: revisiting the Oedipus complex. *International Journal of Psychoanalysis, 90*: 713–732.

Perelberg, R. J. (2011). 'A father is being beaten': constructions in the analysis of some male patients. *International Journal of Psychoanalysis, 92*: 97–116.

Pollock, G. H. (1968). The possible significance of childhood object loss in the Josef Breuer–Bertha Pappenheim (Anna O.)–Sigmund Freud relationship. *Journal of the American Psychoanalytic Association, 16*: 711–739.

Rose, J. (1982). Introduction II. In: J. Mitchell & J. Rose (Eds.), *Feminine Sexuality: Jacques Lacan and The Ecole Freudienne* . London: Macmillan.

Sandler, J. (1959). The background of safety. In: *From Safety to Superego*. London: Karnac, 1987.

Schaeffer, J. (1986). Le rubis a horreur du rouge. *Revue Française de Psychanalyse, 50*: 923–944.

Sedlak, V. (1997). The dream space and countertransference. *International Journal of Psychoanalysis, 78*(2): 295–305.

CHAPTER TWELVE

The use and misuse of transference interpretations

Susan Budd

"An analyst may relate all the material presented to him by the patient in a vague way to the transference such as 'You feel this about me now' or 'You are doing this to me' or they repeat the words of the patient parrot-like and relate them to the session. I think this stereotyped kind of interpretation, which is supposed to be an interpretation of the here-and-now situation, changes Strachey's valuable contribution of the mutative transference into something absurd"

(Rosenfeld, 1972, p. 456)

W hen I began to think about what seems most characteristic of the theory and practice of the Independent Group, two factors stood out above all others. The first is a continuing willingness to consider interventions other than transference interpretations, and the second is to reflect that it might be the context in which interpretations are given which is more important than their content. No clear lines can be drawn between psychoanalytic schools; we all give both transference and other kinds of interpretation. Often, it is the followers who ossify technique; like Marx, Melanie Klein once protested that *she* was not a Kleinian! It is a question of emphasis, but the issue ramifies into every aspect of theory and technique, and so I begin with a brief historical resumé.

When Freud looked back over his brief analysis of "Dora", he concluded that he had overlooked the way in which she had reacted to him as if he were her father, or Herr K. She had *transferred* the feelings that she had about them to him, and, as a result, she had abruptly terminated her analysis in order to win a Pyrrhic victory, not only over him, but over her father and her would-be lover. Her transference was theoretically illuminating, but had fostered a resistance that was clinically disastrous.

This, just over a hundred years ago, might have been the first appearance of the concept of transference in psychoanalytic theory, but Freud pointed out that the phenomenon of transference is universal and age-old. The metaphor that he used was that of the template; we all contain inner shapes, the unconscious residues and expectations of earlier object-relations, and these templates are readily reactivated by new experiences. We will perceive people as authority figures, or remote, or wanting help, and so on, partly because of their "real" characteristics, and partly as if they were figures from our past now lodged within us. One of the purposes of psychoanalysis is to encourage the patient first to form and then to examine the unconscious templates that join their perceptions of their analyst to their experience of other people, either in the past or in their wider lives. This is done by means of the abstinence of the analyst in the setting, and then by transference interpretations, which, in their fullest form, link together the transferences being made to the analyst with those made to parents in the past and other people in the present.

In Dora's case, her feelings and attitudes towards figures in her past and present life were being transferred into her analysis, on to Freud. As the analyst listens to the patient talking about his life outside the session, we scan the material for what it seems to reveal about the analysand's assumptions about the analyst. It is felt that if the patient can understand that when, for example, he talks in a session about someone whom he is irritated with, he is prompted to do so partly because either he is irritated with his analyst, or thinks that his analyst is irritated with him. So, the analyst makes a transference interpretation. "I wonder if, in talking about your fear that your boss will be irritated with you, you mean me . . ."

After the Narcissism paper of 1914, the idea of psychoanalysis as being primarily about recovering repressed knowledge and understanding was replaced, especially in Britain and America, by the idea that psychoanalysis is primarily not about instinct, but about object-relations: about analysing the unconscious projections and introjections that flow between patient and analyst. Again, the analyst scans the material, and his countertransference feelings, to discover the inferences and the assumptions that the patient seems to be making, and tries to get the patient to accept this by the analysis of the transference to the analyst in the session. Such interventions are often referred to as "here and now" interpretations. "Here and now" transference interpretations are often seen as more effective because they are more immediate, and also because the analyst can only really know about the patient's psychic life as it exists inside the session and in relation to himself. In this chapter, I want to question both assumptions, and to argue that transference interpretations are not always desirable or preferable.

Varieties of transference interpretation

No British analyst would dispute that some transference is constantly present between analyst and patient—indeed, as Freud pointed out, it permeates all our relationships. Neither would they dispute that transference interpretations can be very effective, because, by their means, we might be able to convince the patient that we are not as they believe us to be, and so bring to their attention, in that moment and most vividly, the habitual ways of thinking and feeling which cause them to misread their relations with other people. However, I believe that analysts in the British Independent tradition are more inclined than Kleinians to question whether we should always be trying to make a transference interpretation, or, indeed, to make an interpretation at all. This difference of opinion is not confined to Britain; classical Freudians, commoner in the USA, have their own reasons for not always interpreting in the transference, connected both with their views on the role of the instincts, and of the real relationship.

Initially, analysts believed that, indeed, transference will always be present from the beginning of all our relationships, but we might be more or less aware of it, and as the analysis proceeds and the lack of the usual reassurances and inputs from external reality take hold, the transference will become more intense and visible to the analyst, and through interpretation, to the patient. In the classical tradition, it was thought that there was a real perception of the analyst running along-side throughout (the patient has to trust the analyst enough to go on coming, after all), and, thus, at the end of a successful therapy, the transference should have been resolved and the patient able to see and accept the analyst as he is. As is well known, some Kleinian analysts have argued that because the transference is there from the beginning, interpretations of the patient's unconscious can and should be made straight away in order to relieve the overburdened ego. There is, there-fore, no need to build up a "real relationship" with the patient, who, typically, will be too ill to be able to use it anyway. Whatever we do, whatever kind of interpretation we make, however correct, means that we are not doing something else.

To assume that we should only make transference interpretations from the start draws our attention away from needing first of all to learn from the patient about their history and relationships, so that we can relate their transference to us accurately to their past objects, and lessens the interest in stages during an analysis; the way in which interventions that cannot be made at one stage, or will fall on deaf ears, are the right ones to make at another. I think some confusion stems from the assumption that "the history" is like a medical history; in fact, the patient's self-narrative is more like *historia*, something which is constantly changing and being rewritten and reunderstood, and it is its meaning to the patient that is important.

In practice, experienced analysts do mediate their interpretations in terms of what they feel the patient can take in: the metaphor most commonly employed is that of depth, and it is important to emanci-pate ourselves from the assumption that "deep" interpretations are always better and more effective. It is easy for beginners to get the impression that here-and-now transference interpretations, particu-larly about breaks in treatment, are always most likely to be "right". This is partly because we learn to do psychoanalysis largely through an intensive apprenticeship; we absorb the techniques of our analysts and our supervisors, and learn through clinical seminars the kinds of interventions that are and are not currently approved of. Klauber (1981) remarked on how powerfully our own analysis continues to work in us; many years later, he would find himself making inappropriate interpretations under its influence.

We learn to interpret under conditions of some anxiety; unlike many theoretical differences between different psychoanalytic schools, what we believe about interpretation determines what we do, and it will help or hurt a suffering human being. Throughout each and every session, we constantly have to decide whether to speak and what to say. It is comforting to think that there is a theory that can guide us, but, as time goes on and we become more experienced, we learn to trust our own judgement more. Independent analysts have always stressed the incompleteness and indeterminacy of theory, the importance of the partnership between ourselves and every patient that makes every analysis unique, and we see the patient's response to our interventions as the guide to their effectiveness, and to what to say next.

Ironically enough, we can now see, thanks to Elizabeth Spillius's careful examination of Melanie Klein's unpublished lectures and clinical papers, that Klein reminded her students that analytic work is not only interpretation; patients should be given plenty of time to express their thoughts and feelings. She said that she did not make transference interpretations insistently, but tried to bring in the topic at least once a session (Spillius, 2007, pp. 74–75.) When James Strachey summarised her ideas in his landmark paper on the mutative interpretation in 1934, he exaggerated them and made them rather concrete; a common enough process which was to have great repercussions on the development of technique within the British object relations tradition[1] (Ahumada, 1991, p. 683). This question is so central to psychoanalytic theory and practice that it immediately ramifies into a multitude of other issues. I shall try to cling to whether and when we should make transference interpretations as my Ariadne's thread, but we must acknowledge the many other untrodden paths as they snake away into the labyrinth.

In many ways, the pattern of classical analysis, where analyst and patient were able to work together on material thrown up by the patient's unconscious—parapraxes, forgettings, free associations, etc.—can be both more tolerable and more convincing to the patient than interpreting in the transference; the analyst can work with the patient's ego and the patient's unconscious becomes a third. The two-person situation, in which the patient must accept the analyst as the interpreter of the relations between them, triggers the agoraphobic/ claustrophobic dilemma, and requires greater skill in the analyst, and ego-strength in the patient, than either might always be able to muster. By drawing the fire on to himself, so to speak, the analyst might make things more vivid to the patient—or he might, to continue the metaphor, just get shot and the analysis will break down, or the patient will learn to parrot the words of his analyst without really being able to use them.

We have to choose not only whether we should make a transference interpretation or not, but also of what kind. Roth (2004) has given us a clear and illuminating account of how, in the session, the analyst is constantly moving between different levels or areas of interpretation. Working from a piece of clinical material of Peter Giovacchini's about a patient's dream and his handling of it, she distinguished between four different kinds of interpretation which he might have given. The first, historical, interpretation would have been familiar to Freud pre-Dora; the continuing influence on the patient of her father, either the real father or her internal image of him. The second was what Freud was talking about when he discovered transference: about the way in which discrete or particular qualities of the father have been reattributed to the analyst (i.e., "you mean me"). The third kind of interpretation would have been about the repetition of a relationship, both in the dream and in the session. The patient's picture of her relationship with the analyst is being reflected in the dream and relived in the session—a "here and now", "you mean us" interpretation. And, finally, the analyst might have been able to reflect upon and interpret "the ways in which some combination of the patient's pressure, and the difficulties this stirs up in the analyst, lead to an unconsidered response by the analyst" (Roth, 2004, p. 80): that is, there has been a countertransference enactment whereby, in this case, the analyst is repeatedly pressing his questions and interpretations on his patient. These four types of transference interpretation have followed each other in historical succession, and, in Britain, in popularity.

As Roth points out, these four levels are continuously present throughout each session and all our work, and we have to choose which, at any moment, is likely to be the most effective. However, since Strachey's paper on the "mutative" interpretation, it seems that, in Britain, it has become necessary to justify giving the first sort: that is, an historical rather than a transference interpretation. Roth defends it as sometimes being the most helpful, and in Feldman's (2004) discussion of her paper, he, too, underlines how necessary it is to be able to think freely about which sort of interpretation we could most usefully be giving.

The ways in which analysts differ on this point have been substantiated by Hamilton (1996) in a pioneering study of the guiding beliefs of sixty-five psychoanalysts in London, New York, and California, on which I have leaned heavily for evidence for this chapter. In Britain, she found that whereas "Many British independent analysts felt that extra-transference interpretations had intrinsic mutative value, quite distinct from interpretations of the transference", by contrast, "younger Kleinians seemed to feel that . . . nontransference interpretations were seen as signs of weakness or fear aroused by the prospect of making the more probing and mutative transference interpretation" (Hamilton, 1996, pp. 103–104).

"Younger" is significant; as analysts and psychotherapists move beyond training and become more confident, they are likely to allow their own experience to guide them as to when and how they should make particular interventions, and to learn to vary their technique for particular patients. Young analysts are generally so relieved to have spotted anything in their patients' material that they are likely to interpret without considering which kind of intervention they could most usefully make, or, indeed, whether they should say anything at all. Analysts are likely to change their minds during their working lives about how to work most effectively: they see different sorts of patient, the fashionableness of particular concepts changes, and the *zeitgeist* alters. In this chapter, I am mostly addressing the difficulties of beginners, as they try to match what they are doing in the session to what they have been told, and pay tribute here as to how much the psychotherapists whom I have supervised have, in turn, taught me.

Since the Independents are both a group and an intellectual tradition, both with uncertain outlines, I cannot claim to speak for them, or for it. But I do believe that the self-questioning which is at the heart of both the group and its technique, and perhaps a characteristic set of emphases or reflections on the nature of the relationship between analyst and patient, might lead us to be less likely to accept the prevailing hegemony of the transference interpretation. Riley points out that Strachey's original observation about the analyst's resistance to giving transference interpretations has been stood on its head.

Many of us now . . . 'experience a special internal difficulty' in the giving of non-transference interpretations or indeed interventions of any sort which cannot be shown . . . to be preparatory in some way to an transference interpretation. . . . In addition, the increasing weight given to transference interpretation as *the* mutative agent in psychoanalysis signifies by omission the diminishing importance of other factors . . . (Riley, 2000, p. 212)

He argues that we all make many non- and extra-transference interventions, and that they are frequently mutative and important; we need to stop idealising transference interpretations and to bring the two sorts of insight together.

King (2005, pp. 63–64) summed up four different ways of thinking about when we should make transference interpretations. The classical approach was to leave the transference untouched until the patient's flow of free associations was impeded and the transference had become a resistance; the second was to make transference interpretations only when the link between the analyst and the patient's early relationships began to affect the "here and now" analytic situation, the aim being to establish the transference neurosis and give access to unconscious material; the third is where any reference to objects or relationships in the patient's material should be interpreted as soon as possible as referring to the analyst as a part-object, the aim being to help the patient re-experience early conflicts in relation to the analyst, and, by reliving them, resolve them; and, finally, the same thing is done, but no links are made by the analyst to the past sources of the transference neurosis, because the intensity of the patient–analyst relationship might be deflected and defused. She thought that the more forceful approach was suited to the more ill, more narcissistic patients now coming into therapy; but the counter-argument is whether such an approach, without giving time to building up a secure frame and experience of the analyst, might not, of itself, make the patient traumatised and more dependent, and lead to impasses or interminable therapies.

Transference and reality

Now we come to one of the cruxes in psychoanalytic thinking. To what extent can we separate reality-based, extra-transference perceptions of other people (that the boss or the analyst really is irritated) from our conviction that they feel irritated? Freud, and other early analysts, easy in their assumptions about the natural authority of the doctor over the patient, the superior knowledge of the expert, assumed that there was such a thing as objective knowledge, based in the ego, of external reality, which was always there and formed the basis of the "working alliance" between patient and doctor. Indeed, Freud thought, physicians habitually and legitimately used their patients' positive transference to them to help maintain their authority. But, throughout the twentieth century, in discipline after discipline, it has been emphasised that we live in a world which, for all of us, is much more uncertain, fluid, and subjective than we can really imagine. (The strain that accepting such relativism causes us shows in the current hopeful assertion that advances in brain imaging and neuropsychology are going to render the idea of psychic reality, and therefore psychoanalysis, obsolete (Blass & Carmelli, 2007).)

Freud's initial metaphors of the analyst's ideal role—the well-polished mirror, the skilful surgeon—implied that, as in physical medicine, the analyst could and should detach himself from his feelings about his patient. We now accept that this is impossible, but we vary as to how far the analyst's countertransference to his patient is useful: how far it is produced by the analyst's personal reaction to his patient, and how far generated by something the patient has lodged in his analyst. Should the analyst regard it as essentially pathological in him or herself, requiring further work on himself, or, supposing he finds himself feeling angry, does he give the sort of interpretation which begins "you want me to feel how angry you are", or, even worse, "you are putting your anger into me"? (Most analysts would now regard the second sort of formulation as far too attacking and guilt-inducing. It is, of course, likely to be correct; the anger did originate in the patient, but the process was unconscious, and so such interpretations can feel very blaming.) Or should he accept his countertransference as the means by which the patient is trying to communicate something which cannot yet be put into words, and that it might be that it is only by patient, or analyst, acting in within the session that something can be understood? Increasingly, British analysts seem to be converging on this more forgiving point of view, which is more respectful of non-verbal communication. The current trend is for all British analysts to take a more benign view of projective identification as predominantly a means of communication, and, perhaps, even to take more interest in historical reconstruction (Spillius, 1998, p. 7).

However, terminology often long outlives underlying changes in assumptions, and the fact that we still talk about "interpretation" as what the analyst is doing enshrines the feeling that the patient speaks, or acts, and that the analyst can transpose what he is saying into another meta-language of profounder meanings which he alone knows, although he is trying to teach it to the patient to give him "insight". It is quite difficult to get away from this mental framework; it often comes as a shock to students to look at Freud's original description of "interpretation" (Freud, 1913c, p. 135). Think of it, he suggests, as if you are sitting beside the patient in a railway carriage; the patient can see out of the window, but you cannot. The patient will describe to you the flow of free associations that are streaming past the window; you then suggest to the patient ways in which they can be understood. What the patient then says confirms or questions whether your interpretation is right or not. This is a much more collaborative view of building up understanding than that where the patient is seen as unwittingly projecting aspects of himself into his analyst, which the analyst then has to try to expel, so to speak, metabolised in the form of an interpretation. Similarly, the concept of the transference interpretation as the "mutative interpretation" implies that there is only one sort, which can be separated from the other work of an analysis. Hamilton distinguishes between analysts who think of interpretations as revealing psychic truth and those, more often Independents, who think of them as hypotheses, often introducing them with "perhaps" or "maybe" (Hamilton, 1996, p. 65.)

In psychoanalysis, the swing to the subjectivity of meaning has reinforced the view that all knowledge and perception has transference elements; that we can neither experience completely anew, freed from the ghosts of the past, nor can we separate "objective" knowledge from that which is informed by unconscious experience. Indeed, since it is the continuous two-and-fro processes of introjection and projection that links us to the external world in the first place, without these psychic ties we could find little meaning in that world; we can only experience the external world via the internal. This is as true of the analyst as it is of the patient, and the analyst, since he possesses an unconscious, must react to his patient in his turn. Acknowledging the subjectivity of perception does not mean, however, that there is no objective reality, and no point in trying to reach it.

In the beginning, it seemed that it was possible to interpret patients' words and behaviour on the basis that the analyst's clearer view of reality was because he had a comprehensive theory of the developmental sequence of the instincts and their derivatives, and a set of effective defences against being swayed by them in the session. As is well known, another tradition developed inside psychoanalysis in which the patient's inner world was now seen as largely made up of internalised objects. Jung seems to have been the first to realise that this meant that the relationship between patient and doctor had to change (Perry, 1997). Both of them would form transferences to each other, and would modify each other; the search for the truth would be a mutual one. Klein's position was intermediate; all thinking was permeated by our relationships to objects, but these themselves were dominated by the baby's instinctual drives. Because she believed that aggression and annihilation anxiety were such a predominant part of early object-relations and had been obscured by the classical focus on the child's sexual impulses, it became particularly important to ana- lyse the negative transference. Although aggressive phantasies might be exacerbated or modified by real experiences in childhood, the templates were largely set by the instinctual endowments that under- laid object-seeking. But, while we can agree that all relationships, right from the start, contain transference elements, and that the situation in which the analyst remains relatively anonymous will foster them, it does not necessarily follow from this that the most useful interpreta- tions are in the transference. (Again, Klein came to regret the extent to which her views on aggression had been taken up and over-used by her successors, to the detriment of understanding the ways in which aggression can be successfully mediated by love (Spillius, 2007, p. 81).)

The object-relations tradition, in its desire to move away from the biologism of instinct, eagerly embraced the universality of transfer- ence and its interpretation. Payne described how British analysts in the 1920s, before Klein's arrival, were already giving more transfer- ence interpretations than was done in Vienna (Rayner, 1991, p. 182). Klein's view was that transference was present from the very begin- ning of the relationship between patient and analyst, because all thinking is permeated by, and based on, unconscious phantasy. (She never really resolved the issue of how and why the analyst's capacity to see and understand the patient could be separated from the ubiquity of unconscious phantasy, and, hence, of transference from the analyst's side.) My own view is that a false antithesis was created between instincts and object-relations. In human beings, instincts are generally felt and expressed in relation to somebody; object-relations are pretty etiolated if they are not subsumed by instinct (Budd, 2001). Ego-psychologists consider that focusing on the transference is to the detriment of exploring the relationship between ourselves and our instincts, on the one hand, and ourselves in relation to the outside world, on the other. We cannot oppose instinct and object-relations; they are intertwined. And Lacan argued that focusing on the transference in analysis risks deepening the patient's psychosis—a view that, for different reasons, some Independent analysts have also reached.

The universality of transference came to be generally adopted by the object relations school, though sometimes with the caveat that the more ill the patient, the more marked, swift, unqualified, and more total the transference. The analyst was now seen not as the patient's auxiliary ego, but as having had projected into him both the patient's id and part of his superego. It was thought that these archaic introjects could not be loosened by anything except interpretation, and that most effective interpretations were transference interpretations. Over time, the emphasis has shifted from looking at how the patient might have transposed discrete qualities from his other objects on to his analyst to focusing on how a relationship is being recreated in the session, and as to how the analyst is being led to have certain expectations: say, that nothing more can be done for this patient, or that they are very agreeable to work with, or that the analyst feels peculiarly stupid, or virtuous, and so on.

At this point, analysts commonly explain such phenomena by referring to their implicit model of how the child first takes things in. For many Independents, holding and containment are more important than words in both motherhood and the therapeutic relationship, and this, of course, does much to explain how it is that therapists whose views we do not agree with can, none the less, have a positive and therapeutic effect on their patients. It seems likely that many patients are able to introject some of the qualities they attribute to their analysts: capacities for forgiveness, gratitude, curiosity, courage, and so on. These "transference cures" might well be more common, and more effective, than we have assumed. Research on the mutative factors in analysis tends to find that the most important thing is the "fit" between analyst and patient. Patients who have told me about their good experiences of therapy rarely seem to remember much of what their therapists said, though they do retain a strong impression of how therapeutic their attention and concern was. In thinking about to whom to refer a patient, most of us would think about the prospective therapist's personality and attitude to their work, rather than their theoretical position. Hamilton discovered how uneasy analysts can be made at the nearness of these ideas to that of the corrective emotional experience.

Joseph argues that the "you mean me" type of transference explanation, which can be heard by the patient's ego, is not deep enough to effect lasting psychic change (Joseph, 1985). But with each shift toward more unconscious, unspoken, material, the transference becomes harder to spot accurately, and the likelihood that we will get it wrong increases. And, to take up Joseph's point, if an interpretation cannot be heard and used by the ego, where is it heard and how can it be understood (Rosenfeld, 1974)? Is it better to give a more "penetrating" interpretation, at the greater risk of it being wrong but hoping to relieve the patient's anxiety? Or should we wait, and not interpret, or explore with the patient where we think something might be being relived, until we are surer of our ground? Independent analysts, I think, are more likely to stress not only the real nature of the past which the patient is reliving, but also what they themselves are bringing to the party, as well as what is being projected into them.

If we believe that we should be interpreting the shifts in the transference throughout the session, then we will be doing a lot of interpreting. If we believe that we need to wait, because truth can be paradoxical and difficult to reach and that it is most therapeutic for patients to arrive at realisations for themselves, then we are likely to be saying much less. The idea of "space", and being given time, is generally linked to Winnicott, and carries with it the idea that it might be more important not to speak than to interpret, however accurately. Interpreting can often serve to change the subject; Freud's original faith in free association as the key to unconscious processes has been negated if we divert the patient's flow of ideas by repeatedly interpreting in the transference.

The need to return to being guided by the process of free association has been trenchantly argued by Bollas:

There is now a widespread use of what is termed the 'here and now transference interpretation'. This is the view that almost everything the analysand says to the analyst is either a reference to the analyst or an action committed upon the analyst. . . . It is certainly true that from time to time the analysand is unconsciously referring to the psycho-analyst . . . [but] . . . I have no doubt that such a listening perspective collapses the analysand's wish to be unconsciously communicative, and that this often leads the analysand to retreat into an enclave in the hour in order to ward off intense paranoid intrusiveness by the analyst. That such a retreat is seen as evidence of the invidiously destructive ambition of the analysand's negative transference is a profound tragedy, in my view. (Bollas, 2006, p. 138)

If we believe that the work of psychoanalysis is done by interpreta-tion, then that is what we do; if we believe that other factors—the reli-able setting, or the relationship with the analyst, or the experience of being held and listened to—are equally therapeutic, then we feel less pressure to interpret. Those analysts who believe that there is a "real relationship", over and above the transference, are much more likely to value extra-transference interpretations (Hamilton, 1996, p. 103).

(In parentheses, I think that there can be a confusion which arises at this point from the elision between "human" and "humane". It is sometimes asserted that the object-relations tradition is inherently more humane, because we talk to our patients about other people, rather than about their instincts; "bringing men back in". But it seems to me that instinct-based interpretations can be very humane, because they are framed by the knowledge that we all have instincts, and all have to struggle with them. Klein was said by many of her patients to have conveyed this feeling of a common humanity very strongly. (Grosskurth, 1985). Interpreting entirely in terms of object-relations projected outward from the patient can feel very inhumane; as if the patient should somehow have been able to conquer his envy, aggres-sion, greed, etc., in the face of his benign and omniscient analyst.)

The Independent tradition has always laid more emphasis on the importance of the baby's and the child's, and, indeed, the adult's, real experience. However much distorted by phantasy and by unconscious wishes, we all have real parents, or missing parents, who are different from each other, and the events of their lives had an impact on what kind of parents they were and on their children. There were deaths, illnesses, absences, forced migrations, traumatic experiences, different kinds of values, social and economic necessities, there were or were not siblings, and these historical facts, however retranscribed and unconsciously distorted, formed us then and have affected all our subsequent relationships. (It is, of course, important not to slip between using the past to explain something to using it to justify going on behaving in the same way.) Because it is impossible to finally establish what "really" is the case outside the session, either in the past or the present, analysts now tend to focus on what happens in the session, in particular the pressure that the patient seems to be exerting on the analytic relationship, as both the best evidence and also as the clearest, most convincing way of showing the patient, through interpretation of the transference, the gap between what they feel the analyst to be, to be feeling, and the evidence. But I would argue that such interpretations are both powerful and risky.

The first risk is that it is difficult for us, in the heat of the session, to grasp how we are being affected by our patients, on the one hand, and to remain in touch with ourselves and what we are bringing, on the other. To take a simple example: a patient once told me that he thought that I looked ill, as if I might be coming down with 'flu. I said that I did not think that I was and wondered to him if he felt that he was damaging me in some way, only to have to ring up that night and cancel his session for the following day because I really had come down with 'flu. This patient could cope with the fact that I had been wrong about myself; another patient would have been afraid that he had made me ill, or that I was generally out of touch with reality. I will return to the question as to how we respond when a patient really has spotted something about us.

If we rely on interpreting the transference as the main means of therapy, it follows that it is easier to do if the patient knows little or nothing about us. However, since they inevitably know a great deal about us (our surroundings, appearance, tastes, voice, the vocabulary we use, not to mention the gossip that they might have heard, their knowledge of our professional lives if they are therapists themselves), we need to know ourselves well, and to be prepared to acknowledge that our patients' transferences to us are mixed in with their real knowledge of us (Klauber, 1981, pp. 45–62; 123–140). If we do not do this, we are giving the patient the impression that we cannot stand them knowing anything about us, which puts them into a dilemma that might have been all too familiar in childhood, when they had to conceal and pretend not to notice what they really knew. Ferenczi was the first to argue this about children who had been sexually abused (Ferenczi, 1933, p. 159)

It is very difficult to know what it is that has led analyses to break down or be only partially successful. Each analytic "school" has its prejudices about the rightness of its views on technique, which are reinforced by those patients who come on to second analyses complaining about the defects of the first, apparently different, analyst or school. However detached we try to remain in this situation, the seduction of being assumed to be a better sort of analyst is hard to resist. None the less, I have collected quite a lot of anecdotal evidence which suggests that patients feel that if their realistic perceptions about their analysts are denied (one man, for example, told me that he had ended his therapy because he was convinced that his previous therapist had worn a wig, but that when he questioned him, he would not answer), this can lead to a falsity and distrust which can destroy, or at least limit, the therapy. The patient might conclude that the therapist simply cannot face the truth about himself, and so will avoid confronting him. Hamilton points out that if we argue that we avoid making transference interpretations because we fear the transference being brought violently into the session and directed at us, it must be equally true that we might be making them because we are afraid to acknowledge what the patient really has been able to discern about us (Hamilton, 1996, p. 116). Riley drew attention to the embedded pattern of object-relations which is concealed within different types of interpretation: ocnophilic analysts will tend towards transference interpretations; philobats will tend towards extra-transference (Riley, 2000).

It is our borderline, even psychotic, patients who seem to know most about us, though they draw erroneous conclusions; Stewart cites a patient who "knew" when it was his birthday, that he had received a legacy, and even how much it was (Stewart, 1989, p. 221). I used to notice that my most borderline patients were those who knew which car in the street was mine, and almost immediately that I had changed it. They knew most and needed a real relationship most, and yet were terrified of knowing and could not use what they knew; as they grew better, they began to know less, and could experience me as a separate person with a mind and a life of my own. The difficulty of interpreting in the transference to such patients is that they hear everything concretely; they would have thought that they really had given me the 'flu because I had suggested that they thought it. Kohut (1971) wrote extensively about such thin-skinned and narcissistically vulnerable patients; the need for the analyst to empathise with how they are experiencing the analytic session and their intense feelings of shame and annihilation when they see something in us which worries them. Freud's way of putting it was that they are unable to split the ego into an experiencing part, and a part which can ally itself with the analyst to observe and understand it.

The risk in giving such patients transference interpretations, however accurate, is that they are traumatised by them; they cannot face the fact that the analyst is separate from them, and has a mind which observes them. I will never forget interpreting to one of my earliest patients, who had a history of unreliable and rejecting parental figures, that she might feel angry with me. "You don't understand," she said. "I can't afford to think about you as someone separate; I'm falling over a cliff all the time, you are the bush on the edge that I have to cling to. You're all I've got; I can't think about you." She was a gifted writer who was still able to use metaphor; in other patients, this capacity to symbolise has disappeared, or has never been learnt, and so we cannot use it in making interpretations. But she was telling me that she was not yet ready to face the fact that I was not merged with her, and so my interpretation made her intolerably anxious. Britton (1989), describing a patient who became violent when he tried to interpret and shouted at him to stop his fucking thinking, concluded that she experienced his interpretations as being shut out from his mind and that made her feel that she did not exist. Some analysts would have concluded that she could only be helped by his interpreting the transference; he found that he had to keep his interpretations to himself to keep his own mind free, and talk to her about how he understood her to be feeling.

Recent analytic theorising has focused on how, for such very disturbed patients, the analyst has to act as a container, or provide secure holding, for some time before he can begin to interpret. It is only through the passage of time, the experience of the analyst as reliable, enduring, prepared to scrutinise and explain his own habits of mind, that the patient is enabled to develop a self-reflexive function and the capacity to think in words (Tuch, 2007). Again, research into the early mental life of infants has been used to support the view that we should not interpret in the transference to very disturbed patients;

since, like very young children, they are unable to conceive of inter-psychic processes, they experience the analyst as violently intruding into the mind (Bateman & Fonagy, 2003). Such patients might need actively not to be interpreted to until they can hear interpretations as proceeding from someone who is outside their minds and is not omni-scient. It can also be that patients who are unwilling to concede that their analyst has anything to tell them will be more convinced by an intrapsychic event than by a transference interpretation. A patient whose mother had killed herself when he was a child had been compelled to rescue and restore women all his life. My interpretations that he needed to make them, and me, ill or stupid in order to do so fell on deaf ears, until one day he mused, "I now know that I was responsible for my mother's death." He had meant to say the oppo-site; his Freudian slip was more convincing to him than my interpre-tations.

Another risk in the emphasis on transference interpretation is that it can seem as if the analyst really is not interested in what is actually happening to the patient, either in the past or in their current life. Listening to students conscientiously interpreting in the transference to patients who are painfully describing real traumas, in their past or present lives, can feel like a dialogue of the deaf. The justification of this is that everything is related to the transference, and should be interpreted there; I find it hard to believe that it can be helpful to a patient to have their real traumas ignored. Some of what our patients endured as children, or have to live through in their present lives, is so devastating to imagine that we might be tempted to retreat from it into a Pollyannaish world in which important things only happen in the transference and in phantasy. Then the patient might well con-clude that we are not interested in their pasts or in their current dilem-mas, and use the analysis as an enclave in which they can dwell with their omnipresent analyst without having to consider their experi-ences and relationships with everyone else (O'Shaughnessy, 1992; Stewart, 1987). Interpretations about the patient's reactions to breaks in treatment, which students are taught to make, are often of this type, and American and French analysts regard the British as being obsessed with them.

Our preferences for one kind of technique or another are caused by many things. In my own case, it was my fascination with the interplay between the inside and the outside of human lives, the way in which childhood events cast long shadows but can be retranscribed and differently understood, the ambiguity of memory and its continuing influence in our lives, the roots of creativity in illusion, which led me to psychoanalysis in the first place. For me, a psychoanalysis in which both analyst and patient never consider the role of the past, and how its grip can change and loosen, would simply be less interesting. Some patients are not particularly concerned about how they have come to be what they are, but that does not mean that I cannot think and speculate about it to myself.

Boundaries and coming clean

The emphasis on transference and its interpretation has led to the contemporary preoccupation with the maintenance of boundaries. Those who have read about, or remember, classical analysis are often struck by the informality of the relationship. Freud, notoriously, gave people tea as well as a good deal of advice and comment; analysts lent and borrowed books, looked at photographs and letters, told stories to illustrate a point. Students can now seem quite phobic, as if they must never answer a question or betray an opinion for fear of "contaminating" the transference. It is difficult to know how widespread this anxiety is; Pearl King thought it was becoming more marked with each generation. Because Independents are prepared to discuss examples of where departing from strict anonymity seemed fruitful, the group is sometimes accused of lacking proper boundaries. In gossip, the cautionary tales about analysts who were believed to act out quite grossly with their patients (and often did) are revisited again and again, and can come to be seen as being only a more extreme version of someone who might lend an umbrella, or a book.

It is also true that we can be led astray by idealising the special relationship between patient and analyst, and Independents might be more guilty of this than others (Kohon, 1986, p. 54). Often, we can only describe very regressed patients by comparing them with babies and young children, but we are not their parents, and how far we can or should stand in for them is a controversial matter. Jennifer Johns (personal communication) remembers a period when, under the influence of evocative descriptions of successful therapies with gifted but very ill patients, many Independent clinical accounts focused on the justification of unusual therapeutic measures. This is the opposite danger from sticking too rigidly to transference interpretations.

To make a transference interpretation implies a certain self-consciousness; we have to consider ourselves from the outside, so to speak, and think about how the patient may be experiencing us, before we begin to speak. Several Independent analysts have argued that, at times, it can be crucially important for the analyst to be able to be spontaneous, to speak from within ourselves, not quite knowing why we do (Coltart, 1986, pp. 1–14; Klauber et al., 1987, pp. 22–34.) It is risky to do this but it can resolve an impasse, because the patient might be able to make a new beginning with someone whom they can sense is genuine and speaks from the heart. But we have also to bear in mind that it could trigger off a malign regression, in which the patient becomes relentlessly greedy and demanding of more than all that we can really offer, which is our willingness to work as their therapist as well as we can. The discussion of such cases illuminates for me how rapidly questions of technique can become fetishised, and how easy it is to idealise or criticise descriptions of dramatic passages in an analysis, forgetting the patient work that preceded and followed them. There has been confusion between the necessary support of the "real relationship" and Alexander's "corrective emotional experience", and, in consequence, anxiety over any parameters of treatment which are not the provision of interpretation leading to insight. This has only been partially alleviated by reconceptualising the "real relationship" as the "analytic frame".

Coltart (1986) argued that analytic theory is by no means complete; we have to be able to bear the anxiety of setting off into the unknown with patients, of refraining from orthodox interpretation until a new pattern is revealed to us. It is flattering for us when our patients believe that we know all about them; transference interpretations are particularly likely to generate fantasies of the analyst's omnipotence. To guard against this, two concepts are often used: Bion's recommendation to be without memory or desire in the session, and Keats' description of "negative capability", or the capacity to be with patients without striving to make premature sense of the situation to console both us and the patient. Transference interpretations seem particularly likely to produce a premature closure; we often find ourselves giving them out of anxiety as we feel ourselves being overtaken by projective identifications which pull us towards feeling and behaving in ways that we dislike: becoming irritated or sleepy, for example. And, indeed, a well-aimed transference interpretation will often stop these difficult countertransferences developing, but at the cost of a fuller understanding of the situation which will make our interpretations more convincing to the patient. Non-understanding is difficult to tolerate and often drives us to interpret in order to escape, rather than to endure until we think we comprehend enough to speak (Money-Kyrle, 1956).

How should we behave when we have shown something about ourselves or made a mistake? We can carry on interpreting in the transference about how the patient has experienced our forgetfulness, sleepiness, missing a session, irritation, losing the bill, and so on, but I think that this is to implicitly divert attention away from the fact that we really have made the mistake. I believe that if a patient observes that we look tired, and we are tired, we should acknowledge that they are right; if we do not, since everyone is tired sometimes, they might well conclude that we or they are mad. I do not think we should feel that we need to explain to them why we are tired.

If we forget a patient or make a mistake, I think that we should acknowledge it, briefly apologise, and then go on to explore with them what they made of it, and, if we think they can bear it, talk to them about why it might have been that it was with them rather than with someone else that we forgot the session or to give the bill. But I think we have to do this with extreme care, so that we avoid any implication that they somehow chose to make us forgetful or sleepy. We know that our acting out could have been prevented had we forcibly interpreted their projective identification, but it is sometimes better to wait until the situation becomes clearer and the patient feels held enough to receive an interpretation, even at the cost of risking a countertransferential enactment. The patient might not be able to tolerate a transference interpretation if he fundamentally distrusts his analyst. It might be that enlarging the scope of his thinking by talking with him about his past and present object relations is necessary for him to begin to develop a capacity to be curious, and to be able to think about his feelings about his therapist without aborting them or the therapy.

It is remarkably difficult to determine what it is that is therapeutic in an analysis. We hope that innovations in technique will make us better analysts, but there is much disagreement, and we have to concede that other interpretive traditions and early analyses were also, at times, perfectly successful. As Hamilton puts it, "the relationship between theoretical orientation and clinical practice is itself complex and obscure" (Hamilton, 1996). The view that it is only interpretation leading to insight that cures is clear, at least, if not entirely convincing. But the idea that there is something important about the relationship itself, independent of the kinds of interpretation that are offered, does not go away.

Clearly, internationally, a large number of psychoanalysts would agree; in the most frequently cited paper by far in the *International Journal of Psychoanalysis* in the past decade or so, Stern (1998) and his associates argued that something more than interpretation is needed for psychic change, and, partly on the basis of infant research, they posited that it is a mutative relationship between analyst and patient where there are special moments of personal connection between the two, not verbal, but learnt through a shared implicit relationship, where they meet "as persons relatively unbidden by their usual therapeutic roles". Interpretations are more than their content; as Rycroft (1956) pointed out, the act of making an interpretation carries a host of under-meanings; I am here, I am listening, I am interested, not shocked, remembering and thinking about you. Perhaps this sort of basic reassurance is more important than we can easily concede. Klauber (1981) argued that patient and analyst always are in a relationship; both are dependent on the other. He believed that the patient could recover because interpretations take place in the context of this relationship; the patient can introject some of the qualities of the analyst, which he learns about by noticing what and how the analyst chooses to interpret. He also believed that unanalysed interventions could be powerful factors leading to cure or failure of treatment, and that much change took place without immediate or precise interpretations. Not everything can be dealt with, even in a long analysis; the unconscious is more opaque, requires more careful listening and study, than interpretations in the transference can allow.

The emphasis on the therapeutic alliance, the care about making premature transference interpretations, the interest in reconstruction and working through, in the system of defences which make up the individual character, the return to an interest in the unconscious as a separate realm in us all which thinks by its own rules, return us to earlier questions of technique. How can we foster the process by which the patient becomes able to receive news from himself, becomes capable of introspection, takes over our role? Not just through inter-pretation, but through going on being in the same space, through time and silence.

Note

1. In fact, Strachey had stressed in his paper how necessary it is to combine transference with extra-transference interpretations; you cannot make a cake entirely of currants, or move an army forward without making link-ages between the forts of the transference interpretation proper.

References

Ahumada, J. C. (1991). Logical types and ostensive insight. *International Journal of Psychoanalysis, 72*: 683–691.

Bateman, A. W., & Fonagy, P. (2003). The development of an attachment-based treatment programme for borderline personality disorder. *Bulletin of the Menninger Clinic, 67*(2): 187–211.

Blass, R. B., & Carmeli, Z. (2007). The case against neuropsychoanalysis: on fallacies underlying psychoanalysis' latest scientific trend and its negative impact on psychoanalytic discourse. *International Journal of Psychoanalysis, 88*: 19–40.

Bollas, C. (2006). Transformations wrought by the unconscious: creativi-ties of the unconscious. Discussion with V. Bonaminio. *Bulletin of the European Psychoanalytical Federation, 60*: 133–160.

Britton, R. (1989). The missing link: parental sexuality in the Oedipus complex. In: J. Steiner (Ed.), *The Oedipus Complex Today* (pp. 83–102). London: Karnac.

Budd, S. (2001). 'No Sex Please—We're British': sexuality in English and French psychoanalysis. In: C. Harding (Ed.), *Sexuality: Psychoanalytic Perspectives* (pp. 52–68). Hove: Brunner-Routledge.

Coltart, N. E. C. (1986). Slouching towards Bethlehem . . . Or thinking the unthinkable in psychoanalysis. In: G. Kohon (Ed.), *The British School of Psychoanalysis: The Independent Tradition* (pp. 185–199). London: Free Association Books.

Feldman, M. (2004). Discussion. In: E. Hargreaves & A. Varchevker (Eds.), *In Pursuit of Psychic Change; The Betty Joseph Workshop* (pp. 100–103). London: Brunner-Routledge.

Ferenczi, S. (1933). Confusion of tongues between adults and the child. *Final Contributions to The Problems and Methods of Psychoanalysis* (pp. 156–167). New York: Brunner/Mazel.

Freud, S. (1913c). On beginning the treatment. *S.E.*, *12*: 121–143. London: Hogarth.

Freud, S. (1914c). On narcissism. An introduction. *S.E.*, *14*: 67–101. London: Hogarth.

Grosskurth, P. (1985). *Melanie Klein: Her World and Her Work,* Hodder and Stoughton, London.

Hamilton, V. (1996). *The Analyst's Pre-conscious.* Hillsdale, NJ: Analytic Press.

Joseph, B. (1985). Transference: the total situation. *International Journal of Psychoanalysis, 66*: 447–454.

King, P. (2005). *Time Present and Time Past: Selected Papers.* London: Karnac.

Klauber, J. (1981). *Difficulties in the Analytic Encounter.* New York: Jason Aronson.

Klauber, J. et al, (1987). *Illusion and Spontaneity in Psychoanalysis.* London: Free Association Books.

Kohon, G. (1986). *The British School of Psychoanalysis: The Independent Tradition.* London: Free Association Books.

Kohut, H. (1971). *The Analysis of the Self.* New York: International Universities Press.

Money-Kyrle, R. (1956). Normal countertransference and some of its deviations. *International Journal of Psychoanalysis, 37*: 360–366.

O'Shaughnessy, E. (1992). Enclaves and excursions. *International Journal of Psychoanalysis, 73*: 603–611.

Perry, C. (1997). Transference and counter-transference. In: P. Young-Eisendrath & T. Danson (Eds.), *The Cambridge Companion to Jung* (pp. 141–163). Cambridge: Cambridge University Press.

Rayner, E. (1991). *The Independent Mind in British Psychoanalysis.* London: Free Association Books.

Riley, D. W. (2000). On extra-transference dread. In: M. Whelan (Ed.), *Mistress of Her Own Thought: Ella Freeman Sharpe and the Practice of Psychoanalysis* (pp. 211–221). London: Rebus Press.

Rosenfeld, H. (1972). A critical appreciation of James Strachey's paper on the nature of the therapeutic action of psychoanalysis. *International Journal of Psychoanalysis, 53*, 455–461.

Roth, P. (2004). Mapping the landscape: levels of transference interpretation. In: E. Hargreaves, & A. Varchevker (Eds.), *In Pursuit of Psychic Change: the Betty Joseph Workshop* (pp. 85–99). London: Routledge.

Rycroft, C. (1956). The nature and function of the analyst's communications to his patient. *International Journal of Psychoanalysis, 37*: 469–472.

Spillius, E. B. (1998). *Melanie Klein Today, Vol.2, Introduction to Developments in Technique.* London: Routledge.

Spillius, E. B. (2007). *Encounters with Melanie Klein: Selected Papers of Elizabeth Spillius.* London: Routledge.

Stern, D. N., Sander, L. W., Nahum, J. P., Harrison, A. M., Lyons-Ruth, K., Morgan, A. C., Bruschweilerstern, N., & Tronick, E. Z. (1998). Non-interpretive mechanisms in psychoanalytic therapy: the 'something more' than interpretation. *International Journal of Psychoanalysis, 79*: 903–921.

Stewart, H. (1989). Techniques of the Basic Fault. *International Journal of Psychoanalysis, 70*: 221–230.

Tuch, R. H. (2007). Thinking about, and with, patients too scared to think: can non-interpretive manoeuvres stimulate reflective thought? *International Journal of Psychoanalysis, 88*: 91–112.

CHAPTER THIRTEEN

The basic fault and the borderline psychotic transference

Caroline Polmear

T here is a long tradition of independently minded psychoanalysts interested in work with early infantile trauma in their patients. The work often implies a conundrum of how to work in analysis in an essentially pre-verbal and "acting out" area when the traditional language of analysis is the symbolic, three-person language of the Oedipus complex. Many have explored those conditions in which therapeutic regression takes place and have examined the stresses and strains that regressed patients place on "ordinary" psychoanalytic technique. Ferenczi's largely unsuccessful Grand Experiment, in which he attempted to gratify the patient's requirement for complete adjustment to his needs in the analytic situation, is well documented (1932). Winnicott's many writings on the earliest relationship between infant and "object" and "environment" mother explore this area, including the ways in which traumatic impingement in the earliest relationship re-emerges in analysis (1949, 1955, 1960a,b, 1962, 1968). Little's contributions from her own understanding of herself and her analysis (1981, 1985) is illuminating, and Kahn's work on cumulative trauma (1963) also focuses on this area of early infantile trauma.

In recent years, our clinical work as psychoanalysts seems to demand more and more attention to these areas of psychotic functioning in our patients, and technique with patients who are diffi-cult to help in analysis is constantly under review and discussion by analysts of all schools.

In this chapter, I shall return to the particular contribution of Michael Balint in his work on the basic fault, and explore some of the ways in which his understanding and the work of currently practis-ing analysts helps us understand the particular technical challenges of the borderline transference psychosis in its many different forms.[1]

Primary love

Fundamental to Balint's theory of the basic fault is the idea of primary love. In *Thrills and Regressions* (1959) he tells us of man's wish to regress to the earliest object relationship, the state of primary harmony or primary love. It is a state in which only the infant's needs register in the mother–infant relationship. Only one partner, the subject in the relationship, has demands and needs; the object is experienced as an environment in complete harmony with the infant's wishes and claims. Winnicott's observations on primary maternal preoccupation (1956) suggest that he held a similar view that this can be experienced sufficiently in the early days and first weeks of life; the healthy child and healthy mother being well enough in tune with each other so that the same action brings gratification to both. I assume that the internal experience of the infant is a more mixed one, less harmonious than proposed by Balint, but one in which the attunement of the mother plays a crucial part in maintaining the phantasy of harmonious merger.

In *The Basic Fault* (1968), he uses the term "harmonious interpene-trating mix-up" to describe the relationship between foetus and envi-ronment before the interruption of birth. He suggests that birth ruptures this idealised state of one-ness and this rupture creates a fault-line in the ego to which the patient might return in analysis.

Balint seems to speak of an actual state as if it were also a psychic state.

For me, the real value of his concept is as a metaphor which captures graphically the borderline patient's experience of being "untimely ripped" from a desired state of one-ness. It is experienced as a traumatic failure of maternal attunement in the first case, and, later, of the analyst's failure to understand and contain the patient's feeling in the consulting room.

Many other analysts have explored this early developmental failure. For example, Klein (1930) describes it in terms of the experience of a violent and too early intrusion of a third into the mother–baby dyad, and Tustin (1992) describes it, in relation to autistic children, as a devastating and rupturing loss of the ecstasy of one-ness with the mother.

In Klein's description of the development of the ego, the achievement of early splitting into the idealised good breast and the bad breast is essential for the infant to be able to tolerate his destructive greed and envy and, thus, to survive annihilation. This seems to me to be very relevant to the phenomenon that Balint describes. The deep internal rift, or fault, perhaps contains within it a repeated and desperate attempt to achieve the earliest step of splitting against the terror of annihilation by the retaliating bad object.

Balint believes that when birth or early experience such as a lack of attunement ruptures the desired state of harmony before the subject is developmentally prepared, either ocnophilic or philobatic organisations develop. Although Balint did not write in these terms, I think that today we would think of them as rigid defensive organisations against the terror of annihilation, characteristic of the borderline patient, for whom ordinary splitting into good and bad breasts has failed and the task of integration has become impossible as a result. In the case of ocnophilia, the baby of Balint's description clings in anxiety to emerging objects (the other) and fears the spaces between them; in the case of philobatism, he clings to the objectless expanses as safe and friendly spaces between objects, while the objects are felt to be treacherous hazards. The clinging, in both cases, is aimed at keeping the idealised good object relationship in place against the fearful bad one.

Ocnophilia and philobatism

Ocnophils and philobats are not opposites, although they often sound like it in Balint's descriptions. Instead, they are two different attitudes branching from the same stem. They both involve loving and hating. They are both responses to the discovery of "firm and resistant objects", which destroy the world of primary love in which the couple together have the same interest and are in perfect harmony. In other words, they are responses to the abrupt discovery of the "otherness" of the object. Balint suggests that this discovery is traumatic, and, I would add, following Winnicott (1958, 1965), that in a good enough relationship between the mother and child the trauma is moderated by gradual disillusionment and gradual discovery of the self through the creation of transitional space (Winnicott, 1951). However, for those patients who bring borderline features to analysis, the trauma of this stage has not been moderated and has necessitated premature psychic organisation for survival.

So, here lies an important point, which I shall illustrate with clinical work below: that for these particular patients, the emergence of separateness seems to have been experienced as a trauma which could not be contained or moderated and which led to premature psychic organisation. This sequence of events is re-experienced constantly in analysis.

In addition, the aspect of premature sexualisation of the object relationship plays an important part. Balint speaks of the impact of it in a malignant regression in analysis. In fact, he sees it as the factor that differentiates the benign from the malignant regression, where one-ness is achieved in phantasy through sadistic control of the object.

Balint postulates that ocnophilic and philobatic organisations are defensive attempts to recreate the state of primary love and harmonious mix-up. The wish is to force the analyst back into one-ness with them. While I think that he implies that the state of one-ness is both desirable and could actually exist, rather than that it was achieved psychically by splitting, as described above, I do think he indicates a crucial point which I think helps us to understand a familiar clinical situation. Our borderline patients seem compelled to try to bring us into line by any means they can when separateness emerges.

The ocnophil clings to the object, over-cathecting the relationship, turning the object into a mighty and vital person who *must* respond to their clinging with complete care, while the philobat over-cathects his own ego function, developing skills in this way in order to maintain himself alone or with very little help from his objects. In philobatism, human objects are either indifferent or actually dangerous and untrustworthy hazards to be avoided. The development of skills is often directed at regaining the objectless friendly expanses, such as mountains, deserts, sea, and air, of the state of primary love and aim to allay the overwhelming anxiety inherent in human dependency through mastery of skills and the illusion of self-sufficiency.

In both cases, reality must be distorted to maintain the psychic reality required for survival. In both cases, the object is taken for granted and a harmonious two-person relationship is demanded. Although it is two-person, the requirement is for a perfect fit, a one-ness of purpose and desire. It implies a rejection of any third party and, as we know, from our work in the consulting room, it requires a rejection of the third position (Britton, 1998)—in fact, any capacity on the part of the analyst to think about the patient.

While I find Balint's terms unnecessarily obscure, I think of the descriptions as valuable in understanding some of the different forms of borderline defences and helpful in making sense of the similarities we see between the psychopath, the person with autistic pockets and retreats, the psychosomatic person, and the more traditionally recognisable borderline personality. Philobatic people seem to me to be deeply traumatised, suffering an irretrievable and unprocessed loss, who have developed autistic defences or shells which have extended from defensive modes of survival to personalities (Tustin, 1986, 1990). Ocnophilic people, perhaps the more classical, impulse-driven border-line people, are those whose survival depends on tyrannical control of their object, forcing the object to provide (and fail to provide) the harmonious environment that they require to defend themselves against their lack of internal containment and the terrible unprocessed loss of separation.

In analysis, when the patient's fragile ego integration is severely threatened, both types of defensive organisation could emerge. Perhaps, as one defence fails to protect the patient from the intense anxiety of annihilation, another is employed. The patient used to retreating into an autistic shell might become more ocnophilic in an attempt to regain possession of the good object, and the more clinging patient might resort to psychic retreats when left alone.

In analysis, borderline patients often speak of a sense of deficit, of some irreparable damage which they can work around, perhaps learn new pathways to warmer closer relationships, but which remains, as Balint indicates, as a fault-line in their personalities. They also share a deep sense of "fault" in their objects, too; a sense that the failure inherent in the object's separateness is, in fact, the object's fault.

Here, I think, is the beauty of Balint's notion of "the basic fault". It captures both the patients' *experience* of the re-emergence of splits in the ego, which weaken the ego and render it fragile, and the sense of shame, failure, and blame which they also feel. It brings to our attention the part played by the disconnected, ruthless super ego of our borderline patients.

The area of the basic fault

Balint describes the level of the basic fault as the point reached in analysis when language as communication fails. He describes two levels of analytic work: the level in which interpretations are heard for what they are and can be taken in and considered. Anxiety and resistance are worked with and analysis progresses. This he defines as the Oedipal level, or the level of the Oedipus Complex. Relationships are triangular, involving conflict caused by ambivalence. Adult language is a reliable form of communication at this level, as it is linked with meaning and is perceived and received as a meaningful communication.

Balint suggests that in many analyses, there is a point either right from the start or at some stage further into the analysis when this type of communication fails. Adult language becomes misleading and interpretations are no longer heard as interpretations, but as concrete experiences of antagonistic attacks, or loving and soothing gratifications, by the analyst. The relationship is no longer a three-person one in which thinking is possible, and has regressed to the two-person level in which one-ness is demanded.

At this point in the analysis, the atmosphere changes. The intensity, closeness, and antagonism can often become stifling as the lack of the third position (Britton, 1998) removes the possibility of thinking. Discourse has shifted from neurotic to psychotic, from the symbolic to the concrete.

In this state of mind, the patient defends himself against a feeling of irreparable loss of the good object and seeks to regain possession of it in the form of the idealised unconscious phantasy of one-ness. Evidence of the otherness of the object and any third party interference places a heavy strain on the subject. In analysis, this is another indication that the level of the basic fault has been reached. The patient finds intrusions, changes in the setting, sessions starting a shade of a minute early or late, and so on as an intolerable intrusion and destruction of the complete attunement of the required state of union.

While Balint speaks in terms of three-person *vs.* two-person relationships, today, following Klein and Bion, we might see the switch from language as meaning and communication to language as concrete action upon the patient in different terms. The loss of meaning of language is the loss or rejection of the internal third object, and expresses the patient's hatred of the analyst's capacity to think, which itself symbolises the analyst's relationship to another, the one with whom the analyst is internally in conversation. The impasse reached is the patient's vehement resistance to the emergence of the separateness of his object and the existence of a couple.

Balint's ideas can sound somewhat outdated. He seems to interchange internal and external worlds as if they are the same; he suggests, I think, that there really can be an idealised state of one-ness with the primary object and that in analysis there should be periods of such a state. Today, we would not think in these terms. He speaks of birth as a traumatic rupture of the state of one-ness at one point, but implies that a failure in the primary object relationship brings this about at others, and his idea of a fault-line can sound like a geological view of the ego rather than a metaphor which captures something of the experience for both patient and analyst at certain points in the analysis of patients with early developmental disturbance. Yet, in my view, he brings something original and valuable to our understanding. I think he directs us to the experience of the patient struggling with fragile ego integration, who can feel a sudden, terrible, and often shocking experience when integration of the ego fails, extreme anxiety dominates, and the analyst becomes a dangerous object threatening his survival. The atmosphere changes and so does the level of analytic work. Balint's conceptualisation that the area of the basic fault concerns traumatic separation from the primary object and the unbearable existence of a third in the primary dyad is crucial. His attention to the issue of the demand for perfect attunement has important technical implications for the analyst, as does the recognition that at the basic fault the patient unconsciously aims to be in a merged union with the analyst. Finally, his descriptions of two defensive organisations can be helpful in better understanding the patient and in formulating helpful and effective interpretations.

I shall explore these issues further with the help of some clinical material.

Clinical material

Ms A was in her thirties when she came into analysis. In her early infancy, her depressed mother was hospitalised, and Ms A was cared for by a foster mother. As a child, she felt that she never fitted with her family and found being hugged by her mother painful. Yet, she was dependent and clingy, too. She impressed me at the first meeting as both far away, hidden somewhere behind expressionless eyes, and yet strangely biddable.

After an initial honeymoon period of a week in analysis, I, as analyst, fell dramatically from grace. The patient said that she believed that I had "told her to use the couch". She was wary of me to an extreme degree, and treated me as someone dangerous and damaging, someone who had raised her hopes of a perfect attunement only to dash them traumatically, someone to keep well away from. She told me that she had felt that I was a good analyst during the first week and was hopeful that at last she had found someone who could really understand her. But now I had turned out to be a fraud and like everybody else, primarily involved with myself and with forcing her to fit in with me.

I felt shocked and upset. I had been looking forward to seeing this new patient again and felt completely unprepared for this change.

We had discussed her anxiety about using the couch during the first week of the analysis but, when the weekend break intervened, this thoughtful discussion became just a "cover up" for my telling her to use the couch.

Now she either dozed in sessions or let me observe someone who could conduct a whole analysis on her own. But, through her virulent accusations about me, she showed me who I had become: someone who stares blankly, who is dead inside, who is a disappointment and a failure, and who has no connection inside between the different parts of herself. It became clear that in this explosive borderline state, she had projected her whole self into me. Now I could really get to know her self-experience, although at this stage I could not relate it to her as such. In fact, I could barely speak at all, as I had become so dangerous. For the time being, my job was to hold it in me until I could find a way of using it without returning it in this frightening form.

My capacity to damage her in incidents like this became a leitmotif of the analysis. Our survival of them and gradual understanding of each other became the therapeutic narrative of the analysis.

Later in the analysis, my patient was following her thoughts, describing being in a water tank, submerged under the sea. My clumsy mistake was to use the word "illusion" when I spoke to her about this experience. To my patient, it was not a fantasy of an experience or an illusion, it was an actual experience. By speaking the way that I did, I distanced myself into another (non-attuned and three-person) world and was experienced as unable to tolerate her interuterine existence and as evacuating her out of my body in murderous hatred.

A further example follows.

The most devastating occasion was when she asked for a change of time, which I was unable to give her. This felt like the complete breakdown of an environment that needed to remain constant and that had failed her. The consequences were devastating, as I am sure they had been in her infancy when she had lost her already depressed and unavailable mother into hospital for a long period of time. I often felt worried that the analysis would not survive, and that I would have lost a patient who would leave more damaged than she had arrived.

For two weeks she lay on the couch with a blanket over her head, unreachable and despairing. I felt that she was shocked and devastated, while she accused me of failing to recognise what she needed. She "knew" that I had lied about not having another time. But what she also brought back time and again over the months and years following was the belief that I had simply switched off, not cared about her, and had not tried to reach her in her silence. In her mind, I had been out of touch and silent for two months.

I hope to have illustrated my hypothesis that it was the separation brought about by the first weekend break, which she had re-experienced as a primitive, traumatic rupturing separation coming too early for her and overwhelming her fragile ego. On later occasions, as the analytic experience deepened, evidence of my failure of attunement occurred when I was thinking *about* her rather than being in the tank *with* her, and, finally, when I demonstrated my separate life by not giving a required change of time. The feeling of dramatic and shocking breakdown that she communicated and the loss of our capacity to talk to each other in a meaningful way dominated. The atmosphere was one in which we both felt that her very survival was at stake. I experienced a forceful projective identification of her whole self into me, obliterating separateness and thinking, while at the same time she appeared not to need me at all. With the rigid and deep split between good and bad came the violent and sadistic accusation of blame, that the internal rift or fault was clearly my fault and due to my failings as an analyst.

Some issues in the resistance to integration

Balint directs us, as analysts, to a recognition of the level at which the patient is functioning during a regression to the basic fault and to the importance of taking up a position of "unobtrusive analyst", allowing the patient to feel that the analyst can tolerate the one-ness of the patient's world at that point. To do this, the analyst must be aware that language is non-symbolic.

While there are helpful aspects of this conceptualisation, I think the tenacity of the split in borderline patients needs further exploration. Balint can make it sound as if a new beginning will be found by the patient and well-attuned analyst, and all will be plain sailing.

Next, I suggest some of the reasons why I think that the borderline patient finds it so hard to move forward to a more integrated state.

The extraordinary research work of neuro-psychologist Alan Schore (2001a,b) gives us a way of conceptualising the tenacity of the lack of integration. He illuminates the relationship between mind/psyche and brain. He shows how early relational trauma, or failures and impingements in mother–infant relations in the earliest phase of life, impair the development of limbic circuits and, thus, damage the development of right brain functioning. This either results in organised insecure attachments or in the more severe attachment disturbances in which

> the regulatory failures are manifest in the individual's limited capacity
> to modulate, either by auto regulation or interactive regulation, the
> intensity and duration of biologically primitive sympathetic-dominant

affects like terror, rage, excitement and elation, or parasympathetic-dominant affects like shame, disgust, and hopeless despair. Notice that intense positive affect, excitement and joy, is also a stressor to these personalities. (Schore, 2001a, p. 226)

Schore also shows that there are certain developmental windows in which the underdeveloped circuits can be repaired or established for the first time, and this finding is borne out by Rutter and colleagues' work on Romanian baby syndrome (1999). To establish the pathways in the brain later in life after the early opportunities have been missed seems to be a much harder task and a greater achievement. We do know from our patients, however, that finding the bridge between the isolated parts of the self is possible in analysis. However, patients often report a need to "work at" their new, gentler, more integrated ways of relating, and describe the tendency when under pressure to relapse into impulse-driven survival behaviour, unmoderated by a connection with the more benign and thoughtful part of their mind. A neuro-psychological approach makes this all too understandable, and helps us to remain sensitive to the very difficult task that faces our patients.

In analysis, we are faced with a patient who seems to depend for his survival on maintaining the internal split, while the analyst believes that it is this internal rift which weakens the ego. Often, the more the analyst enables the patient to integrate, the more the patient forces himself apart. So, we are forced to conclude that a further trauma is experienced when the analyst offers an interpretation that brings the patient together in some way. A more thoroughly neurotic patient would feel relief, while a borderline patient can feel traumatised. The analyst's experience is that every time they make contact with the patient, they are violently pushed away and become the receptor of horrible, violating, mocking contempt.

It is the nature of the attack on us that gives the clue to one of the processes that makes the patient cling to the split.

Following Bion, I think in the moment of contact the analyst experiences the full force of the "ego destructive superego". The psychotic superego is brought together with a fragile and more moderate ego. At that point, the patient's survival is in jeopardy. The analyst knows this to be true because, in that instant, the superego is projected and the annihilating attack is directed at the analyst. Survival as an analyst at this point is always at stake; were the patient to remain integrated, we must assume his or her survival would also be at stake.

The extreme version of this is illustrated by the psychopath. Symington (1980) describes working with psychopaths who, following therapeutic work facilitating integration, commit violating acts on the therapist or his family outside the therapeutic setting, of which the patient is later unaware. The strength of the violent hatred, when brought together with the loving feelings towards the therapist, would create enormous guilt and shame and would mean that the psychopath would attack himself with equally devastating aggression, and might well not survive the attack. Symington suggests that at the heart of the psychopath's internal world is a mother (often experienced as an abandoning mother) who could not contain his sadism as an infant and child. This is a hated internal mother, who would not survive his attacks on her. In this case, his guilt would be unbearable and suicide the only option. In order to preserve this fragile internal mother, his psychopathic split and disavowal must be maintained.

It is interesting to note that Asperger (1944), in his seminal work on a type of childhood autism, links it with psychopathy. He describes ruthlessness akin to that of the psychopath and brought about by the fact that there is no connection with a concern for another. Although this description has been objected to and questioned by some, it seems to me completely acceptable in Balint's schema of primary love and in Winnicott's similar concept of the early phase of "pre-ruth", or before the capacity for concern emerges with some separation from the object and the possibility of recognition of the "otherness" of the other.

At one phase of Ms A's analysis, I was puzzled by a phenomenon that we came to think of as "cartooning". She would get caught up, in the sessions when she felt hateful towards me for my failure to hold and understand her, in a deeply amusing (for her) stream of associations in pictures of all the things she was doing in her mind to me. She would pick me up by my feet and swing me around in the air, then bang my head against the wall in a rhythmic repetition: bang, bang, bang! She chortled with glee. Or she would describe a large cat flap in the wall of the consulting room behind my chair and she would put me on a little rail track, pushing me out through the flap. Of course, there was meaning in it all (controlling the coming and going of me through the cat flap and on rails, rather than feeling helplessly pulled in when I felt like it and pushed out when I did not want her any more), but the meaning was unavailable for thought and so was the affect that these terrible scenes must surely have contained. I was strangely unaffected feeling that although the cartoon images were clearly about what she was doing to me, they did not actually hurt me. I thought it was similar to the psychopath's need not to know the level of their violent hatred and aggression and a method of dissociating from it. It also meant that the preserving and co-operative part of Ms A was able to bring it into the consulting room, where it appeared regularly until such time as she felt we could survive a more direct awareness of the extreme level of her violent and murderous feelings.

In the later stages of her analysis, Ms A used to arrive and breathlessly report that she had been deeply afraid of how psychopathic (her word) she had been while coming to her session. She would list the violent actions she had or had not managed to stop herself doing and report to me her complete lack of concern for the consequences. She knew that there was someone to whom she could talk who would be worried about this even though she had lost contact internally with that aspect of herself. At this stage of the analysis, she could enlist my help in trying to bring her into a more integrated state. It was usually linked with the feeling that the projected side of her split was the good one and she had to get back to her session to find it in me again. Gradually, she developed a facility to conjure me up in her mind, a whole new experience for her, and to have an internal conversation with me. She would report a conversation in which she would say to herself, "Now what would she say?" The patient could easily provide the answer herself, although at this stage she still attributed it to the "me" in her mind with whom she was conversing.

Balint draws attention to another hindrance to integration when he talks about the difference between "benign" and "malignant" regressions. Here, his terms are beautifully descriptive and, I think, clinically recognisable. While a benign regression will tend to be the seedbed of new growth, the malignant one takes on a stuck and somewhat excited quality, which can come to dominate an analysis and wipe out memory of an ordinary good relationship with a real object. Balint locates the key difference in how far the regression is sexualised; the more sexualised, the more malignant the regression.

I think the question needs to be asked then, what does this sexualisation defend the patient against? Perhaps, through sado-masochism, a connection is established between the traumatising object and the infant, one that protects him against the unmoderated rupture of separation at a point where the object not only separates, but takes part of the subject away with her. A more affectionate and gentler way of relating requires a level of basic trust in which the loved one is separate and can go off, but with the expectation of return before the baby is annihilated.

Understanding this connection between the impossibility of surviving loss and the failure of a capacity to mourn a lost good object (Brenman, 2006) helps the analyst to understand the sexualisation inherent in the malignant regression.

Before leaving the subject of the integration of splits, I would like to take up Balint's idea, developed further by Stewart (1996), of showing the patient what he is doing or has been doing in the psychoanalytic setting. It is implicit in Balint's work that timing is everything in the usefulness or otherwise of showing patients what they are doing. Balint's description of the "unobtrusive analyst" is of an analyst sensitive to the patient's need for a good fit with the environment when in the state of primary love. Clearly, at this point where thinking is not possible, showing the patient what he is doing is not helpful. But there comes a time when the same patient will need something more separate from their analyst. It seems to have twofold value. The first is the obvious manifest one of bringing the split-off parts of the self to the patient's notice and the second is to demonstrate to the patient that their analyst can feel, know about, and survive their aggression and sadism without retaliating and without having to resort to a similar dissociation.

In the next section, I look in more detail at the difficulties for patient and analyst locked in the undifferentiated world of projected parts of the self, and an indeterminate identity where part lives in the analyst and part in the patient.

The world of unharmonious, interpenetrating mix-up

Balint's description of the yearned-for "harmonious interpenetrating mix-up" of the state of primary love is one which I think we seldom experience with our borderline patients. It might be there fleetingly, only to be smashed by the analyst's separate existence. Mostly, what emerges is a loud and vehement objection to the disruption of harmony. The concept of interpenetration is extremely valuable in understanding it, because it is a state where the patient is unable to distinguish the borders between self and other and either projects their whole self or parts of the self violently into the analyst. It is this activity which gives rise to the frequently uncomfortable intensity of work with a borderline patient, often described as the patient getting under your skin. The certainty with which the patient "knows" the analyst's mind puts pressure on the analyst to reveal all in a thinly disguised version of "you've got it wrong, it isn't like that at all". Interpretations aimed at showing the patient what they are doing, or communicating to the analyst or describing to the patient the way the analyst makes them feel at the moment, make little real contact with a patient who is struggling to tell what belongs inside them and what belongs inside the analyst. Those types of interpretation can feel to the patient as if the analyst is attempting to differentiate herself and to get away from something loathsome in the patient, to put herself outside and above the patient's torture. In fact, they can become a re-traumatising of the patient who is clinging to a merged and undifferentiated state, and further evidence to the patient that the analyst cannot tolerate them and their lack of differentiation.

There can frequently be a borderline transference situation where the patient, in a state of heightened anxiety, feeling provoked and impulse driven, will push and push at the analyst in such an infuriating and sadistic way that the analyst feels that the patient seems to want to make the analyst hate him. If the analyst says something hateful under pressure, there can be a sense of triumph which surprises the analyst, whose main concern is that she might have said something cruel or damaging.

Various analysts have grappled with this phenomenon in different ways. Winnicott (1949) suggests that the infant needs to find in the mother/analyst her real hatred for the child. Only then can love grow. If the child can begin to locate this "real" experience of the mother, they have the foundation or building blocks on which a more benign and responsive relationship can develop. Winnicott gives an example of a disturbed child who lived with the Winnicotts for three months. When the child became unbearably disobedient and infuriating and reason was unavailable, Winnicott put him outside the door and said, "Your behaviour has made me hate you." Perhaps, then, the search for the real response of hatred inside the real analyst is a search for this experience and the beginnings of the development of a connection between cause and effect, which is essential to development of a coherent self and of reliable and predictable relationships. Winnicott (1964), I think, adds a further dimension when talking about delinquents. He wrote that "in violence there is an attempt to reactivate firm holding". Perhaps, then, the provocative attacks are attempts to push the analyst to the limit and find out whether or not the patient can find both the hatred of the patient the analyst feels and the containment of that hatred. The technical predicament is that in that impulse-driven state, the patient wants a concrete knowing of the analyst's state of mind and also that the analyst can continue to be an analyst. When the analyst fails in this and retaliates, there is a triumphant moment for the patient: "See, you are no better than I am!", followed by the despair of having an object no better than he is and, therefore, unable to take his sadism and aggression and unable to hold him as he needs to be held.

Stewart (1992) describes a borderline patient who found the ends of sessions hard. She would leave banging the doors so hard that it began to destroy the paintwork. She would then walk down the street shouting obscenities about her analyst. When interpretative work made no difference, Stewart told his patient that if she continued to damage his property he would terminate the analysis. By extraordinary self-control, including tying her hands together with string around her wrists, she managed to stop. However, she then would not leave the consulting room at the end of sessions. She wanted to know why the analyst's family could stay and she could not. Stewart told her that he chose to have his family in his house and he did not choose to have her.

This view of the analyst's mind and thought processes, a mind in which there were real boundaries and a capacity to differentiate between family and patients, seems to have calmed the patient, who managed then to maintain the boundaries of the analysis.

So far, then, we know that the patient is struggling with a fragile self experience, one that is often undifferentiated from another. His projections and introjections are concrete and uncontained, so are potentially annihilating. He believes that he knows the analyst's mind, yet cannot really read it. He is looking for a real sense of the other's mind and, in the absence of real knowledge, experiences it as contemptuous, critical, and as damming as his own superego. He looks to see his impact on the analyst, unsure of what it might be, and, so doing, provokes the analyst to reveal his hatred of the patient. At the same time, he watches his analyst, needing to know how the analyst stands his hatred. Repeatedly, he brings his traumatic early experience, or experience at the basic fault, into his analysis.

Technique at the basic fault

The trauma will not be avoided, and, in my opinion, neither should it be. Instead, it will be the heart of the analysis. The patient's search for the "real" analyst seems crucial. The patient looks for an analyst who knows and feels how hatefully they are being attacked, who experiences this, and survives it as an analyst. It is a search for a mind that understands cause and effect (if you attack me, it makes me hate you), a mind that knows the difference between "me" and "you" and "inside" and "outside" and can go on thinking about the patient's feeling and her own feeling and what all this heated feeling is all about. The challenge is to find ways of showing the patient the analyst's mind at work sufficiently and appropriately, without any boundary-less behaviour. The often provocative pushing into the analyst can nudge her into a rejecting, evacuating, response—one familiar to the patient and, perhaps, in that familiarity, reassuring. But the more hopeful part of the patient is looking to see how the analyst can do what he, the patient, cannot do; he is looking to find a more life-giving object, in Bollas's words, a transformational object (Bollas, 1986). The analyst must find ways of meeting this hope.

In responding to the patient's enquiry about how her mind works, the analyst has a delicate task. Her response must not satisfy the patient's wish for perfect (tyrannical) harmony, but yet must be attuned to the patient's unique needs at each moment and to his particular ways of communicating them. The metaphor of the first-time mother comes to mind. She watches and listens to her baby to learn how to understand what he feels and what he requires to transform that feeling into something bearable and more peaceful. The particular kind of holding of that particular baby is not uniform, and neither is it between analyst and patient.

Each analytic couple will aim to find the kind of holding that works; it is not something that can be prescribed. As with the mother and baby analogy, the holding of the baby and the responsive attunement of the mother, including her firmness and her recognition of when the baby can tolerate separation, so a regressed patient in a borderline psychotic transference will need to feel that the analyst is actually trying to find the attuned response, which reaches him. Listening to the patient's complaints and feeling how it might feel to him is the first essential part of this process.

I suggest that at the moment of the repetition, the patient might be able to continue with analytic work if the analyst accepts for the time being the state of one-ness and moves to interpretations that are objectless and descriptive. I am suggesting that there is a level at which one is required to address the patient for the time being, which is, in fact, not objectless, but which the patient can only bear to hear as objectless. In speaking to the patient in this way, the analyst accepts that any mention of the object will feel to the patient like a violent intrusion. Perhaps these interpretations can be described as pre-patient centred. Just as Steiner (1993) describes the analyst moving from patient-centred interpretation to analyst-centred interpretation, I suggest that the analyst of the regressed patient will first need to move from pre-patient or "objectless" interpretation to patient- and then analyst-centred interpretation.

After a holiday break, Ms A came anxiously into the consulting room. She was not able to acknowledge me, and looked anxiously around, flapping one arm and hand in a panicky evacuating movement while blowing her breath out. She turned around (I thought to leave again) and took up a position beside my desk on the floor near the door and almost out of sight. She was then very quiet, and I thought of a child playing dead.

I later learnt that she had assumed and feared in that moment that I would not accept her new position and would annihilate her. Her silence was one of silent, frozen terror. The room and her analyst had become a terrifying and potentially annihilating environment. I experienced her change of position as an act of freedom, a collapse of the old false self, when she seemed to be in analysis but could not risk any real contact or exposure of her shattered core self. I felt that she had courageously made a truly spontaneous gesture (Winnicott, 1960a) that required an authentic and attuned response, one that was as neutral and exact a description of her feeling state as I could manage. Accompanied by a feeling of being in unknown territory, I found myself reverting to skills that I had learnt in infant observation, describing out loud to myself what I thought she felt and perhaps why. For example, I wondered to myself aloud whether she needed the hard surface of the desk to lean against and act as a barrier to protect her from terrifying intrusiveness that could shatter her. Gradually, she became bolder in showing me some movements, which I took to be like mimes. Sometimes, I just described them and sometimes, when Ms A seemed less terrified of me, I sought to make sense of them. For example, she would appear to be taking hold of a handle of what seemed like an extraordinarily solid (perhaps a safe) door and slightly opening it just a fraction. If I moved too fast or spoke too loudly, she would close it again immediately. At those moments, I wondered to myself out loud whether she was risking letting me in for a moment to see if it were tolerable or annihilating. She later brought in paper to draw on, and when I was able to see the pictures, because she just tilted them enough in my direction, or later when she managed to tell me what she was drawing, they were usually of herself inside various sorts of steel casings, or in thick, padded spacesuits and impermeable protective shells. She might be a dot inside a steel box, safe, but dying from lack of oxygen. She accepted my comment that she could contemplate the need for a feed or oxygen as long as she could control the opening time and my intrusiveness.

From the point of her spontaneous gesture, I felt that we had a real hope of a good outcome of the analysis; we had found how to be an analytic couple both really present and alive and both risking all. For her part, she let me see her raw pre-verbal experience, and for mine, I tried to attend as closely as possible, trying to read her communications, then simply speaking about what I thought I saw from time to time, and listening intently and believing her when I got it wrong.

Clearly, the attunement that one finds with each individual patient is patient led. I take as my model Winnicott's idea, as described above, of the beginning of the emergence of self-experience through the expression of feeling in a spontaneous gesture that is responded to by the attuned mother and, thus, makes the infant's experience real. When this interaction fails, then defensive false-self organisations develop to protect the core self from annihilation. The pleasure of working with the borderline patient is that each patient will find his own particular way of showing us that our preconceptions are wrong and will set us the task of finding precise and tailor-made, and, at the same time, entirely analytic, responses.

The task of finding the right response is doubly difficult when the patient's wish for it is less strong, or at least more hidden, than the force of the vehement attack on the analyst.

In the heat of the moment, a patient might well provoke the analyst into a reaction. I think this is a necessary part of the process of finding out what is inside the analyst. The task is to find a way of showing both that one feels provoked, that is, that the patient is having an impact and is not just hitting against an impervious empty person, and, at the same time, can think about it, even if only to wonder about it and not know the answer. What the analyst is doing is recognising that the patient needs to see the workings of his inner world, both his feeling reaction and his processing of that feeling. Similarly, the patient in a raw borderline state, who is attacking his analyst's mind, will be terrified of that mind in silences. Patients usually communicate over time how much silence they can tolerate and under what circumstances they can think and when they simply feel frozen in terror. As analysts, we learn to respond to this information as best we can. It is, after all, another way in which we can develop a more attuned relationship with the patient. When a silence is of a terrifying kind, the patient is seldom helped by asking for his thoughts, but, in my experience, is helped by the analyst volunteering what is going on in his own mind. So, something like, "In the silence I have been thinking that when you feel as hating of me as you do at the moment, it could also feel very frightening and lonely, not having anyone to talk to about it." The patient might well be contemptuous of our paltry efforts and will certainly tell us if we are thinking about something irrelevant, but even then I find that, despite the disappointment that the analyst has got it wrong, the relief that she is not thinking and feeling such dangerous and hateful thoughts as the patient is usually restores communication.

Sometimes, when there seems to be no way into thinking about the attack on the analyst and one is being invited into a retaliation, I find a comment about the fact that at this moment, in this atmosphere and in this state of mind, it does not feel possible to think about or begin to understand what is so upsetting, or enraging, or provocative. It can sometimes open up the possibility for the patient that he can remember that he does have other states of mind and might, in the future when not feeling so compelled to attack as at present, be able to join with the analyst again in thought. It also shows the workings of the analyst's mind. She is still in contact with the part that can think and feel at the same time. This way, she has survived as an analyst and, therefore, as a potential new object (Baker, 1993; Strachey, 1934) for the patient.

In my opinion, all patients watch their analyst to see how they respond and deal with the pressures of the analytic situation. Perhaps this is the most unacknowledged area of learning in analysis. Basic fault patients particularly need to understand whether they are dealing with someone who can really do it or who, like them, has learnt by copying and doing the "right" thing. The patient wants and, at the same time, does not want the analyst to be different from them. Balint's point about acknowledging one's mistakes is important in this context. There will be times when one is provoked into retaliation. Without this, the patient might feel that they are with an automaton. But they also need to hear an honest answer to their frequent question about what is the analyst's "own stuff" and what is theirs. This is a vital part of sorting out what is "me" and "not me". So, the accusation that the analyst had been sadistic or contemptuous or mocking and that "it is 'your stuff'" needs to be met with a thoughtful acknowledgment that "Yes, I think you are right about that" on an occasion when the analyst had been provoked into retaliation. This opens up the possibility of going back and looking at what went on in that provocation.

In moments when the heat is past, the patient has a new experience to draw on. He develops a relationship with an object who can feel, know that when attacked she can act defensively, can go on thinking about it, can acknowledge her mistakes, repair the damage done, and survive as an analyst doing her best for her patient.

Summary and conclusions

I hope to have shown that while Balint's work on the basic fault has limitations, he does make a unique and valuable contribution to our understanding of the internal structure of a range of borderline transferences. Through this understanding, we can direct our interpretative work to the appropriate developmental level.

First and foremost, he captures the quality and nature of the trauma at the heart of the borderline condition. The essential pre-verbal remembering in the transference concerns a failure or rupture of the earliest state in which the baby requires a harmonious union in which only his needs and demands signify.

The trauma seems to constitute an overwhelming, unprocessed loss of an attuned state of one-ness, a sense of "too much too soon" (Tustin, 1992) of an intrusive third person, with the patient feeling expelled out of his rightful place (Figuerido, 2006).

Balint also opens the way to understanding the range of premature psychic organisations constructed defensively in the face of the failure of manageable separation, and indicates the ways in which premature sexualisation can become a part of the defensive structure. Both the rigidity and the fragility of these internal organisations are recognised. With this conceptualisation of the internal structure comes the recognition that the efforts of the patient to force the analyst into the desired state of perfect attunement play a central part in the analysis of borderline patients.

He captures, too, something of the clinical drama of the shift between levels, from integrated to split or from neurotic to psychotic, and alerts the analyst to the vital importance of recognising and working with those shifts and changes in level. The point of shift to the level of the basic fault requires the analyst to shift too. The interpretative activity of the analyst must shift from interpretations that assume some thinking capacity to interpretations which recognise the patient's desperate wish for one-ness. These moments will be the most fruitful ones for analysis, so the analyst's awareness of their meaning and importance is vital.

From a basis in Balint's work, I explore how best to help patients in analysis regressed to the level of the basic fault.

I have used clinical material to illustrate my view that the essential pre-verbal remembering and repeating in the transference reproduces traumatic failure or rupture of the earliest state of merger with the object, which incorporates within it a failure of containment of the trauma.

In the transference, small acts of lack of perfect attunement, or more obvious separations, repeat the trauma and a vicious circle will be set up. The patient tries to survive by attacking and rejecting all thinking and tries either to force the analyst into harmony and union or rejects the analyst in favour of the harmony he can provide for himself.

While the patient feels that his survival depends on regaining possession of the analyst in a merged union, the analyst is faced with the task of helping the patient to integrate the deep internal split that has been established so early and so firmly.

I suggest that the survival of the analyst is important and, ultimately, therapeutic during phases of regression to the basic fault. While Balint makes it sound rather a harmonious, almost blissful, experience, I think most clinicians would disagree. Certainly, in the case of the more malignant regressions in which sadism plays a significant part, the pressure on the analyst to retaliate and, thus, to comply with the patient by becoming the same as they are, is great. In these phases, I suggest that work is focused on remaining both real and yet as neutral and exact as possible. Having projected himself into the analyst with ferocious intensity, the patient is highly sensitive to the analyst's responses. Too emotional or highly charged a response and he believes he has rid himself of his bad feeling and that the difficulty is all in the analyst and not in himself; too distant and careful, and he thinks that the analyst has removed herself from the patient, distancing and protecting herself from him. He fears that he is too damaging for her to take head on and will have to redouble his efforts to push at her until he finds something hard in the analyst to stop him, to survive him. What I refer to as objectless interpretations, in which the analyst describes the patient's internal experience and thinks aloud about it without relating it to the analyst, shows the patient that the analyst has survived the intensity without shooting it back and without her mind being destroyed.

I hope that I have shown both the complexity of this transference and the ways in which it is possible to work analytically with it.

Additionally, I hope to have shown that the patient searches for a "real" response in the analyst. It might be in order to reactivate firm holding, to both destroy and be stopped from destroying the analyst's capacity for thinking, and to find out how the analyst's mind works. He needs to know that the analyst experiences hatred in response to his attacks and yet can recover her capacity to think about her patient. Interpretations need to acknowledge the patient's fear of having attacked the analyst so hatefully that he is now terrified of his analyst's response. Carrying on as if unaffected by the patient's destructive behaviour makes the patient feel as if the analyst is not real and is not affected, and that patient and analyst are on two different planets.

Finally, I hope to have shown that I believe that with early experience being so central in these analyses, the analyst must find an attuned response to her particular patient, one that is patient led rather than theory or analyst led, at the same time without the analyst ever deserting her analytic stance. The patient needs to experience the analytic position constantly if they are to learn that they can be survived, held, and contained as they gradually relinquish their defensive, false-self organisation and learn to survive separateness.

Note

1.   Harold Stewart (1996) makes the point that although Balint did not spell this out, he is actually describing the borderline psychotic transference in his book *The Basic Fault*.

References

Asperger, H. (1944). 'Autistic psychopathy' in childhood. In: U. Frith (Ed. and Trans.), *Autism and Asperger Syndrome* (pp. 37–92). Cambridge: Cambridge University Press, 1991.

Baker, R. (1993). The patient's discovery of the psychoanalyst as a new object. *International Journal of Psychoanalysis*, 74: 1223–1233.

Balint, M. (1959). *Thrills and Regressions*. London, Hogarth.

Balint, M. (1968). *The Basic Fault; Therapeutic Aspects of Regression*. London: Tavistock.

Bollas, C. (1986). The transformational object. In: G. Kohon (Ed.), *The British School of Psychoanalysis: The Independent Tradition* (pp. 83–100). London: Free Association Books.

Brenman, E. (2006). *Recovery of the Lost Good Object*. London: Routledge, New Library of Psychoanalysis.

Britton, R. (1998). *Belief and Imagination: Explorations in Psychoanalysis*. London: Routledge.

Ferenczi, S. (1932). Notes and fragments. In: *Final Contributions to Psychoanalysis*. London: Hogarth Press, 1955.

Figuerido, L. C. (2006). Sense of reality, reality testing and reality processing in borderline states. *International Journal of Psychoanalysis, 87*(3): 769–788.

Kahn, M. (1963). The concept of cumulative trauma. In: G. Kohon (Ed.), *The British School of Psychoanalysis: The Independent Tradition.* (pp. 117–135). London: Free Association Books.

Klein, M. (1930). The importance of symbol formation in the development of the ego. *International Journal of Psychoanalysis, 11*: 24–39.

Little, M. (1981). *Transference Neurosis and Transference Psychosis*. New York: Jason Aronson.

Little, M. (1985). Winnicott working in areas where psychotic anxieties predominate: a personal record. *Free Associations, 3*: 9–42.

Rutter, M., Andersen-Wood, L., Beckett, C., Bredenkamp, D., Castle, J., Groothues, C., Kreppner, J., Keaveney, L., Lord, C., & O'Connor, T. G. (1999). Quasi-autistic patterns following severe early global privation. *Journal of Child Psychology and Psychiatry, 40*: 537–549.

Schore, A. N. (2001a). The effects of early relational trauma on right brain development, affect regulation and infant mental health. *Infant Mental Health Journal, 22*: 201–269.

Schore, A. N. (2001b). The effects of a secure attachment relationship on right brain development, affect regulation and infant mental health. *Infant Mental Health Journal, 22*: 7–66.

Steiner, J. (1993). Problems of psychoanalytic technique: patient centred and analyst centred interpretations. In: *Psychic Retreats* (pp. 131–146). London: New Library of Psychoanalysis.

Stewart, H. (1992). Technique at the basic fault and regression. In: *Psychic Experience and Problems of Technique* (pp. 111–126). London: The New Library of Psychoanalysis.

Stewart, H. (1996). *Michael Balint: Object Relations Pure and Applied*. London: The New Library of Psychoanalysis.

Strachey, J. (1934). The nature of the therapeutic action of psychoanalysis. *International Journal of Psychoanalysis, 15*: 127–159.

Symington, N. (1980). The response aroused by the psychopath. *International Review of Psychoanalysis, 7*: 291–298. Reprinted as: The origins of rage and aggression, in: C. Cordess & M. Cox (Eds.), *Forensic Psychotherapy* (pp. 187–192). London: Jessica Kingsley, 1996.

Tustin, F. (1986). *Autistic Barriers in Neurotic Patients*. London: Karnac.

Tustin, F. (1990). *The Protective Shell in Children and Adults*. London: Karnac.

Tustin, F. (1992). *Autistic States in Children* (revised edn). London: Routledge.

Winnicott, D. W. (1947). Hate in the counter transference. In: *Collected Papers: Through Paediatrics to Psychoanalysis* (pp. 194–203). London: Hogarth, 1975.

Winnicott, D. W. (1951). Transitional objects and transitional phenomena. In: *Collected Papers: Through Paediatrics to Psychoanalysis* (pp. 229–242). London: Hogarth, 1975.

Winnicott, D. W. (1955). Clinical varieties of transference. In: *Collected Papers: Through Paediatrics to Psychoanalysis* (pp. 295–299). London: Hogarth, 1975.

Winnicott, D. W. (1956). Primary maternal preoccupation. In: *Collected Papers: Through Paediatrics to Psychoanalysis* (pp. 300–305). London: Hogarth, 1975.

Winnicott, D. W. (1960a). Ego distortion in terms of the true and the false self. In: *The Maturational Processes and the Facilitating Environment* (pp. 140–152). Hogarth Press and The Institute of Psychoanalysis, 1965.

Winnicott, D. W. (1960b). The theory of the parent–infant relationship. In: *The Maturational Processes and the Facilitating Environment* (pp. 37–55). Hogarth Press and The Institute of Psychoanalysis, 1965.

Winnicott, D. W. (1962). Ego distortion in child development. In: *The Maturational Processes and the Facilitating Environment* (pp. 56–63. Hogarth Press and The Institute of Psychoanalysis, 1965.

Winnicott, D. W. (1964). Youth will not sleep. In: C. Winnicott, M. Davis, & R. Shepherd, (Eds.), *Deprivation and Delinquency* (pp. 156–160). London: Tavistock.

Winnicott, D. W. (1968). The use of the object and relating through identification. In: *Playing and Reality* (pp. 86–94). London: Tavistock, 1971.

CHAPTER FOURTEEN

Entertaining the body in mind: thoughts on incest, the body, sexuality, and the self

Ann Horne

"There are no brakes on fantasy"

(Winnicott, 1945, p. 153)

To begin at the beginning . . .

There had been several years of concern about the Long family. Mrs Long, whose first marriage had been to an older, cruel, violent, and sexually abusive man, had a son (Robert) from that marriage. It was suspected—indeed, disclosed by Robert then retracted—that Mrs Long had sexually abused him and it also seemed to be a matter of local knowledge that, following the death of her husband, she had frequently entertained a group of young adolescent boys in her house. The first contact the clinic had with the family was a consultation about Robert, whose compulsive, sexualised actions had become extremely hard for his care staff and social worker to manage and understand.

Married again, to a man of her own age who, like her, had learning difficulties, Mrs Long had two further children and was pregnant with a third when *she* was referred. The assessment led the diagnostician to conclude that psychotherapy for Mrs Long was not at that point a treatment of choice; however, the first child of this second marriage, Katiebell, had begun to act in a sexually inappropriate way with her younger brother, being compelled to intrude repeatedly into his bedroom in the middle of the night for this sexual engagement, and a referral was made in relation to this. She had learning difficulties (global developmental delay, functioning on the first centile), was encopretic, still in nappies at night, neglected, and waif-like.

Katiebell had been sexually abused from the age of eighteen months by Robert, then fourteen. The abuse ceased when he was finally taken into care, some two years on, although his mother remained unable (some thought unwilling) to keep him apart from her other children. Katiebell came for her assessment a week after her seventh birthday. I saw her weekly in therapy for over seven years.

Introduction

I would like to explore several themes in this paper, with the help of Katiebell.

- The child and young person's relationship with the body, especially how this is integrated into the psychological sense of self, notably when it carries damage. Winnicott's term "personalisation" is of help here (Winnicott 1945, 1949, 1972), a term he devised to counterpoint the defensive position of depersonalisation, as a positive developmental form:

  > The term *personalization* was intended to draw attention to the fact that the in-dwelling of this other part of the personality in the body, and its firm link with whatever is there which we call psyche, in developmental terms represents an achievement in health. (Winnicott, 1972, p. 7)

  A little further on, he simplifies: "personalization" is "an in-dwelling of psyche in soma" (1972, p. 10).

  One interest, therefore, is the developmental process, while being aware of the insult to it. If the mind is extant throughout the body, as Gaddini reminds us (Gaddini, 1980), then the body becomes complicit in the inability of the traumatised child to process what has been overwhelming to the immature ego and complicit in the mind's constant state of alertness to intrusion of memory or re-enactment of the trauma. For Katiebell, the "S word" (sex) constantly lurked, awaiting an opportunity to bound into her mind, and had to be kept at bay. Indeed, I would posit that the body itself merely functions and "is"; it is to be *not* thought about at all times. Part of the therapeutic process is to enable the child to entertain the body in mind, to have a body image and a concept of body in which she then can belong.

- The child—and the body and sexuality of the child—in the eye and the mind of the mother, especially when there has been an incestuous relationship. The meaning of this in the therapy—how it emerges and how progress is gained—has an impact on our technical approach.

- Sexuality. I take the view that infantile sexuality is proto-sexuality, the capacity for passionate, sensuous, and wholehearted relationships with both sexes, but is a long way away from adult sexuality. Indeed, we must learn greater exactness in our use of concepts in relation to the developing child to ensure that we simply do not elide the one idea to take on equivalence to the other. The intrusion of adult—and perverse—sexuality has to be considered in relation to the nature of the trauma and the defences engaged against this; to the developmental thrust (in Winnicott's terms, "the general inherited tendency that the child has towards integration" (Winnicott, 1945, p. 8)) that is halted or diverted; to the developmental stage of the child at the time of the trauma; and to the capacity to regain a pathway to "normal" development, of which sexuality is a part.

It is not unusual for child and adolescent psychotherapists to work with children where sexual abuse has been an element in their very early childhood: indeed, it is all too common a feature of the work. Less frequently, we engage with children and young people who are driven to enact past abusive and sexually abusive experiences, or to decant the anxiety and shame arising from their memories of such events on to others. This repetition compulsion, identifying with the aggressor in order to relieve one's mind and body of memories of humiliation and victimisation, arrives in the consulting room in a variety of ways: invitation to abuse, seductive overtures, perversion of normal verbal intercourse, and terror of a potentially abusive object. Of course, sometimes sexuality makes its way into the consulting room and is prominent in its absence, but with our awareness of the "shadow of the object" (Bollas, 1987) in the countertransference.

Katiebell arrives

A tall, extremely thin, elfin-looking child sat apart from her heavily pregnant mother in the waiting room. She had fine, mousy brown hair and a tremendous sense of lightness about her, as if somehow she was not certain about having substance. Her grubby NHS spectacles sat aslant her face and were held together with Elastoplast. Nevertheless, she placed herself before me as I introduced myself to both and stared, head on one side, with very direct curiosity. She hesitated as we came down into my basement room, possibly the due anxiety one would expect at a first encounter, but I felt it more to be an uncertainty about what one did. Very soon the session theme of "how do you get things right?" emerged. Already, it seemed, there was a child who was concerned about the state of mind of the object rather than in any way egocentric.

Katiebell flitted carefully around the room as if she could not bear to stop and settle to play with any particular thing there. I showed her the locker that would be hers, with bits and pieces in it—the usual "kit" of paper, felt pens, sellotape, scissors, string, a small doll family, a few farm and wild animals. She was overwhelmed that something had been done with her in mind, that the adult might anticipate her presence. I was reminded of Alvarez's injunction that the good experience can be as overwhelming as the traumatic one and require time to recover in order to integrate it (Alvarez, 1988). She stood in the middle of the room and looked at me. She offered that she was wearing a sweatshirt that she liked. It was a nice sweatshirt, very well washed and rather aged. We were wearing similar colours. She came across to me and compared the tones, then beamed. This seemed to give her the courage to explore. While placing people in the dolls' house, she was insistent that the parents shared a bedroom, but then she seemed a little uncertain about the children sharing a room. I said, with the referral in mind, that she might be finding it awkward when people shared, but she did not respond. Finally, she drew, and volunteered to draw me. The picture was exceptionally primitive. A circle represented the head and she added two eyes and a smiling mouth. Two long lines came down from this, each ending in a foot. Somewhere in the middle, she drew a circle. I was just beginning to feel a sense of relief that it might be a body representation when she said informatively, "That's the belly button!" Looking at me quite carefully, she added, "I think I'll give you arms." This small sign of hope felt hugely affecting in the countertransference. At times, she drifted into another place in her mind, coming back and reminding herself where she was. We talked of her possibly coming every week, a radical but entertaining idea, and she asked about the time, how to know how long we had, packing up when the big hand reached 10. In the waiting room, her mother sat eating biscuits and drinking cola, wearing a huge pair of headphones. She shrieked at Katiebell, who stood like an arthritic crane in front of her, forearms and hands twisted together and one leg wrapped around the other.

In the second assessment session, Katiebell came cautiously downstairs with me. She showed great anxiety, questioning, "Are these your stairs? Is that your kitchen?" She seemed to recognise nothing. I gently drew her attention to her locker and the pictures she had drawn. There were instances when she stood in bizarre, contorted postures, as if the awkwardness of the body position was an attempt to contain anxiety and the discomfort served to remind her of her existence. She peered in the dolls' house, returned to the table and, about ten or fifteen minutes into the session, suddenly looked straight at me and said, "You're *Ann*—I *know* who you are!" It felt once more that she had had no expectation of an attentive object: Katiebell thus struggles to gain any sense of herself, or of the self reflected back from the object, from any of her adults.

In brief, the session was not unlike the previous one, flitting and alighting briefly, living in the moment with no sense of continuity and little sense of "going on being'. I made simple connections, and at one point she darted to me, hugged me, and drifted off once more. She did ask to go to the lavatory, where I waited for her outside a little way off. The odour that accompanied her back to the room made me wonder about her encopresis and its relation to anxiety and abuse. I was left feeling that this child was like a series of atolls surrounded by sea, not joined. There was some glimmer of hope about attachment: the comparison of our clothing, the eventual delighted memory of her previous session, her sense of pride when I noticed her good efforts, and that she could consider that arms could be a good thing. At the end, her mother was very ambivalent about returning, which made Katiebell come very close to me, lifting her head with her lips puckered, silently asking for a goodbye kiss. The discomfort of this episode lay not in the refusal, but in her need for a sexualised approach to mitigate a crisis.

Thinking about Katiebell's arrival

In initial sessions, the themes of a whole analysis are often suggested. This was no exception. The issues that preoccupied her, the meaning of her objects in her internal world, the defences available to her, despite our apparent paucity of conversation, were there in outline. Her preoccupation with her compulsion to abuse, and the great difficulty in thinking about this, giving rise to primitive defensive manoeuvres of denying, ignoring; her constant attendance to the object and how to be acceptable to this, indicative of the lack of any internalised capacity to think of herself as tolerable and the lack of a good-enough reflection of the self back to the child; the absence of any sense of substance and any sense of "going on being"; the immaturity of representations of the body; dissociation and "switching off" as a way of dealing with the possibility of stress; the good experience as a source of engulfment; the use of sexualisation as a way of gaining mastery over anxiety—all were there.

One could also begin to create a theoretical frame, to find the theoretical bricks that would enable us to assemble an understanding of her experience and the internal sense she made of it. In this, we think of the child as a part object to the mother, not a sentient being with integrity and individuality, and recall Welldon's formulation of the perverse female who turns inwards, to the body and the body products, in her annihilation of *her* internal, abusing mother (Welldon, 1988). For the child of such a parent, one revisits Winnicott's comments on the development of the self:

> The self essentially recognises itself in the eyes and facial expression of the mother and in the mirror which can come to represent the mother's face. Eventually the self arrives at a significant relationship

between the child and the sum of the identifications which (after enough incorporation and introjection of mental representations) become organised in the shape of the internal psychic reality. (Winnicott, 1972, p. 16)

We recall Mrs Long, headphones firmly attached, mouth filled with biscuits. Winnicott goes on to emphasise the role of parental expectations in modifying the emerging self, and we recall Mrs Long's ambivalence about her daughter, her exposing her to the son whom she had abused. In therapy, throughout the first months Katiebell played very repetitively at hide and seek, longing and not longing to be found. In the countertransference, hunting behind chairs, under the couch, and in her favourite place beneath my desk (from which I often thought she emerged, brought into life, into a world where she was able to be perceived differently from the perception she saw in her mother's gaze), I felt she was revisiting the dangerous drama of being found by her abuser. Heightened anxiety and adrenalin rush repeated the prefatory body sensations of her infant self. Interpretation centred on the fear that I might be abusive, the wish that this now might be different, and the need constantly to repeat the good experience of being found by a good enough object. As with a small child, the emphasis was on the joy of finding—"*There* you are! How awful it felt not to find and see you!"—and the process of internalising a normal developmental engagement between adult and child. It is such a developmental achievement to know one can make the object pursue and seek one; how much more so when that object can also begin to be internalised as "benign".

Who the child is in the eyes of the incestuous and incest-permitting mother and of the incestuous partner becomes an important question. The absence of any stage of primary narcissism must be part of our construct: there is no experience of the omnipotence that should be part of normal development. Neither is there the straightforward affirmation through gaze between mother and baby:

Of course, the baby does see the mother's smiling face, but this, which is in reality her response to his smiles, reflects back to him his own aliveness: "The mother is looking at the baby and what she looks like is related to what she sees there" (Winnicott 1967: 112). (Wright, 1991, p. 12)

Dio Bleichmar emphasises the look of the seducer which "inhabits the body" and results in an absence of any safe or secret place: looking "in the mirror or when she bathes, there is always another detached pair of eyes looking at her body through her own 'sexualised' eyes" (Dio Bleichmar, 1995). There appears to be little respite from the internalised view of the object, and dissociation (used often by Katiebell in our early days) would seem an obvious defence against exposure and the absence of privacy. Indeed, we should also consider the impact of the loss of shame as a protective function in development.

The very young child is body-centred; the first ego is a body ego.

> Experiences of being-next-to or being-in, characterised by softness and continuity, give rise to what Winnicott describes as going-on-being . . . The lack of such experiences, or the experience of impingements at skin level, threaten the infant/child with a feeling of annihilation. (Grand & Alpert, 1993, p. 332)

This body, Krueger reminds us, "is often the narrator of feelings [patients] cannot bear to hold in conscious thought, much less express in words" (Krueger, 2001, p. 239). Laufer develops this a little further: "Within such a safe space the infant can begin to feel its own body as having the capacity to protect itself from the 'bad' experiences intruding into its own body ego boundaries" (Laufer, 1991, p. 63). She finds that the risk inherent in the distorted body image—the mental representation of the body—lies in that "it forms a psychotic core to the personality in that it must affect the person's relationship to external reality" (ibid., p. 71). Entertaining the body in mind thus becomes of the essence.

Given Katiebell's family history, it is not surprising that I had Fairbairn in mind. As the Independents emphasise, the drive of the child is towards relationships. In Fairbairn's construct, the child will split off the bad parent in an attempt to hold on to an illusory good parent, in the process defining herself as bad, rather than risk loss of the object (Fairbairn, 1952). The process of the therapy, then, with luck, enables the child to perceive herself as motherable.

Finally, there is the place of identification with the mother and "how the mother responds to her daughter's sexuality is of crucial importance for the girl's future relationships" (Klockars & Sirola, 2001,

p. 233). Mrs Long's attitude to Katiebell's body and sexuality was perverse. The child was treated as a part-object, not a separate human being who might be seen as such, and that part-object was offered for abuse to the already abused son. Reliant on the early body-self, Katiebell then evacuated the humiliating memory of abuse on to her little brother via the body. Thought plays no part in such an early process. Developmentally, there is still a struggle to establish an ego ideal, this being dependent on the objects available, and the role of shame in that process is important. Campbell reminds us of the protective function of shame: it takes us out of humiliating situations when, for example, we cover our faces, and once more it is about "seeing" and "being seen", and he points to the absence of this protective shield in abused and abusing young people (Campbell, 1994). Katiebell could not bear to talk of her body, what it got up to, or the over-determined "S" word, for many months, such was the shame she felt. Oedipal resolutions—far ahead in psychological development—are, thus, unsurprisingly few with abused children like Katiebell, and identification with such a mother as Mrs Long—part of the normal Oedipal resolution—also carries its complexities.

Reflecting on technique after the assessment: "First you have to build the house"

Fantasy, in Winnicott's words quoted at the start of this paper, reminds me of the tricycle I was much attached to when I was three, a hand-me-down from my big brother. The pedals were built into the front wheel. There were no brakes ("there are no brakes on fantasy"); to brake, you had to keep your feet firmly on the pedals and stop pedalling, very difficult to achieve when you were speeding downhill. Fortunately, perhaps, I lived in a small village with little traffic. But it required an active *not doing* and a resistance to *doing*. For the child whose immature ego has been overwhelmed by invasive trauma, there are no brakes on memory or fantasy; indeed, the fantasy of assaulting another child comes hard on the heels of the intrusion of memory with its attendants, humiliation and shame. It operates equally outwith control. One aim is, thus, to interpose "thought" between "fantasy" and the compulsion to act. Thought becomes the equivalent of "not pedalling", enabling "not doing".

For Katiebell, this would be part of the therapeutic process, but it was evident from these sessions that the earlier stage of recognising emotional states would be the first essential, before she would be able to think about such states and gain some control over action. This takes us into the arena of fluid and sensitive interaction between a developmental stance and an interpretative, analytic stance—work on the lines of Hurry's (1998) "developmental psychotherapy". Where the capacities for thought, curiosity, feeling, and emotion are limited, whether this be due to conflict (when it appears as a primitive defence) or deficit, "the analyst's task is to engage inhibited or under-developed processes within the analytic encounter" (ibid., p. 67). And, technically,

> ... it is important that the analyst be prepared to move between the developmental/relational stance and the interpretative, as Anna Freud described. ... Both developmental relating and understanding are necessary; each can potentiate and reinforce the effects of the other. (ibid., pp. 71–72)

Hurry's concept of the analyst as *"developmental* object" was to be important in work with Katiebell. Thus, recognising and naming affects was a large part of the early sessions: "Gosh! That was a good goal! You must have felt really pleased!", or equally, "Ouch! That was a sore kick. I think your foot was feeling terribly annoyed with me!", and the emotional states were noted before they could be explored.

As a corollary of this, the therapist has a difficult task with the child whose thinking is still concrete: to talk of what might be in mind can be to seem to give it actuality. In situations like this, work in the displacement gives access to externalised affects and defences. It is, as Anna Freud said, "a way of approaching threatening mental content gradually" (Sandler, Kennedy, & Tyson, 1980, p. 165). So we played with the doll families and reflected on their experiences, thoughts, and feelings, until Katiebell herself could say, "I feel . . ."

Every abused child is hypersensitive to the actions and intentions of the object. This requires the therapist's acute awareness of issues of intimacy and distance, what can be verbalised, what is likely to be experienced as intrusion, and, as Khan reminds us, for the child trau-matised early, there is no internalised protective sense and later impingements may well take on traumatic proportions (Khan, 1963). Intimacy becomes a key therapeutic issue. Indeed, I often find myself waiting when a new child comes for therapy to see where he/she will sit, or I say that I am going to sit over there, by the window, away from the door, leaving a good space in which the child may feel safer. I have found this initial process of finding a manageable distance to be the first indication in the countertransference of traumatic intrusion and psychological safety. With children where a sense of hope might still lurk, the core complex difficulties with intimacy, obliteration, rage, and abandonment are all too readily summoned (Glasser, 1996).

Equally, there is the role of hate and the impact of this in the countertransference. Reading Winnicott is essential:

> an analyst . . . must be able to be so thoroughly aware of the countertransference that he can sort out and study his *objective* reactions to the patient. These will include hate. Countertransference phenomena will at times be the important things in the analysis. (Winnicott, 1947, p. 195)

> Sentimentality is useless . . . as it contains a denial of hate. (ibid., p. 202)

In this paper, Winnicott also alerts us to the need for us to hold on to our experience of hating: for some patients, there comes a point when the process can be discussed; for others it cannot, as "there may be too little good experience in the patient's past to work on" (ibid., p. 198). Therapy then becomes even more a parallel expression of the "good enough" experience.

Four years on

In the Portman Clinic, where I saw Katiebell, one has permission to engage in treatment for four years, after which the therapist presents the work to the clinic team for joint consideration of "what next?" There had been times in the four years when I had discussed Katiebell at clinical meetings; the staff group was not unacquainted with her and had been enormously enriching of the therapy in the understanding they offered. During the four years, Katiebell shifted from dealing with her object through activity, although her bizarre poses took a little time to be abandoned, and she would run and climb around the room. Her encopresis, after one dreadful session when it was combined with car-sickness, slowly vanished, seemingly in parallel with a capacity to contain: contain feelings and think about them, contain body products, and contain the impulse to enact her abuse. Gradually, games of hide and seek were initiated by her, controlling finding and being found, and helping the internalisation of an object who would seek her at her own pace. Those who have read Hopkins' (1996) paper about Paddy, supervised by Winnicott, will recall the slow ego-structuring work necessary before the child can face conflict and conflictual feelings. Katiebell tried out ego strengths and competencies, especially rehearsing with the body in physical struggles at football and rounders, where she had enormous determination and persistence. In this, there was a gradual sense of integration, a body that could function as a whole. This integration was aided by her respite carer, who taught her basic hygiene and self-care and who dressed her appropriately—very different from the often dirty clothes provided by her mother. Splitting off her body for our joint consideration allowed it to begin to be entertained in mind: "Wasn't that interesting what your body did!" encourages the thinking part of the child to ally with the therapist and, thus, both can observe together the infantile part. She allowed curiosity about me to emerge in endless games of "school", where I was often set the writing topic of "What I did at the weekend". For a spell, she would leap on to the couch and sing, and a strong, deep tuneful voice emanated from this slight body, as if she had a total sense of self-in-body while singing. Experiences of being bullied were mastered in games of Ludo, where her generosity in helping me was matched by her aggressive attacks on, and humiliation of, the other two players, in fantasy her two persecutors in school.

Importantly, Katiebell got in touch with anger, aggression, and hate. Ludo could equally be an arena for wiping out my pieces, relishing sending them back to the start. At times, this felt like appropriate rehearsal of the aggression that becomes agency and potency; at others it was deliberately controlling and bloody-minded. The countertransference gave the clue as to which. Waiting while she took turn after turn, manipulating the dice until she threw a six, I could feel distressed for her, but equally there were many times when I felt furious, frustrated, and excluded. This extended to the clinic environment. Katiebell had noticed that, if she lingered on her arrival at the top of the stairs, a teaching group would emerge at the bottom from the room next to mine. Arms across the stairwell from wall to wall, she chose her moment to declare loudly, "I'm coming DOWN!", and watched the adults retreat, leaving her triumphal pathway clear. Endings of sessions could be times of high anxiety, delaying, panic, and opposition. Despite always having warning of the advent of the end of our appointment time, Katiebell often tore around the room, desperately seeking something to take with her, at times shouting and swearing at the top of her voice in order to let any colleagues know how bad a therapist she felt me to be. For most of the therapy, I dreaded such endings. Although practical steps guaranteed some containment (I ensured that the next appointment was always twenty minutes after Katiebell, giving time to focus on the ending, to tidy the room—often in chaos—and for my recovery), I knew that in my countertransference being available to the degree of fury and despair that she felt would mean that I would be drained at the end. Surviving this mattered; resilience in the therapist (who does need ways of becoming available to the next patient) depends greatly on the availability of listening, thinking colleagues, and one wise colleague often came to my room after Katiebell's session offering coffee and a processing ear. All therapists have to survive and still think, even when the thought is about the inability to think.

Her abuse emerged from time to time, as much as she felt she could deal with, and we thought together about Robert's abusing her in the bath—being regularly sent by their mother to bathe Katiebell—and about her body's memories of this, resulting in its trying to do the same to her little brother. She was overwhelmed at the idea that one could explain why she behaved in this way and it led her to develop the concept of her mind as a third person in the room (as I had with her body): "My brain tells me this . . ." became a useful introduction to themes that might have felt infantilising or shameful.

Equally her greater certainty in relationships had led to her telling me that she had a boyfriend, Ruben, who was "Nice. He helps me in class and gives me answers." This was minus any sexual overlay, a very latency relationship. That session continued with "What I did at the weekend", written by Katiebell and illustrated with a drawing of her playing football in the park with another girl. Katiebell explained that the circle in their middles was a belly button. She thought that other people had them, but perhaps they did not. I thought that bodies and differences were in her mind today. "Do you have one as well?" I said that she was thinking about other bodies, about what everybody had and about differences between bodies, especially my grown-up body and her girl's one. "I'm thinking about sex now." I wondered what she might be thinking about, but she drank her cola silently, big-eyed, looking at me. I said that sex had jumped into her mind again with the talk about bodies and belly buttons. She laughed. She shouted, "Freeze!" in a loud, harsh voice. "On you go—you're the teacher—you say 'Freeze!'" I said that the teacher did not seem sure about the muddle about bodies, other bodies, and sexy thoughts. "Go on, *freeze!*" I said that she wanted me to stop thinking about the worrying thoughts about sex, and how these can still pop with surprise into her mind, so she was freezing them out.

This led her to remember her respite carer, and she told me that she did not see her any more. I wondered about that. She said that her Mum hated Irene and had an argument with her. I said that it must be extremely difficult for Katiebell when grown-ups do not get on and make muddles for children. "I hate Mum." There was a pause, a sense of shocking despair. I offered that it was hard to love and hate people, just as she hated me when she thought about breaks and holiday times. She looked at our calendar: we were approaching the Christmas break. "Christmas Day. I couldn't come here on Christmas Day! Ho, ho, ho." I agreed, but added that sometimes we wished we could. She stared and nodded. I said she was thinking about losses today and how angry they can make us feel.

The clinic team supported continuing work with Katiebell until she had achieved puberty, anticipating that the advent of potent sexuality might well be a source of conflict for her.

The last years

During these next three-plus years, Katiebell became, at her own instigation, Kate. Finally, her social worker accommodated her, following grave concern about her mother's neglect and her incapacity to cope with an adolescent whom she, ever more strongly, saw as a sexual rival and with whom she engaged in adolescent fights. Kate moved into a permanent foster home where the foster mother was older, a grandmother, and, because of her age, easier for Kate to love without fear of hurting her mother. Kate also made her transfer to a mainstream secondary school with good special needs staff, such was the improvement in her functioning.

This led to two important sessions.

Kate, almost twelve years old, in foster care with access visits home, played at "parents and children"—several games, all involving the life-size baby doll. The theme was giving birth to a baby, a fairly straightforward and untraumatic event as she played it, followed by "how to grow it properly". She fed and changed it, then settled it carefully to sleep. The mother became ill, had to go into hospital, and the father had the dual worry of being with his wife but also needing to care for the baby. How could these two demands be resolved: does father choose wife or child? That both could be managed was what she sought. In the next session, the extended theme was clearly "How to be a good parent", with the emphasis on which needs of the parents would be forced upon the baby. The baby was dealt with rather roughly as father and mother wanted "to cuddle". Father tried to get mother to put the baby down. "He wants to sex her," said Kate flatly. I wondered what the baby was thinking. Kate looked startled that the baby might have an opinion that could be solicited or inferred. She began to play out both parents trying to have intercourse and the baby being squashed, in the way or otherwise a nuisance. As she looked at me for a reaction, I felt I was being asked to intervene: perhaps the baby would be better in her room, sleeping, and the adults could keep grown-up sexy things just for the grown-ups? She nodded. The baby was settled elsewhere. Darkly, she told me that she hated hearing her parents "sexing". Then, "And I wish they wouldn't go into my bedroom to do it!" This was said very seriously and despairingly. I commented that she had been thinking a lot about what was grown-ups' business and what children were not ready to know about yet. "Yes."

Later, in school, it emerged that Kate had made threats to harm herself and the staff were worried. She entered a group programme of Drama Therapy—which she enjoyed—and in the setting of this could explore issues around adolescence and relationships. One could say that Kate was still articulating distress through the body (the threat had come on the heels of her mother's insisting that Kate should return home, an eventually ineffectual insistence), but at least one could point to her talking of what her feelings were impelling rather than acting it out.

Endings

My informing Kate of my retirement had been delayed for several months by the onset of her menstrual periods. I did not want the potential for her as a woman to become aligned with my perceived rejection in ending. When finally I told Kate that we would be stopping work in nine months' time, she gave an anguished whisper, "But you *know* me!" She tore off to the lavatory. I felt utterly hopeless and inept. On her return, she told me that she had been upset in the toilet. I had a small sense of relief at the maintenance of her capacity for verbalising emotional states. It was not surprising that she began to wonder in subsequent meetings if I had become an abuser, too. (In a sense, I had.) The story of a man who wished to be her boyfriend emerged. He pursued her home. He was her brother. He was everywhere. He was her husband. He would break in—how on earth could she be safe? The tenor was of terrifying fear of rape; thought had become impossible; panic reigned. Words, for several weeks, could not be heard when this theme came into her mind. It felt to me like a film without sound where little was delineated and the depiction was dark and unformed, and Katiebell had lost any expectation of a listener able to hear, think, and begin to process such deep anxiety. Interpretation, when it became possible, was of me as the man, my seduction of her, my abuse of her sense of hope and intimacy, my abandonment of her. The strength of the primitive affect was more than startling; delusion and reality together informed an almost psychotic fantasy. The marked difference was that she could actually attempt to articulate it: somewhere in her mind there *was* the concept of an object who heard even while she thought she could not imagine such a person.

The theme of changing, potent, sexual bodies continued in a later session as she let me know, with her back to me, that she was going shopping for a sports bra with her foster mother. After a pause, she said in a low voice that it was because she was being teased in school. I wondered aloud about this—it sounded as if the other girls might be teasing her about her breasts because theirs had not grown much yet. Maybe they were jealous that she needed a sports bra. Kate slowly turned round and stared at me. A grin appeared and grew wider.

There was much repetition of earlier play—recapitulation is quite usual in child work. This included, "Do you remember when I did singing?" She leapt on to the couch to sing, as she had when a lightweight seven-year-old. The leg of the elderly couch gave way. My countertransference feelings were mainly bound up with the couch. "Do you remember when . . .?" frequently appears in normal parent–child interaction and is part of the process of internalising a sense of going-on-being. There was more work on the intrusion of her memory. "I'm thinking the S word again!" 'And I notice that you can think about it and not have to do something!' She nodded seriously, "Yes, I don't *do* things any more."

In one session, she noticed my hands. A finger came out and almost prodded them but drew back—the loss of elasticity in the skin was evident and she knew of my retirement. "Yuck! You're OLD!" It was as if, in this moment, she realised that I had changed—not into an abuser, but simply old. This was a new adaptation and an appropriate use of aggression in separation. It allowed her distance, while dealing a small blow to my narcissism.

Endings of sessions, while still fraught, became different in two ways. First, Kate had become able to articulate her feelings of letdown and anger, along with her occasional wish to STOP NOW (shouted at me) as a way of dealing with the pain of ending. She no longer resorted to the frantic use of her body, rushing around and hiding. In addition, she developed a ritual for ascending the stairs at the end, the two of us side by side like a three-legged race, and Kate stretching over two, then three, then four and more steps with each pace. It was a laborious ascent that allowed her the physical contact of leaning on my arm as she demonstrated her physical growth and capacities and allowed her to triumph over me as she became the competent one. Colleagues would often encounter this somewhat bizarre sight and would wait until we made it to the top.

Towards the end, during one session, she walked slowly up to the door. My raincoat hung on the hook. There was a long mirror on the wall to the left of it. She reached out—again slowly—as if ready to comply with any prohibition. I watched, not feeling any aggression in this move. She put on the coat. It fitted her perfectly at age 14½. She struggled to fasten the belt but persisted—her own containment—and looked in the mirror. We both felt great sadness. I found myself unable to speak, tears in my eyes. When I could find words, I commented that she was trying out being me and having me wrapped around her in that way; perhaps, though, we both would miss each other but have each other inside our minds.

Conclusion

Technically, the work could be said to have depended mainly on an approach that owed much to Anna Freud and to Winnicott. One can see the adoption of a very Winnicottian position, beginning with the mother who survives the infant's aggression and continuing to the resilient but containing environment he describes especially in work with delinquents. The parallels between the process of therapy and the process of the good enough developmental experience are evident. Within this, one also needs access to the thinking of Anna Freud and her successors on the development of the ego ("First you must build the house before you can throw anyone out of it" is Anna Freud's reference to the need for ego structuring in order later to be able to address a mature enough ego in the therapeutic process). And, of course, both these theoretical clinicians emphasise the necessity of the defences, however apparently maladaptive, and the need to acknowledge and evince curiosity about them rather than immediately to confront.

It is also in the writings of Anna Freud and Winnicott that one finds such an emphasis on the adaptation of psychoanalysis that is psychoanalytic child psychotherapy. The capacity to be responsive to the child—and to develop themes at the child's pace—starts with the in-tune, good-enough mother: Katiebell could gradually risk engaging with curiosity and learnt that she could be met and "known" in this process. Anna Freud equally allows a freedom of therapeutic interaction, an absence of any absolute sense of "right" and "correct" approach that can only be freeing for the therapist: "There is no absolute psychoanalytic technique for use with children, but rather a set of analytic principles which have to be adapted to specific cases" (Sandler, Kennedy, & Tyson, 1980, p. 199).

Perhaps the only argument with Miss Freud at this point would be to note that technique is not "adapted *to*" specific children; rather, it is created in the dyad, in the therapist–child relationship, in the trans-formational space between, while drawing its import from the under-standing that psychoanalysis brings.

This freeing the therapist from institutionalised positions is, for me, as a child psychotherapist, the most evident sign of an Independent: "The key to an understanding of the Independents is their avowed openness to learning from any psychoanalytical theories" (Rayner, 1991, p. 4).

Or, like Winnicott, "I aim to be myself and to behave myself" (Winnicott, 1962, p. 166).

Writing papers, it must be acknowledged, is as much for the writer as it is for one's colleagues, or, indeed, the patients on whom one is reflecting. Kate has been often in my mind. She is left with many issues that will cause struggles for her and probably necessitate the life-long involvement of a wider network. Whether one thinks a mature sexuality will ever be available to her is an open question. To have reached some sense of "an in-dwelling of psyche in soma" and "going-on-being" is an achievement and, perhaps, merely the foundation.

References

Alvarez, A. (1988). Beyond the unpleasure principle: some pre-conditions for thinking through play. *Journal of Child Psychotherapy*, 14(2): 1–13.

Bollas, C. (1987). *The Shadow of the Object: Psychoanalysis of the Unthought Known*. London: Free Association Books.

Campbell, D. (1994). Breaching the shame shield: thoughts on the assessment of adolescent child sexual abusers. *Journal of Child Psychotherapy*, 20(3): 309–326.

Dio Bleichmar, E. (1995). The secret in the constitution of female sexuality: the effects of the adult's sexual look upon the subjectivity of the girl *Journal of Clinical Psychoanalysis*, 4(3): 331–342.

Fairbairn, W. R. (1952). *Psychoanalytic Studies of the Personality*. London: Routledge & Kegan Paul.

Gaddini, E. (1980). Notes on the mind–body question. In: A. Limentani (Ed.), *A Psychoanalytic Theory of Infantile Experience: Conceptual and Clinical Reflections*. London: Tavistock/Routledge, 1992.

Glasser, M. (1996). Aggression and sadism in the perversions. In: I Rosen (Ed.) *Sexual Deviation* (3rd edn) (pp. 279–299). Oxford: Oxford University Press.

Grand, S., & Alpert, J. (1993). The core trauma of incest: an object relations view. *Professional Psychology: Research and Practice*, 24(3): 330–334.

Hopkins, J. (1996). From baby games to let's pretend. *Journal of the British Association of Psychotherapists*, 1(2): 20–27.

Hurry, A. (1998). *Psychoanalysis and Developmental Therapy*. London: Karnac.

Khan, M. M. R. (1963). The concept of cumulative trauma. In: *The Privacy of the Self: Papers on Psychoanalytic Theory and Technique* (pp. 42–58). New York: International Universities Press, 1974.

Klockars, L., & Sirola, R. (2001). The mother–daughter love affair across the generations. *Psychoanalytic Study of the Child, 56*: 219–237.

Krueger, D. W. (2001). Body self: development, psychopathologies and psychoanalytic significance. *The Psychoanalytic Study of the Child, 56*: 238–259.

Laufer, E. (1991). Body image, sexuality and the psychotic core. *International Journal of Psychoanalysis, 72*(1): 63–71.

Rayner, E. (1991). *The Independent Mind in British Psychoanalysis*. London: Free Association Books.

Sandler, J., Kennedy, H., & Tyson, R. (1980). *The Technique of Child Psychoanalysis: Discussions with Anna Freud*. London: Hogarth Press.

Welldon, E. (1988). *Mother, Madonna, Whore: The Idealisation and Denigration of Motherhood*. London: Free Association Books.

Winnicott, D. W. (1945). Primitive emotional development. In *Through Paediatrics to Psychoanalysis* (pp. 145–156). London: Hogarth Press, 1975.

Winnicott, D. W. (1947). Hate in the counter-transference. *Through Paediatrics to Psychoanalysis* (pp. 194–203). London: Hogarth Press, 1975.

Winnicott, D. W. (1949). Mind and its relation to the psyche-soma. In: *Through Paediatrics to Psychoanalysis* (pp. 243–254). London: Hogarth Press, 1975.

Winnicott, D. W. (1962). The aims of psychoanalytical treatment. In: *The Maturational Processes and the Facilitating Environment* (pp. 166–170). London: Hogarth Press, 1965.

Winnicott, D. W. (1967). Mirror-role of mother and family in child development. In: *Playing and Reality* (pp. 111–118). London: Tavistock, 1971.

Winnicott, D. W. (1972). Basis for self in body. *International Journal of Child Psychotherapy, 1*(1): 7–16.

Wright, K. (1991). *Vision and Separation: Between Mother and Baby*. London: Free Association Books.

CHAPTER FIFTEEN

A severe form of breakdown in communication in the psychoanalysis of an ill adolescent

Roger Kennedy

Introduction

Five-times-weekly psychoanalysis of the severely suicidal or psychotic adolescent is difficult and demanding for the patient and the analyst, both of whom require a fair amount of motivation in order to keep going through the many difficult patches. There are bound to be periods in which the patient will feel acutely suicidal, will feel strongly like opting out of the analysis, will make attacks on the setting, or will bring profound difficulties in communicating and relating for understanding. The analyst, in turn, might, not infrequently, feel tempted to relinquish his or her role, to attempt to do something rather than continue to analyse, or might feel hopeless and alone with an unbearable responsibility.

Part of the strain for the analyst might be that there often seems to be an expectation in psychoanalytic treatment that the analyst should always be "in touch" with the analysand in a number of different ways. Put simply, one could say that the analyst's "in touchness" consists of three interlocking elements: an appropriate physical setting, adequate intellectual understanding, and selective emotional responsiveness. While I am not denying the central importance of being in touch with the patient as far as possible, I think that one can say that there are often moments, particularly in the psychoanalysis of psychotic and borderline psychotic subjects, when there are fairly major breakdowns in communication between analyst and analysand. Such moments are perhaps more sustained and serious in those subjects with whom I am particularly concerned in this paper, who have experienced a major interference in functioning, such as a suicide attempt or a serious psychotic breakdown. In this latter group, the three elements of the analyst's in-touchness might be interfered with, so that the setting might no longer be safe, the analyst's intellectual grasp of the analysis might be severely compromised, and/or his emotional awareness blunted. I wish to suggest that there are times when such breakdowns in communication, which threaten the analyst's in-touchness, are useful, even though, at the time of their occurrence, they may be distressing, bewildering, and frustrating for both analyst and analysand.

The purpose of this paper is to describe, with clinical material, what I have called, for convenience, a "core" breakdown in communication in the ill adolescent. I hope that some of the points I make might also be applicable to the analysis of ill adults. In the discussion, I shall distinguish, with references to the literature, this form of breakdown of communication from other, rather less serious, forms of communication problem.

The "core" breakdown in communication

In this rather loose category, I include those who have experienced a real breakdown in mental functioning, such as a severe suicide attempt or one or more psychotic episodes in which the patient loses touch with the real world, or has delusional ideas about themselves, their body, or others. I think that, in this group, a major breakdown in communication is both significant and inevitable at some point in the analysis. It cannot be avoided, however well one analyses, and one could also argue that, unless such difficulties are brought right into the treatment, the patient's pathology will not be significantly shifted. Such a breakdown might be experienced by the analyst in the following way.

Over days, weeks. or even months, there appears to be endless repetition, little sense of the analysis going anywhere, sometimes with unproductive silences, and with a constant strain on the analyst's stamina. A predominant feeling in the analyst, though, strangely, not always in the patient, is of feeling out of touch, or of having only fleeting moments in touch, with the patient. The sessions appear to be dead, and the analyst does not know what is going on, but it is a most uncomfortable and worrying uncertainty. Dreaming might take place, but one begins to doubt its significance and usefulness. The recounting of the dream might itself have an unreal quality, or the patients might be doing all the interpreting themselves, as if they thought they were the analyst; that is, the dream itself and/or the recounting of it to the analyst might disguise a psychotic wish to live in the mind of the analyst.

However much the analyst might persuade him or herself that these phenomena are inevitable, given the degree of the patient's pathology, he or she is, none the less, apparently far from understanding them. The analyst might experience enormous pressure to act, to change the setting, give up the analysis, suggest a termination date, or even persuade themselves that these phenomena are merely the result of the universal death drive and are to be permanently lived with. Such a clinical situation could be understood as the result of the impact on the analyst of the analysand's affects and projections. But I think it is also indicative of a repetition of an essential "core" breakdown of functioning, and the bringing of the more psychotic, or, at any rate, ill, aspects of the subject's personality for understanding. One could use the vague term "breakdown" to cover what Winnicott (1974) described as the "unthinkable state of affairs that underlies the defensive organization". It is, as he thought, a difficult term to define. It seems to involve both external signs that something is very wrong, and a view of the subject's inner experience of bewilderment and chaos. Winnicott also wrote of the fear of breakdown that has already been experienced; while here I am emphasising the reality of the contemporary breakdown. He also wrote of the need for some subjects to experience primitive feelings associated with fear of breakdown, such as emptiness or loss of a sense of reality. Developing this notion, one could say that the clinical phenomena I have outlined cannot be eliminated, however well one analyses, however much transference and countertransference issues are examined, however sensitive the analyst. Indeed, there might even be a danger in being too understanding of the dynamics of the breakdown in communication at the point in the analysis when it first arises, for it might not then be experienced as a phenomenon to be understood. That is, there might be a need for the breakdown to be felt over a longish period by the analyst before it can be made tolerable to the analysand by a slow process of analysis.

The analysis of such ill people in adolescence poses particular clinical problems. While, in common with ill adults, they might be hard to reach, there is, perhaps, more hope of a favourable outcome. At least, in adolescence, there are the additional biological and social forces which are making the subject detach from the parents. Incestuous fantasies are also more readily available, and the adolescent is engaged in an active struggle around developing sexuality and the changing of his or her immature body into a mature sexual body; all of which makes the analytic relationship both crucial to the adolescent's future life and, potentially, very engaging. With the psychotic adolescent, one sees encapsulated a desperate struggle to achieve separation and independence, but one also sees the overwhelming guilt and sense of persecution when this normal developmental task cannot be successfully negotiated. I would see the breakdown of functioning at adolescence as essentially a developmental breakdown, as described by Laufer and Laufer (1984):

> We define developmental breakdown in adolescence as the unconscious rejection of the sexual body and an accompanying feeling of being passive in the face of demands coming from one's own body, with the result that one's genitals are ignored or disowned or, in the more severe cases, the feeling that they are different from what one wanted them to be. It is a breakdown in the process of integrating the physically mature body image into the representation of oneself. Whatever the actual disorder, the specific interference in the developmental process that can be defined as adolescent pathology is contained in the adolescent's distorted view of and relationship to his body. (pp. 22–23)

I would add to this description the need to consider the infantile and childhood precursors of the adolescent breakdown which lay the ground for future disorder, as I shall indicate in the following clinical material.

Clinical material

Introduction

I shall try to highlight the core breakdown in communication in the following clinical material, taken from the psychoanalysis of a self-mutilating adolescent. The analysis has been undertaken at the Centre for Research into Adolescent Breakdown. My concept of a core breakdown arises both from my own case and also from observation of some of the other cases in our research scheme. I noticed that at a certain point in the analysis, several cases appeared to become apparently repetitive, with the same kind of material often being produced, while the analyst felt increasingly frustrated and sometimes tempted to "do" something active about the situation.

"Simon" came into analysis at the age of seventeen, following a suicide attempt. While feeling hopeless and depressed, he had gone to a park and cut his wrists with a razor blade, with the intention of severing his arteries. He reported later that the pain of the cut stopped him. He had made an earlier attempt to cut an artery a year previously. The first overt sign of disturbance had been at puberty at the age of thirteen, when he had also probably attempted suicide, by suffocation in a plastic bag. Before his analysis, he cut himself superficially on his chest, abdomen, arms, and legs. As well as feeling generally depressed, he felt sexually and physically inadequate, particularly following a rejection by a girl he liked, and he was greatly troubled by sexual feelings and fantasies. Related to his sexual anxieties, Simon described intense self-hatred, particularly a hatred of and wish to disown his body, which he felt was too feminine and not masculine enough. He wished at times he could have another body, highlighting the kind of disturbance described above by Laufer and Laufer. However, his desires were never as extreme as to make him wish to want a sex change, as some adolescents might.

Simon felt, during the time he was suicidal, that the barrier between himself and the world was too thin, as if it would not hold, and that this was linked to his wish to cut his skin. He also felt at times that everything was a fairyland, that is, unreal, and that he felt himself inadequate and separated from others, from those with normal sexuality and a normal life, by a glass barrier. He experienced periods of being overwhelmed with aggressive fantasies towards girls: for example, of wanting to rape them violently. Perhaps related to these fantasies, he had some homosexual experiences before analysis, which included oral and mutual masturbation, though apparently not anal penetration, which, in the experience of the Brent Centre, is of more serious prognostic significance with regard to the adolescent's future sexual orientation. Simon's adolescent "rebellious" side was in evidence in the first year or so of the analysis in the way that he dressed garishly and aggressively, with various violent punk slogans daubed all over his clothes, as well as in a preoccupation with far left politics and drugs.

Simon is from a middle-class background. His father had severe alcohol problems when Simon was a child, and he remains a degraded figure in the family. The mother appears more forceful, but still retains an unrealistic attitude towards Simon: for example, she still believes he is going to grow much taller. Neither parent has supported the analysis; they feel that he will simply "grow out" of his problems, and have, unfortunately, chosen to ignore the seriousness of the suicide attempts and the self-mutilation. There is an interesting story about his mother's pregnancy with him, which came up earlier in the analysis as an aside, but whose significance became clearer only later in the analysis, when communication seemed "dead". It was said that his mother had a miscarriage while pregnant with him, yet the pregnancy continued in spite of the expulsion of an umbilical cord: that is, a twin was aborted.

To my surprise, the analysis began smoothly, and Simon developed a fairly strong therapeutic alliance. He usually arrived on time and began to feel that the analysis was the most crucial experience of his life. But after a few months, he began to feel constantly tempted to drop out. He felt that interpretations were aimed at brainwashing him and robbed him of his individuality. He spent many sessions trying to engage me, if not batter me, with a far left extreme political discourse rather than a personal discourse. My attitude to the intensity with which he held his beliefs, as he felt, in opposition to psychoanalysis, was very much coloured by the fact that he was an adolescent and needed to experiment with ideologies. I also tended to respect the defensive aspect of his politics and tried to see what one could find in it that was personal to him. More worryingly with regard to his mental stability, he tended to produce what I called "propaganda for mindlessness", in which psychedelic drug experiences, particularly at weekends, were used repeatedly to eliminate any feelings of separation and dependency. There was, at that time, little sense that he had an awareness of the loss of an object; when I was not in his presence, I was almost completely absent from his mind. It seemed at such times that he was taken over by an idealised identification with a destructive and drunken father, as well as taken over by a mother whom he felt was driving him mad and whom he could not limit.

There was considerable material in the sessions, but quite often I had the feeling that, though he was talking about himself, he was trying to slip out of my reach, yet he also wished me to pursue him. He seemed to be attempting to seduce me into colluding with him: for example, by wishing me to endorse his drug abuse, or agree that homosexual feelings or acts were no problem, or ignore his suicidal impulses. I had to keep reminding myself of the seriousness of his difficulties, particularly around holiday times, as he was a suicide risk for at least the first eighteen months of treatment. I had the impression that as soon as I became a relatively non-persecuting father in the transference, Simon would quickly react by cutting off what he was saying, or would turn to drugs or alcohol outside the sessions, which I think could be understood as having to ward off an awareness of the pre-Oedipal mother. I would suggest that such quick reactions to the transference changes mean having to pay constant attention in a vigilant way to what happens between sessions and from session to session, which one would not normally do with less ill patients.

Core breakdown

As the analysis continued, Simon's more "florid" difficulties appeared to lessen; he did not cut himself, became less acutely suicidal, stopped turning to drugs, and sought some employment. In the first year or so of the analysis, he had short relationships with girls, but they, like him, attacked their bodies in various ways, for example, through drug abuse, repeated abortions, or anorexia nervosa. Subsequently, he formed a relationship that has lasted some years with a somewhat deprived but apparently caring young woman. The atmosphere of the sessions became less of a fight about brainwashing and instead rather more concerned with his inner world.

However, while he was making some moves in the outside world, the analysis began to become increasingly bogged down, an experience common to the analyses of several disturbed adolescents in analysis under the Centre for Research into Adolescent Breakdown. Simon often would not talk, justifying his silences by expressing a wish to overturn any progress, as well as wanting to make me powerless and so paralyse me. He would produce dreams, many of which seemed significant, but he would tend to analyse them himself. The dreams in themselves became a barrier to communication as much as a source of unconscious material. The sessions became increasingly boring and confusing, which could be seen, given his history, as a repetition in the transference of a broken-down father and a confused mother. The move towards heterosexuality with his girlfriend triggered with me a stonewalling attitude, of which he was hardly conscious. He was, however, aware of a dominant wish to lose his individuality, to be almost submerged in me, or dependent on me, "like a leech", as he put it.

In spite of my interpretations, he might endlessly ruminate in a tedious way about things he should or should not do, which seemed to take all the meaning out of things, so much so that I was constantly losing the thread of the communications. This was in contrast to the earlier part of the analysis, when I felt that, in spite of the enormous difficulties, such as having to face the possible risk of suicide or a severe psychotic breakdown, I was, by and large, in touch with what was going on. Simon said that he was like a child who was intent on not budging or moving an inch. He yearned for me to be God-like, to solve his problems, take away his pain, get him a job, and so on.

During a summer break, I took some time to think about what had been happening. I was aware that the other analysts in the research programme had been having somewhat similar experiences. In retrospect, I felt that I had been exposed to a relentless attempt to deaden me, and that it might be important to clarify this process. In addition, I had a fruitful consultation with a senior analyst, something which seems to be necessary on occasions in the treatment of such ill people, and which in this case helped the treatment to move along.

My deadness seemed to be an important phenomenon, as it dominated the sessions from my point of view, and contrasted with the animation I experienced earlier in the analysis. It was as if Simon felt that he could not live without deadening or even destroying the other, and that this might help to account for his terror of living and of growing through adolescence into adulthood. What happened to the analysis at this time is difficult to summarise, as it took several months of slow work to alter the picture. However, there was some immediate relief when I took up his fear that his leaving home and seeking some independence would result in his parents collapsing into a severe depression, and that communication between people contained the threat of death. The boredom of many of the sessions corresponded to how Simon kept his potency and intelligence away from the sessions, displaying them only in dreams. I began to realise that I had often experienced a fight to stay alive in the sessions, while all my "nourishment" was being taken away by some sadistic process.

The next theme that seemed to make an impact on him was that he was living at a price, that he could only just about bear being alive to his body and to others, that too much life was unbearable. The atmosphere of the sessions began to change. In part, this might have been due to my own renewed confidence in the analytic process that had perhaps been compromised by the relentless deadening, but it was also, I believe, because we began to approach the heart of his pathology. I do not think that my renewed confidence could have sustained any significant or long-lasting change in him. One could say that, once he was fully established in the analysis, and also in a long-term relationship with a girl, as well as in employment, his "core" disturbance, around which his symptoms had crystallised, was repeated in the transference.

It was then that the piece of history about his having survived a dead twin seemed to make sense. It appeared that I had become, in the transference, the dead twin, or the mother preoccupied by the dead twin. Rather to my surprise, Simon reacted with relief to this reconstruction, both immediately in one session and subsequent to it. I had imagined that he might not know what I was talking about, but, on the contrary, it seemed to make sense to him in a way that made one feel it had the ring of truth about it. It might have helped to see the themes I have described at an earlier stage, but then the point I am making is that I had to experience the deadness for it to be a clinical phenomenon pressing to be understood. In addition, it is possible that Simon would not have been able to make sense of the reconstruction without having gone through with me the experience of the period of core breakdown. I had taken up, on previous occasions, his murderousness and violence—one could hardly ignore it in view of the attacks on his body through cutting and drug taking, his attraction to violent politics, and the "punk" way he used to dress early on in the analysis—but I had not understood the importance of the dead twin material and neither had it been picked up by discussions at the Brent Centre.

I must emphasise that I am not assigning all his pathology to his early history, but that its emergence in the transference marked an important moment in the analysis. I should also clarify that I am not saying that the patient remembered the dead twin, though its significance rang many bells for him, or that an infant can remember such an event. It is possible that the latter is the case, but I leave the question open. It is more likely that the fact of the aborted twin became an integral part of the family's fantasy life, shaping and distorting their relationships. The change that took place in the analysis was, then, due to a complex mixture of a number of elements: my own understanding had been increased, it was possible to face his deadening within the transference in a way that made sense to him and without him having to deny it or deaden the insight, and it was possible to make what seemed a relevant and emotionally significant reconstruction of his history. All these elements added together brought a sense of relief to both of us and enabled the analysis to progress, although I must emphasise that the analysis remained difficult and, at times, stressful for both of us.

I will present material from two sessions, separated by a few months, both of which contain a dream, in order to convey a feeling of what happened subsequent to the breakdown of communication. In a session after a job interview, Simon began with a vivid dream, which horrified him.

> He was standing outside his parents' house, talking to a three-foot-tall dwarf with incredibly well-developed muscles. As he talked to him, the dwarf shrank, becoming smaller and smaller, until he was six to seven inches high, like some sort of plastic doll, but still with incredible muscles, which the dwarf wanted Simon to inspect. The dwarf kept on talking and all his flesh disappeared, and he ended up as just a few bones which were not human but the remains of someone's dinner, the bones from a lamb chop.

> He thought that the dwarf was a parody of himself—weight-lifting muscles on a small body. I took up how he felt dwarfed by me and belittled. This led on to him saying that I was the dwarf of the dream. He

admired my superiority, but I was made smaller and smaller into a plastic doll, and then I was just like the remains of the dinner, nothing much left at all. I took up his (oral) devouring quality, how he stripped the food he had from me, leaving him feeling empty and only left with the scraps. This uncovered his horrifying wish to devour me, as he put it, in order to get close to me; as well as his fear that I would want to keep him with me and not let him go and get jobs and separate from me; as if I wanted him for me, so that he remain a dwarfed man with a small penis, "an adult trapped in a child-size body", as he put it.

In this frightening world, his fantasy was that I could only survive because of my "good muscles", but he then ate me up, which made him feel disgust and horror. If he took nourishment from me, it was only at the cost of survival. The more he took from the analytic feed, the smaller I became. The plastic doll might have been a reference to the dead girl twin, with whom he was identified in his presenting symptom of self-mutilation. There was also the fear of having a live communication with me. The moment he felt alive in the session, or that I was alive, he tended to cut off the discourse.

Between this session and the next one I shall summarise, Simon changed his job from one in which he was isolated from people to one which involved considerable contact with them. This seemed to parallel an impression I had that he felt rather better, less cut off, less guilt ridden and anxious about communicating. He also survived a break from the analysis rather better than usual, in that he did not have to increase his alcohol consumption dangerously or smoke heavily, as he would usually do.

He began this session with another dream.

He was at his previous [isolated] job. The supervisor he didn't like was in the wrong office. A girl made a mistake, which Simon tried to cover up in order to protect her. He was then at a market stall with a male friend. Some Indian bread turned out to be cake. His friend and he were both smartly dressed and walking across a ploughed field. They were worried about getting their clothes covered in mud.

His associations were that all the images in the dream were somehow inappropriate—the wrong office, the mistake, the wrong food, the wrong clothes. He wondered if he were saying something about here. After a pause, he thought there was something about being blamed for something he did not do, by someone he hated, like the supervisor, who was a bully.

There was a feeling of guilt. The clothes made him feel out of place . . . there was shit on them. Then he recalled that he used to have a strong fear of eating in front of people that had got better recently . . . I then made an interpretation based on both the dream and his associations. I took up the feeling of a lack of fit with me and how he seemed to be feeling guilty and responsible for the lack of fit, as in the mistakes in the dream. He replied by saying that this was a feeling he always carried with him, not fitting in, being different . . . he was to blame for it all. The thing about his clothes not being right also referred to the feeling about his body not being right, which he used to experience a lot. He wondered why he should have difficulty about eating in public. Was it the same?

I was thinking at this time about some recent sessions in which he had brought up quite primitive fears of eating up his mother's goodness, and so I felt fairly confident about bringing up that he might be expressing a fear of showing his aggressiveness in public, and that eating food was somehow linked to eating up his mother's food, and I also at some point linked this with a fear that he was responsible for the death of his twin. He did not, as he might have, greet this latter interpretation with scepticism; instead it reminded him that his mother had often expressed to him, as a child, that she would have liked another child after him. This led to his fear that he had destroyed her babies, and, strangely, he recalled that for years he had hated milk and dairy products. For example, he never took milk in tea or coffee and always hated cheese, the smell of which made him feel sick. He admitted with much hesitation that the eating up of his twin was a lurking fantasy. He blamed himself for his mother not having more children. He was her "cute little boy", which made him grow up feeling like a selfish little monster.

He returned spontaneously to the dream and the sense of inappropriateness. The friend with him always had smart clothes in reality, and Simon had wondered whether or not he were gay, because he came across as effeminate and ambiguous sexually. It made him think that while he himself was a child, it was almost like being a girl. I brought him back to the male supervisor in the dream, and also made some reference to his father. Simon said that this man was actually a homosexual. He was, then, not a good father who could help, or "not a real man", as he put it. And the session ended.

In the following session, Simon described what he had felt about this session, which I thought was quite useful. He said he had felt freer than usual, that usually he feels in a kind of straitjacket when he has to talk about one thing at a time and cannot see the links between things: that he often feels as if he is undergoing an exam, or he is not free, or cannot express himself as "me". But this time he felt he could talk about himself without those feelings, he was less cut off, and less anxious. I certainly thought that he was beginning to work through the issue of separation and independence, the right he had to live, and the dreadful feeling of being responsible for killing off both his twin and his mother's other babies. The new job, which gave him access to people, seemed a concrete manifestation of some inner change.

Discussion

As I suggested in the introduction, it might be useful to distinguish various kinds of breakdown in communication in order to highlight the kind of problem that I have made the theme of the chapter. I should say that one or more of the following kinds of breakdown in communication are bound to arise at various points of an analysis. I also make no claim for exhaustiveness and am merely offering this typology for convenience.

Analysand's resistance

Some breakdowns in communication are usually of short duration, as is the case when the analysand's free associations fail due to a resistance, including a transference resistance. Freud wrote that, at these moments, the associations really cease and are not merely being kept back owing to ordinary feelings of unpleasure.

> . . . if a patient's free associations fail the stoppage can invariably be removed by an assurance that he is being dominated at the moment by an association which is concerned with the doctor himself or with something connected with him. As soon as the explanation is given, the stoppage is removed, or the situation changed from one in which the associations fail into one in which they are being kept back. (1912, p. 104).

I think that the implication of this quotation is that these kinds of breakdown in communication are transient and fairly easily dealt with. Whether or not we would now consider that giving an assurance of the type indicated invariably leads to a freeing of communication is, perhaps, debatable. What seems to be the point is that one's first line of approach is often to think of the breakdown as a resistance. If the breakdown persists for longer, then one might have to reconsider what is going on in the session.

Negative therapeutic reaction

This notion seems to designate a particular clinical phenomenon where an improvement or temporary suspension of symptoms produces in the analysand an exacerbation of their pathology, resistance, or hostility: "the need for illness has got the upper hand . . . over the desire for recovery" (Freud, 1923b, p. 49). Freud considered that the phenomenon was the expression of an unconscious sense of guilt. In Kleinian theory, the phenomenon seems to be the result of an exacerbation of envy of therapeutic progress. Joseph (1982) has described what she calls "addiction to near death" in a small group of patients. They often show a strong negative therapeutic reaction, but this is only part of a broader and more insidious picture. There is a powerful addiction to masochism, and a particular way of communicating this to the analyst.

Some kinds of sado-masochistic transferences might incur repeated negative therapeutic reactions. The sadistic part of the patient cannot tolerate any good being sustained.

Phenomena associated with the negative therapeutic reaction seem to be fairly long-lasting and also do imply that there has to be some kind of improvement in the first place. In the ill adolescent, it is difficult to be certain of any major positive change. One could perhaps describe briefer moments of "undoing" the analytic work, from day to day, or week to week; this is not quite a negative therapeutic reaction, but is, perhaps, related to it.

The analyst's resistance

This category basically describes breakdowns of communication that are to be avoided. Rosenfeld (1987) describes in meticulous detail the kinds of difficulties that the analyst can get into when treating psychotic subjects, and which result in a negative "impasse" or treatment failure. Essentially, he is referring to a kind of impasse in which "severe negative reactions to analysis do not follow real progress and where it would not, therefore, be appropriate to speak of negative feelings being due to envy of therapeutic progress" (Rosenfeld, 1987, p. 139).

He felt that the source of such difficulties often arose in the analyst. They could be due to constantly vague or badly timed interpretations, rigidity, or inflexibility, and above all to unrecognised difficulties in the analyst's countertransference. He thought it important to distinguish between a subject communicating clearly with symbolic language and the confused way of talking of a psychotic subject who has lost their way in the analysis. He writes,

> Most psychotic subjects project their feelings and anxieties very intensely into the analyst when they verbally or non-verbally communicate. This generally helps the analyst to understand better. But if the analyst cannot cope with the patient's projections, he tends to get out of touch. (ibid., p. 51)

Klauber (1981) implied that some kinds of breakdown in communication follow from a lack of sympathy between patient and analyst. This could be a result of inevitable differences in personality, or the analyst failing to recognise his or her unconscious need for sympathy with and from the patient, or, alternatively, that he pitches all his interpretations at one level. Thus, Klauber, like Rosenfeld, is warning analysts not to be too rigid or inflexible in their approach.

Particular kinds of transference

There are particular kinds of transference that run the risk of creating breakdowns in communication between analyst and analysand. For example, with the kind of person who might need the analyst to be a "parent who was not able to tune accurately into his feelings, who was continually concerned with his or her sense of failure or inability to cope, or who was continually criticizing or belittling him" (King, 1978, p. 331).

I myself (Kennedy, 1984) have described that some adult analysands have difficulty with what I have called the "dual aspect" of the transference, the capacity to see the analyst as simultaneously the receiver of the analysand's projections and as different from these projections. Such subjects have difficulty in understanding and tolerating the regressive aspects of the transference experience.

I have also outlined how difficult it might be for the highly disturbed perverse subject to take the step from being in the middle of a perverse transference to being aware, through words, of the perverse relationship to the analyst, and how this could put great strain on the analyst's capacity to think and remain unconfused (Kennedy, 1987).

I have also suggested (Kennedy, 1989) that there is a particular kind of "split transference", in which, to put it simply, the internal parents are not united and are constantly and strongly divided. This internal splitting makes the analysis of such subjects particularly tricky, as they might unconsciously use the split transference to ward off interpretations. The moment one gets close to one aspect of the transference, another aspect is used to cut off any work, and so must be simultaneously addressed.

Finally, there might be breakdowns in communication related to a transference of a psychotic parent who, one could say, never had the analysand in mind, and where there have been major breakdowns in early care.

"Core" breakdown in communication

I have already described the observations that led me to put forward the notion of a core breakdown of communication. Fundamentally, I am describing a transference phenomenon, with possibly multiple origins from early childhood right through to puberty and later adolescence. It is possible that such a phenomenon arises in a definite form only when the personality structure is beginning to become fixed, from about mid-adolescence onwards. I have emphasised that the breakdown needs to be tolerated by the analyst, in the face of temptations to turn to what one could call "false" solutions, such as trying unusual analytic technique or interventions. Part of the origin of the phenomenon could be attributed to primitive areas of the psyche on the lines described both by Winnicott, in his paper "Fear of breakdown" (1974), and also by Balint, in his book *The Basic Fault* (1968). Balint's concept of the basic fault refers to a pre-Oedipal level of the mind, which involves an exclusively two-person relationship. While the patient functions at this level, the analyst might fail to be in touch with the patient, who might then experience feelings of emptiness and deadness. My notion of a core breakdown does not necessarily refer only to such primitive levels of functioning. Indeed, there is no evidence that Simon or the other adolescents in the research were regressed at the point of core breakdown. On the contrary, Simon, for example, was progressing well in the outside world. Presumably, however, this might have allowed him to bring more primitive material to my attention. I am, anyway, calling attention to an apparent interruption in the analytic process, which needs to be worked through. I am also suggesting that the way in which the analyst might be forced to be out of touch with the patient is, in itself, significant. In addition, I am not suggesting that the analyst encourage regression in order to heal the primitive areas of the psyche, though there could be times when this is important. Instead, I am suggesting that, like it or not, the analyst might find himself out of touch when he treats such ill patients, and might mistakenly wish to do something unusual about this. Presumably, at such times, the patient communicates a quality of despair and hopelessness that appears to demand action by someone. The analyst might then feel that his presence in itself is not enough. But it is possible that he might then, if unusual interventions are attempted, miss an opportunity really to grasp the significance of this moment in the analysis and this might then merely repeat some "basic fault" in the patient's early history.

Returning, in summary, to Simon's analysis, it seems to underline a difficult and common dilemma: how to communicate with someone who has great problems in communication. How, one may ask, can one communicate with the primitive, psychotic-like areas, represented, in his case, by the dead twin? That is, putting it metaphorically, how can one get in touch with a dead twin who has been aborted and cannot speak? Simon's discourse seemed to turn round and round this essential dilemma, and also the cost of attempting to communicate—the cost of sanity. The analyst has to bear the psychotic cutting off of emotions, in Simon's case, the dead transference. This transference was composed of several dead figures, not only the dead twin, but also the mother deadened to Simon's needs, her dead babies, and the father anaesthetised by alcohol to Simon's emotions.

In my summary of different kinds of breakdown in communication, I made the point that some kinds of breakdown are inevitable, while others, mainly due to the analyst's resistance, are to be avoided. The point I wish to make is that with the ill adolescent, and, perhaps, the ill adult, the core pathology needs to be experienced in the transference for treatment to be effective, and that the way that this could occur is via a breakdown of communication of the type I have outlined. Rather than the periods of deadness and difficulty being seen as an absence of analytic work, they might, in fact, be indicative of the subject's attempt to work through something, or, at the very least, to bring, unconsciously, to the analyst's attention some important areas that need to be addressed. Other, less ill subjects might be able to do this in a less disordered fashion. There might be many resistances, even the occasional severe breakdown in communication, but not the all-pervasive disturbance in communication. The treatment of the ill adolescent of the kind I have described is very demanding and difficult, for the analyst's own capacity to stay alive and sane is constantly being challenged.

Acknowledgements

My thanks to Dr M. Laufer, the Director of the Research into Adolescent Breakdown, for support and encouragement in the writing of this paper, to my colleagues at the Centre for the help they have provided for the treatment of "Simon", and to Dr D. Pines for her insightful consultations.

References

Balint, M. (1968). *The Basic Fault.* London: Tavistock.

Freud, S. (1912b). The dynamics of the transference. *S.E., 12*: 97–107. London: Hogarth.

Freud, S. (1923b). *The Ego and the Id. S.E., 19*: 3–66. London: Hogarth.

Joseph, B. (1982). Addiction to near death. *International Journal of Psychoanalysis, 63*: 449–456.

Kennedy, R. (1984). A dual aspect of the transference. *International Journal of Psychoanalysis, 65*: 471–483.

Kennedy, R. (1987). Struggling with words: aspects of the psychoanalysis of a male homosexual *International Journal of Psychoanalysis, 68*: 119–128.

Kennedy, R. (1989). Starting an analysis with a self-mutilating adolescent. In: M. Laufer & E. Laufer (Eds.). *Developmental Breakdown and*

Psychoanalytic Treatment in Adolescence: Clinical Studies. New Haven, CT: Yale University Press.

King, P. (1978). Affective response of the analyst to the patient's communications. *International Journal of Psychoanalysis, 59*: 329–334.

Klauber, J. (1981). *Difficulties in the Analytic Encounter.* New York: Jason Aronson.

Laufer, M., & Laufer, E. (1984). *Adolescence and Developmental Breakdown.* New Haven, CT: Yale University Press.

Rosenfeld, H. (1987). *Impasse and Interpretation.* London: Tavistock and the Institute of Psycho-Analysis.

Winnicott, D. W. (1974). Fear of breakdown. *International Journal of Psychoanalysis, 1*: 103–107.

INDEX